PENGUIN BOOKS

Anzac to Amiens

Charles Edwin Woodrow Bean was born in Bathurst, NSW, in 1879. An Oxford graduate in law, he soon turned to writing and joined the *Sydney Morning Herald* as a reporter in 1908. At the outbreak of the First World War in 1914, Bean was appointed war correspondent with the Australian Imperial Force and spent the five years of the war in Europe. In addition to filling countless notebooks with descriptions, interviews and impressions of that time, Bean stayed on after the war to study the relics of battle and learnt, as historian Patsy Adam-Smith has remarked, 'those things that the soldiers could not know while hostilities were taking place.' On his return to Australia in 1919 Bean commenced the enormous task of editing the *Official History of Australia in the War of 1914–18*, the twelfth and final volume of which was published in 1942. Bean was instrumental in establishing the Australian War Memorial, which opened in 1941, and was its guiding spirit between the wars. Much honoured in his lifetime for his contribution to Australian military history, Bean died in 1968.

T0342659

ANZAC
TO AMIENS

C. E. W. BEAN

PENGUIN BOOKS

PENGUIN BOOKS

UK | USA | Canada | Ireland | Australia
India | New Zealand | South Africa | China

Penguin Books is part of the Penguin Random House group of companies
whose addresses can be found at global.penguinrandomhouse.com.

Penguin
Random House
Australia

First published by The Australian War Memorial 1946
First published by Penguin Books Australia Ltd 1993
This edition published by Penguin Group (Australia) 2014

Printed and bound in Australia by Griffin Press,
an accredited ISO AS/NZS 14001 Environmental Management Systems printer.

National Library of Australia Cataloguing-in-Publication data is available.

ISBN: 9780143571674

penguin.com.au

MIX
Paper | Supporting
responsible forestry
FSC® C018684

CONTENTS

MAPS

CHAPTER I

AUSTRALIA IN 1914

IN Australia in 1914, as in England and America, there had been ample warning of the possibility that Europe and the Atlantic would soon be plunged into a great war because of sharpening differences between the big European powers. The Pacific seemed to slumber, because there the leaders of Japan—the one power with a strong urge, and reason, to expand—were for the moment content peacefully to extend their trade while they built up their army, navy and industrial equipment. Japan was at the time the ally of Great Britain, an arrangement which relieved Britain of the necessity for maintaining a powerful fleet in the Pacific, and assured for Japan the time needed for establishing herself as a great power.

But though no breath of quarrel directly associated with the Pacific stirred the air, yet most of the civilised peoples of that ocean were intensely interested in what was happening on the other side of the world. As has generally been the case with civilised peoples, most of them were, in their organisation for defence, bound to other peoples in other regions. Normally it is by such groupings that mankind has, of necessity, defended itself against itself. The motive of any grouping may in the first instance have been trade, or domination, or even the conversion of the pagan—and the group may be an Empire, a federation, or an alliance; but when once its common defence system has been set up, it becomes, among other things, a group for self-protection; and a threat to any part of its body is felt, often acutely, by each of its members.

Australians formed part of the defence group represented by the British Empire; and, like people of the other Dominions, they were keenly sensitive to stirrings of the air of Europe where lay the one power, Germany, which at that moment appeared likely to become an active enemy of their group. A German colony—north-eastern New Guinea and the neighbouring islands—was Australia's nearest neighbour; and many Australians thought that, if war came, the German Pacific squadron would use New Guinea as a base for raiding Australian cities and sea trade.

Nevertheless that local danger was a minor one, and might never arise. The Germans had only slightly developed New Guinea; it possessed no land force except a few volunteers, and the German naval squadron in the Pacific, based on the German port of Tsingtao in China, was not powerful enough to raise serious fears in view of the protection that could fairly soon be brought to all British territories by the British Navy—and, as part of it, the Australian squadron. Australians judged, and judged rightly, that the real danger to themselves existed, if at all, in developments on the other side of the world.

Concerning the daily events of the world Australians were as well informed as most Anglo-Saxon people. The newspapers that city folk received with their breakfast—and country ones up to a week later according to distance from the capitals on the coast—set forth in their "cable pages" a gleaning of the world's news sent by their common agencies in London and Vancouver. The news was wide if rather thin; but among grown citizens and even children the facts of the Kaiser's recent expansion of his navy, of the race of British "Dreadnought" building to meet it, and of the German sabre-rattling in Morocco and the Balkan wars, were at least as well known as among their cousins in Great Britain. The average Australian family was as well aware as the average London one of the German goods—generally held to be inferior—

2

which because of their cheapness and of thoughtful, untiring salesmanship, had of late been "peacefully penetrating" the British Empire; and of the German steamers which—helped, it was said, by German government subsidies—were shouldering British ships from many berths in Australian harbours. German shipping arrangements had virtually, though not formally, closed to the British-Australian steamship lines the old traffic with German New Guinea and its neighbouring islands.

The Australian of every class felt, as keenly as most, the excitement maintained by aggressive newspapers in England and Germany, dealing each other blow for blow (and greatly increasing their sales) in a warfare of words that obviously was likely to end in actions tragic for everybody; and the Australian tried, as conscientiously as did the Peace Movement in Europe, to see the right and wrong behind it all. In the Peace Movement far-sighted leaders in many countries were striving to avert the catastrophe that seemed to be needlessly approaching. To this end they were following up the establishment of the World Court of Arbitration at the Hague by trying to spread the habit of peaceful arbitration. The British Minister for War, Lord Haldane, had visited Germany to see if he could not bring about a friendly understanding with the German government and people. It was felt that, behind their governments (and, in the case of Germany, their military staffs), the peoples had not the least wish for war, nor had they any intention or desire to pursue aims that would harm other peoples; and that, if only their suspicions of each other could be allayed, there was no reason why the gigantic armament race of the last few years should not cease.

But Germany's great and sudden expansion of her fleet provoked uneasiness which would not be allayed. All the great nations were, in consequence, feverishly increasing their forces, especially their navies. Obviously this race could not go on indefinitely. As men of Lord

Haldane's wisdom realiséd, not even any of the autocratic rulers wanted war; they disliked and feared the prospect of it. But there are degrees in dislike. Few rulers, especially among the autocrats, hated war as much as did their peoples; and, when once the rulers had built their huge armaments, there was always an increasing chance that in the next crisis, instead of waiting to reason, one of them would say: "What are this army and navy for? I will negotiate no longer."

Nevertheless, though in Australia as in England everyone was intellectually aware of these dangers, the general run of men and women of all classes, having grown up in the splendid stability of Anglo-Saxondom in the nineteenth century, found it hard to feel that a general upheaval might be immediately ahead of them. The British Navy had lain between them and the past when such things happened. But not many realised that only the Navy had prevented these things from continuing. As in all the Anglo-Saxon countries at that time, the grown citizen going to his business, just as much as the schoolboy at his desk, felt that the ruthless action and bad faith of Napoleon's time could hardly occur nowadays—Western nations and governments, on the whole, were too civilised. There might be local wars; but as for a world war—even among those who spoke of its possibility the conscious or unconscious conviction often was that in 1815 the world had finally entered the age of general, and almost perpetual, peace.

In Australia this feeling was all the more natural as war never had happened there. In the 126 years, from the day when Captain Arthur Phillip's eleven ships landed their 1100 white folk in the strange silence of grass and gum trees at Sydney Cove, to that on which the same foreshore clanged with the whirl of trams and crowds in the hub of Sydney's 800,000 people—for four generations pioneers, squatters, farmers, city folk had gone their ways without a serious thought of being inter-

4

fered with except within the law. The serious business of their lives—to carve homesteads from the intact bush; to organise the carriage of most of their necessities from the growing coastal capitals or the smaller ports, and the carriage thither of their products in return; to establish the machinery of sales, shipping, land transport and—in the latest generation—of manufacture; their recreations, some of these already grown to extensive businesses; their education, their fashions, their holidays; and not least their "White Australia Policy"—a vehement effort to maintain a high Western standard of economy, society and culture (necessitating certainly, at that stage, however it might be camouflaged, the rigid exclusion of Oriental peoples)—all these had been carried on without the least realisation that some great jackboot might smash down within a year or two the whole careful and careless structure, overturn every rule, tear husband from wife, son from parent, savings from those who had spent a lifetime in patient thrift.

In 1914 Australians were only 126 years from their first settlement in this continent—even when these words are written Europeans have been here less than half the time that the Romans were in Britain; in 1914 we were only 101 years from the first crossing of the Blue Mountains, only 63 from the first gold rush, 58 from the first establishment here of democratic self-government. Some Australians who went to the war had ancestors still alive who could remember some of the first generation of their countrymen; many had grandparents or great grandparents who could tell them of the gold rush, the bushrangers, the later explorers and the imported convicts. Even among the men who went to the First World War not a few had childish recollections of some old shepherd seen sleeping off his liquor outside a country town, to whom the whisper, that he was an "old lag", gave an awesome halo of romance and crime that sent a childish head deep under the blankets at night.

Yet, though many of the older men and women had actually lived in them, the colonial days were, by 1914, almost as extinct as those of William the Conqueror. The people of the six colonies, which had federated only fourteen years before, regarded themselves as being in the forefront of human progress and, indeed, in some not unimportant respects they had reason to do so. When emigrating from Britain most of their ancestors had half-consciously tried to cast off what they vaguely felt to be elements of inequality and injustice in the inherited social systems of Europe. They were disrespectful of old methods, eager to try out new ones. They had of late deliberately changed the whole basis of their wages system, in an effort to adjust it to the public conscience in place of the uncontrolled results of supply and demand. They had made many mistakes, due to vague thinking and inadequate study, but they had achieved something. They had established at least one very great and successful industry—that of wool production—and had managed so to spread its profits that real wages were then possibly higher in Australia than anywhere else in the world; at all events the life of the ordinary man, woman and child contained probably more healthy recreation than anywhere else.[1] Public education then compared favourably with that of any people except perhaps those of Scandinavia; in the enjoyment of such modern material benefits as telephones and electric light Australians were ahead of the British though behind the Americans.

Probably nowhere were the less wealthy folk more truly free, or on such terms of genuine social equality with the rich, in dress, habits and intercourse. Such class distinction as existed among Australians was perhaps chiefly based on their schools; but comparatively few boys, even from the most expensive schools, thought of entering the war-time army or navy except as privates or

---

[1] For a brilliant sketch of Australian motives and economy see Professor W. K. Hancock's *Australia*.

6

ordinary seamen. In the ranks of the Australian Forces that went to the Sudan, the South African War, and the Boxer rebellion, no private would think of explaining to you why he was a "ranker". While some officers undoubtedly were picked for their education, or up-bringing, the average Australian who enlisted, from whatever class, assumed that his job was with all other recruits—in the ranks.

It is true that in one respect living conditions in Australia—as in most newly-settled lands, even the United States—differed widely from those in older countries: a vast gap existed between the conditions in country and city. In the cities life was not markedly different from that of any great European or American town; but country life was in many parts still set in almost pioneering environment. Beyond the railways mail coaches still ran, changing horses every thirty miles or so; the motor car was only just reducing—by three quarters or more—the time occupied in outback travel.[2]

Yet the outback homesteads often contained surprising evidence of culture. It was much more than a superficial sign that the women who drove in to meet the mail train at a distant siding often dressed in the fashion of Paris, London, or New York. And if in the bars and hotels even of the big cities at racetimes and on holidays there was sometimes evidence of the Wild West, there was little inferiority complex about the people of this particularly free country. Its universities were in many ways progressive; its governments were launching into social experiments. Its business and political leaders thoroughly believed in its future and, with only 4½ million white people (and perhaps 100,000 Australian blacks) in the continent, they borrowed freely from overseas to launch into industrial and social enterprises. The

---

[2] Few aeroplanes had yet been seen in Australia. Wireless telegraphy had come into use between ships and shore; the Navy was establishing many stations. Wireless telephony and broadcasting were not brought in till 1923-5.

country was humming with this activity, much increased by the inflow of immigrants, mainly well-chosen British people, then reaching 40,000 yearly.

The old colonialism lingered on mainly in the fairly general belief that not only British clothes and boots but British leaders in business, or in army, navy, teaching, and other services, were necessarily better than Australian ones. Partly in reaction to this, there was much incisive and often exaggerated criticism of the mother country in nationalist newspapers such as the Sydney *Bulletin*, and among nationalist groups such as the Australian Natives' Association. Even the gentle Joseph Furphy was stung into giving an absurdly exaggerated picture of Englishmen in his incomparable portrayal of our country folk in *Such is Life*. Many young Australians tended to condemn the English immigrant for his comparative slowness and lack of confidence in dealing with unknown men and conditions, and were irritated by his certitude as to the superiority of the methods of the "old country". On the other hand Britons, and a large part of the older Australian citizens, felt that any patriotism that centred on Australia was a breach of the old loyalty to Great Britain or even to the Empire, to which nine-tenths of Australians were fervently attached. As a result, at this stage enthusiasm for the Empire and enthusiasm for Australia were often forced into competition, although in the greatest of Australian nationalists, Alfred Deakin, they ran wholeheartedly parallel.

The historian, who tries to discover what motive most powerfully moved the Australian people at that interesting stage, will probably come to the conclusion that tradition—such as is consciously or unconsciously handed down in almost every word or action by parents and teachers to children, by priests and pastors, professional, trades and business men to their successors, by writers to readers, even by older children to younger—was immensely strong and enduring. The tradition was largely British; homelife was similar to that of the British and American provinces. But with the British standards were mingled those of the pioneers—the backwoodsmen, and the men of the great runs and the mining fields. It was to these last that Australians owed their resourcefulness and readiness to grapple with their objectives even against authority, and also their basic creed, in industry as in war, that a man must at all costs stand by his mate. Contrary to the then current economic creed of "devil take the hindmost", they clung to the principle of standing by the weaker brother. As in Great Britain, the moral influence of games—especially of cricket—was very strong. The Australian ballad writers, Gordon, Lawson, Paterson, Ogilvie and others, were constantly read and quoted. The people were not formally religious, but there was a marked comradeliness in their outlook, and no degree of economic pressure could induce them to abandon it.

Their attitude towards the profession of arms was almost purely British. It is true that Australians had brought back from the South African War—and from the Maori Wars long before that—the impression that the regular British army was unduly rigid in thought and method for colonial warfare. Yet the old British military tradition was cited by Australian soldiers as proudly as by the British Army itself. Australians, almost as much as the English, had been brought up on tales of Crécy and Agincourt, Trafalgar, Waterloo, the Indian Mutiny and the Crimean, Afghan, Zulu and other British wars; and bound volumes of the English illustrated papers, with pictures of some of these campaigns, were in constant use in many homes.

The people, newly federated, were at this stage very consciously intent upon building themselves into a great nation. Without giving the matter much thought, most Australians assumed that the development of their country would be similar to that of the United States.

To suggest a doubt whether this continent had the rainfall or other conditions on which America's development was based was considered unpatriotic. Though a few students, notably Professor Griffith Taylor, pointed courageously to the fact that most of Australia was necessarily pastoral, it was the fashion to speak of her "unlimited potentialities", and with easy optimism Australians anticipated that within a century or so her 5 million people would be increased to 60 if not 100 million. They foresaw her as the possible centre of the British Empire.

The political leaders were as genuine as the people in their enthusiasm for this future; and on the strength of these expectations governments and industrial leaders had launched into a campaign of borrowing heavily in Great Britain to finance the country's development. The British government helped by including Dominion loans among the stocks in which British trustees might invest the monies in their care.

Australians were thus intent upon the great increase in their wool sales, the improvement of their wheat, meat, fruit and butter export, the building of their secondary industries behind the new Australian tariff, the construction of their great public works, dams for water storage and irrigation; their first transcontinental railway from east to west (which was to be largely financed by the Federal government's original note issue); the opening of new universities—of Queensland in 1911 and Western Australia in 1912. Other projects were those for a north-south transcontinental railway, and for weirs and locks for irrigation and navigation along more than 2000 miles of the Murray-Darling river system. Canberra had already been chosen as the capital of Australia, and its building was another project—the subject of much dissension. The war of course resulted in the postponement of this task, and Melbourne therefore still remained the seat of government.

But one of the biggest projects of the federation was already well advanced—the establishment of a new, all-Australian defence system. A main reason for federation had been the obvious need to replace the small separate naval and military forces of the six colonies by one military and one naval force, with single control. Small though they were, the forces of the six colonies had been seriously regarded, at least by the enthusiastic officers and men who had composed them; the chief Australian leaders in the war—Bridges, White, Monash, Chauvel—all came from them.

Ever since the Australian colonies had been assured of future control of their own revenue, just before the Crimean War, they had accepted some responsibility for land and harbour defence, a task previously borne for them with growing unwillingness by Great Britain, which in addition to her ubiquitous navy had to maintain regular garrisons. Only in war scares had Australians felt how empty and defenceless their big island was. In the Crimean War the chief colonies raised small citizen forces, and some forts were built. The effort soon flagged, but received another impulse in the Second Maori War (1860), when an appeal for troops was received and some of the regular garrison as well as volunteers were sent. The final withdrawal of the British garrisons from Australia in 1870 led to requests to Great Britain for advice, and by 1884, largely on the careful recommendations of a British Commission, the colonies adopted a co-ordinated scheme of local defence; certain harbour or coastal defence ships were obtained, and naval reservists trained to man them, and small military forces were raised, generally comprising a permanent nucleus backed by paid and unpaid volunteers.

At that stage the military effort of Australia really began to take shape. In January 1885 the shock of the news of British reverses in the Sudan and of General Gordon's death caused the people and government of one

State, New South Wales, to create what, even at the time, was realised as being a most important precedent in Empire defence, by offering a force of 750 infantry and artillery, who were raised, shipped and disembarked in the Sudan within two months. A scare of war with Russia suddenly closed the Sudan Campaign, and the contingent, after an experience far more interesting than is generally realised, was back within five months of Gordon's death. But the Russian scare caused another spurt in Australian defence and by March 1901, when they were absorbed in a single Federal force, the military forces—militia and volunteers—of the six colonies were nearly 30,000 strong.

The federation of Australia occurred in the midst of the South African War, for which all the colonies enthusiastically offered contingents; 16,632 Australians were sent, some 12,000 before Federation and 4000 after it. Nearly all belonged to the typical Australian arm, mounted infantry; and the few infantry, sent on suggestion from the War Office, were also mounted soon after arrival. Campaigning in country very similar to their own, the colonial mounted troops were, to the surprise of the British authorities, found more suitable than regular cavalry. Their casualties including deaths through action (251) and disease (267) were 1400.[3] The Australians returned by 1902 with a wide reputation for dash and skill in action and for some wildness when unengaged. Except for patriotic funds there was little public effort to rehabilitate them, and a proportion found it most difficult to settle down in civil life.

The development of the Australian naval forces was much slower. The almost absolute protection afforded by the British Navy had, as already mentioned, generally helped to prevent the realisation of danger. In the scares of war with Russia, however, the colonists were always

---

3 An accurate short account of the Australian part in this war is in the *Australian Encyclopaedia*, under "South Africa". For the Sudan, see *The Sudan Contingent* by Stanley Brogden.

sensitive as to their coastal cities. In 1886 Admiral Tryon advised the Admiralty that the right solution was personal service by the colonists in ships controlled by them in peace-time, but he was ahead of his time. Until Federation in 1901 the naval effort of the Australian colonies—apart from pure harbour defence—consisted in subsidising the British Navy to keep some small cruisers on the coast for local defence and for training the local reserves which helped to man them.

But when Australians federated there was alive in a great part of the people a spirit which these efforts did not satisfy. The younger nationalists of the kind that supported the then active Australian Natives' Association desired to see their nation equipped with fighting services manned and controlled by Australians, enabling the country to pull its full weight in an emergency, though it was generally realised that the nation would not be able to stand by itself. Among this section there was keen dissatisfaction when the imperial conference of 1902 merely adopted a scheme for subsidising the British Navy to provide a bigger squadron for the local defence of Australia and New Zealand. But the British Admiralty (supported in this by conservative opinion in Australia), was against any individual naval effort by the colonies, and steadily opposed the project for an Australian navy.

In 1907, however, the Australian Prime Minister, Alfred Deakin, managed to secure Admiralty approval for a flotilla of torpedo-boats and submarines. This was a whittling down of a cherished scheme of Australia's Director of Naval Forces, Captain W. R. Creswell—the real founder of the Australian Navy—and the Australian naval advisers wisely objected to the class of vessel now proposed. The Deakin government accordingly decided to provide destroyers, and the Labour government under Andrew Fisher, which followed it in 1908-9, ordered three of them to be built in England.

Just then, in 1909, the whole Empire was swept by a

13

war scare following the sudden realisation that the German Emperor's programme of naval expansion was on a scale to challenge Britain's one real defence—her command of the sea. From most parts of the Empire there flowed offers of naval help. Canada, which in fact was largely protected by the Monroe doctrine of the United States and had therefore been less interested than Australia in naval projects, was now ready to form its own navy. In the other Dominions there were proposals to present battleships to the British Navy. Australia was keenly divided on the question of method, but was all eager to help. A special Imperial Defence Conference was accordingly held in London in order to thrash out the most useful and practicable action.

This conference approved of a scheme for a strong "Eastern Fleet" to be maintained by the Empire in the Pacific. It would comprise three "fleet-units", two to be maintained by Great Britain (in place of her old East Indies and China squadrons), and one by Australia (in place of the old British squadron in Australian waters). Each fleet unit would comprise a battle-cruiser, three light cruisers, six destroyers and three submarines. Canada, being interested in the Atlantic also, decided to provide in the Pacific for the time being only light cruisers and destroyers. New Zealand had already offered Great Britain the money for a battleship or battle-cruiser; the Admiralty now promised that this ship should be allotted as one of the three battle-cruisers for the Pacific Fleet. Arrangements were also made for training New Zealand seamen to serve in British ships.

During this period the Australian government was constantly changed, but all governments, Liberal and Labour, were determined on these projects; and, as happened in the case of many big national plans of that generation, it was a Labour government, coming into power in 1910 under Andrew Fisher and William Morris

14

Hughes, that took most of the steps actually finalising the scheme.

The final adoption of this plan for the first considerable Dominion navy had been due to Australia's insistence. The real basis of the Admiralty's agreement to it was the condition that ships, officers and men must be trained and maintained at the standards of the British Navy. The fact that the Admiralty, with its conservative tradition, now trusted the Dominion's undertaking to do this—a trust which Admiral Tryon had shown in 1887— and, that on the basis of that pledge Dominion ships were permitted to fly the famous White Ensign, marks an immense step in co-operation between the Mother Country and the Dominions.

The Australian naval effort thus planned was not, it is true, proportionate to the naval effort of the British people; but it was a solid, considerable factor in the British Empire's naval defence. Even many of those Australians who had opposed Deakin's plan for a "tin-pot navy" (as they called it), and had wanted instead to present the Mother Country with a Dreadnought, became hearty supporters of this scheme.

Australia's new army which, as it happened, was finally shaped in the same year, 1910, was planned with equal vigour but with a different object. The sea, and therefore the Navy, had no boundaries. But, to many Australians of that time, to contemplate the operations of an army on any soil except Australia's smacked of "aggression". Their political leaders, therefore, feared to plan or prepare, even provisionally, for joining in the Empire's land wars. It was not enough that, if such war came, the Dominion's relation to the Mother Country left Australians entirely free to keep both their army and navy out of the war. (The moral basis for that apparently one-sided arrangement was that the British government then alone had the responsibility for conducting foreign relations and the power of declaring war.) Australian political leaders felt that, though their peoples would doubtless help the Motherland in emergency, as they had done in the South African war, the provision for this must be left until the emergency arose: Hitler had not then proved that almost any nation which limits itself to defending its own doorstep has already voluntarily abandoned its defence.

Accordingly, not only did the other Dominions at the conference in 1909 reject a proposal by New Zealand for the maintenance of special army reserves in the Dominions in case they were again required as in South Africa, but the Australian government would not allow its staff even to prepare plans against the possibility that such a force might be required.

To one proposal, however, put forward with admirable tact and restraint by the British general staff, all the Dominions agreed. Since the South African War fierce publicity, and intelligent criticism by some military leaders, had brought about in the British Army many reforms, among which the establishment of a general staff and of a staff college was perhaps the chief. Though the War Office was still the butt of newspaper critics, some exceedingly able men, civil and military, were met there by Australians who subsequently had dealings with them in 1914-18. On this occasion in 1909 the British general staff, accepting the lesson of past rebuffs, most wisely limited its proposals for co-operation to one by which the several forces of the Empire should be, as far as possible, armed, organised and trained in the same way, so as to be interchangeable; that officers should be exchanged; and that the British General Staff should be in some measure combined with those of the Dominions into an Imperial General Staff, to study problems, exchange information, and tender advice. This proposal was enthusiastically adopted—and the value of the step, when the British and oversea forces eventually co-operated in the two World Wars, was beyond estimation.

As a result of the feeling above described, the Australian Army was enlisted for home service only; but after the 1907 Conference the danger of Australia's isolated position was sufficiently understood to result in the Federal government's using its power of forcing the citizens to train for home defence. Service was made "universal"—or, more accurately, compulsory for all fit citizens in the more closely settled regions—and a military college was to be set up. This scheme, mainly the work of Colonel J. G. Legge, was expanded in 1910 when, at Australia's request, Lord Kitchener, then retiring from command of the Indian Army, inspected the Australian defences, and recommended that the settled regions be divided not merely into the six military districts (practically the six States) but into 215 military areas, each with an "area officer"—ultimately to be drawn from the 350 highly trained military college graduates. Successive Federal governments—Deakin-Cook (Liberal) and Fisher (Labour)—keenly supported these schemes, but Fisher went farthest and laid it down that the training at Australian Military and Naval Colleges should be free of expense for any of the youngsters chosen for future officers. The two colleges were hard at work—though their first classes had not yet graduated—when the First World War broke out.

By then the main part of the Australian "fleet-unit" was in Australian waters—battle-cruiser *Australia*, light cruisers *Sydney* and *Melbourne*, destroyers *Parramatta*, *Yarra*, *Warrego*, and submarines *AE1* and *AE2*, in addition to the light cruiser *Encounter* and small cruiser *Pioneer* (the first lent, the second given, by the Admiralty). The crews were about half Australian, half British, under an arrangement by which the Admiralty helped until Australia (in her college at Jervis Bay and the training ship *Tingira* and elsewhere) had produced her full crews. The army was only half-way to its new stage, but comprised 45,000 men, mainly youngsters of nineteen to

3—os

17

twenty-one years but with a remnant of the old militia. They were trained for sixteen to twenty-five days each year and partly organised in brigades. For future recruits they were backed by an excellent reservoir in the mass of Australian boys, of whom some 150,000 of twelve to seventeen years were trained for an hour or more weekly in the junior and senior cadets. There were also 35,000, mainly older, men enrolled in rifle clubs. Most Australians had some of the soldier's skills, in shooting, camping, foraging or finding their way. A government factory was just beginning to turn out rifles at Lithgow in the Blue Mountains; government cordite, harness, clothing and woollen factories were already at work in Victoria; the old naval yards and depots at Sydney, Melbourne and elsewhere—by then under Australian control—were operating, and others were under construction at Fremantle and near Western Port. The first Australian military flying school was about to start at Point Cook.

Such was the military side of the preparation that Australians were busily making for their nation's future. Many wondered what part this southern white people would play in the future of the British Empire or of mankind; many believed that it would some day prove a valuable link between the British and American peoples. In the new country as well as the old, on the other hand, some critics saw danger in the Australian's independence of outlook and action. Increasing awareness of the German threat had diminished the loose talk, current in the previous generation of Australians, about "cutting the painter"; but there remained enough of it to cause some conservative minds to believe and say that the small navy which Australians were now establishing was meant to be used against Britain. A much more general belief was that it was an expensive gesture unlikely to prove useful in practice.

Actually, every step by which the Mother Country increased the self-government of the Dominions strengthened the invisible bond between herself and them, and increased their readiness to provide for common defence.

There were some Australians who half consciously longed for the day when their untried people would be pitted against the fighters of other nations; when, as Henry Lawson wrote, "the Star of the South shall rise— in the lurid clouds of war"; not a few young Australians dreamt of that "rush with the Bush Brigades" when "the cavalry charge again". It is true that Australians had served in the Sudan and South Africa—and these were impelled by some of the same motives that were to stir them in 1914, excitement in adventure, desire for Australian achievement, and determination to stand by the old country in crisis. But, despite the very stout showing at Eland's River and elsewhere, those really serious tests were regarded by Australians, and by such of the outside world as were interested, as something of a picnic. Such conscious feeling of nationhood as Australians possessed centred as much on their test matches, and the quality of their sheep and racehorses, as on their achievements in art, poetry, politics or social progress. The names of Victor Trumper, and Carbine undoubtedly struck a national chord, perhaps as deeply as those of Henry Lawson or Alfred Deakin. And, in truth, Australian sportsmen, like her poets and the best of her writers, stood for something fine and free; but as a people Australians lacked the confidence that has come to most nations only from a trial that this people had never yet undergone.

CHAPTER II

THE FIRST WORLD WAR BREAKS OUT

In the last week of July 1914 the Australian newspapers were busy with the crisis in Ireland, where the objection of Northern Irishmen to be included in the home rule given by the British Parliament to the whole island seemed about to precipitate civil war; with the win by the Australian and New Zealand tennis pair over Canada in the Davis Cup match at Chicago; with the exciting flights of Guillaux, a French aviator, in Australia; with the approaching meeting in Australia of the British Association for the Advancement of Science; with the high cost of recent immigration; with the coming Australian Federal election, in which the Liberal Prime Minister, Mr Joseph Cook, and his party, who had won office just a year before, were trying by a "double dissolution" to get rid of a Labour majority in the Senate which was thwarting the will of the Liberal majority in the lower house.[1]

The papers of July 24th included a paragraph reporting that the Chamber of Commerce of Hamburg had invited the boys of the Young Australia League to pay a goodwill visit to Germany. On July 27th the main news was the failure of the conference called by King George V at Buckingham Palace in an endeavour to settle the Irish Home Rule crisis. Reports of tension between Austria and Serbia—and, in the background, between Germany, Austria's ally, and Russia, which supported Serbia—had

[1] The Federal Parliament had been dissolved on June 27th and the elections were to be held on September 5th. For the details of this and the matters that follow, see *Vol. XI, pp. 7-26*, and *Vol. I, pp. 20-32*.

continued ever since the cables of June 30th, telling of the murder of the Austrian Crown Prince and his wife by a Serb at Sarajevo. Australians were, of course, aware that France was allied with Russia, and that Great Britain was loosely committed to France; and on July 27th the *Sydney Morning Herald*, in a leading article headed "Is it war?" mentioned the suspicion that Britain's immersion in the Home Rule crisis, and Russia's in a bitter political strike, might have led Austria deliberately to choose this opportunity for settling her old accounts with Serbia in the belief that these powers would be too engrossed with their own troubles to interfere. The article said that on the hope that Germany would bring pressure to bear on Austria and Britain on Russia "perhaps may hang the peace of the world".

That was the last day of Australia's feeling of secure remoteness—it is never likely to return. On July 28th news of the almost impossible demands made by Austria on Serbia, and of Russia's resentment, brought the realisation that unless Sir Edward Grey, the British Foreign Minister, could arrange a conference of the powers, war was certain between Austria and Germany on the one hand and Russia and France on the other.

Australians now followed with tense anxiety the cables posted outside the newspaper offices. On July 30th Austria declared war on Serbia. Russia ordered her army to mobilise. Germany, after futile last-minute gestures by her emperor who, too late, threatened to withdraw his support from Austria, on August 2nd declared war on Russia. That France would be involved was now certain, and for two days most Australians like most Englishmen were filled with an intense, but changed, anxiety—lest the British government, in which certain Ministers were known to be firmly opposed to war, might fail to support the French.

British governments had been most careful in the past to avoid giving the French any promise beyond that of

consultation if war should threaten, which promise had
been all that opinion in Great Britain would permit; but
her people now felt that, however strong the opposite
intention, the French had been led to expect British
support, and that the British people could never again
hold up their heads if they failed to give it. When on
August 2nd German armies—as the easiest way of attacking France—marched on Belgium which Germany,
like France and Britain, was herself pledged by treaty to
protect against any invasion, this anxiety became still
keener.

But the invasion of Belgium cleared the difficulty. In
the British Cabinet the party that opposed full support
for France now dwindled to a few, who resigned; the
remainder resolved to help Belgium and France. At
11 p.m. on August 4th, English time, Britain declared
war on Germany which was already invading those two
countries.[2]

The present writer can remember how, after the following night's work at a newspaper office, as he walked
home in the small hours through Macquarie Street,
Sydney, the clouds, dimly piled high in the four quarters
of the dark sky above, seemed to him like the pillared
structure of the world's civilisation, of which some shock
had broken the keystones. The wide gap overhead seemed
to show where one great pillar after another had crashed
as the mutual support had failed; and, as the sky peered
through, the last masses seemed to sway above the abyss.
The stable world of the nineteenth century was coming
down in chaos: security was gone. For the first time since
Trafalgar, 109 years before, the British fleet was at sea
on a mission of life or death for all British nations. Yet
people's feeling, in Australia and New Zealand as in

---

2 It is not, of course, implied that these events were the *cause* of the war.
So far as is known to the writer, the best account of the events that immedi-
ately led up to the First World War is in *The Coming of the War, 1914* by
Bernadotte E. Schmitt.

England, was one of relief from that latest and worst anxiety. Had Britain, despite her pledges, held out of the war, the loyalty of the oversea Dominions to her would hardly have survived the shock to the Empire's honour.

In the days when that decision was doubtful, and when it was obviously desirable that Britain's influence in any negotiations or decisions should carry the greatest possible weight, all the great self-governing Dominions independently decided to strengthen her hand by free offers of military support. Although in the international conditions of that time all their foreign relations were conducted through Great Britain, and each Dominion would automatically be at war if the Mother Country was so, not one of them was obliged to raise a soldier or sailor or move a ship or an ounce of merchandise in any effort against the common enemy. But when, on July 29th, each Dominion received from Britain a telegram (in the form specified in their defence schemes) warning them that war was imminent, and that certain precautions should be taken, it became obvious that, if the British government was to be assured of support, the assurance should be given at once. Next day, on July 30th, New Zealand—regularly first in such crises—offered to send a force of troops if need arose. On July 31st the Canadian government promised the fullest aid. In Australia Cabinet Ministers were busy electioneering; the Minister for Defence, Senator E. D. Millen, promised that Australia "was no fair-weather partner" in the Empire; but of all Australians it was the leader of the Labour opposition, Mr Andrew Fisher, who—though presumably he knew nothing of the warning message—gave the Mother Country the most comforting pledge, that Australia was with her to the "last man and last shilling". That day the Governor-General, Sir Ronald Munro-Ferguson, suggested to the Prime Minister, Mr Joseph Cook, that he should call a Cabinet meeting in order that the British

23

government might know what support it might expect from the Australian government.

Meanwhile the preliminary steps were taken. The Australian squadron was directed to Sydney for coaling and other preparation. On August 2nd the "first stage" of mobilisation was ordered. On the 3rd the Federal Cabinet met in Melbourne and called in representatives of its Army and Navy. The Canadian government was reported to have offered to send 30,000 troops.[3] The Prime Minister now asked the military staff officer at the Cabinet meeting whether any plans existed for sending an expeditionary force from Australia.

Australia was quite remarkably fortunate in the leaders of her small professional military staff at that time, but it chanced that the two most distinguished of them—Brig.-General William Throsby Bridges and Colonel J. G. Legge—were away from Melbourne. Most happily, however, throughout this crisis the acting-head of the general staff at the Defence Department was Major Cyril Brudenell White, a young Queenslander, who, despite the exceptional quality of the two absent leaders, was beginning to be recognised as the most brilliant soldier the Australian permanent service had produced. Son of a courageous Irish-Australian pastoralist, who thrice quietly faced the wreckage of his fortune in the back country, Cyril White had had to struggle for his education. But, when once in the Army, his power of instantly grasping a situation, his unerring sense of proportion, the strength of his will, and the outstanding charm of his personality—helped by his training under a remarkable British leader, General Hutton—took him quickly to important work. After a term at the Staff College in England his services were asked for by the British War Office for three years to lecture and train its regular troops. As an organiser he was no whit inferior to the

---

3 Actually Canada had offered 20,000, though this was soon increased to 33,000.

other Australian who was to achieve great distinction during the war, John Monash.

A military defence scheme for Australia had, partly on suggestion from the Imperial General Staff, been worked on, first by Brig.-General Bridges, but of late by Major White. It dealt, however, purely with precautions to be taken in Australia; White had not been allowed to work at any scheme for supporting Britain. But one Labour Minister, Senator George Foster Pearce, who had charge of the Defence Department during the Fisher regime, had agreed to his elaborating a scheme for joint defence with New Zealand. Under this, Australia and New Zealand would furnish between them one infantry division—the only force of such size envisaged in the defence plans of these southern Dominions. This division would comprise 18,000 men—6000 from New Zealand and 12,000 from Australia. White now told the Prime Minister of this plan for despatching 12,000. Sir Joseph Cook, however, was determined that Australia's contribution should be on a larger scale, and he asked if 20,000 could be sent. White replied that they could, and that there was fair prospect of their being ready in six weeks. The Ministers accordingly decided that Australia should offer to—

(1) place her Navy under the British Admiralty; and to

(2) despatch "a force of 20,000 men of any suggested composition to any destination desired by the Home government", and to maintain it there.

The offer was immediately announced, and was accepted by the British government, which on August 6th telegraphed asking that the force should be sent as soon as possible. The Australian government appointed General Bridges, who had been the first commandant of Australia's Military College, and had lately been made inspector-general, to organise and command it. He chose White for the chief of his staff.

Bridges was a deep student of his profession, a man of first-rate brain and wide learning, of great physical and moral courage, and of grim determination, though he was shy in intercourse. He had been born in Scotland, son of a naval officer who married an Australian, and he had been trained at Kingston Military College in Canada. In 1885 he joined the New South Wales permanent forces, in which the school of gunnery at Middle Head gave scope for his technical interests and enthusiasm. He served with the British Cavalry Division in South Africa, and later went to London as Australia's representative on the Imperial General Staff. The standards and tradition of Australia's new military college at Duntroon were almost entirely of his making.

Now, faced with the task of producing an Australian force for service abroad, he was determined that it should serve as a compact national contribution. The British War Office had suggested that it should be composed of brigades of separate services—infantry, light horse, and artillery—a request which indicated an intention of the British staff to distribute these separately among British divisions. Bridges telegraphed that he had begun organising an Australian infantry division and one light horse brigade, to sail in six weeks. Did the British Army Council concur? The Army Council agreed, and the principle that Australia should supply—so far as the Army was concerned—a compact Australian force, and not one to be split up among other particles forming a British army, was thus settled at the outset. Australian hospitals were the chief exception to this; throughout the war they served all troops though Australian patients largely passed through them.

In ordinary times it would have been possible to create this force by obtaining volunteer detachments from the existing home-service battalions, batteries, and other units all over Australia, and so linking the home-service army with the contingent for overseas. New Zealand's force—a brigade of infantry and one of mounted rifles—was so raised, and Brudenell White would greatly have preferred this course. But the Australian citizen forces were then so largely composed of youths, in their first or second year of training under the new Kitchener scheme, that Bridges and he decided that the only method then possible was to create a special force by enlistment from the whole population. The scheme was ready by August 8th, and on the 10th recruiting was opened by proclamation. Bridges, with an eye on the initials which he knew would be used for its name, called the new army the Australian Imperial Force, the "A.I.F.". It was intended to sail for Europe on September 12th.

CHAPTER III

THE NAVY—AND NEW GUINEA

ALL that time the world was waiting to hear from Europe, at any hour, of a great battle between the British and German fleets, on the result of which the course of the war was expected largely to depend. More than once came rumours of it; and, the normal sources of information having for the first time in Australian history been suddenly closed by censorship, rumours eddied round Australia as to happenings to her own ships also.

All that was known of the Australian squadron was—it was at sea. Formerly, when opposing the creation of an Australian navy, the British Admiralty had argued that the naval defence policy of Great Britain always necessarily took the form of seeking out the enemy fleet and attacking it, whereas Australians seemed to require a squadron to be kept in their home waters. Now, however, when the test came, Admiral Patey commanding the Australian squadron, decided—and continued strongly to urge, so long as the decision could be influenced by him and by the Australian Naval Board—that the supreme duty of his ships was to find and beat the German Pacific squadron.

Immeasurably the strongest fleet in the Pacific was that of Japan; but, though allied to Great Britain and bound to help if Britain was aggressively attacked in India or East Asia, Japan was not yet in the war. Her fleet was at the moment neutral; at that stage the main belligerents in the Pacific were the German Pacific quadron on the one hand and the British China and East Indies squadrons and the Australian squadron on the other. Only the Australian squadron had been brought up to the strength arranged for in the Imperial Conferences of 1909 and 1911,[1] and the very efficient German squadron, with its strong pair of armoured cruisers—the *Scharnhorst* and *Gneisenau*—and several good light cruisers might well prove more powerful than the British China and East Indies squadrons combined. The battle-cruiser *Australia*, on the other hand, should be more than a match for the two German armoured cruisers; and if, as was expected to happen in a few days, Japan came into the war, the balance of strength in the Pacific would be overwhelmingly against Germany.

The commander of the German squadron, Admiral von Spee, of course, made his plans with this probability in view, and during the past month had deliberately taken his squadron into hiding in the Pacific islands. Its position was unknown, but some of its wireless messages had been heard; they certainly came from not more than 2000 miles north of Australia, and were thought to come from 1000 miles, probably from New Guinea waters. The German government was suspected of having made some preparation for war at its New Guinea capital, Rabaul, in New Britain. It was thought very probable that the German squadron might actually be in the fine harbour there (Simpsonshafen), and Admiral Patey obtained leave to search it forthwith.

He accordingly ordered his squadron to concentrate off New Guinea, and after dark on August 11th the light cruiser *Sydney* and three destroyers were sent to Blanche Bay, the innermost waters of which form that harbour. Patey with the *Australia* remained near by, in the channel between New Britain and New Ireland; the *Sydney*

---

[1] The danger from Germany had led the British government to keep the promised battle-cruisers in European waters. The old battleship *Triumph* was sent out instead. In view of the urgent situation in Europe the Australian government raised no objection. But it did not send the battle-cruiser *Australia* to the Atlantic, as the First Lord of the Admiralty, Mr Winston Churchill, suggested that it should do (*see Vol. IX, p. xxxvii*).

went to the entrance of Blanche Bay. In the night, which was very dark, the destroyers went in, the *Yarra* searching the outer bay while the *Warrego* and *Parramatta* entered the inner harbour and made straight for Rabaul anchorage with orders to attack the German squadron if found. It was expected to comprise the *Gneisenau* and *Scharnhorst*, the light cruiser *Nürnberg* and perhaps some small ships. But after a breathless search the *Warrego* found itself right against Rabaul jetty without an enemy ship being seen. Actually the German squadron after hiding for three weeks at Ponape,[2] one of the Caroline Islands 950 miles north-east of Rabaul, had that day reached Pagan in the Mariannes, 1600 miles north of Rabaul.

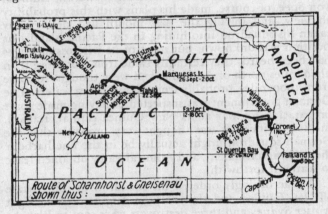

At daylight the destroyers entered Rabaul harbour again in order to find and destroy the wireless station which could be heard sending reports of their movements to the German naval squadron at its unknown position. But though an Australian party landed at Rabaul the station could not be found, having evidently been moved

[2] It had previously been at Truk in the same islands (*see Vol. IX*, *pp. 25-8*).

into the jungle. The Australian squadron, being short of coal and oil, then withdrew to Port Moresby in the Australian colony of Papua (the south-eastern section of New Guinea) and elsewhere to refill preparatory to seeking the German squadron in the more distant islands.

On August 6th, however, the British government had asked the Australian government, as "a great and urgent imperial service", to seize and destroy the German wireless stations in the south-west Pacific, at Yap in the western Carolines (700 miles north of Dutch New Guinea), at Nauru (700 miles north-east of the Solomons), and in the region of New Guinea. The message said that any territory occupied by this expedition must be held at the disposal of the Imperial government for the purposes of the peace settlement. Other Dominions, it added, were acting in a similar way. New Zealand had been asked to take action as to Samoa.

The Australian and New Zealand governments at once agreed to send the expeditions desired—which forthwith became enterprises for the occupation of the German colonies. They were to start almost at once. The Australian government decided to raise a special mixed force, to be known as the Australian Naval and Military Expeditionary Force; and while General Bridges with White organised the A.I.F., Colonel Legge, taking up on August 8th his appointment of chief of the general staff in the Defence Department at Melbourne, separately organised this smaller volunteer force—generally known as the A.N. & M.E.F. It comprised a battalion (1000 strong) of infantry specially enlisted in Sydney, another (500 strong) of naval reservists and ex-seamen, to serve as infantry, and a third comprising part of a young citizen-force battalion from northern Queensland which, under the defence scheme, had been hurriedly sent in a commandeered coastal liner, the *Kanowna*, to garrison Thursday Island, and 500 of which now volunteered to serve outside Australia. The Sydney battalion was raised from men mostly untrained but of first-rate quality, who rushed to enlist. Command of all troops for New Guinea was given to Colonel William Holmes, in peace-time the secretary of the Sydney Water Board, a capable militia officer of fine character and with experience of war in South Africa.

The sailing of this expedition for New Guinea, and of the similar New Zealand expedition for Samoa, while the powerful enemy cruiser squadron was at some place unknown in the Pacific Ocean ahead of them, entirely changed the plans for using the battle-cruiser *Australia* to find and destroy the German squadron. Messages from Great Britain urged speed in sending the troops, and the Admiralty ordered Admiral Patey to cover them with the *Australia*. Reluctantly he had to divert his battle-cruiser from what he felt should be her first task. The *Australia* and *Melbourne* met the French cruiser *Montcalm* at New Caledonia on August 21st, and escorted the New Zealand expedition from there to Samoa, which was occupied on the 30th. On the 23rd the Japanese came into the war. They at once blockaded the German base of Tsingtao (in the Kiao Chao territory, "leased" from China), and began to search for the German squadron.

In the meantime most of the Australian troops for New Guinea had embarked in the P. & O. liner *Berrima* and had steamed up the Australian coast to Palm Island near Townsville, where they were exercised. As soon as Samoa was taken the Australian expedition moved to Moresby in Papua (New Guinea), where the Queensland citizen-force battalion had been waiting in its transport the *Kanowna*. Colonel Holmes formed the opinion that this youthful battalion was unsuitable for the task. No adequate preparation had been possible for its training, equipment, provisioning or transport. The Admiral decided that it should accompany the force; but, after the expedition left Moresby for German New Guinea on September 7th, trouble with the stokers of the *Kanowna*—

which had been taken from her run without warning at the outbreak of war—led to this battalion's being left behind, though the young soldiers volunteered to stoke the ship.[3]

At the Louisiades, off the eastern end of New Guinea, the A.N. & M.E.F., escorted by the light cruiser *Sydney*, met the *Australia*, back from Samoa, and other ships that were to escort the expedition to Rabaul. The *Melbourne* was away, having been detached from the squadron after the occupation of Samoa to destroy the wireless station on Nauru. The ships approached Blanche Bay at daylight on September 11th, and after the *Sydney* and destroyers had reported it to be free from enemy ships, and that the *Berrima* could lie at Rabaul jetty, the expedition moved in. The *Berrima* was to land her soldiers at Rabaul. But as she moved into Blanche Bay there came word that stiff fighting had been met by one of two small parties of naval reservists, who had been transferred to the *Sydney* and to destroyers, and had been landed at Kabakaul and Herbertshöhe (settlements on the south-east shore of the bay) with orders to destroy the wireless stations which

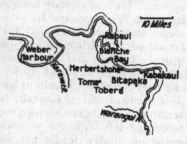

were believed to be four or five miles back in the country behind those places. Admiral Patey ordered the *Berrima* to Kabakaul to land reinforcements for these parties.

The party of reservists that had pushed inland from Herbertshöhe along the road towards Toma (in the hills some ten miles away) went through the jungle half way to that place without seeing any wireless station or any

---

[3] And did stoke her to Australia (see *Vol. X, pp. 31-3, Vol. IX, pp. 76-8*).

4—os

enemy except a body of armed natives who at once disappeared among the trees. But the party which had
landed at Kabakaul under Lieutenant Bowen had barely
passed the comparatively open plantations when two of
its scouts, working round and into the first dense patch
of the jungle, came from the rear upon an armed party
of twenty natives under a white man. They also saw two
white men farther away, crouching by the roadside and
watching the approach of Bowen's party. The leading
scout, Petty Officer Palmer, shot and wounded the nearest
German, whose troops scattered into shelter. On Palmer's
covering him the German surrendered and ordered his
troops to cease fire. The two white men on the road were
captured by a ruse, and proved to be two of the chief
German officers who had come forward to reconnoitre.

On the prisoners were found maps of the road which
showed Bowen that his party would be systematically
opposed. He had already been reinforced by a dozen men
from the *Warrego*, and he now sent for more reinforcements and pushed on. Sixty men of the destroyer crews,
armed partly with rifles and partly with revolvers, were
quickly landed, and at 10 a.m. reached Bowen's party,
which by then was held up by fire from a trench across
the road. Several Australians had been killed or wounded.
The medical officer, Captain B. C. A. Pockley, after attending to one,[4] gave his own red cross brassard to a stoker
whom he left with the wounded man, and himself was
going on, under deadly fire, to rejoin the front troops,
when he too was mortally wounded. Bowen now decided
to creep round the enemy's flanks, but he himself was soon
wounded and the outflanking had not yet been completed
at 1 o'clock when another reinforcement, Lieut.-Com-
mander Elwell with fifty naval reservists from the *Ber-*

---

[4] A seaman, W. G. V. Williams, an employee of Melbourne City Council
and apparently the first Australian to be hit. He died the same day. For the
details of these operations see *Vol. IX, pp. 78-99*, and *Vol. X, pp. 52-81*; for
the German forces, *Vol. X, pp. 47-9.*

rima, came up. Elwell took control of one flank and at once charged the enemy trench. He was killed, but the Germans' native troops were terrified, their fears being increased by a statement (shouted by the first German prisoner, whom Bowen forced to do so) that 800 troops had been landed. The Germans also believed this. A white flag was presently raised and three German officers came from the trench to ask for terms. They were taken to Commander Beresford who had arrived in rear with another fifty naval reservists. After long discussion the German officers agreed to the surrender of their whole force, which was protecting the wireless station. Six Germans and twenty natives in the trench surrendered, and Lieutenant Bond and twenty-five Australians were sent on with the senior German officer to enforce these terms on other defenders farther back. Partly by bold action, partly by bluff Bond succeeded. The great wireless mast was found at Bitapaka, destroyed, but the instruments were captured. The German commander afterwards reported to his Governor that the defenders had underestimated the skill of the Australians in jungle fighting; it had been expected that they would be confined to the roads.

Meanwhile little news of either of the undertakings ashore had reached Colonel Holmes in the *Berrima.* In the afternoon she had landed half her infantry at Herbertshöhe. He and Admiral Patey decided to land the other half at Kabakaul, withdraw the advanced troops to the coast, and, at dawn, attack from both places after a naval bombardment of the hills behind. After dark, however, came full reports which showed this attack to be now unnecessary. The Herbertshöhe landing party had carried a letter from Admiral Patey to the German Acting-Governor, Dr Haber, demanding the surrender of the colony. A German civilian had agreed to carry it to Haber, who had previously transferred the seat of government to Toma. At 6 p.m. an answer had arrived. Haber said he had no authority to surrender the territory, but that Herbertshöhe and Rabaul were unprotected. Patey decided to occupy those two places next day.

Accordingly on September 12th the naval reserve marched from Kabakaul to Herbertshöhe, and the *Berrima* took the military battalion to Rabaul and reaching it about nightfall landed a garrison. Next afternoon, Sunday, September 13th, at a stately ceremony in what was afterwards known as Proclamation Square, the British flag was hoisted, and the occupation of New Britain was proclaimed. A translation told the natives: "All boys belongira one place, you savvy big master he come now, he new feller master, . . . he look out good you feller. Now he like you feller look out good alonga him. . . . No more 'Um Kaiser. God Save 'Um King."

Patey had written to Haber that any further communication should be made to Colonel Holmes. Haber replied to the effect that he had no objection to discussing the situation with Holmes. Holmes concluded that Haber was merely making time in order to withdraw his government farther, into the Baining mountains, and therefore decided to send a force to arrest him. With Patey's agreement at dawn on the 14th the *Encounter* shelled a ridge shown in the captured map to be the main defence line of Toma, and half a battalion with a naval field-gun then advanced along the Toma road. A few German native police were scattered by the field-gun, and this display had the desired effect. A flag of truce came down the road. Toma was occupied, and on the 15th Haber visited Holmes in Herbertshöhe and, after discussion, returned to Toma with a draft of the terms. His military commander reported that the native troops were "thoroughly terrified", and many of the white soldiers disabled by dysentery and malaria. After inspecting them at Vunadidir, Haber took the military commander back with him to Herbertshohe and on September 17th the terms were signed. All military resistance in German New Guinea (which was defined as meaning all German possessions previously administered by Haber from Rabaul) was to cease at once, and the armed German forces then in the field were to be surrendered on September 21st, Holmes granting them "military honours". Haber would be allowed to return to Germany on condition that he took no further part in the war. German civilians who took the oath of neutrality could remain in their homes and present occupations except the civil servants, of whom some might be required to assist the government. Those of them who refused to take the oath of neutrality would be sent to Australia, but allowed to return from there to Germany as soon as possible. The native constabulary then serving in the German defence force was, for the safety of the whites, to be transferred to the new administration.

Holmes was strongly criticised in Australia for the lenience of the terms. But his special instructions were to occupy, not annex, the German colony and his actions have since been generally approved. The occupation was accomplished with very slight loss, the most important being that of the submarine *AE1* and her crew. After patrolling near Rabaul on September 14th they did not return and were never again heard of.

On September 21st 40 German white soldiers and 110 natives formally marched in and, at a parade in which they exchanged salutes with the Australian force, laid down their arms. There were still left German officials in other islands, and at the main settlement, Madang (then known as Friedrich Wilhelm Harbour), on the New Guinea mainland. On the 22nd, therefore, Holmes sailed thither in the *Berrima*, escorted by the *Australia*, *Montcalm*, and *Encounter*, and two days later the British flag was hoisted and a garrison of a couple of companies was left there. Until the German naval history was published after the war it was not known that, while Holmes was at Madang on September 24th, a German merchant cruiser was in hiding at Port Alexis, twelve miles away. The admiral of the German Pacific squadron, Count Spee, had ordered two merchant cruisers to combine in attacking trade routes in Western Australian waters. They had met on the way to Western Australia, but owing to the destruction of German wireless stations, could get no coal there. It was therefore decided to raid traffic off the east coast of Australia, the two ships meeting for this purpose in Port Alexis. One of them, the *Cormoran* (formerly the Russian merchant cruiser *Riasan*), arrived there on the 24th; being concealed in a winding channel, she was not seen, though one of the Australian warships apparently searched the entrance. After dark that evening the *Cormoran* left hurriedly. The other merchant cruiser —the liner *Prinz Eitel Friedrich*—arrived four days later, with coal urgently needed by the *Cormoran*. She called the *Cormoran* repeatedly with her wireless, but the only answer was the wireless of British ships "all around us . . . in particular the battle-cruiser *Australia*". Actually the Australian squadron was back in Rabaul by the 26th. But the British arrangements were making it almost impossible for the Germans to get either coal or news, and the captain of the *Prinz Eitel Friedrich* therefore gave up his task and sailed for South America. Meanwhile the *Cormoran* had run to Yap and was taking aboard the naval garrison of that island with the object of returning to New Guinea for a surprise attack on Madang. On approaching that place, however, these Germans, too, apparently imagined that they detected "five ships lying off the place, including the *Australia*", and gave up the expedition. The *Cormoran* went into hiding in the Pacific.[5]

Colonel Holmes had returned to Rabaul, where he

---

[5] The small cruiser *Geier* also was in those waters. For details of these events see *Vol. IX, p. 39*. The beautiful German naval yacht, *Komet*, which eventually hid on the coast of New Britain, was captured in October and rechristened *H.M.A.S. Una* (see *Vol. IX, pp. 114-21*).

now set up a government, finding from among his troops all the necessary officials, for Treasury, Works, Lands and Survey, Post and Telephones, Native Affairs, and even for the printing office. In the next two months Holmes sent out detachments, mostly in small captured German steamers, to occupy the remaining German islands south of the Equator—New Ireland, the Admiralty Islands, Western Islands, Bougainville and the German Solomons. Nauru, where a party from the *Melbourne* on September 9th had put out of action the wireless station, was visited during November in a commandeered merchant steamer by Holmes, who removed the German officials and left an Australian garrison.

While these events, which drew little attention in Australia, were proceeding in the islands north of her, the great expected sea battle between the German and British fleets in European waters had not happened. The Germans apparently saw no hope of success in it, and consequently kept their main fleet in port, with the British blockading all approaches from the North Sea and Atlantic.

The sea war in Europe thus turned into one of blockade, minefields, and German submarine attack (aircraft had as yet no significant part in it). In Australia the people's attention was meanwhile chiefly concentrated on two chains of incidents—the unexpected, sweeping advance of the German Army through northern France until the Marne battle, in which it was turned and the crystallisation of the Western Front began; and the raising and despatch of their own force, the A.I.F. The expectation was that the A.I.F. would help the British and French finally to beat back the German onrush, against which in October these allies were desperately fighting with their backs to the wall at Ypres.

CHAPTER IV

THE FIRST CONTINGENT SAILS

FEW Australians—indeed comparatively few Anglo-Saxons—in July 1914 knew what a "division" of cavalry or infantry was; and to the stream of ill-assorted men who poured like ants into the barrack squares of the main Australian cities on 10th August 1914, eager to enlist, the title 1st Australian Division meant almost nothing. Probably those who applied to enter the 1st Australian Light Horse Brigade knew a little more. It was into the Light Horse or other mounted arms—horse transport and artillery—that Australians of that day tended to rush; that generation of them had no fondness for walking. "Hiking" had not come into vogue among city folk, and, if caste existed in the country, the "footman" was on its lowest rung. The old "sundowner" only tramped because he had to; and anyone who (like the famous *Times* correspondent, "Chinese" Morrison, and certain professors and poets) willingly walked, when he could avoid it, was genuinely regarded there as "queer". Part even of the city population could then still ride—or at least had made some attempt at it during country holidays.

So there was a natural rush for the mounted arm. But so keen was the desire to enlist that many fine horsemen, fearing to be shut out, went straight into the infantry.

From before the first official day of enlistment there streamed to the military headquarters in each State numbers of the keen-spirited youngsters—and also many over the limit of nineteen to thirty-eight years—to whom

the British connection had always been sacred. There
crowded to them also all the adventurous spirits, rather
numerous in Australia, that *must* be in anything that was
moving. For some time the only centres for enlistment
were in the great coastal cities, and, partly through inexperience, the medical and dental standards were at that
stage absurdly rigorous. Men who had abandoned their
jobs, some who had sold their small farms and businesses,
or left them to their neighbours, or had simply locked
the doors and made the long journeys to the capitals,
found themselves rejected for defects of teeth, eyesight,
feet and so on, which a few months later were readily
passed over as either immaterial or amenable to treatment. It was said that some men even broke into tears
on such rejection; many were advised to have the defect
treated and to apply again. In dealing with mental and
moral defects on the other hand, the admission was perhaps too wide, and a severe process of discarding unsuit-
ables had to be carried out by at least one brigade before
leaving Australia, and by the whole force after arrival
overseas.

One difficulty of organising a force for overseas was
that, whereas the Australian Army was organised in local
units, when a force had to be sent abroad it must represent all Australia. When the first contingent was raised
it seemed likely that it would be the only large Australian
force to be sent abroad for a considerable time; men of
every State would naturally demand to serve in it. Consequently in the creation of the 1st Australian Infantry
Division, each of the two most populous States, New
South Wales and Victoria, supplied an infantry brigade,
and the four "outer" States together supplied a third. As
each brigade then comprised four battalions (each of 1017
officers and men) the composition of the 1st Division was:

> 1st Brigade (1, 2, 3 and 4 Bns), New South Wales.
> 2nd Brigade (5, 6, 7 and 8 Bns), Victoria.

3rd Brigade: 9 Bn, Queensland; 10 Bn, South Australia; 11 Bn, Western Australia; 12 Bn, half, Tasmania—half, Western and South Australia.

Besides the 12,000 infantry thus furnished, the division had its own regiment of Light Horse, the 4th (546 strong, from Victoria); its own artillery (3 brigades—in the Second World War we called them regiments—each of 3 four-gun batteries), totalling 36 field-guns, all drawn by six-horse teams; an "ammunition column", also horse-drawn, to bring ammunition for artillery and infantry; 3 field companies of engineers; 3 field ambulances; and a divisional train (horse transport). The total strength was 18,000 men.

The 1st Light Horse Brigade (2226 strong) also represented most of Australia as follows:

1st Regiment, New South Wales,
2nd Regiment, Queensland,
3rd Regiment, South Australia and Tasmania,

and included also its signal troop, field ambulance (and, later, a field troop of engineers) and brigade train.

The composition of all later divisions and brigades was in general much the same, except that in the 4th Infantry Division the "outer" States were more strongly represented.

The only automobiles with the original force were five motor cars given by their owners for the 1st Division's staff; but a "reserve park" of motor transport for the 1st Division was raised almost at once, and a few gifts of motor ambulances were received. (These motor ambulances later arriving in Egypt filled a big gap in the British provision there; and the reserve park, going on to England, served with the British in Belgium long before the Australian infantry was sent there.) The A.I.F.'s guns were then all 18-pounders, the standard British field-guns of that day, and were drawn from those

of the citizen forces. Later it had two siege batteries;
but the heavies supporting it were almost always British.

Before the battalions, batteries, engineer and other
companies could be formed, their commanders had to be
chosen. The main staff and the artillery and infantry
brigade commanders were selected by Bridges and White.
For the three infantry brigades they chose Henry Mac-
Laurin, a young Sydney barrister, a fine product of
Sydney University; James Whiteside M'Cay, a Victorian
lawyer, one of a brilliant family, and for a short while
Federal Minister for Defence—both of these were highly
trained militiamen; and E. G. Sinclair-MacLagan, a
British regular officer who had been right-hand to Bridges
in shaping the military college at Duntroon, and whose
interest in men and sense of humour, as well as his
efficiency, made him a suitable commander of Australians.
To command the 1st Light Horse Brigade Bridges chose
Colonel Henry George Chauvel,[1] then Australian representative on the Imperial General Staff in London. For
his chief artillery officer he selected Colonel Talbot
Hobbs, a keen little expert from the militia, in civil life
an architect in Western Australia. The two officers chosen
for the heads of his medical service proved, before long,
to be inadequate for the exacting demands of the highest
positions and were successively displaced by a dynamic
personality, Colonel Neville R. Howse, a country surgeon
who had won a V.C. in South Africa and who, through
the influence given him by that decoration, managed to
return from the A.N. & M.E.F. in New Guinea just in
time to secure a special post as "supernumerary medical
officer" with Bridges' staff. The staff included, besides
several British specialist officers who were in Australia on
loan or exchange, Captain John Gellibrand, a Tasmanian
apple-grower, formerly in the British regular Army and

---

[1] At this time all infantry and light-horse brigade commanders of the
First A.I.F. were given the rank of colonel; in and after the Gallipoli Campaign all were made brigadier-generals.

a contemporary of White at the Staff College; and Captain Tom Griffiths, formerly gunner in the Victorian Permanent Artillery, who became Bridges' "military secretary", dealing with the administration of the force as a whole as distinct from that of the 1st Division. None could then foretell that this tiny branch of Bridges' staff would eventually develop into an oversea miniature of the British War Office, with a staff of several thousands.

The first task of the brigadiers was to choose their battalion commanders, who then picked their company officers. These included but few "regular" soldiers. It is true that cadets of the military college, sergeants of the permanent instructional staff, and "area officers" under Kitchener's scheme were usually allotted to battalions as adjutants, machine-gun officers, quartermasters, regimental sergeant-majors and so forth. Some of these posts were also given to former officers or N.C.O.'s of the British regular Army who had emigrated to Australia, and a sprinkling of these was also among the company officers. But for the most part each commander staffed his battalion, battery, field company or other unit with officers from the Australian militia, and it was on the old militia far more than on any other body that the leading and training of the A.I.F. fell.

By about August 17th this choice of leaders was sufficiently complete for the units to be embodied; and on prescribed mornings the selected officers reported in their militia uniforms to the State headquarters, where the parade ground was crowded with men in every kind of civilian dress. As in the New Guinea force, so in the A.I.F. it was never afterwards difficult to find representatives of any calling required—dentists, labourers, surveyors, farmers, engineers, navigators, artists, masons, mechanics, chemists, even clergymen, and fine ones at that. On this first day the officers were allotted to their companies; a few sharp commands—enough of the men knew enough of their drill for the whole to be pushed

into their places; and on a final order a nondescript
column, perhaps 20 officers and 300 men, marched off,
winding through the barracks gate and out along the
dusty road to some camp, showground or racecourse on
the city's outskirts. Here among the windy tents or grand-
stands it began its camp life; and a collection of strangers,
who arrived there meaning no more to one another than
do fellow-passengers in a suburban train, began within
a week or two of feverish registering, examining, and
equipping, and some rough and ready training, to become the 1st, 9th, 12th or other battalion with its individual spirit and manner, easily recognisable in the
later history of the A.I.F.

For Australia as it then was, the equipping of this
force within a month of its enrolment, the manufacture
of waggons, harness and uniforms, the refitting of passenger liners and freighters to carry troops and horses,
the provisioning of fleet and army with food, stores and
medical equipment so that it should be ready to sail by
September 21st, was a proof—too little recognised—of the
realism and ability of the small military and naval staffs
built up in peace-time, as well as of the resourcefulness
of Australian workers and manufacturers.[2]

By mid-September the newly formed brigades and
battalions were sufficiently trained to march through the
streets where their relations and friends proudly crowded
the kerbs to see them. Not all citizens were equally
impressed. The loose pea-soup coloured, dull-buttoned
khaki uniforms of the A.I.F., though more workmanlike
than those of any other army within the A.I.F.'s subsequent experience, appeared slovenly to critics who compared them with the traditional tight-stuffed, twinkling,
gold-braided, brass-buttoned uniforms of peace-time; and
there was an unevenness about these big, early troops

---

[2] It is noteworthy that the contingent raised in New South Wales in 1885
to serve in the Sudan War embarked three weeks after its formation was
suggested. See *The Sudan Contingent*, by Stanley Brogden.

that caused one onlooker to say: "They'll never make soldiers of this lot. The light horse may be all right, but they've got the ragtag and bobtail of Australia in this infantry." "Going to the front!" said the manager of a great Sydney newspaper. "They'll keep the trained British regular Army for the front; the nearest these'll get to it will be the line of communications!"

The pay of Australian privates was estimated to yield to each man the same return as the wages of the average worker, and was the highest in that war—6s. a day, of which 1s. was "deferred", to be paid on discharge. A nickname of this force in those early days—with a laugh at their supposed motive of seeing the world—was the "Six-bob-a-day Tourists".

However, promptly in the fourth week of September, orders were given to the battalions to embark. A couple were already steaming round the coast on the way to the rendezvous in Western Australia, when the orders were cancelled and the ships brought into port.

This was due to the appearance off Samoa of the two main cruisers of the German Pacific fleet, *Gneisenau* and *Scharnhorst*, at dawn on September 14th. The German official history says that the raid was undertaken in the hope of making a dawn attack upon any warships of the Allies—"even the *Australia*"—or any transports, found in harbour. But none were there, and without uselessly hitting the natives Spee could not fire on the khaki figures of the New Zealanders seen ashore. He therefore left a few hours later, steering north-west.

Thus the German squadron was now definitely known to have been on that date in the south-west Pacific, 2400 miles from the Australian coast. The Admiralty ordered the *Australia* to finish its work at New Guinea and then search for the two big German cruisers. Meanwhile a strong escort, the British armoured cruiser, *Minotaur*, and the much more powerful Japanese cruiser, *Ibuki*, would go to Western Australia to protect the convoy, which would assemble there, in King George's Sound, for the voyage to Europe. Australian and New Zealand Ministers, however, were racked by deep doubts as to whether it was safe for their unescorted transports to venture yet on the voyage to Western Australia seeing that the German cruisers might already be entering the Tasman Sea. Perceiving—and sharing—these doubts, the Governor-General of Australia, Sir Ronald Munro-Ferguson, wisely took on himself the responsibility of telegraphing an intimation of them to the Governor-General of New Zealand, and the British Colonial Office. Although the Admiralty believed that the transports would be safe, his action caused it to send the escort all the way to New Zealand, to pick up the New Zealand transports; the Australian ones would join it as it returned.

The sailing of Australian transports was therefore cancelled; those already at sea were ordered to port and their troops into camp. On September 30th arrived news that the German cruisers on September 22nd had raided Papeete,[3] 1000 miles more distant than Samoa. The New Zealand government, having by then promised its people that the troops would be escorted, insisted that the escort should come for them as arranged. The Australian government, believing the danger to be ended (and being 1000 miles farther away), ordered its transports to start or resume their voyages individually to Western Australia. The battle-cruiser *Australia*, having finished its task in New Guinea waters, went by the Admiralty's order to Fiji to search for the big German cruisers. Most of the Australian squadron was directed thither.

General Bridges had protested against the delay in sailing, feeling that it diminished the value of the help to be given by his force in the crisis on the Western Front. The anti-climax was also a severe test for the discipline of the troops: at this stage Melbourne and Sydney were

---

[3] The French there acted most vigorously and the Germans did not land. (*Vol. IX, p. 107.*)

nightly thronged by men supposed to be in camp. It was
a relief to them and to their leaders when, in mid-
October, the embarkation order was renewed.

From October 24th there began to arrive in King
George's Sound, the great, safe, lonely harbour of Albany
in the south-western corner of Australia, transport after
transport carrying men, horses, guns. The troops were
not allowed to land. On the 26th came in the Orient liner
Orvieto, now transporting General Bridges, his staff, and
over 1000 men from Melbourne. On the 28th, when
nearly 30 Australian transports were in port, all in their
peace-time paint, 14 ships entered—the New Zealand
transports, painted grey, and their powerful escort. Four
days later, at 6.45 a.m. on November 1st, the *Orvieto* led
the transports out from the harbour heads. The 26 Australian transports formed up first, in three divisions,
steaming parallel with a mile between them, each division
in "line ahead" (or, as the Army would say, in "single
file"). The 10 New Zealand ships in two similar divisions
followed, and the warships escorted. Two days later 2
Western Australian transports met the fleet at sea. Then
with the British cruiser *Minotaur* five miles ahead, the
Ibuki and *Melbourne* four miles out on either beam, and
the *Sydney* far astern, the 38 transports headed for Suez
en route to England.

CHAPTER V

EARLY PROBLEMS OF THE HOME FRONT

For most Australians except those whose near relatives or friends had enlisted, even the raising of the A.I.F. was hardly more than a side issue as compared with the progress of the war in Europe on which—as even in the Second World War—they felt that their fate and the fate of most other nations primarily depended. Never, perhaps, was a general election less welcome than that which occurred throughout Australia on September 5th. The Liberals (the party of the Right), who were in office, had expected success largely on the ground that in an "Empire" crisis, and for the conduct of such a war, the floating voter would trust them rather than the Left. But in this issue the Labour party was immensely helped by the character of its two main leaders. Its official leader, Andrew Fisher—a Scot, and like his opponent, Joseph Cook, formerly a miner—was known to be a man of high integrity and, for all his Australian nationalism, a firm supporter of the British Commonwealth. The genius of the party, William Morris Hughes—a Welshman born, who had tried many trades and succeeded remarkably in his later ones, as trades-union leader, politician, barrister, and journalist—had, long before this war, placed beyond doubt his enthusiasm for the common defence of the Empire. A courageous realist, he had flung himself into the movement for universal service. Throughout the election, while most others spoke of local issues, he asked for unity in the war effort and suggested a truce between the parties, and the cancelling of the dissolution—which his opponents refused.

To an extent that surprised even its own supporters, Labour swept the polls, winning 31 of the 36 seats in the Senate and 42 of the 75 in the House of Representatives. Andrew Fisher became Prime Minister and Treasurer, and W. M. Hughes Attorney-General. The Defence Department was given to Senator George Foster Pearce, a much abler head than was generally recognised, most careful in giving his decisions, and thereafter most loyal to those charged with carrying them out.[1] Mr F. G. Tudor became Minister for Trade and Customs—a post of much importance in view of the vast changes due to transport needs and the eventual system of priorities in the Empire's trade, the immense world-wide organisation of embargoes, "black" and "white" lists, and the other means gradually developed in order to direct supplies to the Allies and to enforce the blockade of Germany.

For, though, as stated above, in the exciting news from Paris and the Marne many Australians barely noted events on their local stage, both this government and the one that it displaced had almost daily to face unprecedented problems. It was commonly supposed that the outbreak of a great war would bring financial crisis. The Stock Exchanges closed (and remained so for six or seven weeks, until the situation was clearer). Almost automatically there came the beginning of a rush of nervous depositors on the savings banks; many folk, however, paid in their money again almost immediately—a few were reported to have had it stolen before they could do so. The people's good sense quickly ended this agitation. But in the last days of peace and the first days of war a great part of oversea shipping came to a standstill, German steamers fleeing to their own or neutral ports, British ones waiting till the command of the seas and conditions of insurance became clearer. Sea freights rose. The wool

---

[1] From July 1915 the Navy Department was separated from Defence, and given to another Minister. For short biographies of these ministers see Vol. XI, pp. 38 and 42-51.

trade with Germany ceased; other European buyers cancelled their orders. Wool prices fell and sales were postponed. Industries dependent on wool became slack and unemployment increased. Many other exports stopped—the oversea coal trade, the trade in metals between Broken Hill and Germany, the export of pearl shell and opals. On the other hand Australian importing houses began to cancel their purchases of British cottons and other goods. The danger of panic, or at least of wild speculation, might have been extreme.

Throughout this, as in later crises of the war, the loosely knit organisation of the British Empire worked extraordinarily well. The Dominion governments and peoples usually looked to the British government for guidance, themselves keeping their heads and quietly meeting each problem as it arose—always in close consultation with the Mother Country. At the request of the British government, Australian importers were asked not "unduly or hurriedly" to reduce their orders—"if we tide over the next few weeks things will probably improve". Thus began the policy of "business as usual", an admirable rule in that crisis although later it became dangerous and was modified or abandoned.

Most fortunately for all concerned the British Committee of Imperial Defence had recently studied the problems of trade and shipping, and was able to recommend well-considered solutions. One of its plans, approved and announced on the night when war began, brought immediate relief in the most vital matter of the Empire's shipping. Premiums for insurance against war risks at sea rose at one stage to as high as 20 per cent, but the problem was solved by the British government's undertaking to shoulder four-fifths of the risk—an undertaking which, on request, it extended to ships registered in other parts of the Empire. As stated in the previous chapter, the sea battle that was to decide the command of the sea never came; the German staff decided that it could not take the risk, and kept its High Seas fleet in port so that it would remain a constant threat—the British Navy had to keep watch on it and to clear German cruisers from the seas. Despite all dangers the sea remained open for British traffic which, with the British scheme of insurance, presently moved almost as freely as in peace-time.

Second to maintaining the flow of materials for the Allies was the task of stopping the flow to their enemies. On the first day of the war the British government by proclamation made direct trade with the enemy illegal. To prevent materials of war from reaching him through neutrals, lists of "absolute" and "conditional" contraband were published. But the Committee of Imperial Defence had also studied beforehand the question of what foodstuffs and raw materials were likely to be most urgently needed at home or by an enemy, and on the same day it prohibited or restricted the export from Britain of any of these. Shortly afterwards, as the Empire's sea trade was moving again, it asked the Dominion governments to take certain similar steps—Australia was requested in mid-August to hold up any cargo of wool destined for European neutrals unless satisfied that the wool was not intended for Germany or Austria; and to send Australia's surplus foodstuffs to England.

There had been a bad season in Australia; the government was anxious as to food supplies, and immediately after the outbreak of war the Cook government took the very wise step of calling the Premiers of the six States, as well as the Opposition leaders, Mr Fisher and Mr Hughes, into conference in Melbourne on August 11th-14th to consider this and other problems. An important object was to prevent any "cornering" or other speculation in foodstuffs. The power to do so at that time lay with the States. The government of New South Wales set up, by a special law, a commission to control "necessary commodities"; and the Federal government appointed a royal commission, with Alfred Deakin as chairman, to

study the food supply. On its advice the appeals from
Great Britain were met by forbidding, except with special
leave, the export of meat to countries outside the Empire,
and of wheat and flour to any country except Britain. In
general similar restrictions were later applied to wool,
wheat, hides and most of the important exports, the
restrictions being tightened or relaxed according to
British or Australian needs. At times Australian wool
was allowed to be sold to the United States, a neutral
power, the best customer at that time outside Great
Britain; American manufacturers agreed to use it in their
own mills and, further, to discourage the export even of
American wool.

The urgent need of such measures may be illustrated
by the fact that, in the Pacific, German staff agencies,
established in neutral islands and in countries bordering
that ocean, were then making desperate efforts to coal
the cruisers and merchant cruisers that for some time
infested it—and two of which were ordered to raid Australian trade; and it was reported that coal from Newcastle in New South Wales, exported, of course, to neutral
countries, had come into German possession. The necessity for another measure, the strict censorship maintained
in Australia as to *troop movements*, is illustrated by the
fact that through some leakage—possibly through neutrals
reaching Java—reports of the projected sailing of the
Australian and New Zealand contingent reached newspapers, apparently in the islands, and carried the information to the most dangerous German raider in the
Pacific, the *Emden*, but fortunately gave her captain no
useful clue as to the time or the route.[2]

Other precautions never before taken in Australia,

---

[2] Her Captain, von Müller, himself wrote afterwards: "From newspapers
which had been found in the ships we had met, and from utterances of the
hangers-on of the crews of the captured ships, I concluded that, after the
outbreak of war, transport of troops from India to France had taken place,
and that troops would be shipped thither also from Australia and New
Zealand."

but for which the need quickly became obvious, were the internment of German and other enemy reservists then in Australia and the keeping of at least some kind of contact with other enemy citizens. At first many of the reservists were set free again on giving their parole, and other enemy nationals were merely ordered to give their addresses to the police. But as the methods adopted by the German leaders in Europe took on some of the uglier characteristics of "total" war, the precautions became stricter. All reservists, and others whose conduct was unsatisfactory or suspicious, were interned. On New Year's Day 1915, a murderous outbreak by two Turks at Broken Hill[3] stirred feeling there against aliens. But, despite the efforts of the German government to keep Germans in other countries under its own influence and allegiance, there was—except in America—no "fifth column" activity comparable to that organised by the Nazis in and before World War II; consequently registration of all aliens was not introduced in Australia until the third year of war.

Far more vigorous was the campaign against German trade; in this respect Australia led the Allies, the heart and soul of the activity being, from first to last, W. M. Hughes. Before the war German trade throughout the British Empire—which, in general, was free to it—had advanced with such leaps that it was a current joke that Germany before long would "possess" the Empire by peaceful penetration. Mr Hughes was determined to rid Australia—and, if possible, the Empire—of German commercial influences, both by transferring the local agencies to British control and by establishing in British lands those industries in which Germans held a monopoly. Above all he objected to the control won by German companies over the Australian base-metal industry. This control had been obtained by very high skill, both in

---

[3] The details of this fight are given in *Vol. XI, p. 111.*

treating ores and in establishing world-wide organisation, and it had probably helped the German government to build up stocks important for war manufacture. Mr Hughes was determined not merely to stop the traffic with Germany but to transfer the industry to British or Australian hands.

These drastic steps could be completed only by inducing the Australian and British Parliaments to pass special laws—in which Mr Hughes eventually succeeded. But for most war-time measures the Federal government relied on the War Precautions Act, brought in by the Fisher Ministry two months after the outbreak of war in order to enable it to take all kinds of precautions never thought of in peace-time—and indeed beyond its peace-time powers. The Australian Federal constitution proved admirably flexible for the extraordinary needs of war, for which a federation is normally too weak and slow in action. Fortunately the clause giving to the Federal Parliament power to make laws for the country's defence enabled the government to be virtually unified in war-time; and by the War Precautions Act—similar to the famous DORA (Defence of Realm Act) in Great Britain—the Federal Parliament practically handed on that power to the central government during the war. From 29th October 1914, when the act was passed, the Federal government could make and enforce almost any regulation that it desired, provided that the projected action was not disallowed by the High Court of Australia as unconstitutional.

It was not at first clear how far the High Court would agree with the government as to what action was genuinely helpful for defence. In 1916, however, when a lawsuit arose over its fixing of the price of bread,[4] and the High Court upheld the regulation, it became evident that the High Court would confirm the government's

---

[4] In the case of *Farey v. Burvett. See Vol. XI, pp. 642-3.*

power to regulate in respect of everything that might reasonably be held to contribute to victory or defence. In the case in question, obviously the price of bread by affecting public health or morale might affect the result of the war.

Price-fixing, however, did not come until 1916; in the early days the declaration of the Federal and State governments that they would allow no cornering or profiteering in foodstuffs and other necessaries possibly helped somewhat to keep prices from rising steeply in the early months of the war.

Mr Joseph Cook and the State Premiers when they met on August 11th-14th had to face also some big problems of finance. As already mentioned, the Australian States had of late been rapidly developing their railways, irrigation dams and other national facilities with money borrowed in London. They could not suddenly close down these works without creating waste and unemployment. At that time the appeal from Britain was for business as usual for the next few weeks. The Australian government telegraphed that it would continue public works "at their full current volume" and, if necessary, place its credit behind the States and banks to encourage employment. It soon became clear to the succeeding Prime Minister and Treasurer, Mr Fisher, that London would need all its money for the huge effort of war; the British government was refusing to authorise much proposed expenditure on works required by British towns and counties. Eventually it agreed to lend the Australian government for war purposes £18 million from the next British loan; this enabled the Australian government to lend its States the same amount from the Australian note issue. Later the British government permitted the State governments of Australia to borrow in London to complete works already started, or to meet earlier loans when due, but not for new works or extensions—these being the same restrictions that were imposed on local

government bodies in Great Britain. Ultimately the
Federal government undertook all borrowings in London
on behalf of most of the Australian States—New South
Wales alone standing out.

With the cost of the war to the Mother Country
growing enormously from month to month, the British
Chancellor of the Exchequer was forced in June 1915
to point out that there must be in the Dominions considerable private funds which were not being invested
for war purposes, which might readily be subscribed for
local war loans. The British government offered to
guarantee such loans, if desired.

The Federal government did not take advantage of
this offer. Actually it had already decided to float a loan
in Australia and it now realised that for its main war
expenditure it would have to rely on its own people. In
war, as previously in the building up of the Australian
Navy, Andrew Fisher was determined to pay as much as
possible of the cost out of revenue. But as the Federal
revenue had till then been derived almost entirely from
customs (of which part was returned as a subsidy to the
States) he now had to introduce several direct taxes, the
first of these, brought in early in the war, being a succession duty—a Federal income tax was not thought necessary until 1915-16. In the first year of war the Federal
government's own revenue was £22 million, of which
only £1 million was spent on war services, £14 million
of the total war cost for that year (£15 million) coming
from the British loan.

But the narrative of the home front has here far out-
paced that of the fighting services. At the beginning of
November 1914, when the first contingent left Albany,
questions of taxation and finance, and even of trade,
caused little concern to the Australian public. The attention of the whole people, irrespective of class, religion,
race, or any other normal division, was concentrated, as
already stated on the shocking initial disasters of the

war in Europe, the retreat from Mons, the heartening
recovery—by a bare margin—on the Marne, the horrors
in Belgium, the swift advance and then stoppage of the
Russian "steam roller", the first struggle at Ypres. Australians were still rushing to enlist; fresh troops—a
fourth infantry brigade, two more light horse brigades,
hospitals, veterinary, bakery, and butchery units were
sent. Funds were started for relief of Belgians and
for Red Cross aid for the British and, almost by afterthought, for Australia's own troops. By Christmas 1914
over £1 million had been collected, and these funds
rapidly grew. An Australian branch of the British Red
Cross Society, with a division in each State, was launched
by Lady Helen Munro-Ferguson, wife of the Governor-
General; all over Australia women made comforts for
the troops in the battle that swayed on the Western
Front.

Meanwhile, without the least doubt as to the out-
come of that desperate struggle but eager to be in it
before the main fighting of the war should be over, the
Australian and New Zealand soldiers on their transports
drilled and were lectured on the decks, or groomed and
exercised their horses and cleaned the stalls, as the
thirty-eight ships slowly heaved and dipped in the
tropical seas.

CHAPTER VI

TO THE WAR THEATRES

THE convoy carrying with it towards the Western Front so many of Australia's hopes, fears and interests, was heading into waters in which it was not likely to meet serious dangers. The German cruiser squadron, last heard of when at Papeete on September 22nd, was unlikely to have sailed far back towards the Indian Ocean. The only German cruisers believed to be there were the *Emden*, whose tall, taciturn, half-French captain, von Müller, had been brilliantly raiding British traffic in Malayan and Indian waters, and the *Königsberg*; and both these sisterships, though somewhat similar to the *Sydney* and *Melbourne*, were older, much smaller, and armed with ten 4.1-inch guns against the eight 6-inchers of the Australian light cruisers.

On November 7th there reached the convoy news that the main German cruiser squadron, coming to light off the west coast of South America, had been attacked by a British cruiser squadron, a degree less powerful than itself, and had sunk the two biggest of the attacking ships—the cruisers *Good Hope* and *Monmouth*. This grievous disaster brought one advantage—it definitely located the German squadron—and a regrouping of the British Navy immediately followed. Among other changes, the *Minotaur* was at once ordered to leave the Australian convoy which would henceforth be in charge of Captain Silver of the *Melbourne*. The convoy held on its course with the *Melbourne* ahead, *Sydney* away out to the west and *Ibuki* to the east.

It was getting into waters where the chief danger was from the vigorous *Emden*.

This light German cruiser had sunk or captured twenty-five allied steamers and two warships, raided Penang, and shelled the oil tanks at Madras in India, and was at the moment paralysing Britain's far Eastern sea-trade. The Australian and New Zealand convoy was learning to sail without lights. The big staff-ship, *Orvieto*, still sometimes twinkled (as the others complained) "like a hotel"; but this discipline was already becoming strict and effective when, on the night of November 8th, the convoy approached the solitary Cocos Islands, keeping fifty miles to the east in case the *Emden* was near.

The convoy had steamed quietly through the night and at dawn was just altering course to bend round the islands, which lay out of sight over the western horizon, when many wireless operators in the transports picked up, very loud and clear, a short coded signal of a wireless which some of them recognised as the *Emden*'s. The Cocos Islands wireless was heard asking for the code and then telegraphing, "Strange warship approaching."[1] This came again, with an "SOS", and then silence. Captain Silver at once started with the *Melbourne* to make for Cocos, but immedi-ately afterwards, real-ising that his main responsibility was the conduct of the con-voy, ordered the *Syd*-

ney to hasten thither instead. The *Sydney*'s engines were in splendid condition and she quickly disappeared, the *Melbourne* moving to westward of the transports, as did the *Ibuki* whose captain had to be restrained from racing westwards to join in the fight. Several hours later some of the troops drilling on the transports' decks heard now

---

[1] The *Emden* had set up a fourth funnel, a sham one, before appearing off Cocos, but afterwards removed it.

and again the distant thud of guns. At 9.30 a wireless message came from the *Sydney*, that she had sighted the enemy steaming northward. At 10.45 she reported, "Am briskly engaging enemy"; and at 11.10, "*Emden* beached and done for."

Captain John Glossop of the *Sydney*, while his highly efficient engineer was driving her at her full 25 knots towards the *Emden*, had with his gunnery officer decided to open fire at 9500 yards, which he believed to be beyond the *Emden's* range. What was his surprise when, having sighted the three-funnelled cruiser about eight miles away, and quickly closed to 10,500 yards and swung on to a parallel course, he saw the enemy open fire and a salvo burst in the sea 200 yards away. A second fell closer, and of the third two shells struck the *Sydney*. For ten minutes the *Sydney* raced through showers of shell bursts, the *Emden* firing with speed and accuracy. The *Sydney* took longer to find the range and her salvoes were less regular; but her heavier shells soon told. The *Emden* quickly hit her fifteen times, though only five shells burst. From then onwards she did not hit again. The *Sydney's* crew—about half Australian, including many boys—worked most steadily through the action. The *Emden's* forward funnel went over the side; then the foremast and main fire-control station. As the *Emden* showed signs of suffering, the *Sydney* closed to 5500 yards and fired a torpedo, which ran short. The *Emden's* captain had throughout been trying to damage the *Sydney* sufficiently to enable him to attack with torpedo, but the *Sydney's* speed always foiled him. The *Sydney's* 100-lb. shells were inflicting much greater damage than the *Emden's* 38-pounders had done.[2] The *Emden* was on fire, another funnel was shot down, one ammunition-room flooded; the steering gear was destroyed and Müller had to steer

---

[2] For details of the fight see *Vol. IX, pp. 179 et seq.* (Captain von Müller's account, *pp. 193-202*); also *Vol. I; pp. 103-8.*

the ship by her screws; half his crew was disabled and, having left 3 officers and 40 men at Cocos Islands to destroy the cable station, he had no reserves. Through stoppage of ventilation the engineers were at times driven from their engines. By about 11 a.m. only one gun was firing. As the *Sydney* was almost undamaged, Müller at last gave up the fight. Keeling Island, a northern member of the Cocos group, happened then to be nearer to him than to the *Sydney*, and he therefore ran his ship at its highest speed on to the coral reef.

The *Sydney* left at once to chase the *Emden's* collier, which was forthwith scuttled by her crew. Returning at 4 p.m. the *Sydney* stood off and forced Captain Müller to haul down his flag and put up a white flag—two salvoes unfortunately being necessary.[3] The *Emden's* landing party at Cocos was found to have escaped at nightfall in a schooner—in an adventurous voyage they ultimately reached Arabia, and thence Germany. The *Sydney* next day returned to the *Emden*, took aboard the survivors, about 190 in number, and sailed with them to Colombo.

The convoy meanwhile had held steadily on its course. For one more night it sailed without lights; then news that the other German light cruiser in the Indian Ocean, the *Königsberg*, had been cornered in East Africa freed it from all serious danger.[4]

The faster ships went on straight to Colombo and were lining that harbour on November 15th when the victorious *Sydney* steamed in between them. Eight German officers and 126 of other ranks—besides 4 of the *Sydney's* crew—had been killed in the battle, and aboard the *Sydney* were 65 wounded Germans, many of them seriously ill. Captain Glossop telegraphed a special re-

---

[3] Glossop was blamed by Müller for such precaution; but it may have been precisely for want of it that the second *Sydney* was lost with all hands in the Second World War.

[4] The *Königsberg* was eventually destroyed in July 1915 in her shelter in the Rufigi River south of Dar-es-Salaam, after operations in which the small Australian cruiser *Pioneer* played a full part.

quest from the *Sydney* that, out of consideration for these maimed and dying men, there should be no cheering when his ship passed through.

The Western Pacific and the Indian Ocean now being known to be free of all important German ships, the *Sydney* and *Melbourne* were at once ordered by the Admiralty to Malta and thence were sent across the Atlantic to the American coast, where at first they helped to force German raiders into port, and later kept watch on contraband. The *Australia* was sent to the Pacific coast of America to block the German cruiser squadron if it should attempt to make towards Canada, a Japanese squadron joining her on the way. Near Panama news reached her that on December 8th the German squadron had been fought, and its big ships and their admiral[5] destroyed, by two British battle-cruisers off the Falkland Islands in the South Atlantic. The *Australia* was, with the Australian government's consent, ordered to Great Britain to become flagship of the Second Battle Cruiser Squadron keeping watch on the main enemy, the German High Seas Fleet. She arrived at Rosyth, after docking, in February 1915 and for the rest of the war took her part with the British "Grand Fleet" in the North Sea. But the light cruisers *Melbourne* and *Sydney* were destined to work for nearly two years on their North and South American beats before they similarly joined the Grand Fleet towards the end of 1916.

The clearing of the German cruisers left the oceans for the time being relatively safe. The mere sinking of the *Emden* caused British insurance rates for war risks on Eastern cargoes to fall from 60s. to 40s., and they soon afterwards dropped below 30s. The Australian and New Zealand contingents continued their voyage, the transports now sailing in separate groups according to their speed. Reaching Aden at the end of November they

---

[5] For some details of this brave and chivalrous man see *Vol. IX, p. 106.*

found the harbour under the dazzling sun crowded with transports on the way to and from India. The Australians and New Zealanders had heard during their voyage that Turkey had entered the war, and they now half expected to receive orders to disembark in Egypt and defend that country. And, surely enough, almost immediately after the ships left Aden a signal was received from the Australian High Commissioner in London, Sir George Reid, saying that the force was to

train in Egypt and go to the front from there. The Australians and New Zealanders are to form a corps under General Birdwood. The locality of the camp is near Cairo.

Only later was it known that the reason for this change of plan was that in England great difficulty had occurred in building winter camps even for British troops and for the Canadian contingent already there; the camp sites were deep in mud and training was hampered by these unexpected miseries and by the discontent that inevitably resulted. Sir George Reid, fearing the effect on the Australians, interviewed the British Secretary of State for War, Lord Kitchener, and found him already of opinion that the Australians should be stopped in Egypt. The Australian government agreed and the decision came just in time.

From November 30th for several days and nights the Australian and New Zealand transports moved through the Suez Canal. On its eastern bank was post after post of Indian troops behind breastworks and barbed wire. At night the flicker of a campfire and the shapes of a few tents would bring "cooees" from the transports. Dark figures would appear on the bank. "Who are you?" from some young English officer there. "Australians—who are you?" "Indian Army. Where are you going?" "Cairo." "You'll be here soon!" "No, thank you!" And amid cheers and counter-cheers the ships would glide on towards another post. By December 3rd the Australians were disembarking at Alexandria; and after a railway journey through the teeming flats of the Nile Delta, sections of the force marched daily and nightly through Cairo, across the Kasr-el-Nil bridge over the Nile, and thence five miles out to the edge of the Libyan desert close by the Pyramids. Here, with headquarters camped behind Mena House Hotel, they settled into a huge tented camp which quickly sprang up as, for the first time, the 1st Australian Division was brought together on land. The New Zealand Infantry and Mounted Rifles Brigades, under Maj.-General Sir A. J. Godley (of the British Army), camped on the other side of Cairo, on the desert's edge at Zeitoun, and the 1st Light Horse Brigade in a similar position at Maadi.

It was nearly mid-December before the last unit of the 1st Division marched to Mena Camp, and the task of welding the division into a single instrument of war was in full swing. In the first weeks most of the Australians there, with Arab guides or children chattering behind them, climbed the Pyramids where some left their names inscribed beside those of Napoleon's soldiers of 1798; and the sight of the camp far below—with the tents of its headquarters, three infantry brigades, artillery, transport, and ambulances, all neatly spaced as on a map—was to some men the first lesson as to the structure of a division. Quickly on certain spaces near the lines there sprang up Arab or other tents labelled "Australians System Afternoon Tea", or tenanted by hairdressers, newspaper vendors, tobacconists, tailors, photographers, and sellers of souvenirs.

Under the bright winter sun, with the desert dragging at their boots, the troops, strikingly tall and generally perfect in physique, trained with grim earnestness under their militia officers and under brigade and divisional staffs, staffs as efficient and vigorous as any they were henceforth to meet in that war. General Bridges and Colonel White insisted on thoroughness; not till

6—o,

February were the troops exercised as brigades, and then they marched, bivouacked and fought for days on end in exercises sometimes as tiring as real operations. In one respect, it is true, the staff lacked experience; though a large Y.M.C.A. room was erected in camp, and several chaplains, especially "Padre" McKenzie of the Salvation Army, tried to organise some amusement, the recreation of the troops was not seriously taken in hand in the sense in which Colonel White, General Monash and others grappled with those problems later in the war. Cairo with its bright, teeming streets, and amusements descending to any degree of filth, beckoned to the troops in their short leisure hours. Trams, motors, carriages streamed thither, crammed and tasselled with men, and a blight of disease was quickly the upshot. Desertion and absence without leave became rife, especially among a certain class of old soldiers who appeared to have been unsettled in habit since the South African war. Eventually General Bridges took the step, already adopted in the New Zealand force, of returning a large number of the more troublesome men to Australia, and this remained for nearly two years the supreme punishment in the A.I.F.; but, through the overwork of the staff in its task of training the troops, the constructive (but then unusual) task of providing mental and physical recreation for the troops was not adequately undertaken till much later.

Lord Kitchener had decided, with the agreement of their governments, to weld the Australian and New Zealand contingents into an improvised Army Corps. To create and command the corps he chose William Riddell Birdwood, a British cavalry officer, short and dapper in figure, a vigorous, brave, upright and understanding leader of fighting men. Though he was a commander rather than an organiser he had served on Kitchener's staff in South Africa and India and was completely trusted by his great chief. Given the temporary rank of lieutenant-general, he arrived in Egypt from India with his staff on

December 21st, and at once proposed to Lord Kitchener
to organise the corps as follows:

> *Corps Headquarters* (this was a British unit with
> a staff of British officers selected by Birdwood
> in India);
>
> *1st Australian Division*;
> "*New Zealand and Australian Division*".

This last (usually known as the N.Z. and A. Division)
would be constituted under General Godley from the

> New Zealand Infantry Brigade;
> 4th Australian Infantry Brigade (under Colonel
> Monash) which was then just leaving Australia;
> 1st Australian Light Horse Brigade;
> New Zealand Mounted Rifles Brigade.

The only artillery of the N.Z. and A. Division was a
single New Zealand Field Artillery Brigade.

The second Australian contingent, comprising Monash's (4th) Infantry Brigade, the 2nd Australian Light
Horse Brigade under Colonel Ryrie—a bluff Australian
pastoralist, politician and pugilist—and other troops,
began arriving on February 1st and camped next to the
New Zealanders. It had required no other escort than
the Australian submarine, *AE2*, towed by the *Berrima*.
When these ships came through the Suez Canal an adventurous Turkish expedition under one of the main
Turkish leaders, Djemal Pasha, was only a few days'
marches away east of the Canal, and was rapidly approaching, but no shot was fired at the transports. The
Turks were coming across the desert in three widely
separated columns, later ascertained to comprise in all,
about four divisions. On February 1st the Indian posts
near the northern end of the Canal saw troops moving
among the distant sandhills; and twenty miles to the south,
beyond Ismailia, before dawn on February 3rd Indian
sentries detected several boats being launched on the

Canal. Only one reached the western bank, and that, like
the others, was riddled with fire from the Indians and
a detachment of New Zealanders.[6] Before nightfall the
expedition had been driven back into the Sinai desert
and in the next few days it withdrew by the desert routes
by which it had come. The Indian cavalry on the Canal
could not follow it; but the ease with which these Turks
had been defeated, suffering probably ten times greater
loss than the British, caused their army to be more lightly
estimated than hitherto.

No Australian infantry was employed in this fight,
though immediately after it two battalions, 7th and 8th,
were hurried from Mena to the Canal and temporarily
put into trenches there. But momentous naval operations
were already brewing in the eastern Mediterranean. On
2nd January 1915 there had reached the British government an appeal from the Russian government, whose
troops in the Caucasus were being hard pressed by
Turkish divisions there. The Russians asked that, in
order to draw away Turkish forces, the British should
make a demonstration in some other quarter, and "spread
reports" which might cause the Turks to withdraw some
of their troops.

Lord Kitchener, to whom the Russian request was
immediately referred, strongly desired to help, especially
as early in the war the Russians, despite their lack of preparation, had loyally assisted France by invading East
Prussia, and had themselves suffered disaster in consequence. Assuming that the Turks now attacking the
Russians were being withdrawn from the Turkish forces
near Constantinople (then capital of Turkey), Kitchener
decided that the only reasonable place for a feint attack
designed to stop this transfer was the famous sea approach
from the Mediterranean to Constantinople—the straits

---

[6] The pontoons used in this heroic attempt, and some heavy guns, had
been dragged across Sinai. One pontoon is now in the Australian War
Memorial at Canberra.

of the Dardanelles. These straits reach, like a long, winding river, between the narrow rugged Gallipoli Peninsula and the neighbouring slopes of Asia Minor, eventually opening into the Sea of Marmora, at the other end of which, on the similar straits of the Bosporus, leading to the Black Sea, lies Constantinople. An attack on the Dardanelles would, of course, be interpreted by the Turks as an attempt to get warships through to Constantinople. An attack on forts such as those fringing both sides of the Dardanelles was not generally regarded as an operation suitable for

ships alone, but Kitchener felt that he could not spare any land troops owing to the critical fighting in Flanders. If, therefore, a demonstration was to be made it must be by the Navy alone.

Kitchener thrashed out his conclusions at an immediate consultation with his younger colleague, Winston Churchill, then First Lord of the Admiralty. Churchill undertook that the demonstration should be made. Ever since he suspected that Turkey would enter the war Churchill had been interested in the notion of attacking the Dardanelles—upon her entry he had ordered the Navy to bombard the forts there, which it did on 3rd November 1914.

He now became intensely attracted by the present project. The war in France and Flanders had reached a deadlock. In the first five months each side had failed to get around the other's flank, the obvious method for reaching an early decision. The Western Front now

stretched from the Swiss border to the North Sea—leaving
no exposed flank for either side to envelop. The western
armies were stagnant; henceforth, unless either side was
prepared to invade a neutral country—Holland or
Switzerland—the only way to get behind its opponent on
land was to break through the opposing line from the
front—a costly, difficult process. The navies were equally
stagnant, the British blockading the German. Churchill,
whose vigorous spirit was impatient with this inactivity,
had seized on a proposal that the British Army should
attack along the Flemish coast under cover of the guns
of the Fleet. In the early weeks of the war the Allies had
been surprised by the German Army's bringing up heavy
artillery, and using it—with astonishing effect, at least
psychologically—to crush the resistance of the Belgian
forts at Liège. The British Navy had many old battleships with heavier artillery than the German Army, and
Churchill believed that these, working beside the Army
along the Flemish coast, could give the Army "absolutely
devastating support".

When the demonstration at the Dardanelles was
decided on, a note from Lord Fisher, then professional
head at the Admiralty, caused Churchill to conceive that
he might obtain Fisher's support for a project in which
old battleships, attacking alone without Army support
(which Kitchener would not then give), would force the
passage of the Dardanelles and reach and overawe the
Turkish capital at Constantinople.[7] This would be no
demonstration—it would be a momentous stroke against
the Turks and, if it succeeded, it might swing the
then wavering Balkan States—especially Bulgaria—into
deciding to join the Allies. It would open up a route for
arms and munitions to reach Russia and for Russian
wheat to come in return. With these objects Churchill

7 Lord Fisher's letter in enthusiastic terms suggested that, as part of a vast
plan of combined operations—which Churchill saw to be impracticable as a
whole—old battleships should force the Dardanelles.

had previously advocated the seizure of the Dardanelles with the help of Greece. The proposal had been rejected largely through Russia's jealousy of Greece. Now there appeared another opportunity of undertaking it, with ships alone. Churchill was full of eagerness—but all depended on whether it was practicable.

With the agreement of naval experts in London, Churchill put this question to the British naval commander on the spot, Vice-Admiral Carden. Carden replied that the Dardanelles could not be rushed but "might be forced by extended operations" with a large number of ships. The significant word "might" was apparently assumed to mean "could". The Chief of Staff at the Admiralty and Admiral Sir Henry Jackson, who was studying naval problems of that region, held that a step by step reduction of the Dardanelles forts by the fleet was possible. Churchill informed Carden of this and asked him for his detailed plan. On January 11th it arrived. The attack was to be made in four stages which were, in effect, as follows: (1) reduce forts at entrance; (2) clear defences of the next ten miles up to the Narrows (a section of the channel, about three miles long and from one to two miles wide, with a zigzag course); (3) reduce forts at Narrows; (4) clear a way through the minefield, pass Narrows, reduce further forts, pass through the remaining twenty-five miles of the channel, and enter the Sea of Marmora. Churchill and his naval advisers decided to add to the fleet for these operations several stronger ships—including the new battleship *Queen Elizabeth*, which would try out her 15-inch guns on the Turkish forts. These forts were expected to be reduced within a few weeks.

Churchill's project was not one of any demonstration; it was to be a major operation "to bombard and take the Gallipoli Peninsula with Constantinople as its objective". By January 28th the British government had agreed to

71

make the attack. If it failed, it could be treated as a mere demonstration, and the attempt abandoned.

So it was that on 20th February 1915 Australians training in Egypt were electrified by the news that a British fleet (mainly of old battleships gathered from various quarters) and a French squadron had bombarded the forts at the Dardanelles. The attack was heralded in Britain and all over the world by excited newspaper comment. Great hopes were raised and encouraged, and few Australians then in Egypt will forget the chill of disillusionment that slowly followed when week after week went by with the ships still apparently unable to penetrate farther than the mouth of the straits. Guns at

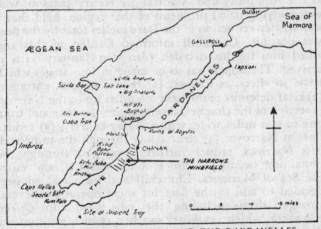

THE GALLIPOLI PENINSULA AND THE DARDANELLES

Helles and Seddel Bahr, north of the entrance, and Kum Kale south of it were put out of action and were eventually destroyed by parties of marines who, during several of the earlier bombardments, were easily landed and re-embarked. On March 4th however they were bitterly opposed and, though in greater force than before, were withdrawn only with loss.

The second phase under the plan began on March 2nd, and on March 11th Churchill suggested to Admiral Carden to press more vigorously, incurring any necessary losses, and attack the Narrows—the third stage. Carden, who was genuinely ill, was succeeded by Vice-Admiral de Robeck with the dynamic Commodore Roger Keyes as chief of staff. The passage of the Narrows was attempted on March 18th. Before the approach to them had been reached two old British battleships and one French one were sunk or sinking and the Dreadnought cruiser *Inflexible* badly hit—all, as it was found later, by a line of mines newly laid far down the straits—and the attack was called off.

At the beginning of the attacks, and in anticipation that they would succeed and the captured forts would have to be occupied, the Admiralty had moved some of its special troops—part of the Royal Naval Division—to Lemnos Island near by, the use of which had been offered to the Allies by the Greek Premier, Venizelos.[8] Kitchener agreed to send for the same purpose General Birdwood's army corps from Egypt. The French would add a division, and Kitchener had also agreed to send the 29th British Division, lately formed in England from British regular troops recalled from garrison duties oversea. It was at first intended to place General Birdwood in charge of the whole force but, as the French Commander happened to be a senior general, Sir Ian Hamilton, a fighting leader of higher rank, who had been chief of Kitchener's staff in the South African War, was finally selected and sent out from England. On March 4th General Birdwood and on March 18th, while the Navy's attempt to force

---

[8] Venizelos afterwards had to resign, as the Greek king, Constantine, repudiated his Prime Minister's offers of naval and military help to the Allies. The reason for the repudiation was the Russian government's objection to any approach by the Greeks to Constantinople.

the passage was actually going on, Sir Ian Hamilton visited the straits. Both came to the conclusion that the passage could be forced only by landing an army to help the fleet.

Actually the big guns of the forts in the Narrows had used most of their ammunition and the British fleet which was preparing for a fresh attempt, could soon have forced them to spend the remainder. But they were only part of the obstacle; the most important was the main minefield, about six miles deep and not yet reached, which had to be cleared. The fishing craft and crews on whom the task of minesweeping had hitherto mainly fallen, had on March 18th retired when fired on by howitzers hidden on the shores. Destroyers and their crews, on the other hand, faced this fire without flinching, and it was now proposed to use them in a new attempt planned for April 4th.

But meanwhile Vice-Admiral de Robeck also swung to the generals' view. At a conference on the *Queen Elizabeth* on March 22nd he fully agreed with them. The naval attempt planned for April 4th was never made. Commodore Keyes remained firmly convinced that it would have succeeded; but few Australians who recall how vulnerable were destroyers to field artillery will share his confidence, seeing how easily the sweepers could have been brought under direct fire from field-guns with ample ammunition, shooting almost with impunity at point-blank range from behind thorn bushes or houses on either side of the straits or the walls or gardens of Chanak.

The British Cabinet accepted the admiral's view, but now, after all the publicity that accompanied the naval attacks, there was no talk of breaking off the operations. Lord Kitchener undertook that the Army should attempt a very different task from the secondary role hitherto intended for it—it would endeavour to seize the Gallipoli Peninsula.

Only the naval operations, not, of course, the plans, were known to the troops training in the desert. But when on February 28th, on sudden orders, the 3rd Australian Infantry Brigade, with some engineers, an ambulance and certain other troops, disappeared from Mena Camp, their destination was rumoured to be the island of Lemnos; and the rumour proved true. The troops were to be used, if required, for occupying the battered forts at the neighbouring Dardanelles. Other signs followed. Sturdy British regulars in sun helmets—the 29th Division, previously held back in England by Kitchener—began to arrive in Alexandria, as did French white and native troops. Sir Ian Hamilton appeared in Cairo and reviewed each of the oversea divisions. The nurses at one of the hospitals were ordered to obtain sun hats.

Then on April 1st, like a bolt from the blue, came the order: "All leave stopped!" The 1st Australian Division was ordered to the front—but what front? The N.Z. and A. Division was ordered to follow it. On April 3rd camp began to be struck[9]; black kitbags were piled in thousands on the sand beside the Mena tramway terminus. At night the incinerators blazed all over the camp. Throughout days and nights battalion after battalion quietly entrained in Cairo for Alexandria, and filed aboard their transports which sailed one by one without escort as the ships filled. In Egypt only the camps of the light horse and mounted rifles, and those of a few British troops, stood forlornly on the desert. The infantry, artillery, engineers, ambulances in their ships, one by one, steamed off to join a great naval concourse accumulating in the huge, bare, circular harbour of Lemnos, sixty miles from the Dardanelles. The orders to the transport-captains had been sealed, but they knew Lemnos to be their destination. One forgot to open his orders until

---

[9] On April 2nd (Good Friday) there occurred a not very creditable riot of troops of both divisions in a low quarter of Cairo (the Haret el Wasser). The details are given in *Vol. I, p. 130n.*

three hours out of port; "then," as he said, "I found we were going to the right place."

Everyone in that region—including the Turks—now knew that the Peninsula, or the Asiatic coast south of it, was to be seized. While the troops, still in their transports, were instructed and occasionally practised in getting into boats and landing, the staffs in the headquarters ships settled down to the drawing of plans.

Sir Ian Hamilton's army—now known as the Mediterranean Expeditionary Force—was to attempt to land in two places, the regular 29th Division at several beaches below or between the cliffs at Cape Helles and Seddel Bahr, at the end or toe of the Peninsula, and the Australian and New Zealand Army Corps under Birdwood on its outer coast at a beach thirteen miles farther north.

Here the Peninsula was little over four miles wide, and its rugged backbone was broken by a comparatively low, grassy neck reaching from the promontory of Gaba Tepe to the Narrows. North of this a maze of gullies and ridges ran gradually up to a main hill four and a half miles away and about 1000 feet high, known to the British as Hill 971 and to the Turks as Koja Chemen Tepe (Hill of the Great Pasture). This rugged mass formed the backbone of the Peninsula opposite the northern end of the Narrows, and from all its main crest-line parts of the Narrows were visible. If some of its main heights were seized the artillery observers should be able to direct the fire of heavy guns on to the forts guarding the straits. The 1st Australian Division was accordingly to land on a beach about a mile north of the promontory of Gaba Tepe (which itself was the southernmost end of the range, and was fortified) and would try to seize on the first day the whole range, from Gaba Tepe to the summit. The N.Z. and A. Division, coming ashore after the 1st, would then push inland through it, and their united forces would advance to a prominent conical hill, Mal Tepe, more closely overlooking the Narrows.

The toe of the Peninsula, where the 29th Division would try to land, was much more level—but far from as level as it appeared from the sea, for there were several rough, hidden gullies. It led gradually up to a smooth height, Achi Baba, that resembled a human neck and shoulders barring the way up the Peninsula. The 29th Division was to seize this on the first day. Later this southern force helped by General Birdwood's Corps from the north would move against the massive bastion of hill, Kilid Bahr Plateau, which

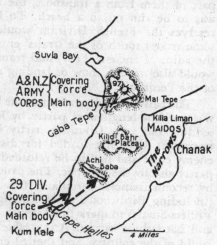

Final objective for the 29th Division was Kilid Bahr Plateau, but only Achi Baba was to be reached on the first day.

would then lie between them, like a vast square castle directly covering the southern end of the Narrows.

The first landing of each of these two forces would be made by a fraction of each—in the Australian case by

77

the 3rd Infantry Brigade—which would seize the heights protecting the landing places. Both landings would be made at dawn; but Birdwood, like other commanders of Dominion troops throughout the war, desired to strike by surprise and therefore would attack just before the first light, without any bombardment. On the other hand at Cape Helles, where opposition would probably be stronger, the ships would bombard the Turkish positions at dawn; immediately afterwards the troops would land— part of them from a transport, the *River Clyde*, which was to be run on to a beach. To keep away Turkish reserves the French Division would temporarily land some troops south of the straits' entrance (not far from the ruins of ancient Troy) and transports and warships would also make a show of landing at the northern end of the Peninsula.

The pause that occurred after the battle of March 18th was perhaps lengthened partly by Kitchener's delay in sending the 29th Division; partly by the fact that its transports were not loaded for disembarkation on an enemy coast and had to be reloaded in Alexandria; but partly also by the weather. The pause was usefully filled by reconnaissances: aeroplanes flew over with observers (including Birdwood's chief intelligence officer, Major Villiers-Stuart) to mark the Turkish trenches and camps; and battleships carried Army officers to see what they could of the country, and shelled enemy positions. The force could hardly, in any case, have been prepared to land before mid-April. As it was, by April 22nd the 200 or more ships at Lemnos were ready but the weather was unsuitable. Next day it improved and some of the Australian transports and the warships with their covering force made certain preliminary moves. After dark on the 24th the whole flotilla sailed.

Eight months from their earliest enrolments, straight

from their training camps, the first contingents from Australia and New Zealand were, together with their British and French comrades, about to be tried in one of the most crucial and difficult tasks of the war. They had come at last to the ancient test; and in the mind of each man was the question—how would they react to it?

CHAPTER VII

THE LANDING, 25th APRIL 1915

THEY made a certainty of it from the start. During the early part of the night of April 24th the whole force had rested about the decks while their ships slipped through the black, quiet sea. Except for the subdued reflection of a shaded sternlight on the ruffled wake of the next ship ahead, no vessel was visible from any others. Here and there two mates quietly talked. In the *Minnewaska*, which carried the headquarters of Generals Birdwood and Bridges, and also the 1st Battalion, from some corner came a snatch of song:

> What 'o for a life on the sea!
> So give it a chance,
> Come an' 'ave a dance,
> Come and dance along with me.

Later all was quiet; everyone knew he needed all possible rest for the coming day. High on some land to starboard—presumably Imbros Island—a single light swam by. Presently another appeared low ahead. It was on a stationary warship. The transports carrying the main body of the 1st Australian Division turned round it and (to describe the action in unnautical language) headed very slowly at right angles to the right.

On the water ahead of them, unseen, was another concentration—the warships and transports of the 3rd Brigade which was to make the first landing. Its 4000 troops were to be taken close inshore by warships, since these were less vulnerable to shellfire than merchant ships: 1500 men, who were to land first, had been brought from Imbros in three old battleships which would steam with them to within 2½ miles of the land; somewhere in the dark the remainder, 2500, were now climbing down rope ladders from their transports on to the decks of seven destroyers which would take them as near to land as possible, and then send them ashore close behind the 1500 from the battleships. The last stage of the journey to the land would be made in rowing boats: twelve strings of these—three in each string (or "tow") with a small steamboat towing them—would be sent off by the three battleships; and other rowing boats, collected in the dark from the transports, would be towed by each destroyer.

The men and officers of the battleships had for that night given up their sleeping quarters to the Australians carried in their ships; had insisted on feeding them and providing extras from the ships' canteens; and, when the troops were awakened, had carried round to them hot cocoa, also a gift of the Navy. Each infantryman carried, besides his rifle, 200 rounds of ammunition, two extra days' rations (in small white bags), and full packs so fastened that they could easily be slipped off if a boat was sunk.

At 11 p.m. the destroyers, creeping up to their proper transports, took aboard their troops and then closed slowly towards the shadowy battleships, whose infantry was then climbing down rope ladders into the rowing boats alongside. Many a British naval officer afterwards remarked how orderly and silent, now that the test had come, were these troops whose reputed doings had shocked Cairo. In the destroyer *Ribble* the commander had told them: "You fellows can smoke and talk quietly. But I expect all lights to be put out and absolute silence to be kept when I give the order."

So arrived the famous morning of Sunday, 25th April 1915. Until 3 a.m., when the moon sank, the shape of the land could be dimly seen, several miles ahead. The battleships were still slowly towing their boats which had dropped behind them. At 3.30 the battleships stopped.

The small steamboats tugged away each towing three
boats. It had become very dark; except for the stars, sea
and sky were sheer black, and it was often impossible for
soldiers in any of the twelve tows to see even the tow
abreast of them. For half an hour the small engines
throbbed, and the hawsers tugged. Once many hearts in
the crowded boats seemed to stand still when, far ahead,
a long pencil of pale light suddenly shot into the sky. It
was a Turkish searchlight. A second pencil joined it and
for a few moments the two moved restlessly about. But it
was seen that they came from behind a barrier of hilly
land; evidently they were in the Narrows, behind the
Peninsula.

In the silent crowded boats the tension was extreme.
Did the Turks suspect? Were they posted on those invisible hills and on the beaches? Would they detect the
landing? Would they resist it in force? When would the
first shot come?

After half an hour's towing there was seen against
the night sky, as it began to pale with the earliest approach of dawn, the black outline of land, now high
above the boats and close ahead. Among the destroyers
in the dark two miles astern the *Ribble's* commander
said to his Australians of the second wave: "Lights out,
men, and stop talking; we're going in now." In the first
wave the twelve tows, when near the silent land, had
slightly changed their course and then straightened again,
and the tiny steamboats began to cast off the rowing boats.
In each were a sailor at the tiller and four seamen at the
oars, with a naval officer in the steamboat ahead and a
midshipman in the last boat of each tow. The boats rowed
independently ahead, and the first had just grated on
shingle a few yards off the beach and the first men were
climbing out in three or four feet of water and wading
ashore,[1] when there came signs of life from the land. A

---

1 The first man ashore was probably Lieutenant D. Chapman (of Mary-
borough, Queensland), 9th Battalion. He was killed in 1916 at Pozières.

yellow flame, evidently of a beacon, flared on a height not far to the south; on the skyline, towering 300 feet above the beach, a figure moved. A shot from there plunged into the water, near the boats, followed by a group of four or five shots—the flashes seen along the skyline above. Then there broke out a constant fire along the crest, the flashes sparkling like a necklace, while from other heights on the flanks, seen and unseen, other rifles and a machine-gun, or perhaps two, joined in.

Men in the boats began to be hit in fair numbers but this stage was quickly over when they ran across the shingle and sheltered under the bank. Neither then nor at any later time was that beach the inferno of bursting shells, barbed wire entanglements, and falling men that has sometimes been described or painted.[2] A hot rifle fire struck sparks from the shingle in the dark. Fortunately there was no barbed wire entanglement such as officers, searching with their glasses from a battleship some days before, had seen bristling along the beach (and even in the sea) near Gaba Tepe promontory, two miles to the south. Far out on the black satin of the sea, where the main body of transports was moving into place, four behind four in the night, that flare was seen at exactly 4.29 a.m.—it resembled a signal lamp flashing from the shore—and a minute later there was heard across the miles of water the sound of distant shots growing to a continuous bubbling like that of water in a seething cauldron. It was sustained minute after minute. Had the advanced force in the boats been able to land? Sky and sea gradually turned to a clear lemon yellow, smooth as silk. A ship's boat was passed, floating bottom up, the sign of an accident that had cost several lives. Then, with a buffet that shook every transport, a battleship opened fire and others followed. At 4.45, the whine of Turkish shells was heard for the first time, and their fleecy white

---

[2] As will be told later, much the heaviest loss was suffered by a few boatloads that rowed in much farther north.

shrapnel puffs appeared high over the water—the first of a slow succession of salvoes. "Hey!" said one of the onlookers, "they're carrying this joke too far—they're using ball ammunition!" On the purple band of hills no movement could yet be detected by those in the transports. On their decks some of the waiting troops munched their morning meal; the officers went down to breakfast in the saloons where the naval gun flashes intermittently flushed with raw orange the white deck girders above, and the ships' stewards, napkins on arms, went round quietly asking, "Porridge or fish, sir?"

To many on the transports the first definite news of the landing came when there approached, slowly circling to alongside, one of the destroyers that had discharged the second wave of the landing force and were now to begin taking off the main body from the transports. On the deck close beside the destroyer's funnels several seamen were bending carefully over something that lay there. It was presently seen to be a badly wounded man, very white and still, wrapped in brown blankets. First of many, he was lifted on to a transport with tender care. Yes, the sailors said, the force was ashore all right—and gradually news came from the Navy, in terms glowing with enthusiasm. "The way those chaps went up the hill" had strikingly impressed the handful of naval men who could see them; it should be also said that the handful of naval men including the midshipmen—mere children to the Australians—who helped the soldiers in the boats had made an impression which those whom they took to the shore were never to forget—that day or later.

What had happened on shore only gradually became known. But at 7 o'clock men on the transports, scanning the horizon through whatever glasses were available, saw along the crest of the hills ahead a line of men standing talking and digging, in those easy carefree poses by which Australians came constantly to be recognised on fifty later battlefields of the First World War. A weight of anxiety was lifted from the onlookers. It was clear that, however difficult this coast, for the moment at any rate the Australians had made good their landing.

As already stated, the infantry brigade chosen to land first—the 3rd, from the outer States—had made a certainty from the start. As officers and men tumbled out of the grating boats and waded ashore, they found themselves faced by a country utterly different from that which had been described to them in the previous lectures as to their tasks. They had been told to rush across the beach and shelter under a bank such as lines nearly all beaches. They were to drop their packs there, quickly form up, fix bayonets, load their magazines, close the cut-offs—as there was to be no firing till daylight—and then advance over a belt of open land to a comparatively low ridge which they would climb. On top of this they were to reorganise, and then push off again towards specified points on a long ridge about a mile inland.

But that was nothing like the country in which they landed. They found themselves on the foot of an exceedingly steep, almost precipitous hill 300 feet high which, except for a minor lower knoll around which the boats grounded, rose straight from the bank that bordered the shingle. How this happened was made clear—to a few who happened to be within earshot—by the voice of the naval commander in charge of the tows, just before the first shots: "Explain to the colonel that the dam' fools have taken us a mile too far north!"

Actually the boats landed on part of the coast which Birdwood and Australian officers had scanned from a warship a few days before and considered "impossible" for an attempt at landing in the dark.

Fortunately, however, the beach ended in the usual bank. The Australians ran across to it, some fixing bayonets as they ran. They dropped their packs; then, after three minutes for taking breath in shelter from the strong Turkish fire, came the crucial moment of decision

what to do. Each party could see only dimly beyond its
own members, but nearly all leaders took them at once
straight up that long
precipitous height. It
was too steep for nor-
mal hill-climbing—they
had to help themselves
by their rifle butts and
haul themselves by the
stems and roots of the
low holly and arbutus
scrub that thickly cov-
ered the slope. The
height took some quar-
ter of an hour to climb.
In that light men could
be seen only if they
moved. In that respect
the Turks had the ad-
vantage and a fair num-

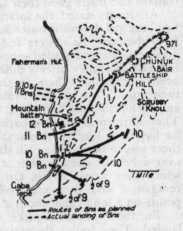

ber of the climbing men were wounded and left hanging
among the scrub. The medical officer of the 9th, Captain
A. Graham Butler, attended to them there while he urged
the rest on. The fire continued until they almost reached
the summit, but as they neared it the Turks there began
to disappear. A few had been routed out of a post on the
lower knoll—known as Ari Burnu (Bee Point)—and a few
others stayed for an actual scuffle with the leading Australians on the summit.

It was by then light with the grey of dawn. The summit was found to be a small plateau covered with low
scrub through which the last of those Turks who were
not killed ran off to plunge immediately down a very
steep slope on the farther edge of the plateau. The Australians following them found themselves looking out
on a tangled, deeply folded country almost entirely
covered with dark, knee- or waist-deep holly oak scrub.

Below them and to right and left opened a deep, tortuous valley rising to a second, slightly higher ridge 600 yards away—hidden beyond which was a third ridge which would shut out any view of the straits even from the second ridge, and which, joining the main ridge at Chunuk Bair, was the principal objective intended to be seized that morning by this brigade.

All this time other parties came panting to the top of the first ridge. The dislodged Turks could still dimly be seen running and jumping far down the near hillside and then padding at a steady trot up a faintly showing path on the opposite slope. After standing firing at them, the Australian scouts, in accordance with the plans, plunged down the same track; on the small plateau behind them the bulk of the first companies attempted a hurried reorganisation.

By this time part of the second wave from the destroyers was reaching them. The destroyers had steamed in on a much wider front than the tows. They came to within about 100 yards of the shore, and their troops began to get into the rowing boats just as the Turks began firing at the first wave, which must then have been scrambling ashore at Ari Burnu. The troops on the destroyers heard a cheer somewhere on the land ahead. On the southernmost destroyers bullets from Ari Burnu and from the heights ahead rattled on the fo'c'sle sides before the troops were all in their boats; and there and also north of Ari Burnu the boatloads of the second wave were rowed to land through bullets churning the water and thudding into the boats.

It is impossible in this history to enter into the details of that long day's fighting. Readers who wish to know precisely where each destroyer's troops landed—some of them farther south near the point originally intended, to climb the second ridge there; how a battery at Gaba Tepe promontory, which jutted into the sea a mile to the south, opened up again and again on the crowded destroyers and boats moving in to the Beach; how the British cruiser *Bacchante* several times pushed forward till she almost grounded, and smothered the neighbourhood of the battery with the dust and smoke of her salvoes; and how the Turkish guns—really sheltered by a quarry—always opened again when more boats came in, though in the whole day only one or two of their shells burst over a boat; how the great *Queen Elizabeth* (with Sir Ian Hamilton aboard, though none of the troops knew of his presence) came in early among the warships, for a look at things; how the balloon ship *Manica* out near the transports sent up her big grub-like balloon to peer over the hills into the Narrows; and what were the experiences of the Australian scouts and other troops, some of whom, as planned, overran two Turkish field batteries and reached the Third Ridge—the one that the covering force had been intended to seize—and some of whom even looked out on the Narrows; how in this strange country, amid the sweet smelling thyme on the uplands on that beautiful bright spring day, the fight which, after the first rush, had seemed almost over, gradually became intense again and swayed hour after hour on the Second Ridge until the factor that wins or loses battles—the strain upon nerves—became almost unbearable so that to many brave men the smell of thyme long afterwards brought a shudder—for the intimate experiences of the Australians and of the Turks who faced them in that famous fight the reader must be referred to the *Australian Official History*,[3] which devotes two hundred pages to that day. Nevertheless that famous and difficult fight may justifiably be described here somewhat more fully than the many great battles that followed.

The Australians instead of landing opposite the comparatively low and smooth southern end of the ridges, north of Gaba Tepe, came ashore nearer the centre of

---

3 *Vol. 1, pp. 245-443. For the Turks' experiences, pp. 444-81.*

the 971 Hill-chain, where two knolls, Ari Burnu to the
north and Hell Spit about half a mile south, led up to
the northern and southern end respectively of a small,
steep plateau, the three heights partly enclosing a curving
bay with half a mile of beach. (This summit was called,
after a New Zealand commander, Plugge's Plateau—pro-
nounced Pluggey's.)

The Turks' plan of defence had lately been changed
by the German general, Liman von Sanders, who
after the naval attempt on March 18th was sent by the
Turkish government from Constantinople to command
at the Dardanelles. Till then the Turkish forces had been
scattered all round the coast. Liman von Sanders most
wisely stationed only outposts on or above the beaches,
to do what they could in stopping invasion and to give
warning, but he held the main forces of his six infantry
divisions concentrated at several points in rear from
which they could be directed against the main invasion
wherever it happened. After his reorganisation the whole
coastline of the southern third of the Peninsula, from
north of the Australian landing place right round to the
straits, was held by four battalions—actually by less than
half of one division (the 9th) of which the greater part
was kept in reserve. A second division (the 19th) was
camped ready near the Narrows. Two others (5th and
7th) were kept twenty-five miles away near the neck of
the Peninsula at Bulair, where von Sanders expected the
attack although the defences there were strong. The 3rd
and 11th Divisions were south of the straits.

The coast at and for four miles north of Gaba Tepe
promontory was held by one Turkish battalion, which
had to cover with one company, supported by some
machine-guns and three or four batteries of artillery, the
section of shore on which the Australian landing was
actually made. It was part of this company that fired from
the top of the ridge above the beach and was rushed off
it by the climbing Australians. These Turks fled back

through two of their batteries stationed with some machine-gunners on a wide plateau (400 feet high) of the Second Ridge, and thence over the longer Third Ridge. So broken was the country that, as will presently be seen, although some of the Australian scouts and advanced parties chased these Turks very fast, it took the scouts three or four hours to fight and climb their way to the Third Ridge; and the main part of the covering brigade, split up by landing in separate boatloads on so rough a coast and by advancing over sheer ridges and through gullies and ravines, took almost as long to reach the Second Ridge and, in a scattered way, to reorganise. On the wide plateau there (known as the 400 Plateau) the scouts were to search for some Turkish guns, which, according to the plans, the 10th Battalion was to seize.

Most of the carefully laid plans had been torn to shreds by the current that had carried the tows too far northward, and the human error that caused them to cluster into less than half the front intended. Not only were the troops in country indescribably rougher than any leader had expected, but nearly all platoons were intermingled with platoons of other companies, and in the case of the 9th Battalion the two companies in the second wave came ashore three quarters of a mile south of the two in the first wave. All had to go straight on as they were, with only four or five minutes for the roughest reorganisation under the bank of the beach in the dark.

Yet it was noticeable that, at every interval in the attack, the officers and N.C.O.'s—as they had learnt in their desert training—reorganised the troops whom they found near them; and that in spite of the nerve-racking confusion of that day, which might have wrecked the whole undertaking and the force, frequent and clear reports from some of the scattered, furiously fighting parties ahead quickly reached the commanders. The commanders in turn were often able to locate and confer with each other and to send their orders forward to at least some of the advanced troops, and so to influence the fight sufficiently to prevent its being at any time entirely beyond their control.

The action which most influenced the day was taken very early by the brigadier of the covering force, Colonel E. G. Sinclair-MacLagan. He and his staff landed with the second wave (from the destroyers), but before landing he realised that his brigade had been disembarked too far north and in extraordinarily difficult country. His troops would be much farther than intended from the part of the Third Ridge which his right flank battalion, the 9th, was to seize—that is to say its southern half, from Gaba Tepe for two miles north-eastwards. He therefore at once, from the beach, sent his brigade major, Major C. H. Brand, to take control of the troops who were pushing in that direction. He then climbed the southern shoulder of Plugge's Plateau immediately above him (thenceforth called MacLagan's Ridge).

At 5.30 MacLagan, looking from Plugge's Plateau upon the crumpled folds and slopes of the Second Ridge, which spread for a mile and a half right and left before his eyes, instantly realised that the four miles' expanse of the Third Ridge, hidden beyond it, would be most difficult for his scattered companies to reach and retain. But he also saw that the Second Ridge, though it would give no glimpse of the straits, offered a strong position to hold at least temporarily, provided that he also held the half-bare, higher hill in which it ended on the left. This hill rose from the northern end of the

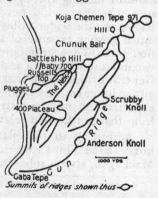

(Note: Gun Ridge was Third Ridge.)

valley that lay in front of him (Shrapnel and Monash valleys). It was known as Baby 700, and was the first prominent summit of the gradually rising chain of the main ridge, the northernmost being Hill 971.[4]

From Plugge's Plateau the 10th Battalion and half of the 9th had already moved into Shrapnel Valley, and MacLagan could see them making through the scrub towards the easily recognised 400 Plateau to carry out their set tasks. But on Plugge's beside MacLagan there was still most of the 11th Battalion being organised by one of its company commanders, Major E. A. Drake-Brockman (in later years a well-known Australian judge). The set objective of the 11th was Big 700 and the northern end of the Third Ridge, which joined the main range at Chunuk Bair. The 2nd Brigade when it landed was to push northwards through the 11th Battalion and seize Chunuk and the farther summits.

But MacLagan watching the 9th and 10th, a mere handful moving through the wide, scrubby slopes, felt sure that they could never seize and cross the Second Ridge and the wider valley beyond, and then capture the much greater expanse of the Third Ridge, not to mention Gaba Tepe promontory, which jutted into the sea two miles south of him and was strongly fortified. He and General Bridges knew that Turkish reserves were camped on the lower country inland of Gaba Tepe, and all leaders expected the first and strongest counter-blow to come from that southerly direction.

According to the plans, the 9th Battalion was to hurry to the Third Ridge there and hold off these Turks. MacLagan, always solicitous for his troops, felt that they

---

4 Baby 700 was marked as just over 700 feet high. The next summit was Big 700, later known (after shelling by the battleships) as Battleship Hill. The next, Chunuk (or Dchonk) Bair, was over 800 feet. Then came the two slightly higher summits of Hill Q; and then Hill 971. The whole range was called, by the British, Sari Bair ("Yellow Slope"), but that was really the name of the gravel cliffs of which the centre feature was "the Sphinx", just north of Plugge's Plateau.

were heading out on a completely impossible task. One step, and one only, could now save the situation on that flank—the switching thither of the 2nd Brigade while there was yet time.

However, if that was to be done, he and the 3rd Brigade must make sure of the northern flank, for which the 2nd Brigade was to have been responsible. He therefore directed Drake-Brockman to take the 11th Battalion northward along both valley and heights; part of it, moving up Monash Valley, was to seize and hold a succession of indentations on the Second Ridge along the eastern side of that valley, and part to go on from the head of the valley and seize Baby 700.

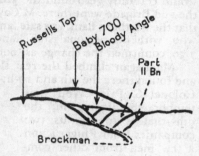

By 5.50 MacLagan had imparted his decisions to Major Duncan Glasfurd of the divisional staff, who, under the original plan, was to meet and direct the troops now landing, and also to Lieut.-Colonel H. E. ("Pompey") Elliott of the 7th Battalion, whose stalwart form panted up to him as some of the first troops of the 2nd Brigade landed. MacLagan himself then descended into Shrapnel Valley in order to follow the 9th and 10th to the Second Ridge before placing his headquarters farther north, about the centre of that ridge,[5] directly opposite Plugge's Plateau. He sent his signallers straight thither so that the telephone might be through from the Beach when he arrived.

[5] That part was later called MacLaurin's Ridge, after the young commander of the 1st Brigade, who was killed there two days later after relieving MacLagan.

On the slope from Plugge's MacLagan met Colonel M'Cay, commanding the 2nd Brigade, and asked his agreement to the change of plan. M'Cay pointed out that this was asking him, as his first act, to disobey orders, and suggested that he should see the position for himself. "There isn't time," MacLagan answered; the Turks would certainly get round the 3rd Brigade's right unless the 2nd Brigade went there. M'Cay asked for an assurance that the northern flank was safe, and then agreed. Bridges, who, with his personal staff, landed from a trawler at 7.30, confirmed the change as soon as he heard of it.

MacLagan climbed the rear slope of the 400 Plateau and found there the 9th and 10th; the 10th, under Lieut.-Colonel S. Price Weir, was temporarily digging in; the 9th—that is to say, its two companies from Plugge's and a few men from other companies which had landed farther south and were still clearing the summit of the 400 Plateau and part of the ridges south of it—was being reorganised by the two leaders who had brought it from Plugge's, a young major, A. G. Salisbury (one of the many who immediately took charge on that day when their com-

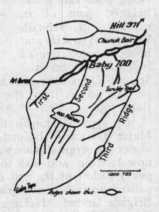

manders fell or failed) and a high-spirited, capable sergeant, M. Wilder-Neligan, who was acting as adjutant.

The 400 Plateau was a wide hump, about a square half-mile in area, into which the Second Ridge expanded much as the stem of an onion does into its bulb. Its scrubby surface was almost flat except for a gully (known as Owen's) leading eastwards from its centre and dividing it into two lobes. From the middle of the southern and larger of these there then stood out a single small pine, which later gave that half the name of Lone Pine. The resemblance of the plateau to a bulb was increased by four lower, subsidiary ridges which, as well as the main one, extended southwards, like roots, from its southern side.

The first troops to reach the 400 Plateau, largely parts of companies from the southern destroyers, were out ahead completing the clearing of the Plateau. Some of them had seized at 6.30 a.m. a Turkish field battery which tried to escape through an unsuspected, cup-shaped hollow close behind the lone pine tree. Most of these parties were now at the far side of the Plateau. From its slopes (clad there with taller scrub, low pine trees and arbutus) they looked over Legge Valley, the grassy flat between the Second and Third Ridges. Searching for these parties, and trying to co-ordinate their action, was Major Brand, the staff officer whom MacLagan had sent from the Beach.

At this stage Brand, like MacLagan, became convinced that the scattered parties, if they tried to climb and seize the wide expanse of the Third Ridge, would run great danger of being cut off. It is true that for a month previously every leader from Birdwood downwards had dinned into them: "Keep going at all costs! Go as fast as you can!" Brand himself had told some of the first parties he met, "Keep going; others will be sent on after you." But now the Third Ridge, with its many spurs facing him, seemed much too wide and distant. He could see 500 yards behind him on the Plateau the main line of the 9th and 10th digging in. He therefore sent back a scout to MacLagan with word that the advanced parties on the Plateau were about a company strong, and asked whether he should keep them out there or withdraw them. MacLagan decided that his main force should for the present dig in across the rear half of the Plateau. He therefore ordered Brand to keep the advanced parties forward to cover the digging. He apparently intended that, when the 2nd Brigade came up on his right, the advance should, if conditions were suitable, be resumed.

It was then about 8 o'clock. Since before seven there had been a lull in the fighting, not only on the 400 Plateau but on the main range to the north and the low ridges to the south. The sun had risen on a glorious spring morning, and only scattered, distant shots now broke the silence on most of the battlefield. Men felt that the greatest difficulties were past.

But though neither MacLagan nor Brand knew of it, both on the Third Ridge to the east and on the main ridge to the north were parties of Australians under vigorous leaders who, in accordance with their original

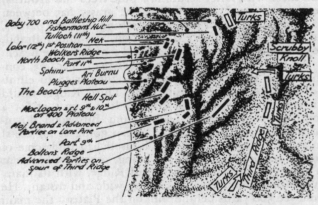

The situation just before 9 a.m., 25th April 1915.

orders, had "kept going" towards their objectives. They were largely beyond the reach of MacLagan's or Brand's orders, and had carried forward a fight which must now be described.

A prominent hump on the Third Ridge, Scrubby Knoll, nearly a mile north-east of the 400 Plateau, was at about 8 o'clock reached by a few keen men of the 10th

Battalion.[6] For a brief interval these looked out on part
of the goal of all hopes, the water of the Narrows. But
the first pair of scouts had barely reached the height before they saw numbers of Turks moving through the
valley east of it. By the time some thirty men, under
Lieutenants Loutit and J. L. Haig, had crossed from the
400 Plateau a little farther south to a height which they
found to be not the true Third Ridge but a spur of it
not marked on their maps, these Turks were already
lining the top of the Third Ridge 400 yards in front of
them. Both sides lay in the scrub for some time firing intensely. The Australians called up from the 400 Plateau a
second party about equal to their own, under Captain
J. F. Ryder.

But presently shots whipping in from Scrubby Knoll,
high on their left, showed that Turks were crossing the
Third Ridge north of them. Men began to be killed. The
Turks on the north were driving past. After sending
many messages for support, the young leaders had, about
9.30, to withdraw their parties in extreme danger of
being cut off. But it was skilfully done. On the most
dangerous left flank it became a race, the Australians
bolting from the last foothill to cross Legge Valley shortly
after 10 o'clock, just as the Turks raced for that foothill.
Thence the Australians withdrew up Wire Gully, north
of the 400 Plateau to reach the main line at its head
about 11 a.m. The Turks following them, and other
Turks now streaming across the ridges farther north,
met a whirlwind of fire from the Second Ridge. They
sank into the scrub, and, from their side, poured a stream
of fire over the 400 Plateau and the ridges.

---

6 The first were two scouts, L.-Cpl P. de Q. Robin (killed three days
later) and Pte A. S. Blackburn (who afterwards won the V.C. at Pozières, and
in the Second World War commanded, as brigadier, the Australian troops
left behind, and captured, in Java). These two circled Scrubby Knoll, which
a little later was climbed by Lieut. (now Brig.) N. M. Loutit and two com-
panions. A mile farther south the crest of the Third Ridge seems to have
been reached by a party going very fast, as ordered, under Lieut. (now
Maj.-Gen.) F. C. P. Plant.

8—os

Troops on the 400 Plateau had heard, about 8.30, the sound of furious firing somewhere ahead. The forward parties had reported that the Turks were trying to out-flank them. A little later there appeared on the southern end of the Third Ridge another battalion of Turks, marching, with mule teams and guns, steadily north-wards along the crest. There were estimated to be 2000-3000 of the enemy at this time on the Third Ridge. About 9 o'clock MacLagan, realising that a powerful counter-attack was developing, and seeing that parts of the 2nd Brigade had come up on his right and other parts were following, judged it safe to send forward the 9th Battalion across the 400 Plateau—apparently to re-inforce the advanced parties there who were calling for support to meet this threat. He gave the order to Salis-bury, whose men had taken off their equipment while digging. They put it on again and advanced.

MacLagan then walked northwards to settle his head-quarters at the point where the Second Ridge ran into the 400 Plateau. On his way he passed the 10th Battalion digging. Its commander, Lieut.-Colonel Price Weir, told him, on the strength of reports from the advanced parties, that there was now no chance of the 10th's seizing, as planned, certain guns supposed to be on the Third Ridge. MacLagan was even more impressed by what he saw him-self—that, of the Australian reinforcements that con-stantly came over Plugge's Plateau and plunged into Shrapnel Valley, barely 20 in every 100 reached him at the 400 Plateau; the rest seemed to be sucked in by urgent calls coming from parts of the line where he had less need of them. He had hoped, when reinforcements should have arrived, to continue the attempt to seize the Third Ridge. But with the few men now reaching him that task would be impossible.

From that moment, between 9.30 and 10 a.m., Mac-Lagan gave up all notion of capturing the Third Ridge

that day. He ordered that no attempt should be made to
advance beyond the Second Ridge. The arriving troops
must dig themselves in there. And he sent word to Major
Brand to withdraw all the advanced parties to the firing
line.

So far as concerned the longer front, facing inland,
MacLagan's directions were now complete. As he reached
his headquarters, probably a little after 10 o'clock, he saw
that, to the north, on Baby 700 hill, beyond the head
of Monash Valley and the Second Ridge, a crucial fight
was in progress. As stated above, the progress of the foremost parties up the main ridge to the north was unknown
to MacLagan, as it was to most of the A.I.F., until after
the war. The events there were as follows.

The first Australians to reach that part of the range[7]
were boatloads comprising parts of the 11th and 12th
Battalions, whose destroyers approached the shore north
of Ari Burnu. These troops landed under sharp fire including that of a machine-gun from some Turkish post
along the beach farther north, and were also fired on by
Turks looking down from the semicircle of almost sheer
gravel cliffs, 250-400 feet high, which here, like an amphi-
theatre, hemmed in the mounds of hummocky foreshore
above the "North Beach".

Immediately north of Ari Burnu Point the bank of
this beach gave no shelter from the flanking fire. Several
leaders afterwards well known were with the troops there.
Some leaders, especially among the older men, failed that
day; but Colonel L. F. Clarke, the 57-year-old colonel
of the 12th Battalion, a Hobart business man and the
oldest battalion commander in the force, acted here
with vigour and skill. His battalion, as brigade reserve,

---

[7] Russell's Top was in effect the seaward end of the main chain since
the saddle connecting it with Plugge's (the lowest height in the chain) had
been weathered down to a knife-edge along whose crest a man could barely
walk.

was to have assembled a mile southwards, on the
400 Plateau. As that plan was out of the question, Clarke,
to whom some of the young officers of both battalions
attached themselves, sent a party along the beach to
silence the machine-gun, which was harassing the later
boats as they rowed in, and then with his troops set out
straight up the cliffs ahead. The original orders were very
different, as Lieutenant R. A. Rafferty, whom he sent to
silence the machine-gun, reminded him. "I can't help
that," was the firm reply.

The younger officers with their men, scrambling over
the sandy debris, and then on hands and knees up a slant
on the gravel face, at first outdistanced the colonel; but,
to their surprise, when they worked out on to the fairly
level hilltop (later called Russell's Top) and searched
around to gather about fifty men, they found the colonel
and a companion already there. Almost at once, not far
from the prominent cliff afterwards known as the Sphinx,
which jutted out from the centre of the semicircle, they
saw their first Turks, about thirty, lining a trench. With
a leap the Tasmanians made at them, but the Turks
clambered out and ran off northward. A shout from
Clarke, "Steady, you fellows, and clear the bush as you
go," brought the Tasmanians into a rough line.

They pushed northwards along the height until it
began to narrow to a neck (afterwards known as The
Nek) 150 yards wide, narrowing to 70, between steep
gullies descending to the sea on the left and to Monash
Valley on the right. The saddle between led straight up
to the long, more open crest of Baby 700. Towards this
saddle there curved through the scrub a white foot track.
The men fired at the Turks as these trundled heavily
away up the hill to settle in the scrub 1000 yards farther
on. Clarke standing on the track, writing a message to
MacLagan, was presently shot dead. His batman, who had
been ready to take the message, was killed by a second

shot. His second-in-command, Major C. H. Elliott,[8] came up and was at once badly wounded.

But the junior officers (one of them a Hobart school-master, Lieutenant I. S. Margetts) sent their scouts across The Nek, while other parties arriving reorganised with them. The commander was now Captain E. W. Tulloch, who, with about a platoon of the 11th, had landed farther north than Clarke and fought his way quickly up a steep, tortuous spur, later known as Walker's Ridge, from North Beach almost to The Nek. They were about to advance again towards Baby 700 when there came up another party of the 12th under Captain J. P. Lalor, a grandson of Peter Lalor, the cultured Irishman who as a goldminer on the Eureka lead in 1854 headed the only armed revolt in Australian history.

Lalor was now senior officer of the 12th in that area. His whole fiery nature favoured an advance (it was typical of him that, in spite of regula-tions, he carried a treasured family sword); but he knew that the 12th was brigade reserve. Accordingly, while Tulloch with about one company, mainly of the 11th, pushed forward over The Nek and up Baby 700, Lalor with a similar force of the 12th, remained digging a semi-circular line of rifle-pits—the first stage of a trench—just short of The Nek, obviously a posi-tion of great value against any Turkish counter-attack on that flank.

1 Lalor   2. Tulloch

Tulloch's company had been reorganised in platoons and sections, each with its allotted commander. Sending

<hr />

8 Lieut.-Col. S. Hawley, the previous second-in-command, had been shot through the spine when leaving his boat. He survived, paralysed for life. For these episodes see *Vol. I, pp. 269 et seq.*

Lieutenant S. H. Jackson with a platoon to the seaward slope of the range, Tulloch (in private life a Melbourne brewer) pushed on with the remaining sixty in a widely extended line through the knee-deep scrub on the inland shoulder. At first the whole expanse of dark, scrub-covered hills and valleys around showed no sign of life, though firing could be heard far behind, probably on the 400 Plateau. The hillside was folded with the upper ends of valleys and ridges, and on the second rise the party was met by fire from about sixty Turks and a machine-gun somewhere on the next fold. By carefully controlled shooting they beat down this fire. The Turks disappeared and Tulloch's party moved on to the next ridge, the inland shoulder of Big 700 (Battleship Hill). Here they met much heavier fire, but by rushes they reached shortly after 9 o'clock the slope leading to the next valley, beyond which rose the inland shoulder of the next main summit, Chunuk Bair, actually the most important height of the range.

Tulloch's men were firing admirably, directed—as in their desert training—by orders passed verbally along the line by Lieutenant Mordaunt Reid, a born leader, and others. Their waterbottles were almost untouched, a sign of first-rate control. But there were now Turks strongly posted before the first foothill of Chunuk Bair, others were visible high up its slopes, and others far south behind the right flank. After half an hour bullets began to come from the left flank also. The rattle of heavy fire on the seaward side of the range showed that the Turks were infiltrating behind the flank that Jackson had been sent to guard. Mordaunt Reid and a number of Tulloch's men had been hit. The party, now reduced to about forty, was in great danger of being enveloped. He therefore withdrew, two sections alternately firing to cover two retiring; about 10.30 he reached the seaward slope of The Nek, to find that a tense struggle had been in progress there.

Captain Lalor had been left entrenching just in rear of The Nek, and for an hour and a half he had stayed there watching the lifeless summit ahead, and knowing nothing of what was happening beyond it. Major S. B. Robertson of the 9th, who had missed most of his own company, had come up, and at 8.30 he and Lalor had decided that they must get closer to the scene of action. Most of the company accordingly moved over the crest of Baby 700, but Lalor, still discharging his duty as reserve, stayed with part of the troops a little beyond The Nek. The forward line under Robertson lay down in the scrub under scattered fire. Beyond rose Battleship Hill, and to right and left those near the summit could see the Narrows and the open sea respectively. It was then precisely 9 o'clock.[9]

The seaward side of Baby 700 sloped evenly down until it broke into four jagged gravel spurs, which zig-zagged steeply to the beach. Through the scrub on the smooth upper part of this descent ran some Turkish trenches, in rough continuation of a similar digging on the seaward slope of Battleship Hill. The trenches on Baby 700 held Turks, as did the head of the next gully behind them, and with these Turks Major Robertson's line was at once sharply engaged. The struggle grew in intensity. Between 9

1 Robertson 2 Margetts 3. Tulloch
Turks

and 10 o'clock other Turks were seen approaching

[9] The time of this event, and the time (10 a.m.) at which the parties on the Third Ridge were being driven back towards Legge Valley, are certain, events related to them having been noted by Lieut. Margetts and Capt. Peck (11th Bn) respectively.

through the distant trench on Battleship Hill. Meanwhile the seaward slope of Baby 700 had first been cleared and then lost again; and when it was lost Lieutenant Margetts on the summit had to withdraw his line part of the way down the rear slope. Shortly afterwards a Turkish battery began to burst its shrapnel regularly down the heads of the valleys on the Australian side of the hill.

It was this withdrawal on Baby 700 that MacLagan saw as he reached his headquarters three-quarters of a mile farther south. As mentioned above, he recognised this hill, looking down the upper slopes of Monash and Shrapnel Valleys behind the Second Ridge, as the key to the Second Ridge position, as indeed it was to the whole Australian "bridgehead" on Gallipoli. He now saw the fight there turning against the Australians. Henceforth

he concentrated his effort upon directing thither all reinforcements that came within his influence, and impressing the position on General Bridges, whose headquarters on the Beach was in telephone communication with both MacLagan and M'Cay. The troops whom Mac-Lagan had originally sent to the northern flank under Major Drake-Brock-

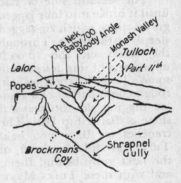

man had already arrived; others, as ordered, had lined the niches on the Second Ridge where it led up to that height and were now being fiercely attacked by Turks who had flowed across the Third Ridge north of Scrubby Knoll. The fire against this end of the Second Ridge was terrific, but that ridge was a very strong position. Some parties of Australians had thrust and were still thrusting

beyond it, to the head of the next spur of Baby 700,
Mortar Ridge. The plight of these advanced parties
gradually became precarious, but the only real danger to
the posts on the Second Ridge behind them lay in the
chance of the Turks' seizing all Baby 700, above and
behind the left flank of the posts.

From one danger the Australians were now free:
there was no chance of the Turks' penetrating along the
northern beach or foreshore, on the west side of the
range. A most powerful deterrent was the direct observation of the warships. It is true that the Turks had
originally held
trenches on the
knolls above
Fisherman's Hut,
and had fired
thence on boats
rowing in from the
northernmost des-
troyers. The party
sent by Colonel
Clarke to suppress
this fire noticed, as
it went, four still

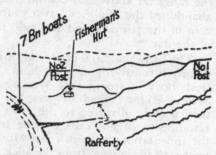

(Note: Posts 1 and 2 were then Turkish.)

more northerly boats rowing directly towards this post.
They came from a transport of the 2nd Brigade, the
Galeka, whose eager captain had brought her much closer
to shore than any other transport.

As the rowers were obviously heading for a death-
trap, the parties sent by Clarke charged forward to a spur
from which they might shoot effectively. In this charge
they lost half their men by fire from higher knolls on
their right, and the survivors reached the spur only to see
the boats already grounded, and a number of Australians
lying on the sand in front of them. A Tasmanian miner,
A. H. Stubbings, managed to run to the boats and found
behind them four men, who told him—as they believed—

that the cargoes were all dead or wounded. They were part of the 7th Battalion, which was to land on this flank, and they had come into a zone of terrible fire. Many of the rowers had been shot; others seized the oars and rowed the boats ashore; but of 140 officers and men only some 35 managed to cross the beach and shelter behind the low grassy hummocks.

However, at this stage the fire suddenly ceased. Apparently the Turks on the knoll, seeing Australians coming from several directions, especially those thrusting along the range far above and behind them, took fright. They abandoned the knoll, and two young officers and thirty men of the 7th occupied and held the position for most of the day.[10]

On Baby 700, high in rear of this scene, the fight continued furiously, hour after hour. Unfortunately, each fresh body of troops that MacLagan, waving from the Second Ridge, urged to press on up Monash Valley, tended to be diverted to the posts along that valley in response to urgent calls coming from officers high up the indentations or even from Mortar Ridge. Baby 700 projected like a head from the apex of the triangle which the Australian foothold now formed. The Turkish attack naturally tended to drive at the two shoulders, and henceforth increasingly against the inland one. The fight in the whole sector now fell more and more upon the reinforcements, which here came, first, from the 1st Brigade (reserve of the 1st Division), and, from the late morning onwards, from the New Zealanders. Despite all difficulties these fresh troops did intermittently reach that flank, and, whenever the line was driven from the crest of Baby 700,

---

10 The officers were Capt. H. T. C. Layh and Lieut. J. J. Scanlan. The wounded were sent off in some boats by the 3rd Field Ambulance, which had landed with heavy loss half a mile to the south. Next day it was noticed that some men remaining in the boats had moved slightly. The Turks were then back in the foothills, but a magnificent series of rescues was carried out. (See Vol. I, pp. 330-2. For the losses in boats, see pp. 325-9.)

another brave advance from the neighbourhood of The Nek would take it back again.

All the morning and most of the afternoon a tense battle, fought with unsurpassed courage on both sides, swayed backwards and forwards over that height. Meanwhile a mile to the south across the 400 Plateau there raged through all that long day an equally bitter struggle, but one that MacLagan had not intended. Here he had apparently meant the 2nd Brigade to dig in at least temporarily, prolonging southwards the line of his brigade somewhat behind the centre of the Plateau. Many parties of the 2nd Brigade, hurrying to their newly allotted front, inevitably missed all orders except the one that switched them to the south of the 3rd Brigade, and merely understood that they were to advance on that flank as far as they could. Yet many others did hear that they were to reinforce or extend southwards the line of the 3rd Brigade, and the order might well have achieved its object, if there had been a definite line to extend.

But where was the line of the 3rd Brigade? MacLagan's order to the 9th Battalion to advance and meet the counter-attack had caused most of his line on that flank to push forward through the intense fire that now swept the Plateau whenever a party moved there. Such was the torrent of bullets that, although parties of the 9th gradually reached the farther end of the Plateau, they did so as isolated fragments; in this battle the 9th was never together again. Successive companies of the 2nd Brigade, as they came up, found no line on the 400 Plateau or on the spurs south of it, and pressed on seeking for one. The stream of bullets that grazed the plateau, decimated each of these parties also. It is true that by about noon a considerable section of line had been formed on the Plateau by later companies of the 2nd Brigade about where MacLagan wished, just sheltered by the slight curve of its summit; and Lieutenant Alf Derham, a fine young officer from one of the decimated companies on the forward slope, urged that this line should remain there; but at that moment a call of "There they (the Turks) are!" and an excited rush led by a junior officer caused this line also to advance, with the same result as before; and Derham, who was wounded, had to limp after it.

Shortly before noon the strain had been greatly increased by the arrival of salvoes from two Turkish batteries, one probably being the battery that had already shelled the Australians on Baby 700, and which now directly enfiladed the line on the Second Ridge, and the other a mountain battery on Scrubby Knoll. The only ways for the troops to protect themselves from this fire were to dig in or to withdraw to the gullies. To withdraw would mean to let the Turks come on. Yet if men stood up to dig they were caught by the whirlwind of rifle and machine-gun fire across the Plateau; and when they lay down the salvoes of shrapnel burst, as regularly as the striking of a clock—every couple of minutes—over their defenceless backs. Neither here nor, as a rule, on Baby 700 could the Australians see the Turks who were now shooting at them. The fire seemed to pour out from whole hillsides. At rare intervals a dark grey or brown form might be detected moving, like a feeding rabbit, across some bare patch, from one bush to another, but few men saw even this. What they *did* note was that occasional rusty coloured streaks through the holly scrub were places to beware of—they denoted the dry scrub strewn as camouflage on the flat parapets of Turkish earthworks.

Now that the trial arrived the warships' guns, of which so much had been hoped, were at most stages completely powerless to help: the observers for them, afloat and ashore, could not tell where were the Turks and where their own men. The Australian field artillery, though some guns were brought to the Beach, could not in that steep country find positions from which to fire them. The Australians in this first battle had simply to hold on hour after hour to their exposed positions out on the ridges while the enemy artillery burst its shrapnel mercilessly and steadily over their backs, but no gun on their own side answered.

This was much the heaviest trial of that day and the real test of the men's mettle. They were steadied by fine leaders in their line, such as Major F. J. Kindon, stolidly puffing his pipe on Baby 700, Major R. Saker, taking grip on the 400 Plateau, and Lieutenant R. C. G. Prisk, Sergeant A. R. Knightley, or Major H. G. Bennett on the spurs south of it where part of the 2nd Brigade, in stiff fighting which cannot even be outlined here, managed temporarily to seize the furthest spur, Pine Ridge, while reserves dug in on Bolton's Ridge (a continuation of the main Second Ridge) behind them. On Pine Ridge a second battery, abandoned by the Turks, was captured.

Just before noon there came a temporary relief. One of the two Indian Mountain Batteries attached to the Corps had climbed with its mules on to the rear part of the 400 Plateau and opened fire vigorously. Its commander detected a few Turks moving on the Third Ridge and, in default of a more definite target, he shelled that ridge. To the Australians and New Zealanders all round the front the bang of those guns came like a cool drink to a parched man. Their spirits leapt. But the Indian battery, though it could not itself detect the Turkish batteries on the hills around, could be seen by them. It was quickly answered by a battery in the north and presently by another, now in position on Gun Ridge to the south-east. A murderous crossfire swept the Indians' gun positions and by 2.30, after great loss, the battery, threatened with extinction, was withdrawn to shelter.

From that time until sundown the infantry had to endure the unanswered fire of the Turkish batteries. The stream of wounded to the Beach was continuous; and many unwounded men, some believing themselves to be

cut off or the sole survivors of their units, others unable
to stand the strain, trickled back to the gullies or even to
the Beach. Once or twice a dangerous backward rush of
men occurred; but there was almost always some keen
officer or man to rally them and lead them forward again.

But on the left at about 4 p.m. the line on the crest
of Baby 700 was finally driven in. Major Robertson,
Captain Lalor,[11] and many other leaders had been killed;
and this time no reserve was at hand to carry the line
forward again. Several New Zealand battalions had been
sent thither, but there had been a delay in the arrival of
the transports, and some big shells coming over in pairs,
evidently from a Turkish warship in the Dardanelles,
had caused these ships to anchor farther out. General
Bridges had long kept one Australian battalion, the 4th,
in reserve. Ever since midday he had received urgent
requests for reinforcements from Colonel M'Cay, whose
advanced parties still held the Lone Pine lobe of the 400
Plateau but had lost heavily and were now being attacked
and gradually driven in on the spurs south of the Plateau.
The Turks now threatened to penetrate to the thin line
on Bolton's Ridge, behind those spurs. Major T. A.
Blamey, a young staff officer sent by Bridges to M'Cay,
confirmed that the need on that flank was extreme.
Bridges knew that MacLagan also urgently required help
for the northern flank; but at 4.45, on M'Cay's assurance
that the danger of losing the southern flank was absolute,
he sent the 4th Battalion thither. It found the line
immediately south of the 400 Plateau held by very few
men and was soon afterwards attacked there. Far out on
Pine Ridge at dusk parties of the 2nd Brigade were still
fighting. The Australian Historical Mission which visited
Gallipoli early in 1919 found their remains still there, in
the little crescent-shaped groups in which they fought it

---

11 For a note as to the career of this brave officer see *Vol. I, p. 291*. His
sword had been lost. It was picked up by L.-Cpl Harry Freame, a famous
Australian scout of half-Japanese blood, but was dropped again and is said
to be in a Turkish museum.

out, and with their battalion colours still visible on their sleeves.

Thus for Baby 700 on the opposite flank no reinforcements were available. The Australians and New Zealanders there had been driven into the heads of the valleys at its southern end. Nearly all leaders had been killed or wounded and the surviving men were in small parties unaware of each other's existence or of what was happening elsewhere. At nightfall Turks penetrated across The Nek and actually filtered across Russell's Top, far behind the northern end of the Australian line on the Second Ridge.

The position was exceedingly serious. General Bridges knew that his force had failed to achieve the object of the Landing, and MacLagan told him that the troops had been demoralised by the day-long shrapnel fire and that he doubted whether they could now hold if strongly attacked. It is true that 16,000 men and great quantities of stores had been landed and the 4th Australian Infantry Brigade under Colonel John Monash was being put ashore and sent straight to the threatened centre; but great numbers of wounded, and of others who had lost their units, had flowed back to the Beach. The mountain artillery had again clambered on to the heights but few other guns had been landed—at sunset the crowd of wounded lying at the southern end of the Beach cheered as a straining horse team urged by its drivers tugged the first Australian fieldpiece through them along the heavy sand, to be manhandled up the knoll there.

The day's losses were, at the time, estimated at 2000—actually they had been greater. The left flank had been forced back to Walker's Ridge. Instead of driving 1½ miles inland with a front of 4 miles the troops were clinging to a bare foothold on the Second Ridge little more than a ½ mile inland on a front of a mile and, even in the centre, with only one ridge between them and their landing place.

But it was on the condition of the troops that the brigadiers' fears were chiefly based. As always in the toughest fighting, commanders and staffs in rear saw chiefly the non-combatants and the weaker elements, the wounded, the shaken, and those who had lost their units. It is doubtful if most parts of the line would have obeyed an order to retire—certainly troops and officers would have questioned it.

But General Bridges knew that his force had achieved much less than was intended. So far as he knew the 29th Division at Cape Helles had succeeded, and the best use of his troops might be to abandon the task in which they had failed, and to support the 29th. Accordingly, after conference with the New Zealand commander, General Godley, Bridges sent for General Birdwood, who was to have landed later, and placed before him the question of a withdrawal. Birdwood was shocked but, in the end, like Bridges, he was impressed, and he referred the matter to General Hamilton who was in the *Queen Elizabeth*.

It happened that this great warship immediately afterwards arrived off Gaba Tepe, and Admiral Thursby, whose squadron had escorted the Australians and New Zealanders, took the message aboard her. On Hamilton's asking what was to be done about it, Thursby, who had already ordered all warships to lower their boats in readiness, spoke his opinion—that surviving boats now available were too few and the time too short to take off the troops before dawn or next morning. Hamilton therefore wrote to Birdwood: "There is nothing for it but to dig yourselves right in and stick it out."

He added that the 29th Division (which had landed at Cape Helles—but at some points was pinned more tightly than the Australians and New Zealanders) would be advancing next day and diverting pressure from Birdwood's force; and the Australian submarine *AE2* had got through the Narrows and torpedoed a Turkish gun-boat there.[12]

The night had fallen wet—one of the rare wet spells in the whole campaign—and the lantern in General Bridges' shelter glinted on the wet raincoats and shingle as the leaders on the Beach awaited Hamilton's message. From the hills came a ceaseless rattle of rifle fire. The troops who were the subject of these anxious discussions had, of course, not the least knowledge of them and would have been shocked had they known. For with nightfall there had come everywhere along the front a blessed and wholly unexpected relief. The Turkish batteries ceased firing, and the rifle and machine-gun fire became badly aimed and relatively harmless. Men could now stand and dig almost with impunity, and they quickly shovelled out trenches which, though as yet cramped, shallow and unconnected, afforded almost complete protection.

It is true that on the left, where the main range ran in, the Turks had penetrated across The Nek on to Russell's Top, behind the general Australian line; but they were few and no force followed them. We know now that here the two sides had fought each other to exhaustion, and, though the Turkish force had been ordered to attack, officers and men could not carry out the advance.

---

[12] In the Sea of Marmora she was joined by the British Submarine, *E14*, but on April 30th was sunk by the Turks. Her crew was saved.

9—os

113

CHAPTER VIII

"ANZAC" AND HELLES

MUCH else that had happened on the Turkish side was learnt four years later by the Australian Historical Mission. As mentioned above, the coastline of the southern half of the Peninsula had been held by the 9th Turkish Division, which placed four battalions around the seaboard and held the other five in reserve. The actual landing places had been garrisoned on the Australian front by one company, and on the 29th Division's front by two, in each case assisted by machine-gunners and some artillery. The main local reserve, the 19th Turkish Division, was camped two miles from the Narrows and three or four miles from the Australian landing place.

News of the Australian landing reached headquarters of the 9th Turkish Division, at Maidos on the Narrows, probably about daybreak. Its commander, Khalil Sami, at once sent off the two reserve battalions of the regiment (27th) whose other battalion was holding that part of the coast. They were to attack from Kojadere, a village just behind what may be called the Fourth Ridge. They started at 7.30 and were the troops who drove back the advanced parties near Scrubby Knoll and some also were later seen marching up the Third Ridge. For further reinforcement Khalil appealed to the 19th Division—apparently keeping the rest of his own reserve, three battalions, in case of need for the southern end of the Peninsula, whither they were eventually sent.

The 19th Division to which he appealed consisted of one Turkish regiment (57th), and two Arab ones (72nd and 77th) which the Turks regarded as of less value. It happened that the divisional commander, Major Mustafa Kemal, had arranged to exercise the 57th Regiment that morning over precisely the ground that the Australians were to seize. The regiment assembled at 5.30 and was on parade when Khalil's message reached Mustafa Kemal. It said that a force of "about one battalion" had landed at Ari Burnu and gone towards Hill 971; and Khalil asked Kemal to send a battalion from his camp to Ari Burnu to meet this thrust.

Kemal instantly conjectured that, if his opponents were making for Hill 971, the attack was no mere feint by a single battalion, but a major offensive. He therefore decided to throw in not one battalion but the whole of the 57th Regiment, and himself started off at once across country, map in hand, striding out with the leading company of the regiment, and with its leading battalion commander, Zeki Bey, beside him.[1] As he reached the eastern slope of Scrubby Knoll on the Third Ridge, a number of Turks scattered by the Australian advance came tumbling down the slope. Mustafa Kemal climbed this ridge immediately north of the knoll and sent two battalions of the 57th straight against the Australians. Captain Tulloch's men, several ridges away, by Battleship Hill could then be seen by the Turks, and the tough fight began. The Australian fire, said Zeki Bey afterwards, was heavy and accurate. Zeki Bey's battalion advanced on the inland side of the main range and the sister battalion down the seaward side—it was the latter attack that eventually drove the Australians from Baby 700.

A little farther south the advance against the 400 Plateau and the spurs south of it had been made by Khalil's 27th Regiment. The 27th barely reached the Plateau and in the southern spurs it fought all day against advanced parties of M'Cay's 2nd Brigade holding the

---

[1] For the Turkish side of the story, as told to the Australian Historical Mission which went over the ground carefully with Zeki Bey in 1919, see *Vol. I. pp. 447-52, and 476-9* and *Gallipoli Mission* by the present author.

farthest spur (Pine Ridge). By dusk it had overrun the
last of them. To fill a gap between the 57th and 27th
Regiments Mustafa Kemal had by then brought up his
second regiment, the 77th (Arab); but its troops, attacking
at nightfall or after, became hopelessly scattered, many
of them firing from Third Ridge upon the other Turkish
regiments in front. Part of Kemal's third regiment, the
72nd (Arab) he brought round during the night to the
main range to support the 57th, whose last battalion had
been put in on Baby 700 and had driven the last Australians there across The Nek. Here the Turks were
unknowingly helped by the erroneous belief of some of
the Australians that Indian infantry was fighting beside
them, which caused them at certain critical moments to
cease fire on the Turks whom they mistook for Indians.

After nightfall the Turks, using a third battalion of
the 57th, had outflanked and captured The Nek. The
reports from some Turkish commanders on this front
to Mustafa Kemal had been as alarming as those from
the brigadiers MacLagan and M'Cay to Bridges; but the
commander of this battalion, who was up with his troops
at the Nek, reported that, though he was in touch with
only eighty or ninety of them, and feared that, if attacked,
they might not be able to hold their own, he believed
their opponents also were too exhausted to attack.

During this night at both ends of the Second Ridge
the Turks assaulted in the dark, but their rushes were
always preceded by a sudden wild chorus of "Allah!
Allah!" which gave warning of each attempt, and they
were easily mown down by rifles and machine-guns. All
night parties crept up and sniped or tried to assemble for
closer rushes, but were constantly scared back by short
charges of Australians and New Zealanders with their
bayonets. From dark to dawn both sides maintained a
terrific and perhaps largely useless rifle fire. Alternately
firing and digging, the Australians and New Zealanders
had barely time to notice the drizzling rain. The crucial

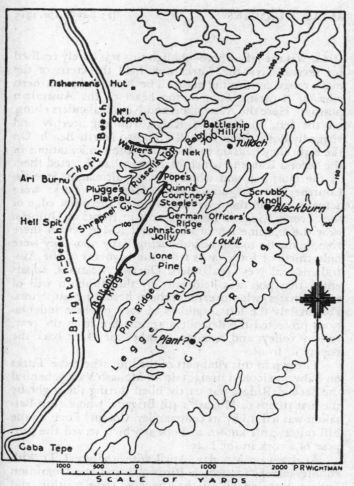

THE BATTLE OF THE LANDING, 25th APRIL 1915

(Though two of the northern outposts are here marked, the effort to establish them was not made till a later stage. Loutit's name marks his party's position—he himself reached Scrubby Knoll.)

Map from "The Empire at War" (50 metre contours).

sector was the left, where—though this was barely realised
for several days—the Turks now held the crests of the
main range continuing across The Nek to the northern
edge of Russell's Top, in the heart of the Australian
position. Here the Australians and New Zealanders clung,
on the left, to Walker's Ridge, running steeply and
ruggedly down from Russell's Top to North Beach. On
the right they held on to the heads of the indentations in
the Second Ridge to which MacLagan had directed them
in the morning, and which became ultimately Steele's,
Courtney's, and Quinn's Posts. Here the Turks were
actually behind them, as well as lining the other edge of
the Second Ridge, a biscuit throw in front; at Quinn's,
near the extreme left of the Second Ridge, which there
rose gradually to the neighbouring Baby 700, they were
only thirty or forty yards from the bayonets of the Australians and New Zealanders. On two occasions, apparently, that post was held only by the stubborn will of
subordinates who overrode their hesitating superiors.
Fortunately the left shoulders of each of these indentations protected the defenders against fire from the rear,
and by volleys and occasional rushes they kept back the
enemy in front.

The gap in this vital part of the line, where the Turks
on Baby 700 looked straight down Monash Valley, behind
the Second Ridge, was partly filled during the night by
the first troops of Monash's 4th Brigade, whose 16th Battalion was led up by its commander, Colonel Pope, to the
hill (afterwards known as Pope's) which served the purpose of a cork in the hole.

At dawn on Monday, April 26th, the great Turkish
counter-attack, for which Birdwood and the Dominion
leaders—and indeed all their troops—were waiting. did
not come. What the Dominion leaders did not realise was
that the Turks were as tired as their opponents, and had
lost very heavily; in the 27th and 57th Regiments alone
there had been 2000 casualties—an astonishing proof of

the accurate fire of the Dominion troops. Later on the 26th a body of Turks attempting to move down the wide summit of Baby 700 towards Pope's Hill was caught and shattered by shells from the *Queen Elizabeth* and other battleships; their fire had been mostly ineffective hitherto, but they pounded the Turkish positions that morning, largely in order to cheer the troops. The twelve Indian mountain guns and a few of the Anzac field artillery were by then in position. The only other visible movement that day was made from near the southern end of the front by the 4th Australian Battalion which, on receiving a verbal order to straighten a section of its line, mistook this for the order for a general advance which many troops were expecting. The 4th swept over the 400 Plateau, recapturing most of the southern lobe (Lone Pine), from which Australians had been withdrawn during the previous night. The rest of the force did not even know till afterwards that this second advance had occurred. Few Turks were there, but the plateau was swept by an intense fire of shrapnel and small arms, and after heavy loss the remnants were that night again brought back into the old line.

On the third day, April 27th, Mustafa Kemal, having been reinforced by two regiments, attempted a general counter-attack. But the warships' guns caught the main attack as it tried to move down Baby 700 and scattered the Turks like ants on a disturbed anthill—after this experience never again until August did the Turks at Anzac attempt to move down slopes exposed to the warships' guns. At Quinn's and the posts south of it they were mown down by rifle fire; and on the right, where they again attacked by night, an Australian battery, which by then Lieut.-Colonel C. Rosenthal had managed to have dragged to the firing line, helped to sweep other assaulting lines away.

Along much of the front the garrison was not even aware it had been attacked. The one sector in which real

119

danger existed was at The Nek—now in possession of the Turks—where the main range ran in. But here three days' constant fighting, under Brig.-General H. B. Walker (chief of Birdwood's staff who temporarily commanded the New Zealand infantry) and Lieut.-Colonel G. F. Braund of the 2nd Australian Battalion, established a line facing the Turks at The Nek. The gap at this apex of the position was not quite closed—the Turks still held Baby 700, the key of the Anzac position, but they could not get further past or round the posts, though they could still fire into the back of Quinn's, Courtney's and Steele's. This day Colonel H. N. MacLaurin, the young Australian brigadier who relieved MacLagan with a view to the remustering of the 3rd Brigade, was killed—as was his brigade major—by a Turkish sniper from the left rear.

In all this time the Australians and New Zealanders had hardly seen an aircraft. The balloon ship *Manica* had done most of the observing from the air. On the evening of the 28th, when Turks were seen on Nibrunesi Point, which jutted out four miles to the north, a seaplane from the *Ark Royal* flew low along the Beach and reported that men were at work on that point. It was feared that they were emplacing a howitzer to shell the Beach. The warships battered the point with their shells. No gun was ever emplaced there, but raiding parties (on April 30th and May 2nd) destroyed the post, the New Zealanders capturing fifteen prisoners there.

Birdwood's Corps had thus established a foothold—it would now be called a bridgehead—on the Peninsula, and by May 1st forty-four of his sixty-four guns had been hauled into position, mainly on the hilltops close behind the front line. The New Zealand and Australian Division under General Godley was allotted the left third of the front, and the 1st Australian Division under General Bridges the remaining two-thirds. Birdwood obtained leave to call the place by the code-name of his corps, ANZAC—Australian and New Zealand Army Corps—and that famous name, though originally devised by one of Birdwood's English clerks, Lieutenant A. T. White, while the Corps was at Cairo, now first came into general use. The bay and the half-mile of beach between the two sheltering knolls, already crammed like a busy port with the food, fodder, ammunition, engineers' stores, dressing stations, pack mules and offices of the Corps, were named Anzac Cove. The warships, the hospital ships and a crowd of transports (still having aboard much of the artillery and nearly all the transport and their horses), as well as trawlers and small craft still lay a few miles off it and a similar collection off Cape Helles, with battleships, cruisers and destroyers guarding them.

At Cape Helles the 29th Division had landed in face of greater difficulties than the "Anzacs"; the heavy naval bombardment there had not suppressed the Turks,[2] but had warned them that the infantry would land. The attempt to disembark at Seddel Bahr from the beached transport, *River Clyde*, miscarried with great loss, and those who here reached shore were pinned all day to the beach or near it, as were those at the next beach to the north, Lancashire Landing. Fortunately on other beaches opposition was much less and the southern effort was helped by the fact that the northern landing, at Anzac, drew to itself for two days nearly all the Turkish reserves; but even on the third day, the first objective for the 29th Division, Achi Baba peak, was still farther off than was the objective, Mal Tepe, at Anzac, and the troops at Helles were as exhausted as the Anzacs.

Sir Ian Hamilton had neither artillery nor infantry enough to push on at both Anzac and Helles. But at Helles the fleet could better support him on both flanks and his land artillery had room for its positions. Chiefly for these reasons he decided to concentrate upon his effort there. On April 27th the French division which had made

---

[2] Throughout the campaign the flat trajectory of most naval guns rendered them largely ineffective against troops in trenches.

the feint south of the straits, and had now been withdrawn, took over the right of the front, at Seddel Bahr, and next day the 29th Division advanced. But, though it greatly improved the foothold by carrying the front to nearly 3 miles from the Cape, it was still 3½ miles short of Achi Baba and over 2 from Krithia village at the foot of that height.

Hamilton now decided to use all available forces—including whatever could be spared from Anzac—in trying to reach Achi Baba peak before the Turkish force ahead of him was too strong and too well dug in. He himself wished to approach the enemy here at night and attack at dawn, but the Commander of the 29th Division, General Hunter-Weston, dreaded the confusion of operations in the dark now that his infantry had lost many good officers.

On May 3rd Hamilton summoned Birdwood and asked him to send to Helles as much of his force as he could spare. Birdwood sent at once the two infantry brigades that had been least heavily tried—the New Zealand and the 2nd Australian—and Hamilton also brought down twenty Anzac field-guns which were still in their ships. The two brigades were transported in fleet-sweepers on the night of the 5th, and landed at dawn next day beside the stranded *River Clyde*, now serving as part of the breakwater and pier at Seddel Bahr. There on May 6th, in a countryside wholly different from the rugged Anzac, they presently watched from amid olive groves and flowery meadows in brilliant sunlight a formal attack, beginning at 10.30 a.m. with a bombardment, the distant infantry, French and 29th Division, advancing on either flank at 11 o'clock. Between the two a "composite" brigade of 29th Division and Royal Naval Division troops was to keep touch. From a quarter to half a mile was gained that day, but two similar attacks next day added very little to this. On the third morning the New Zealand Brigade, lent to the 29th Division, renewed the attack on

the left; its orders arrived late and again little ground
was gained. General Hunter-Weston of the 29th Division
had no better plan than to order it to attack again in
the afternoon.

But here Sir Ian Hamilton stepped in. In nearly three
days the army in its costly advance had not yet reached
or, for the most part, even seen the Turkish positions.
His reserves were almost expended. But it was still believed that, if once reached and pierced, the whole
Turkish line would collapse. Accordingly Hamilton
resolved to put in the 2nd Australian Brigade where the
composite brigade had been; at 5.30 p.m., after fifteen
minutes' bombardment by the ships and land artillery,
the whole Allied line was to fix bayonets and advance.

The 2nd Australian Brigade had just been brought
round over a streamlet and through flowery meadows to
bivouac, so it thought, for the night 600 to 900 yards
behind the British centre. Its men were digging themselves shelter and cooking their evening meal when at
4.55, without warning, the order arrived. Colonel M'Cay
was away, visiting the New Zealand brigadier, and it was
doubtful whether it was physically possible for the
brigade to be in attack formation crossing the front line
within thirty-five minutes. Messengers were sent to the
four battalions and to M'Cay and at 5.5 M'Cay issued his
order—the 7th and 6th Battalions to advance side by side
over the level country ahead of them, with their flanks
on two streams and with the 5th and 8th Battalions
similarly following in support.

The men, then settling to their tea, were hurried
away, with packs on, the battalions making across country
from their bivouacs to pick up position, Major Gordon
Bennett and Lieut.-Colonel McNicoll directing the left
(with which went M'Cay) and the brigade major, W. E.
H. Cass, leading the right. With the Allied guns thundering, the hurrying companies crossed a slight dip and
a trench full of Indians and then emerged through the

123

scattered olive trees on to a wide, dry, level grassland that reached ahead to the distant Achi Baba peak. The moment they appeared, bullets fired at long range fell among them. Presently Turkish shrapnel began to burst over the right, raising tawny clouds as the pellets whipped up the dust. But each time, when it cleared, the platoons were seen marching as before. The fire of small arms increased but the heavily loaded brigade hurried straight on, heads down, as if into fierce rain, some men holding their shovels before their faces like umbrellas in a thunderstorm. The left battalion, 6th, had already extended into successive lines, as it moved, and the right, 7th, now did the same.

Five hundred yards after passing over the Indian trench the troops reached, suddenly and quite unexpectedly, another trench, filled with British soldiers. In the A.I.F. it was ever afterwards known as "The Tommies' Trench". The leading lines jumped into it or lay down behind it, panting from the speed of the advance and wondering if they were to go farther. After about three minutes, as later lines came up, M'Cay jumped out on the parapet and called, "Now then, Australians! On, Australians!"

The fire was by then intense, spurts of dust rising from the plain like drops splashing in a thunder-shower. But line after line of the 2nd Brigade clambered out and hurried forward. Their swift advance was the spectacle of the battlefield. For another 500 yards they hastened on, men falling constantly, until the lines were so thin that it was clear that the front was too weak to push farther. The stone houses of Krithia were still 2000 yards away, but in advancing 1000 yards the brigade, already reduced at Anzac to 2900 men, lost in one short hour another 1000. On higher ground on the far right of the Allied line the Turkish trenches were reached—the French were seen leaping into them. Some Australians at the end of the advance could make out Turkish earthworks 400 yards ahead. On the left the New Zealanders had gained but little ground at heavy cost. After dark touch was found with them. Three weeks later the inexperienced 42nd Division, advancing by night as Hamilton had wished, approached another 200 yards nearer to the Turkish position almost without casualties.

The two Anzac brigades were sent back to their own force. The time when the Turkish line across the south of the Peninsula was still largely unentrenched had passed; and, with the Turks digging in solidly and reinforcements reaching them, there vanished the hope that their defence could be penetrated, and the objectives dominating the straits gained, by Hamilton's present force and method. So far the military attempt as well as the naval had failed.

CHAPTER IX

HOLDING ON AT ANZAC

At both Anzac and Helles the Allies were now faced with complete trench lines, strongly held. Until these could be broken through, the possibility of "open warfare" had passed. The obvious means of breaking through was artillery bombardment, and Hamilton decided to use this in making step by step advances, partly at night. Relying now on artillery, he naturally still adhered to his plan of attacking at Helles. Birdwood and his corps at Anzac were ordered to attempt only minor attacks so as to facilitate any advance that might be planned later and to keep busy a large force of Turks.

There were ample tasks confronting the Anzac troops if their position was even to be held. First, the apex of the position, Baby 700 with The Nek leading to it, was held by the Turks. Already, exactly a week after the Landing, when the troops had been reorganised (partly by the loan of four battalions of "marines"—actually raw troops lately raised by Churchill) the Anzac Corps had endeavoured to close this gap by seizing Baby 700 and the extreme upper end of the Second Ridge north of Quinn's Post. At nightfall on Sunday May 2nd, after a heavy bombardment of that angle by naval and land artillery, Monash's 4th Brigade climbed the right branch of the head of Monash Valley, with orders to link with the New Zealand Infantry Brigade, which was to climb the left branch and thence move across Baby 700.

The Australians attacked with great spirit. Monash and his headquarters, far down the valley, could hear the cheers as the attack topped its edge and with the cheers came the sound of the supports singing "Tipperary" and "Australia will be there".

But the approach march of the New Zealanders around the crowded Beach and up Shrapnel and Monash Valleys took twice as long as planned. They attacked nearly two hours late, to be met by a tempest of fire which had already swept the unsupported flank of the Australians. Useless attempts were made during the night to carry out the plan in the face of the now thoroughly awakened Turks—even at dawn some of the Marines were thrown in; the bodies of some of them crowning the last knuckle in Monash Valley, beyond Pope's, gave their name to "Dead Man's" Ridge. The whole effort achieved nothing and cost 1000 casualties.

With its apex thus firmly in Turkish hands, the Anzac position was difficult to hold; indeed, many tacticians would probably call it "untenable". The Anzacs clung barely to the inner edge of the Second Ridge—and, at The Nek, not even to that—with the Turks on the other edge of it. At Quinn's the Turks, only forty yards away, were digging, and perhaps mining, closer. They held the continuation of this spur to Baby 700, and had thrust forward to Dead Man's Ridge, which not only commanded part of the rear of Quinn's but looked straight down Monash Valley, up the stream bed of which—normally dry—came all traffic and supplies for that part of the Anzac line.

It was also at Quinn's, and on Russell's Top (facing The Nek on the main ridge) that the Turks had thrown missiles like black iron cricket balls. The Australians and New Zealanders had heard of bombs being used on the Western Front but had never seen one, and at first had none to reply with. Moreover, as trench periscopes were unknown to them until the Marines brought a few, the Anzac sentries had to observe by watching through loopholes or with heads over the parapets; but as the Turkish positions looked into Quinn's from three sides it was

almost certain death to expose one's head there by day
for three seconds. As already stated, it seems that Quinn's
was twice being abandoned when a junior overcame the
decision of his superior and was allowed to hold it.

In the following weeks the suspicion that the Turks
would tunnel under Quinn's and blow it up induced
General Godley to order the seizure of the Turkish
trenches on the reverse slope. The first attempt was made
by three parties of the 15th Battalion on the night of
May 9th. But though the parties (totalling 100 men) in
furious fighting took the trenches opposite them, and
three communication trenches were dug from Quinn's
to the new positions, the Australians, having no bombs,
were in the morning bombed and shot out by flank
attacks—10 officers being killed and 200 casualties suffered among the attacking parties and their supports
who became involved in the effort.

The situation there was now very difficult. The three
communication trenches had been left joining Quinn's
and "Turkish Quinn's" (as it was called); and, using part
of these, the Turks in the next week were able to shower
bombs day and night into the Australian trenches there.
The Quinn's garrison—by then consisting of light horsemen, who had just been brought to Anzac without their
horses—had learnt from the infantry to catch the Turkish
bombs before they burst and throw them back, or else to
smother them with an overcoat or sandbag. Also bombs
improvised from jam tins filled with snippets of metal
were now being manufactured on Anzac Beach and a
shower of these quietened the Turks—but not for long.

Accordingly, on the night of May 14th, several parties
of the 2nd Light Horse Regiment charged out in a
planned attempt to fill in the three saps and their
entrances. This time the Turks were ready; of the 60
Australians nearly 50 were at once hit and the attempt
failed.

On the morning after this attack the fire of Turkish snipers down Monash Valley increased in severity. Losses being high, big sandbag buttresses were built at intervals across the valley bed, but snipers fired at men moving from buttress to buttress, and on this day they mortally wounded General Bridges there. Wishing good-bye to a friend in the hospital ship, "Anyhow," he said, "I have commanded an Australian Division."[1]

On May 18th the Turkish rifle fire, which had been constant since the Landing, almost ceased, but the Turkish artillery fire—hitherto mainly light shrapnel, and painful only at certain vulnerable parts of the line and valleys—became constant and included some heavy shells. It had little effect, but a British aviator, who that day happened to make one of the rare flights over that area, detected Turkish troops massed in the valleys behind the Turkish line. A second airman sent out saw other Turks arriving across the straits. As the Navy and the Anzac observers also reported unusual movements the garrison was warned to expect attack.

In the small hours next morning expectant Australians, peering down the gloomy depth of Wire Gully (north of the 400 Plateau), noticed there the faint reflection of light from sheaves of moving bayonets. Heavy fire was opened on these, and shortly afterwards choruses of "Allah, Allah!" were heard, first from there, and successively from most other parts of the front, and charging Turks came dimly into view. In some parts they were deliberately allowed to advance until very close and then the Australians opened a terrible fire, shouting tags of slang learnt in Egypt: "Saida!" "Backsheesh!" "Eggs-a-cook!" Everywhere the attacking lines withered under this fusillade. Here and there machine-guns and, on the right, a field-gun added to the effect. The assault was

---

[1] See Vol. II, pp. 128-30. Bridges died in the hospital ship but his body was taken to Australia and buried on the hilltop above Australia's Military College which he had founded. General Walker was temporarily appointed in his place while General Legge was being sent from Australia.

exceedingly brave and persistent; a few—a very few—
stubborn men reached the parapets and even the trenches.
At Courtney's Post, south of Quinn s, Turkish bombs
cleared one bay and nine of the enemy entered it; but,
after several deadly· attempts to clear them, a Victorian
private, Albert Jacka, cleverly taking the necessary risks,
leapt into the bay while the enemy's attention was held
by his mates, killed six, and wounded and captured one.[2]

The ill-co-ordinated attacks had been launched from
3.30 onwards, at different times against different sectors.
It was after daylight when, at 4.20, an effort was made to
rush Quinn's. Though the trenches there were now, at
one point, only fifteen yards apart, no Turk managed to
get through the crossfire of machine-guns protecting the
post. Later efforts were equally fruitless.

The Anzac troops had only 628 men hit—mostly
through exposing themselves too eagerly after daylight.
But no-man's-land was strewn with Turks. Of the 42,000
—two old and two fresh divisions—that attacked, 10,000
were hit, 3000 (it is said) being killed. One reaction to
this immense slaughter—which was mainly the work of
the Australian riflemen—was that the attitude of the
troops towards this enemy entirely changed; from being
bitter and suspicious they became admirers and almost
friends of the Turks—"Jacko" or "Abdul", as they called
them—and so they remained to the end of the war. An
attempt by Australians on May 20th to rescue some of the
Turkish wounded led, first, to a short informal armistice,
and later, on May 24th, to a formal truce lasting nearly
all day, at which the dead were buried—and incidentally
the embarrassing saps between the opposing trenches at
Quinn's were used as graves and conveniently filled in,
to the relief, probably, of both sides.

This greatest effort, made by order of the Turkish
government and Liman von Sanders, to have done once

---

[2] He was the first Australian to win the Victoria Cross in that war. For
the details see *Vol. II, pp. 148-50.*

and for all with the invaders at Anzac, had thus ended disastrously for the Turks. It is true that the small triangular foothold, with the Turks looking down the valley in its centre, was a difficult one to hold. On May 29th the Turks by tunnelling (which Australian miners had heard but the engineer staff disregarded till too late) blew up and captured part of Quinn's; but after a furious and tensely exciting fight they were quickly driven out again. On June 4th—when, down at Cape Helles, General Hamilton continued his effort to "hammer away", step by step, with bombardment, towards Achi Baba—the Anzacs, being asked to pull their weight, again assaulted the Turkish Quinn's. This time the New Zealand infantry attacked.[3] The enterprise at first went well, but after daybreak the place became a reeking inferno of bombing, and, though jam-tin bombs were now being made in increasing numbers at the improvised factory on the Beach, the supply was still insufficient. The flanking fire of Turkish machine-guns from other posts on both flanks was, as always, most deadly. In an attempt to stop it on the southern flank the Australians now made a swift trench-raid—a party under Lieutenant Longfield Lloyd suddenly dashing to German Officers' Trench and back. But the trench was found to be partly roofed over and little could be effected. At Quinn's the Turks forced their way towards the new communication trench just dug by the New Zealanders and, by 6.30 a.m., to avoid being cut off, the survivors of the New Zealand attack were withdrawn. The brigade lost over 100 men and the Turks twice as many.

This ended for the present all attempts by the Anzacs to make safe the apex of their position by open attack. Instead they safeguarded their posts by mining, while the Turkish sniping that was taking such toll in Monash

---

[3] See *Vol. II, pp. 200, 203, and 206-21.* The final clearing of the crater on May 30th was heroically covered by a young Australian machine-gunner, Pte T. Arnott; see *Vol. II, p. 225.*

Valley was met by counter-sniping. In this the Anzac snipers were helped by the invention, by a man of the 2nd Battalion, of a periscope-rifle; the apparatus was manufactured on the Beach and could be safely fired from shelter in the most dangerous posts. Within a few weeks the tables had been completely turned on the Turkish snipers; Monash Valley became safe;[4] even the Indian mule train were able to go up it by day without a shot being fired at them, the Turkish snipers being prevented from shooting down it until after dark, when they could hit only by chance. For pedestrian traffic a trench was dug along the whole western side of the valley, a little above its bed.

In addition the Anzacs obtained on May 20th four highly effective Japanese trench mortars, which inflicted such loss that the Turks began to roof over their important posts with logs and earth—a practice which is said to have turned their trenches into death-traps when shelled by howitzers later in the campaign. Meanwhile in order to gain ground, as the Anzacs were still clinging to little more than the edge of the Second Ridge, shallow tunnels were pushed out from most parts of that front, and ground was safely won by secretly breaking through from these tunnels to the surface closer to the Turkish front line. For low-level mining, deep tunnels also were begun, heading beneath the Turkish line.

Yet in the centre—where the main ridge ran down through Baby 700, The Nek, and Russell's Top, to end in Plugge's Plateau 300 feet above Anzac Beach—any advance by the Turks must have been fatal: by driving even 300 yards across Russell's Top they would place themselves in direct rear of the vital Anzac posts on the Second Ridge and would look down on North Beach.

---

[4] The details of this classic contest of marksmen are described in *Vol. II, pp. 248 and 285-7.* The snipers were organised first by Lieut. T. M. P. Grace, N.Z. Mounted Rifles, later by Sgt F. M. Mack, Australian Light Horse. Periscopes also were now manufactured on Anzac Beach.

Mustafa Kemal, who then commanded this flank of Essad Pasha's Corps at Anzac, was not one to miss such a chance—and on the night of June 29th he attacked from The Nek, using a well-trained regiment, fresh from Constantinople. It was met by the dismounted 3rd Light Horse Brigade, partly in the new secretly tunnelled defences, and was defeated so disastrously that the attempt was never repeated. Instead the Turks continued to furrow the wide brow of Baby 700 with line after line of trenches barring the way up the main ridge, and fighting went on underground in the deeper tunnels with which each side tried to undermine the other.

The British and French at the toe of the Peninsula made little progress in their attempts to push to Achi Baba by means of artillery support. On June 4th, June 21st, June 28th and July 12th major attacks were launched by the British or French or both. In most of these desperate efforts the attacking troops, after a first success, were left with only one line of Turkish trench, or part of it, in their hands. This fighting had some value; the repeated counter-attacks by the Turks after June 4th and 21st are said to have cost them 25,000 men, and, at a time when Hamilton had other plans maturing, the Turkish leaders were induced to believe that Helles was the danger point—but at a cost to the British which grievously affected the later efforts. During these operations the Anzac staff tried to tie the local Turkish reserves to Anzac by numerous "demonstrations". These ranged from actual attacks, and difficult, costly sorties against the enemy's parapet or a crater in no-man's-land, down to sham concentrations in which a platoon or two with bayonets showing above the parapets ran like stage soldiers round and round a circuit in the trenches to give the appearance of a battalion assembling to attack; this last method was possibly the most effective.

The heavy work, monotonous diet, and widespread infection—of which the main carriers, the swarms of flies, were insufficiently recognised—were straining the troops. Undoubtedly immense casualties were averted through the men's previous inoculation for typhoid, but diarrhoea, dysentery and paratyphoid attacked thousands. Only serious cases were evacuated—or were willing to be evacuated. The rest struggled on, gaunt and weakened, infecting others, sometimes even fainting at their posts, but indomitably eager. Their uniform was like no other in the war, any degree of undress being sufficient for the men[5] and allowed by their officers. Half-naked, they dug, tunnelled, carried food, water, and ammunition up the dusty, precipitous tracks, swept their trenches free of refuse, or patiently searched their clothes for the vermin that nightly plagued them. Occasionally a visit to the beach gave even men from the front line the chance of a bathe from the piers and the crowded shingle. Men whose duty was on or near the beach bathed daily—and when they had this opportunity intermittent shrapnel could never keep them long out of the water.

Life at Anzac—as at Tobruk in the Second World War—differed from experience on the main fronts in that the troops were nowhere away from shellfire and had practically no chance of rest in peaceful conditions. In the gullies where most of them lived, immediately behind the front line, they were plagued, part of the time, by Turkish rocket bombs (sometimes known as broomstick bombs) arriving with a loud hiss and a bang. The Turks even used a few spherical iron shells from old-time mortars—the Anzacs had their four good Japanese trench mortars, others improvised in Egypt with metal tubing, and also catapults resembling crossbows.

It is true that some battalions were taken, one at a time, to Imbros Island, eleven miles away, but at this stage the rest was only for 3-6 days. Until late in the campaign no regular canteen and no Red Cross stores

---

[5] See Wallace Anderson's figure of "Anzac" in the War Memorial, Canberra.

reached Anzac. The Australian mail, which came fort-
nightly, and the more frequent English mail, brought
news for which men hungered; the very rare sight of an
aeroplane, British or German, or the spectacle of a warship bombarding, were the chief other excitements. The
nights were pestilential with fleas and, in the trenches,
lice, for which no delousing apparatus existed at Anzac.
A few dentists—mostly unearthed from the fighting ranks
—tried to meet the hundreds of dental troubles for most
of which, however, men were either not treated or were
sent to Alexandria, against their will. By the end of July,
of 25,000 men at Anzac, 200 were being sént away sick
each day. In Egypt the Australian hospitals, though
immensely expanded since the Landing, were over-
crowded and their staffs at times worked almost to
exhaustion.

Anzac Beach was a sight perhaps never before seen in
modern war—a crowded, busy base within half a mile of
the centre of the front line; and that strongly marked and
definite entity, the Anzac tradition, had, from the first
morning, been partly created there. From the moment of
launching the campaign it was the resolve of those Australian soldiers who would usually be regarded as non-
combatants to show themselves not a hairsbreadth behind
the combatants in hardihood. Wherever a call went
up for "stretcher-bearers" the company bearers would as
a matter of course try to reach it. The first time the writer
heard that call, amid the whine of bullets on an exposed
slope on April 25th, two men instantly rose, pipe in
mouth, stretcher on shoulder, and sauntered casually in
the direction of the voice—a doubtless intentional
example to the crouching infantry around them.

Later one bearer, Private Simpson—his civil name was
Kirkpatrick—annexed one of the donkeys (landed to take
water up the hills but never so used) and for three weeks
carried on it down Monash and Shrapnel valleys men

wounded in the legs. As well as the sniping, the shelling of this route by shrapnel from the south was sometimes severe, and on May 19th a burst of it killed him and his patient. Another bearer,[6] who was seen to pass, without stopping, under a shrapnel burst, carried his patient to the dressing tent, sat quietly in the waiting ranks for the doctor to come to him, and fell dead without having mentioned his wound. The "beach parties" under an old Anglo-American soldier, Captain C. A. Littler, and the naval men who also helped in the landing of men and stores, carried on under almost any fire. Even the military offenders, set on the open decks of the water barges to pump water into the tanks on the Beach, were too proud to turn their heads when shells burst over them. Part of the tradition set, at the Landing on Anzac Beach, by all hands, from naval landing officer to private, from Birdwood to the youngest reinforcement, was—to carry on under shellfire completely heedless, as if the shrapnel was a summer shower.

Within a week visitors were arriving at Anzac to see this sight. Not long afterwards several heavy bombardments from Turkish batteries (afterwards known as "Beachy Bill"), emplaced at the "Olive Grove" on the flats beyond the right flank, made this procedure too costly to continue, and a battery near Anafarta on the northern flank later added a dangerous crossfire. The mule- and horse-lines had hurriedly to be moved off the Beach into the gullies that opened on to it. The Turks had observation posts on both flanks—at Nibrunesi Point and Gaba Tepe—from both of which capes they could see part of the Beach. Yet these batteries never succeeded in stopping work or bathing for more than a short spell. The Anzac field-guns fought Homeric duels with the Olive Grove and Gaba Tepe batteries whenever these opened fire. The piles of stores and ammunition and the

---

[6] L.-Cpl G. T Hill, captain of a Sydney swimming club.

dressing stations remained on the Beach from first to last, with Birdwood's and other headquarters on the slope close above them.

No craft larger than a picket boat could by daylight safely approach Watson's Pier or the other jetties built by the Anzacs—shells from the Olive Grove would at once fall on or around them with unfailing accuracy; and from May 13th the submarine threat had driven away all craft that used to anchor in the offing except the two destroyers always watching the flanks, a few small craft, and the white hospital ship which, relieved every few days by a sister ship, used to lie there, a beautiful thing with her bright motionless lights at night, and the blazing Aegean sky and sunsets, and clustered mountain tops of Imbros and Samothrace, as her background by day. No Turkish shot or German torpedo ever threatened her.[7]

From the first, Generals Birdwood and Bridges wished to be rid of the nuisance afforded by the presence of Turkish observers on the projecting capes on either flank. Accordingly on May 4th an attempt was made by about 100 men under Major Ray Leane of the 11th Battalion to seize or raid the promontory of Gaba Tepe. They were landed from destroyers on its beach, but were at once pinned to the bank there by a whirlwind of fire from its crowded trenches. They were most bravely taken off again by the Navy in boats under cover of vicious bombardment

Raids on Gaba Tepe and Nibrunesi

2 Miles

------

[7] It was on her decks that women—including a few Australian nurses—made their only approach to Anzac.

from the destroyers' guns.[8] This southern flank of the
Anzac position was explored in the early days by some
Tasmanians, who passed round the Turkish flank and
spent a night and day on the Third Ridge close behind
the Turks; but when they tried with Major Blamey to
repeat this achievement they ran into a Turkish patrol
and sentry line, and after a rough and tumble fight
withdrew.

The southern flank had thus been closed by the
Turks; but any danger of their attacking from there was
offset by two facts: first, the valleys and ridges there could
be raked by naval fire; and though on May 25th the
battleship *Triumph* was torpedoed and sunk off Gaba
Tepe in full view of the Anzac lines, warships would
always come if urgently required, and daily (and nightly
with its searchlight) a destroyer kept watch off each flank.
Second, from mid-June the 2nd Light Horse Brigade,
dismounted, under its stout-hearted leader, Brig.-General
G. de L. Ryrie, carried out with the neighbouring infantry an astonishing extension of the defences on to the
neighbouring "Holly Ridge", and from that time, with
these troops in such positions, Birdwood never had any
anxiety as to this flank.

North of Anzac the Turkish observation post at
Nibrunesi Point (Suvla Bay) was, as already mentioned,
raided and temporarily destroyed. On that flank the spurs
of the main range were so steep and sheer that the Turkish
Corps Commander, Essad Pasha, hardly troubled to hold
them. Here the lower ends of two spurs north and south
of Fisherman's Hut were occupied by New Zealanders on
April 30th, and were named Nos. 1 and 2 Outposts.
Scouts of the New Zealand Mounted Rifles found they
could work up the wild gullies north of these. Major

---

[8] About a third, including Leane, were hit. Four men got back to Anzac
along the beach, wading round the Turkish wire. Two more, isolated and
left behind, were gallantly rescued by naval boat. The Turks did not fire
when the wounded were being helped to the boat. *See Vol. I, pp. 558-62.*

Overton crept up part of the main spur, Rhododendron, almost to Chunuk Bair, and Lieut. Blackett, landing from a trawler beyond Suvla Bay watched from the "W" Hills one of the Anafarta batteries while he munched his sandwiches.[9] Also, into No. 2 Post there found their way some Greek villagers from the north who said the country was almost empty of Turkish troops. Birdwood's chief of staff, Brig.-General Skeen, a tall, brave, highly educated Anglo-Indian soldier, leapt at the prospect of a way out of the Gallipoli deadlock—the Anzacs, reinforced by Gurkhas and others, were just the kind of troops who could storm by night up the valleys north of Anzac and thus seize the summits of the main range.

Possibly through the activity of the New Zealand scouts, the Turks began to place additional or stronger posts on these ridges. Birdwood and Skeen, therefore, decided to lull their opponents into false security by showing no activity on this northern flank. Unfortunately, without their authority the nearest Turkish post, 400 yards above No. 2, was seized by the New Zealand Mounted Rifles on the night of May 28th. It was to be converted into a "No. 3" Post; but from dawn next day Turkish snipers in the wild country around prevented all digging, and on the following night a body of the enemy cut off and re-took the post, its garrison being saved by a gallant sortie from No. 2 post.

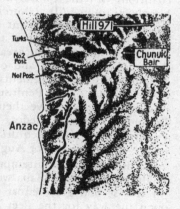

---

[9] See Vol. II, pp. 176 et seq.

Although after this the Turks placed extra posts on the foothills and extended their trenches along part of the crest of the main range, Birdwood and Skeen were convinced that the Anzacs could break out here; they laid their plan before Hamilton on May 30th. He was a leader with the priceless quality of imagination and, after study, he accepted it with enthusiasm. Certain reinforcements, he knew, were coming to him. On May 14th, after the Battle of Krithia, the British government had resolved frankly to face the position, and had inquired how many fresh divisions he needed in order to guarantee success. He had then asked for two army corps, each of two divisions, and full reinforcements for the divisions already with him. After this answer a delay had occurred, due to the decision of the Liberal government, under Mr Asquith, to strengthen itself by forming a coalition with the Conservatives. At last, on June 7th, largely through Mr Churchill's persuasion of Lord Kitchener, the government promised him three divisions[10]—some of the first of the "New Army" raised by Kitchener since the outbreak of war. Two territorial divisions—one English and one Welsh—were afterwards added to these reinforcements. There was no space for all these divisions on the Peninsula bridgeheads, but Hamilton intended to receive them on neighbouring islands, Lemnos, Imbros, Tenedos, and to land them on the Peninsula only when required, which now could not be before the beginning of August.

While the costly attempts to "hammer away" from Helles towards Achi Baba were still going on, the plans for this second great effort to seize the Peninsula and open the way for the fleet were completed. Hamilton decided to make the main effort from Anzac, and would use one New Army division (13th) and two detached brigades (one of them Indian) to reinforce the troops

---

10 A Scottish territorial division also, 52nd, had already been promised.

there; but, as a separate operation which would help the Anzac attempt, the IX Corps (10th and 11th New Army divisions) would be landed at Suvla Bay in the projecting flats four miles north of Anzac, and would try to seize the semicircle of hills five miles inland of their landing place. Their chances were good since the whole area was occupied by only three Turkish battalions, and the Anzac attack should draw to itself most of the Turkish reserves. In order to attract these reserves towards the south and away from the north, a feint attack would be made by the British at Cape Helles; and the Australians at Anzac would seize the now strong Turkish position at Lone Pine, on the southern and bigger half of the 400 Plateau.

Immense labour was forthwith undertaken at Anzac in making shelves for extra water tanks, hauling them to position, installing pump and engine; preparing new ledges, shelters and other facilities to receive twenty battalions, ambulances, and headquarters; and widening the long trench to No. 2 Outpost in order to make a hidden road for the nightly convoy of mule carts.

By July all this work, together with the tunnelling of underground trenches ready for the coming feint at Lone Pine and elsewhere, had aroused expectation among the Anzacs; and leakage of information through commanders and clerks caused the troops gradually to realise that a second great attempt was impending. On the tried, gaunt men who nine months before had left Australia and New Zealand with such enthusiasm and with visions of returning full of experience—as many had done from South Africa—to march through cheering crowds in their home towns, and regale their families with strange tales and "souvenirs"—on these troops this new realisation had a perceptible effect. On many there dawned for the first time the fact that for them the prospect of return was vanishing.

The vision was now one of battle after battle after

battle. Men felt themselves to be between two long walls
from which there seemed to be no turning except death,
or disabling wounds. These feelings were rarely expressed;
the tussle in each man's mind as he faced the grim fact
was a silent one. It could be guessed only from a certain
quietness of demeanour or from an occasional remark.
New battalions had been arriving in Egypt from Australia and were just then being formed there into a 2nd
Australian Division. The men of the older ones at Anzac
read in newspapers, brought by the mail, the current
comment in Australia—that, whereas they themselves had
joined the army largely through love of adventure, these
new troops were enlisting from sober conviction. So the
old ones, or their friends at home, labelled the new lot
"The Dinkum Australians"—the genuine breed. And at
Anzac, when someone, referring to a feat of the 11th
Battalion, said: "Western Australia will be proud of
this," the instant answer was: "This! The 28th (the battalion last raised in Western Australia) will get the
cheering for this!"

The fond dream of the return home was silently
surrendered by many without a word, or a sign in their
letters. The ambitions of civil life had been given up;
men's keenness now was for the A.I.F.—for their regiment, battalion, company—and for the credit of Australia.
Not that these or other tried soldiers were at normal
times eager for battle—in most men that enthusiasm was
more than satisfied by such a fight as that of the Landing;
whatever the newspapers might say, few men looked forward to a second such struggle without some underlying
dread, varying with the character and experience of
each man.

Yet, as the hour for this and later offensives approached, there did come over most Australian troops—
even over the young infantry officers who knew that their
chance of surviving three or four such battles was almost

nil—a keenness to make another stroke for the Allies' success. They had set their hand to this contest; they could see no hope for the future happiness, or perhaps existence, of their nation if they failed. The war had to be carried through to victory—that it would end victoriously not one Anzac in a hundred doubted; indeed—except in the worst days in France—each fresh Allied offensive was approached with glowing hopes of breaking through. A few more days, it seemed, would find the Army pushing through into previously untouched country and a campaign of swift movement would open.

So, as the appointed day, August 6th, drew near, and young British troops[11] in their pith helmets and cotton uniforms began to land by night and camp on the ledges, the Anzac sick parades diminished; men already evacuated tried to "desert" back from ship, hospital or base; and few of the thin, much-tried garrison doubted that one more hard fight would bring them into control of the Narrows.

A week before making this great second attempt General Birdwood had an opportunity of further attracting Turkish attention to his southern flank. The Turks tried to establish a position on a subsidiary spur there, Holly Ridge, on to which the Light Horse and Tasmanians had extended their trenches. On the night of July 31st parties of the 11th Battalion under Major Ray Leane, after an explosion of mines, seized by a determined attack the trench newly made by the enemy along the other edge of the spur. At dawn on August 6th—the very day on which the great offensive was later to begin—the Turks, counter-attacking by surprise, retook part of the position (now known as Leane's Trench). But in the following hours by several brave counter-rushes it was cleared of them.

By this date the German commander, Liman von

---

[11] Of the 13th and part of the 10th Divisions of "Kitchener's" Army.

Sanders, had heard from Salonica rumours that a new offensive was coming in Gallipoli, but he did not know where. From July 31st to August 5th he sent out German airmen daily over Anzac, sometimes in the early dawn. Several times they dropped bombs on Quinn's Post and near other positions. There were then no anti-aircraft guns at Anzac to drive them away but they flew high and apparently observed no important changes.[12]

---

[12] Earlier in the campaign an enemy aeroplane had dropped showers of small steel darts, the size of pencils. They did no harm at Anzac. At dawn on August 7th a German airman tried to attack the balloon of the *Manica*, which was off Gallipoli that day; the German turned back on the appearance of two British machines.

CHAPTER X

THE CLIMAX AT ANZAC

THE second attempt to seize control of the Dardanelles was to begin that afternoon, August 6th, starting with a feint at Helles where, at 3.50 p.m., after a short bombardment, part of the 29th Division attacked a section of the Turkish trenches. At Anzac, after Lone Pine and other parts of the old Turkish line had been bombarded in slow shoots at intervals for three days, the rate of fire was increased at 4.30 p.m.

The 1st Australian Infantry Brigade about to attack Lone Pine, was then filing into the trenches facing it and into the newly-opened tunnelled front line ahead of them, from parts of which the shallow lid of turf had just been secretly removed. The tangle of Turkish trenches where the Lone Pine had formerly stood was being slowly bombarded by eight guns and howitzers. Three small mines had been exploded in no-man's-land close to the enemy front with the purpose of increasing the cover for the troops crossing. By 5 o'clock the 1st Brigade was in position, crowding below the openings in the underground line and on the firestep of the old, deep, open trenches fifty yards behind. "Can you find room for me beside Jim here?" said an Australian who had been searching along the bays. "Him and me are mates an' we're going over together.'

At 5.30, with the sun sinking behind them, pouring golden rays over the ridges and parapets, and gilding the white armbands and the calico square on each man's back

(a provision for recognition in the coming night) the
troops scrambled out and ran for the Turkish line.

It took a few seconds for the Turks' rifle fire to begin
and a few more for their machine-guns. By then the foremost running figures were nearing the Turkish trenches.
There, to the astonishment of onlookers, they bunched,
and, as others came up, a crowd gradually lined out along
the low mole-hill of enemy parapet like spectators along
a street-kerb. For the moment, they had passed beyond
the field of vision of most
Turks observing from
loop-holes but they found
the Turkish front trenches
here so roofed over with
thick pine logs covered
with earth that the attacking lines could not at once
get in.[1] Quickly, however,
one man after another ran
over them and jumped
into the open communi-
cation trenches some dis-
tance beyond. On the
right a line of men lay
down along the parapet
and stayed there; only after a quarter of an hour did
onlookers realise that a Turkish machine-gun had caught
them and they would never rise again.

Turkish trenches at Lone Pine.
(Attack indicated by arrows.)

By then the men entering the Turkish communication trenches and at a few uncovered lengths of the
front line were clearing out the garrison mainly by rifle
and bayonet; positions of friend and foe were too vague
for much bombing, bombs very few, and men unskilled

[1] The situation is admirably shown in a picture-model in the Australian
War Memorial. It is doubtful, however, if any men prized up the head
cover; the legend that this was done started at the time, but was generally
denied by the troops themselves.

Some had charged right over, and through, the network of trenches till they suddenly came to the deep unsuspected Cup in the Plateau, where the Turkish battery had been at the Landing, and where now on ledge after ledge were the local battalion headquarters, and the shelters of the Turkish supports. Beside these headquarters an Australian officer and two or three men were killed—no others came quite so far; the Turks fleeing from the front or rushing up from the valleys were able to hold the ends of the saps opening into this cup.

But the main network was cleared; the bombardment, though to onlookers it seemed slight, had killed or wounded half the Turkish garrison and the bloody fight in the trenches quickly killed, drove out, or captured the rest. Finally ten or a dozen posts were formed by different Australian parties, blocking the communication trenches with sandbag barriers—one vital post being established by Major Iven Mackay (4th Battalion), who held the place alone with his rifle and bayonet while his men threw sandbags across the continuations of the trenches.[2]

By 6 p.m. Lone Pine had been taken; as the wounded came out the reserve battalion (1st) was being fed into it—the earliest of a long series of reinforcements; the old mine tunnels were now used as part-way communication trenches. With the reinforcements went ammunition, stretcher parties, and a few jars of rum. As in most later battles, the Australian leaders deliberately reserved the rum for use when the men were tired, some hours after the attack, and not before it.

The Turkish reserves at Anzac at once began to be directed to Lone Pine. First to arrive was a battalion of Mustafa Kemal's division; it had been just moving out from a neighbouring post to rest behind the lines. It was immediately turned round, and with its arrival began the

---

[2] For this and other incidents see *Vol II, pp. 511 et seq.*

long Turkish attempt to retake the trenches by bombing. From dark on August 6th until the night of the 9th the bombfight went on almost continuously, flaring up four times into many hours of desperate fighting when successive Turkish reinforcements were thrown in.

The bombfighting was such as Australians had never known even at Quinn's Post. Noting that the Turkish bombs had long fuses, the Australians constantly caught them and threw them back before they burst. The Turks then learnt to shorten the fuses and many boys' hands were blown off, and others were blinded or killed. Hundreds of times bombs falling into the trenches were smothered with half-filled sandbags; but others burst, killing and wounding the groups behind the barricades, and the stream of wounded was continuous.

At intervals when Turks were clearly massing behind the barriers the Australians would clear them, exposing themselves above the parapet in the process, and with rifles or a machine-gun sweeping down the enemy. The Turks dynamited a barricade, but the Australians rushed and re-established it. The Turks set fire to the logs of the head cover. The Australians twice extinguished it. The Turks twice penetrated far into the trenches they had lost; the Australians turned them and chased them back. Jam-tin bombs, though pouring from the factory on the Beach, were still in far from sufficient supply. But on both sides the dead clogged many of the trenches till the garrison gave them such burial as it could—underfoot or in the parapet—or dragged them clear. On the enemy's side, the Turkish dead, with a few big Australians at their head, were laid out in a horrifying procession beside the pathway leading up through the Cup, along which Turkish reinforcements had to climb; on the Australian side the wounded and the heap of salvaged rifles, crowded the corresponding depression of Brown's Dip. When on August 10th fighting ceased in the Pine, six Australian battalions had lost, in all, 80 officers and 2197 men,[3] and the Turks (according to their most active commander there) 5000.

The feint which instantly developed into this terrific fight had, of course, only just been begun when, at dark on August 6th, the forces for the real thrust, into the wild country north of Anzac, assembled to begin their night march northward along the grassy foreshore and then inland up the steep ravines to the main ridge. Ahead of them, at 8.30 p.m., the four unmounted regiments of the New Zealand Mounted Rifles, which since May had been holding outposts along the northern beach, marched out by various routes to clear the several strong Turkish posts perched on the steep foothills.

The strongest of these posts—the "Old No. 3 Post" captured on May 29th by the Turks—was rushed by a ruse of General Birdwood's: a destroyer had fired on it nightly for six weeks at 9 p.m., driving the garrison to shelter. When the bombardment ceased this night the Turks found the New Zealanders on top of them, the precipitous slopes having been climbed under cover of the noise. The Turkish supports, in the ravine beyond, fled off into the dark. A Turkish post on Table Top, an even more precipitous position, was scaled partly by cutting steps in the sheer gravel face. While this was being done a Turkish flare shot up and then fell, setting fire to a tuft of scrub and lighting the valley side—but every New Zealander at once stood still; they were unseen and the summit was quickly seized, part of its garrison having been drawn towards other fighting. On Bauchop's Hill, the next ridge to the north, part of the New Zealanders, obeying strictly the order that only bayonets were to be used and there must be no cheers, emerged suddenly and

---

[3] The 3rd had every officer hit except the quartermaster. The battalions of the 1st Brigade lost so heavily that few witnesses of its efforts remained. Consequently of the seven Victoria Crosses awarded after this fight, four went to a reinforcing battalion, the 7th.

silently through the dark upon post after post, coming on them from unexpected directions and even wrestling with the Turks in some cases, since the New Zealanders' rifles were unloaded. By 1 o'clock they had seized that strongly occupied position, completing the most brilliant operation in the whole offensive.

At the same time a brigade (the 40th) of the new British troops, had marched northwards along the foreshore and, to guard the left flank, had seized the comparatively low, seaward end of the spur north of Bauchop's. A Turkish post was rushed, and 200 Turks afterwards surrendered.

The Turkish outposts in the foothills having thus been cleared by the two "covering" columns, the columns of infantry, that had been slowly following in order to attack the main range, now headed into the deep, black gullies leading variously to those heights. There were really three of these columns; nearest to Anzac the New Zealand infantry brigade was to work mostly up the second gully, the Chailak Dere, on to Rhododendron Ridge and thence along its upper length to Chunuk Bair, the main objective of the offensive. This was known as the "right assaulting column". Pushing on separately farther north along the foreshore, the 29th Indian Infantry Brigade, of Gurkhas and Sikhs, would turn into the third gully, Aghyl Dere, and then work up one of its nearer branches to the foot of the twin summits north of Chunuk Bair known as Hill Q, which the brigade would then climb and seize. The 4th Australian Infantry Brigade under General Monash after threading a farther branch of the Aghyl Dere, and crossing a gully beyond it, would reach the last spur of the range, Abdel Rahman Bair, and then follow its crest to the most northerly and highest summit of the main range, Hill 971. The commander of the Indian Brigade, a brave, dour leader, General H. V. Cox, was given the higher direction of these last two brigades, which together were known as the "left assaulting

column". This part of the plan was an afterthought—
Birdwood and Skeen had not originally intended to seize
Hill 971, which was separated from Q by a very narrow
neck; but when they heard that their reinforcements
would be larger than had been expected they had extended
their plan to include the main summit. The IX Corps,
to be landed a few miles farther north, at Suvla Bay, was
intended to reach the next, separate hill-mass, north
of 971.

Although the clearing of the foothills had taken two
hours longer than was planned, there were still three
hours of dark when the main part of the New Zealand
Infantry Brigade turned up the Chailak Dere; and
though, like other columns, it here and there met close
fire from parties of Turks who had been missed or scattered by the Mounted Rifles, the leading battalion, Otago,
reached Table Top and thence Rhododendron Ridge
just as dawn was beginning to break. Chunuk Bair, the
main goal of the offensive, was only 1000 yards away up
the comparatively easily graded crest of the spur. Canterbury Battalion coming by an even steeper, more southerly
valley, was to have met Otago on Rhododendron, and
together they were to seize the summit. At the head of
Otago was the very officer for the enterprise, a bold,
reliable leader, Major F. H. Statham. But there was no
sign of Canterbury—it had started late and lost its way.
The more senior officers decided to wait, and full daylight found them still waiting.

The more northerly columns—Monash's, followed by
the Indian brigade—had been fired on by Turks missed
or scattered by the Mounted Rifles. It was a startling
experience in the dark; and, not knowing whether the
opposition was slight or serious, they had halted while
sending parties to clear it. Moreover a Greek guide had
led the head of these columns into a steep, narrow gully
forming a short cut to the Aghyl Dere, up which both
brigades were to turn. The result was that dawn

found them still working up the Aghyl Dere, far from
their main objective on the heights.

They were exceedingly tired with the shuffle, halt,
and shuffle of the night march, most exhausting for half-
sick men. Monash's brigade, after he himself had gone to
its head in order to overcome one stoppage, fought its
weary way against scattered parties of Turks through the
northern foothills to a ridge which it mistook for Abdel
Rahman Bair, but which was really the second ridge
south of that—indeed the same that was held, nearer to
the coast, by the British brigade. Three miles away to
the left front lay Suvla Bay and its extensive flats; and
off it, on the peaceful sea in the now bright morning
light, could be seen a British fleet escorting transports
which were disembarking troops and stores. Monash's
men, whose officers felt them to be too exhausted to push
farther at the moment, were allowed to dig in. The Indian
column, heading straight up the Aghyl Dere for the main
range, climbed part way up the steep slope; while the
morning was still early the brave New Zealand guide,
Major Overton, was shot as he directed the Indians up
the several spurs.

According to the plan of Birdwood and Skeen, this
hour, dawn, was to be the one for the final breaking of the
old Turkish position on the main range north of Anzac.
It was expected that by then the New Zealanders would
have taken Chunuk Bair. From that foothold on the top
of the range they would attack downwards along its spine
towards Anzac while the Anzac garrison broke out from
Russell's Top to drive up the range towards them by
attacking the formidable series of trenches that, since
April, had barred the way across The Nek and Baby 700.
Some eight successive trench lines now seamed that bare
slope and its approach, the two nearest being on the
Australian side of The Nek less than a stone's throw
from the Australian front.

This attack was to be made by the dismounted 3rd

Light Horse Brigade; it was recognised that, if "unaided", the effort was "almost hopeless". But it was to be helped by the New Zealand attack on the Turkish rear and also by the seizure of the three vital Turkish posts next to The Nek on the south. First, at midnight the 6th Battalion was to assault the southern of these, German Officers' Trench. Later, at dawn, when the 3rd Light Horse Brigade attacked across The Nek, the 1st Light Horse Brigade would simultaneously attack from Quinn's and Pope's.

Since the first two months of the campaign no attempt had been made to launch serious attacks from these posts, it being recognised that the crossfire of the flanking machine-guns was too strong. By seizing German Officers' first, however, some of the machine-guns enfilading Quinn's would be silenced. The attack on German Officers' was to be made from the network of tunnelled trenches, and would follow the firing of three mines.[4] These explosions aroused sharp artillery fire which blocked several trenches and trench openings. This caused the attack to be late; the Turks expected it, and the crowded young troops, largely reinforcements, who had to wait in and move through the black tunnels, and then scramble out from twenty-one bays (where the turf had that day been removed from below) were not in the spirit that could have carried off so tough a task. Some hesitated or lost touch in the tunnels; though brave leaders reached the Turkish parapet others were shot down as they emerged. The openings were congested with wounded. The attack completely failed as did a second, attempted two hours later.

Thus, when the time approached for the assault across The Nek against the main Turkish position, Birdwood and Skeen knew that the chief operations by which it was to have been assisted would not help it. The attack on

---

[4] These had to be exploded beforehand in case they shook down the tunnelled trenches, which were not timbered. Actually the mines did not injure the tunnels.

German Officers' had failed; the New Zealand Infantry Brigade was known to be so far behind its programme that it could not reach Chunuk Bair in time to help. But the attack at The Nek, though part of the main operation, was also intended to keep the Turks' attention riveted on their centre and prevent reinforcements from moving north to oppose the New Zealanders at Chunuk Bair. The news for which Birdwood and Skeen—and General Godley at No. 2 Post in charge of the northern operations—were waiting with almost desperate anxiety at that crucial moment was that of the New Zealanders' progress on Rhododendron Ridge leading to the seizure of Chunuk Bair. Anything that could help this main effort had to be done; and without hesitation it was decided that the attacks on the Turkish centre must go forward, though now serving primarily as feints to keep the Turks from Chunuk Bair.

Men of the two Australian Light Horse Brigades on Russell's Top and Pope's Hill had during the previous afternoon watched with enthusiasm the 1st Infantry Brigade, far to their right and below, seize the Turkish trench network at Lone Pine, and were full of confidence that they would simi-larly seize the network ahead of them. They were to be helped by half-an-hour's previous bombardment by all available land guns, as well as by those of destroyers, culminating in three minutes' intense bombardment from

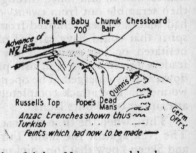

4.27 to 4.30; at 4.30 the Light Horse would charge.

At The Nek this shelling was terrific; it largely missed the front Turkish trench, only twenty to sixty yards from the Australian, but it covered Baby 700 with a cloud of smoke and dust slowly drifting across the low, pale streak of dawn. The attack was to be made by four lines, each of 150 men (there was no room for more on The Nek), following each other at several minutes' intervals.

The first line stood with its feet on pegs in the trench walls, ready to leap out. But for some reason that may now never be discovered—probably an error in timing watches—this shelling suddenly ceased when the watches of the Light Horse officers showed only 4.23—that is, seven minutes before the time for the attack; and when, at 4.30, Lieut.-Colonel A. H. White of the 8th Light Horse gave the word "Go", and, followed eagerly by the 150 men of the first line, scrambled from the deep trenches, there burst out within three or four seconds from the Turkish trenches, packed with men, such a torrent of rifle fire, growing quickly to a continuous roar, as soldiers can seldom have faced. The Australian line, now charging, was seen suddenly to grow limp, and then sink to the earth, as though (said an eye-witness) "the men's limbs had become string". Except those wounded whom bullets had knocked back into the trench, or who managed to crawl a few yards and drop into it, almost the whole line fell dead or dying within the first ten yards. White and every other officer was killed. Three or four men reached the Turkish parapet and the burst of their bombs was heard above the uproar.

The second line, waiting in the trench to start, listening to the tempest that swept its parapet, and helping the wounded, now knew what it must face, but knew also that the moment was a supreme one of the campaign, and that the fate of other troops in that vital effort might also depend on it. When, at 4.33, the whistle was blown, the second line leapt out instantly.

The fusillade, which had slightly abated, instantly rose again to a roar as if some player had opened the swell-box of an organ. The second line, running hard, got a little beyond the first before being mown down. On the right some men reached the Turkish trench. Bombs were again heard, and amid the dust of machine-gun fire one of the small red and yellow flags, carried by the light horsemen to mark their position, was seen on the Turkish parapet.

Both lines of the 8th Light Horse having now charged, the 10th, from Western Australia, filed into the trench which the 8th had left. Its commander questioned the wisdom of continuing the attack—Colonel White, who could have added his advice, alas lay dead. The brigade major, having heard that men had entered the Turkish line, ruled that they must be supported. Accordingly, at a signal at 4.45, the third line leapt out. A survivor said afterwards he knew death was almost certain but had determined to race with all his speed to meet it. The roar which had died into silence immediately rose again, and this line too was mown down. The fourth line was held for half an hour, while a further decision was sought. But at that stage apparently there reached the waiting troops on the right an officer who knew nothing of this and asked why the men had not gone forward. Believing that the charge had been ordered to continue, the men there clambered out. The tempest broke out again. With a call "By God! the right has gone!" other leaders leapt out with their men, and the fourth line went, and most of it was swept away like the others.

Probably the attack on The Nek effected its purpose of holding temporarily near Baby 700 at least part of the Turkish reinforcements which were just then streaming northward towards Chunuk Bair. In any case the light horsemen were not men to hesitate at what was certainly one of the crucial moments of the whole war; if in that decisive hour any advantage was to be gained by their effort they would make it whatever the cost. The flower of the youth of Victoria and Western Australia fell in that attempt. The cost to the smaller population of the

West was especially severe—hardly a pioneer family but
mourned its one or more dead.

At the same hour there occurred the attacks from the
neighbouring posts, Quinn's and Pope's. Each was to be
made by 200 men. At Quinn's the whole of the first
charging line of fifty Queenslanders, except one man, fell
killed or wounded within the first ten yards and the other
lines were consequently held back. At Pope's the New
South Welshmen led by Major T. W. Glasgow captured
three lines of trenches on Dead Man's Ridge; but eventually, running short of bombs and seeing that the other
attacks (including a brave one made from Monash Valley
by Welsh Fusiliers of the New Army) had failed, Glasgow
wisely and ably withdrew his men. According to the
proud tradition of Australian fighting leaders, he was
with the last of them to return.

In all these attacks 800 officers and men—probably
4 out of every 5 who actually entered the fight—were
killed or wounded. They failed to win any ground—the
Lone Pine attack had too well warned the enemy. But
they may have succeeded in hindering until about 7 a.m.
the passing of Turkish reinforcements northwards from
Anzac to summits of the main range. At all events it was
in the hours about dawn that day that there opened the
supreme chance of seizing those vital heights. What was
the progress of the columns trying to reach the summits?

At dawn—4.30—the three leading companies of the
Otago Battalion under Major Statham had reached
Rhododendron Ridge where, 1000 yards from Chunuk
Bair, they were to wait for the Canterbury Battalion.
Canterbury was late, but about 5 o'clock it began climbing
that ridge behind Statham's right as did the rest of the
brigade behind his left. In all the war that place and
moment were actually those in which weary leaders and
troops should have summoned every ounce of energy and
taken every risk. But not till 7 o'clock did the brigadier,
Colonel F. E. Johnston, with the Auckland and Welling-

ton battalions, continue the advance up the crest of
Rhododendron Ridge. At 7.30, on reaching an intermediate knoll,
known as the Apex,
the column was fired
at from the southern
shoulder of Chunuk
Bair, a quarter of a
mile ahead. It could
be seen that none of
the other columns
had reached the
main ridge. Johns-
ton accordingly
halted his column
in shelter of the Apex and signalled to General Godley
(in charge of the offensive north of Anzac) recommending
a halt until after dark.

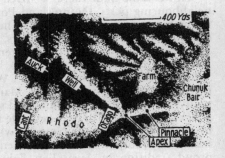

He was forthwith ordered to attack at once. The warships and the Anzac guns bombarded Chunuk Bair at
10.15; and at 11 a.m. the Auckland Battalion and some
Gurkhas on their flank advanced, but were now met by
a whirlwind of fire that swept away line after line. A
Turkish gun on the ridges a mile to the left enfiladed
them. The advance ended at a second knoll, the Pinnacle,
300 yards from Chunuk Bair.

It is now known that until 7 a.m. Chunuk Bair
lay empty except for a single Turkish platoon. At 5.30
Mustafa Kemal on Battleship Hill heard of the New
Zealanders reaching Rhododendron, and sent two Arab
companies to Chunuk Bair. They arrived there at 7, but
fled at the sight of the New Zealanders coming up the
spur. The fire on the New Zealanders at that hour
apparently came from twenty men who were guarding
the headquarters of a battery. The Arab companies withdrawing behind the hill were met by a German commander (Colonel Kannengiesser) whose Turkish division,

the 9th, had been called from the south to Anzac when
Lone Pine was attacked, and, not being needed there, was
at 5.30 a.m. ordered to occupy the main ridge, Chunuk
Bair—Hill 971. The German had come on ahead of his
men. On reaching the summit he found the small battery
guard and ordered it to fire on the New Zealanders, who
seemed to him very tired. He had rallied the Arabs, and
soon afterwards, possibly by 9 o'clock, his own regiments
arrived in good time to stop the New Zealanders' next
attempt at 11 a.m.

The advance was thus everywhere held up till dark.
The other columns had dug in in the foothills; a British
New Army brigade, under Brig.-General Cayley, sent by
General Cox to carry the advance farther, lost its way in
the maze of gullies behind the front.

In spite of the failure to reach the summits, and of the
weariness of the troops, the Anzacs' spirits were high.
The unaccustomed spaciousness of this wild, interesting
country—several square miles of it in contrast with the
crowded slopes of Anzac—was a relief and a call to adventure. Moreover high, confident hopes were raised by the
sight of the transports and warships crowded off Suvla
Bay four miles to the north, with boats and slow motor
lighters (nicknamed "beetles") continually plying to the
shore. The landing of water and stores was being helped
by a Bridging Train of Australian naval reservists. How
far the two New Army divisions, which had been coming
ashore since 11 p.m. the night before, had penetrated the
wide flats and the hills beyond these, the Anzac leaders
did not know.

The summits of the range had nowhere been attained,
but, especially on Rhododendron Ridge, great progress
had been made, and the positions reached would form
a foothold from which the crests might still be gained if
the attempts could be resumed before the Turks could
rush thither sufficient reserves. An attempt was therefore
to be made by all three assaulting columns at 3 a.m. on

August 8th, after the warships had heavily shelled the crest. Accordingly, next morning Monash's (4th) brigade, half an hour late and still believing it was nearer to Abdel Rahman than was the case, crossed a small gully and began to advance along the next spur—actually that running up from "Hill 60". Here part of the brigade was caught in the open by Turkish machine-guns emplaced on the next ridge ahead, the real Abdel Rahman, and after very heavy loss was eventually driven back pell-mell. The Indian Brigade reinforced by parts of two British New Army brigades (38th and 39th) was to seize the summits north of Chunuk, but the British brigades were so scattered, tired, and uncertain of their position that hardly any advance was made. The 1/6th Gurkhas under Major C. J. L. Allanson, however, at 8 a.m. scaled the steep slope to within 300 feet of Q summit before being stopped. Together with some New Army troops they held on, far up the slope.

High on Rhododendron the Wellington Battalion, attacking for the New Zealand Brigade, also started late, as night was just paling to dawn; anxious eyes from below watched its men as they went up the spur, outlined against the sky. To the astonishment of all, the advancing figures reached the crest at the southern shoulder of Chunuk

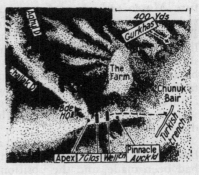

Bair without meeting a shot. The Turks, who (it is now known) now had some 5000 men posted along most of the main ridge had, in that sector, withdrawn, struck by some unexplained panic. The New Zealanders looked

down on the inner slopes, the road, the straits, and, in distant valleys to the right, the worn paths, ledges and shelters indicating the rear of the Turkish positions at Anzac. They began to dig in, making use of an abandoned Turkish trench a foot or two deep.

For this day's attack the New Zealand Infantry Brigade had been reinforced by two new British battalions. These followed the Wellington Battalion; but by that time, with the light clearer and the Turks on the crest to left and right thoroughly alarmed, there poured in such a flanking fire of small arms and of a few well-posted field-guns that most of the British were forced into the deep gullies on either side of Rhododendron. Only a few reached the two flanks of the Wellington Battalion and held on there. The Maori Battalion, which tried to follow, was driven into the Aghyl Dere; the Auckland Mounted Rifles managed to trickle through, but not till afternoon and with very heavy loss.

By 9 a.m. this fire coupled with direct attacks had wiped out the two companies of Wellington on or beyond the crest; and from that hour parts of two Turkish divisions, assembling behind the crest where the New Zealanders had reached it, tried to drive the support line (of the Wellingtons and the remnant of British) from its lofty foothold a few yards west of the crestline. But under Colonel Malone the Wellingtons charged again and again, clearing their front.

This day it was realised by Hamilton that at Suvla Bay—though the important hills overlooking the place were still actually open—through the senility of the command and the inexperience of the troops no attempt had yet been made to occupy them and the last chances of success were slipping away. Nevertheless opportunity was still present both there and at Chunuk Bair. Here Malone was killed; but dusk on the 8th still found his men unshaken from their position a few yards from the crestline.

12—os

At nightfall, as often in battle, the tension there greatly eased, and supplies and reinforcements from Rhododendron moved safely to the front line. The exhausted troops there were relieved. Wellington Battalion which went in 760 strong came out with only 70 unwounded—but its relief was effected without difficulty. Approach by night was easy; and the plan of Generals Godley and Birdwood for the next day's resumption of the Anzac offensive centred on this circumstance. Monash's brigade was to stand still. The left of the attack would be made by the Indian brigade clambering from its vantage point only 150 yards from (and 90 feet below) Hill Q, to seize that summit. On the right, half a mile to the south, the New Zealand brigade, from its position a few yards below the crestline, would seize the crest. In the centre, a composite brigade of five British New Army battalions under Brig.-General Baldwin, would form up in the night close behind the New Zealanders and, attacking northwards, would seize the summit of Chunuk Bair, 200 yards away, and the crest from there to Q. The crest would be shelled by land and naval artillery from 4.30 a.m. to 5.15, when these attacks would be simultaneously launched.

To finalise these plans General Godley was to meet Baldwin and the New Zealand brigadier high on Rhododendron on the afternoon of the 8th. Tragically, Godley could not get there and, though Major A. C. Temperley of the New Zealand brigade staff explained to Baldwin the obvious method, the commander of the New

Zealand Brigade—a brave man, afterwards killed in France, but habitually unreliable for such a time of over-strain—was, after forty-eight hours of terrible tension, in no condition for clear judgment or exposition. Baldwin gathered that his column should descend into the abyss of the Aghyl Dere and thence climb straight up, past a ledge and hut known as the Farm, to Chunuk Bair. Temperley could not dissuade him.

At dawn on August 9th, when the heavy bombard-ment ended, the 6th Gurkhas and a South Lancashire battalion rushed the neck between Q and Chunuk Bair above them. The Turks had evacuated the crest during the shelling, and now fell back farther.

At that moment Baldwin's battalions should have been advancing over Chunuk Bair. But the valley, the Chailak Dere, up which early in the night they tried to climb towards the New Zealanders, had been so blocked with wounded and other traffic coming down, and the pace was so slow that Baldwin had to turn his men about and ultimately led them to the depths of the Aghyl Dere by another, longer, route. At 5.15 after many mishaps, they were still toiling through the deep valley below the Farm. As they were nowhere in sight, the New Zealanders, high on the southern shoulder of Chunuk Bair, were kept in their trench. The Gurkhas and South Lancashire, who had reached the crest near Q were pre-sently shelled from it by some of the guns at Anzac, and fell back; their gallant leaders[5] after trying to recall them (which, if Baldwin's men had appeared, would not have been difficult), flung a last look at the straits, and followed their men to their starting point.

Hours late, at about 8 a.m., when nothing else was moving, portions of Baldwin's force tried to attack from the Farm. Four years later members of the Australian Historical Mission found the remains of its officers and

---

[5] Maj. C. J. L. Allanson (wounded), Lieut. J. W. J. Le Marchand (killed) and others.

men, killed that day and the next, still littered in hundreds over the ridges.

So ended the last—and perhaps the best—chance in Gallipoli. That night the exhausted New Zealanders in their perch on Chunuk Bair were relieved by British New Army troops. At dawn next morning Turks suddenly swarmed over the whole crestline. Liman von Sanders had, in the crisis on August 8th, become dissatisfied with the slowness of the reserves that he had summoned from the north. He had therefore transferred the command north of Anzac to Mustafa Kemal. He had also summoned up his last reserves, leaving the Asiatic side of the Dardanelles almost ungarrisoned. Kemal operated against both Suvla and Anzac. On August 9th he had tried to drive in the extreme northern flank of the Anzac forces, but these had stopped the attack so easily that they hardly realised it had occurred.

Now, at dawn on August 10th, however, he personally led the Turkish reserves on the main range up to the crest. As line after line of them poured over Chunuk Bair the weary British garrisons at Chunuk and the Pinnacle broke back; and, though the guns of the warships, and the machine-guns of the New Zealanders at the Apex, devastated the enemy's ranks, Turks continually filtered down the slopes and ridges. The Summit, the Pinnacle, the Farm and the Indian brigade's foothold on the ascent to Q were eventually lost; Baldwin and a dozen other senior leaders were killed and the line fell back to where a lower spur, Cheshire Ridge, afforded a convenient front. The 5th Connaught Rangers that afternoon retook the Farm, but being then a useless position it was given up. The 6th Leinster and New Zealanders held the Apex.

The Anzac offensive had failed; and on August 9th Turkish reinforcements arriving from the north—practically the last reserves that the Turks could muster—had occupied the commanding heights which the IX British Corps at Suvla Bay had not succeeded in seizing. The

Anzac force had used its last reserve and had lost 12,000 men, British and Dominion, in four days.

Sir Ian Hamilton was of opinion that the hills at Suvla were not yet strongly held by the Turks. Their strength, however, was growing. The two fresh British territorial divisions, 53rd and 54th, were landed there, but were unskilled; belated gains of ground made by them were immediately reversed. To help to subdue the Turkish marksmen, 100 Anzac snipers were selected and sent to Suvla. Lieut.-General Sir F. W. Stopford, the British commander there, and several other leaders were changed, younger and more vigorous men taking their places. But Hamilton now saw that, with the enemy reinforced and everywhere digging in, it was questionable whether the Gallipoli expedition would succeed: only very large reinforce-

Suvla-Anzac position on Aug 20
Arrows show intended attack.

ments could render possible another attempt. On August 17th he telegraphed to Lord Kitchener, that, for early success, he would need another 100,000 men.

Meanwhile his position, with the two bridgeheads at Anzac and Suvla connected only by a thin strip of fore-shore, had to be improved by seizing the southern end of the Suvla hills (an almost detached foothill known from its markings as the "W" Hills) near Anafarta. For this operation he strength-

ened the Suvla force with the Dismounted Yeomanry
Division (5000 strong) brought from Egypt, and the 29th
Division from Helles. The Anzac force would swing up
its left to the extreme north-western end of the foothills
of Hill 971—a low rise known as Hill 60—so as to connect
with the right flank of the Suvla force.[6]

This attempt to round off the line took place on
August 21st. As so often before and afterwards, the
British commanders preferred to advance by day, relying
on their artillery fire to protect their troops rather than
on the dark, in which they feared the advance would lose
direction. But by the standards of the Western Front
their artillery was exceedingly weak. The W Hills were
not reached, and though Scimitar Hill, a northern outlier, was seized and lost, first by the 29th Division and
later by the Yeomanry, hastily thrown in, the effort failed.
Only at Anzac, where a mixed force—of New Zealand
Mounted Rifles, Monash's brigade, Connaught Rangers
and Gurkhas—swung up the flank across part of Hill 60
and the plain beyond, was any ground gained. Even here
the cap of the rise, seamed with hastily dug trenches,
remained in Turkish hands.

It happened that within the last few days the leading
brigade, 5th, of a new Australian division—the 2nd—had
reached Anzac from Egypt, where this division had been
organised from three newly arrived infantry brigades by
General Legge and a staff partly sent with him from
Anzac. Many members of the leading brigade had served
in New Guinea with their present commander, Brig.
General Holmes. They were only half trained, though
considered sufficiently instructed for trench warfare. But
their great, healthy bodies and hearty manner brought
cheerfulness wherever they were seen by the thin, worn
men on the Anzac slopes; and the New Zealand staff,

---

6 Messengers, the only mounted ones at Anzac, occasionally galloped
between Anzac and Suvla. (Hill 60 should not be confused with the more
famous "hill" of the same name on the Ypres battlefield in Belgium.)

being in urgent need to seize the top of Hill 60, asked for these reinforcements.

After at first refusing, General Godley agreed. The 18th Battalion was brought round in a hurry through the newly won gullies and out on to the flats to make a dawn attack. As happened on other such occasions, the arrangements were inadequate, and the time too short, and the battalion far too untrained. It attacked bravely, with little notion of what it was to do, and, though at first extending the New Zealanders' gain, it was gradually driven back on them after losing half its men killed or wounded.

The effort to complete the seizure of Hill 60 was renewed on the afternoon of August 27th after bombardment. What appeared to be the intended objective—a tangled knot of trenches—was taken, partly lost, and again taken after a three days' fight by parties of Mounted Rifles, Connaught Rangers and 100 men of the 18th Australian Battalion, and light horsemen from Western and South Australia.[7] On the southern side of the hill, where by some error the Turks had not been shelled, parties of Monash's brigade were stopped by Turkish fire as they emerged, losing most of their officers and men. After the fight it was found that the top of Hill 60 still lay beyond the ground captured; but all the reserves having been drained, the gain was judged sufficient for safeguarding, for the present, the junction with the Suvla force.

The Allied troops at the Dardanelles had, for the time being, exhausted their powers of attack.

---

[7] The 9th and 10th Light Horse Regiments. Here Capt. H. V. H. Throssell won the Victoria Cross. With Monash's brigade were 100 of the 17th Battalion.

CHAPTER XI

THE LAST PHASE IN GALLIPOLI

IMMEDIATELY after the failure of the attempt on August 21st to take the W Hills, Hamilton shocked the Asquith government in Great Britain by a telegram reporting that, owing to casualties and sickness, he would probably have to give up either the old Anzac position or Suvla, and possibly to withdraw even farther at a later date. Neither the British Cabinet nor the French had any intention of abandoning Gallipoli, but the expedition had now become involved in a tangle of external considerations by which any clear decision was made most difficult.

Both governments were already suspecting that the offensive plans of their commanders on the Western Front would lead, as heretofore, only to vast losses with little gain of ground. On July 6th, in a flash of inspired eloquence, Lord Kitchener had persuaded the French government to envisage no further big offensive there until Britain and France had their programme of new armaments and reinforcements sufficiently complete—that is, until the spring of 1916. But the French Commander-in-Chief, Joffre, still pressed for his plans; the supporters of his rival, General Sarrail, whom Joffre dismissed, agitated for Sarrail's promotion, and in this difficulty the French government desired to create some army, outside of France, for him to lead. For a passing moment it was proposed to send him, with six French divisions, to land south of the Dardanelles.

But Hamilton's August offensive had brought about results which now turned the eyes of the Allies to a new quarter. The German chief-of-staff, Falkenhayn, fearing that the Dardanelles might be forced by the Allies, decided that Germany must crush her way through to Constantinople, which would mean, in the first place, attacking Serbia. Bulgaria which, after the failure of Hamilton's offensive, swung to the German side, agreed on September 6th to help the German Army in the attack on Serbia. The Premier of Greece, Venizelos, and the Serbian government appealed to Britain and France for 150,000 troops, who could land at the nearest Greek port, Salonica. The Greek King, Constantine, afterwards repudiated Venizelos' action. But both France and Britain had by then agreed, though the project was opposed by the British army staff, which could see no prospect of success for this expedition.

By this time Joffre had obtained reversal of the Allies' decision against present offensives on the Western Front.[1] The offensives which followed diminished and delayed the help that the Allies could send to Serbia and Greece, and ended presently in the gain of a few miles at the cost of vast casualties of which a small minority, 45,000, were British.[2] Meanwhile, in order to make up the force promised for Serbia, a British and a French division had to be taken from Gallipoli.

Hamilton had by then received his new generals and the promise of about 25,000 reinforcements, and decided that with these he could hold his three present positions, Helles, Anzac and Suvla. But, with the growing threat that German guns, trench mortars, and troops might reach Gallipoli, there was evident danger that by sheer weight of ammunition the Allies might be blown from

---

[1] In 1915 the Germans had inflicted crushing defeats on the Russians, taking Warsaw. Joffre argued that inactivity on the Western Front would dangerously depress the Russians. Curiously enough, at the same time Falkenhayn was easing the effort against Russia in order to strike at the Dardanelles. He was undeterred by the threat of an Allied offensive in the West.

[2] The British generals, French and Haig, who earlier had opposed the offensive, later, after its launching, wanted it maintained—some of its results were considered hopeful.

their narrow foothold—especially as, during the coming winter, rough seas would often prevent the landing of supplies for the defence. The advisability of evacuating Gallipoli now became, for the first time, a matter of general discussion, the question being even raised in the House of Lords. On the other hand most British Ministers feared that an attempt to withdraw might end in disaster, and that the admission of failure after so much sacrifice would shock the East and possibly the Dominions. Moreover the Turkish troops set free might move against Egypt. It was therefore decided to send six British divisions from France to Egypt and to defer for the moment the question whether they should be used in Gallipoli or in Greece and Serbia. A British general from France, Sir Charles Monro, was to be sent at once to the eastern Mediterranean to advise whether Gallipoli should be held.

At this juncture the British government received several criticisms of Sir Ian Hamilton's leadership, including one from an Australian press correspondent, Keith Murdoch, who by Hamilton's leave had paid a short visit to Anzac. His statement, though overcoloured and in part inaccurate, contained some important truths, and—as Hamilton refused to sacrifice his chief-of-staff— the government decided to transfer the chief command to Monro, Hamilton being recalled and Birdwood acting in his place until Monro arrived.

Hamilton had estimated that, if evacuation was attempted, the government must reckon on losing "not less than half the total force". Monro was already a strong believer in the policy of concentration on the Western Front. In a brief visit he was impressed by the fact that, "except the Australian and New Zealand Corps", the troops were not equal to a sustained effort, and for this and other reasons he recommended on October 30th that the Gallipoli expedition should be withdrawn. To Lord Kitchener in London this recommendation came as a shock. He telegraphed for the views of the local commanders at Helles, Anzac, and Suvla, and found that Birdwood, though he alone of them, was against evacuation.

At this juncture there had arrived in London Commodore Keyes, the chief-of-staff to Vice-Admiral de
Robeck at the Dardanelles. Keyes had always been convinced that the fleet could force the straits, and his chief,
though disagreeing, had now given him leave to urge
that proposal, which included, this time, the use of smoke
screens. Kitchener persuaded the government to postpone its judgment on Monro's report, and telegraphed to
Birdwood to plan very vigorous support for the Navy's
attack. With this in view Kitchener actually transferred
Monro to the separate command of the Salonica Force,
temporarily placed Birdwood (against this leader's own
will) in command of the Mediterranean Expeditionary
Force, and decided himself to visit immediately the
Dardanelles. On November 4th, however, the Ministers'
opinion was against making the naval attempt unless the
Army could attack again. But the Army had no troops for
this, General Joffre having visited England and threatened
that if the British divisions from France were not sent to
Salonica he would resign, and the whole alliance would
be imperilled.

Kitchener accordingly set out for the Dardanelles that
night feeling that a secret evacuation was probably the
most reasonable course. On November 9th he reached
Lemnos and, on the 13th, Australian reserves, camped
like sandmartins in holes all round the semicircle of
gravel cliffs overlooking North Beach, saw approaching
North Pier a small picket-boat from which stepped the
familiar, dapper, figure of General Birdwood with a tall,
rather ungainly figure, instantly recognised, stalking up
the pier beside him. Kitchener strode straight up the
300-foot height. He was deeply impressed by the Anzac
defences but tended to conclude that the foothold was

too narrow to be safely held, and that a withdrawal would—as Monro and Birdwood now held—be less costly than Hamilton had at first thought; it must, however, be carried out before the storms of late December.

The most difficult question was as to the effect of a withdrawal on British prestige in the East. Lord Kitchener was attracted by various schemes—to strike, first, near Alexandretta, where the Turkish road to Egypt could be barred, and then to evacuate Gallipoli; and to abandon Suvla and Anzac only, and retain Helles which was much easier to defend. Kitchener—and almost all the other leaders—swung from one opinion to another; but Monro steadily advised withdrawal. On November 23rd, as the British Cabinet's "War Committee" decided to recommend evacuation of all three bridgeheads, Kitchener ordered Monro to prepare for this. But in London the pleas of Lord Curzon and Colonel Hankey, and an offer by Admiral Wemyss, then in charge, to smash a way through the straits, swung the government back again: instead, it proposed to withdraw from Salonica and renew the Suvla attack. On December 4th the French government reluctantly agreed, but next day reversed its attitude. The generals at the Dardanelles were doubtful of success at Suvla. Consequently on December 7th the British government, after five weeks of hesitation, finally decided on withdrawal.

Neither then nor at any time since the failure of the great second effort, in August, had the British, Anzac, or French troops in Gallipoli any notion that the abandonment of their effort was really probable. At Anzac the 2nd Australian Division,[3] which arrived in August and September without artillery, had long been holding the most vital parts of the old Anzac position (and, for a time, the Apex on Rhododendron Spur), and a British terri-

---

[3] Part of a new brigade, the 6th, in the transport *Southland* was torpedoed by a U-boat, but the troops behaved very coolly; some helped to stoke the crippled ship into port.

torial division from Suvla, the 54th (East Anglian), helped to hold the flank extended towards Hill 60.

The fighting was now almost confined to the mine tunnels which, especially on the old Anzac front, were ceaselessly extended.[4] At Lone Pine and The Nek the Australians on a number of occasions broke into the Turkish network of tunnels; along at least one of these tunnels, at Lone Pine, the miners crawled to within sight of its entrance in the Turkish trenches, where the legs of the Turkish garrison could be seen. In The Nek area one Australian tunnel, "Arnall's Folly", was dug very deep with the purpose of breaking out behind the Turks in some future offensive. The Turkish miners were everywhere outdug and outfought, and by December at every main post several Anzac tunnels were under or near the Turkish front line, ready charged for explosion. As reinforcements sufficient for a normal form of attack were lacking, men at Anzac discussed other means—a favourite suggestion being that, during a storm, when Turkish vigilance was low, the front-line garrison should simply walk over. A hint also came that "land battleships" were being prepared in England—a first whisper of the designing of tanks. Fortunately the Turks had no modern heavy trench mortars, and used no gas or smoke. Any of these would have rendered defence difficult.

The dangers and hardships of winter were foreseen, and from September preparations were made against them. The system of deep dugouts excavated in the Anzac trenches afforded such shelter that various troops were for a time brought thrice weekly by ferry from Suvla and Helles and conducted round them. When on two rough days in October moderate seas smashed parts of the piers and water pipes, arrangements were made for much increased stores, a water-condensing plant, and extra hospitals on North Beach. In mid-November came a rougher spell and on the 27th a blizzard which covered Anzac

---

[4] *Vol. II, pp. 815-20.* There were mines also at the Apex and Hill 60.

with snow—much to the interest of the troops in spite of
their discomfort—but played havoc with the Suvla force
whose low-lying trenches were flooded, some men even
being drowned. Dysentery and enteric had almost
vanished with the cooler weather and diminution of flies;
but after this blizzard 15,800 troops were evacuated from
the Peninsula sick, 11,000 of them from Suvla. For two
days the Anzac water ration was reduced to a nominal
two pints a day—actually in many cases to a cupful of
water in the morning, and another in the evening.[5] The
small craft had sunk or were sheltering at Imbros, and
only one dinghy was available at Anzac.

It was just before this, on November 23rd, that
Kitchener had advised the government to withdraw its
forces from Anzac and Suvla, and had warned the leaders
on the spot. At Birdwood's request he again placed
General Monro in charge of the British armies at the
Dardanelles and Salonica with Birdwood under him
commanding the "Dardanelles Army"; but the actual
carrying out of the evacuation was to be left entirely
to Birdwood. The Australian and New Zealand Army
Corps was now under General Godley, with Brudenell
White as chief of his general staff, Skeen having been
invalided. Already, on Kitchener's instructions, surplus
stores were being sent away—professedly because they
would not be needed in a purely defensive winter cam
paign. Monro had by arrangement with the admiral
appointed a joint committee to plan a withdrawal. For
several reasons—shortage of boats being one—it was eventually decided to withdraw in the first place only from
Anzac and Suvla. The committee had advised that this
should be done in three stages: (1) preliminary stage:
reduction of present forces at Anzac (41,000) and Suvla
(51,000), and their material, to those required for winter;

---

[5] For the winter, water was to be pumped from the flats near Suvla,
where the supply was ample. At Anzac within two days of the Landing
twenty wells had been dug, but many became unsafe for drinking or ran dry.

(2) intermediate stage: withdrawal of all men and material not required to hold the position for the last two days—about 20,000 would be needed for each position; (3) final stage: withdrawal of this remainder in two nights. Monro had also laid it down that no lives were to be sacrificed in an effort to save guns.

Although for a fortnight no final decision arrived from England, Birdwood at once began with the first stage—reduction to winter garrison; and as early as November 22nd, when Kitchener held his final conference at Lemnos, Birdwood warned Godley at Anzac to prepare for evacuation. General Brudenell White, chief-of-staff at Anzac, immediately put in action a plan, which he had already tested, for accustoming the Turks to periods of cessation of fire from the Anzac troops. From 6 p.m. on November 24th until a time fixed eventually at midnight on the 27th no shots or shells were to be fired or bombs thrown from Anzac except in case of danger or upon exceptional targets. The Turks became puzzled and nervous. On the second day four of them were allowed to approach Quinn's Post and one even boldly walked along the trench there until killed. Elsewhere on the third day larger parties emerged—some coming close were suddenly shot down. On the night of the 27th came the blizzard. The Turkish staff had at first suspected a partial withdrawal, but later concluded that the Anzacs wanted quiet while preparing winter quarters—which they themselves were doing.

This incident was known as "The Silent Stunt". Shorter silences were thenceforward repeated almost every night, so that the Turks became thoroughly used to them. The arrival of new artillery for the Turks, or at least of ammunition, was possibly the reason for a sudden concentrated bombardment by them of the Lone Pine trenches on November 29th, when one battalion of the 6th Brigade was being relieved by another. The very deep, narrow trenches, and the shallow tunnels of the

Anzac system there, collapsed in many places, burying many men, and exhibiting a grave danger, not previously realised by the Anzacs.

Meanwhile the Anzac plan of evacuation had been drafted by General White. The normal method, to fall back by stages to successive positions, was out of the question there, because the Turks in the centre, if once warned of what was happening, had only to thrust 300 yards in order to overlook the embarkation piers at North Beach. The only possible method was to deceive the enemy by holding all the front-line posts, however lightly, till the latest possible moment, and then to withdraw their garrisons in one final concerted movement.

White had to fight hard to secure the general adoption of this plan, since General Byng, in command at Suvla, thought there was little chance of deceiving the Turks, and desired to employ the normal method which was feasible at Suvla, but, if used there, might betray the Anzac withdrawal. By an appeal to Birdwood, White ultimately carried his point. General Monro asked that two other devices be considered—the preparation of mines, and the delivery of attacks to cover the withdrawal. White strongly opposed both, as each would disturb the normal conditions and warn the enemy. For success, he urged, they must rely on deceiving the Turks by the maintenance of "normality".

Indeed "normality" became the key principle of those members of the staff who knew what was afoot. A Christmas souvenir book, *The Anzac Book*, for the troops at Anzac had been planned, and contributions poured in for it and literary competitions were held. In order to deceive even most of the staff and the clerks through whose hands the movement orders passed, preparation for winter was generally given as the reason for these orders. The blizzard caused stores to be short and some had to be sent back to the Peninsula; but it also gave a good ostensible reason for some of the withdrawals.

When, on December 8th, the final secret order came, the force at Anzac had been reduced to 36,000 men[6] and 97 guns, and that at Suvla to 41,000 men and 91 guns.

The intermediate stage now began, the same reason, "lightening" the garrison for winter, being alleged. The troops were to be reduced to 20,000 by a date which General Birdwood eventually fixed at December 18th; then the two final days would begin. To ensure that the final movement should be simultaneous, General White persuaded G.H.Q. to have the left flank troops of Anzac embarked at Suvla.

Every night now, beginning at dusk, troops and stores were continuously leaving. The British, Maltese and Egyptian labour units, field ambulances, and a proportion of the artillery were withdrawn, but hospitals were maintained or increased and some troops were landed by day. Nightly the Turks could hear sounds of traffic by land and water, but could not tell whether troops and stores were embarking or disembarking. A steamer was sunk off North Beach to serve as breakwater. About December 11th rumours of evacuation began among the Anzac troops, but even some brigadiers had no inkling of it till several days later.

The news then came as a shock, but naturally to none so sharply as to the Australians and New Zealanders, to whom this first great test of their nations in war had meant so much. Many believed, from various signs, that the Turks facing them were now beaten men, and, like Birdwood himself, some of them would rather have staked their chance on blowing up the mines and rushing the Turkish trenches. A greater part, on the other hand, recognised that the "heads" knew the position better than they, and that the decision was probably wise. But on one point they felt unanimously—what hurt all, and hurt most deeply, was to leave behind to an enemy not only

---

[6] The 54th Division and Essex Garrison Battalion had been withdrawn.

13—os

the heights and valleys that so much effort had won, but the bodies of the mates who had given their lives in that effort. From December 12th onwards the cemeteries of Anzac were never without men, in twos or threes or singly, "tidying" up the grave of some dear, dead friend, and repairing or renewing the little packing-wood crosses and rough inscriptions. "I hope *they* won't hear us marching down the *deres*," said one to Birdwood on the final day.

The last 20,000 men left at each area, Anzac and Suvla, were to be withdrawn on the nights of December 18th and 19th, 10,000 on each night. By the scheme of the Anzac withdrawal—drawn by General White in a paper which has been described as "a model of precision and clear thinking",[7] and carried out under his close supervision the last 10,000 on the night of December 19th were to be withdrawn by three successive thinnings of the front-line garrison, 4100 leaving their posts at nightfall (5.15-5.30 p.m.), 3000 at 8.30-11.30, and the last 2800 in three instalments between 1.30 and 3.15 a.m. Of the sixteen mines then lying ready-charged beneath the Turkish line on the old Anzac front, none except two at The Nek were to be fired unless the Turks attacked. The Nek mines might be exploded at the very end of the operation in order to prevent the Turks from following up.

During the making of the plans the staff became convinced that the withdrawal might be effected with much less than the 50 per cent casualties expected by Hamilton or even the 30 per cent expected by Monro. It was still, however, believed likely to be a costly operation, and hospital accommodation for 2000 was to be left at each place, Suvla and Anzac, to receive the wounded. Nevertheless, from the first rumour of the plans, men and regiments at Anzac demanded "as a right" to be included in the last parties: "I was here first and I have a right to be last!" was a frequent argument. On refusal, some men

---

[7] *British Official History of the Gallipoli Campaign, Vol. II, p. 444,* by Brig.-Gen. Aspinall-Oglander, who himself was C.G.S. to Birdwood and one of the very able committee appointed by Monro to draw the main plans.

asked to be paraded before their commanding officers in order to discover "what they had done" to be denied this "right". The eventual selection was carefully and well carried out.

On Birdwood's insistence the Navy undertook only by night all necessary movement of transports and small craft from the island of Imbros, ten miles away. The Turks did notice an unusual amount of steamer smoke arising from that distant shelter before dark, but this might have indicated many other activities. The weather remained perfect, and the intermediate stage and the work on the first of the two final nights was completed without any hitch, or any sign of Turkish suspicion. Command at Anzac was then handed over to Maj.-General A. H. Russell of the N.Z. and A. Division, in charge of the "rearguard".

On that last day, Sunday, December 19th, Anzac seemed strangely desolate and empty, except at a few points visible to the Turks, where movement was specially maintained. Many of the guns were gone but the others, mostly old pieces, fired for them—no more and no less than usual. Curiously enough, that day strange, fairly heavy Turkish shells, with an ugly black smoke, burst occasionally over Suvla and others near Lone Pine—first sign of the arrival of new guns or ammunition for the Turks.

At dusk the first parties began, with padded feet, to move to the beaches. Except for a few on the flanks, who embarked from specially made piers, they wound along the well-known paths and trenches—all carefully marked for this night—to Anzac Cove and North Beach.[8] As there had so far been no casualties, General Russell sent away also half of his hospital staff. After midnight the eleven miles of Anzac front were held by only 1500 men. These moved from loophole to loophole, keeping up normal fire and bombing. At 1.30 Russell handed over the com-

---

[8] A destroyer's searchlight beam, steadily laid (as often before) beyond the southern flank, hampered observation from Gaba Tepe.

mand to Lieut.-Colonel J. Paton, in charge of an "inner line" previously organised (from Plugge's Plateau to The Nek and No. 1 Outpost), and the final withdrawal began, at the distant northern flank.

Here and there was left a rifle which, by varying devices, would fire up to half an hour after the troops had gone.

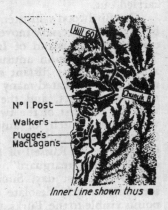

Inner Line shown thus ■

So, gradually, the Anzac front was uncovered. At 2.25 the withdrawal began from the southern flank also. At 2.40 the last men left their loopholes at Lone Pine, and at 2.55 at Quinn's, where for seven months the bombfight had continued every night and day. At all usual points the desultory firing and bombing by the Turks still went on, and at this stage Colonel Paton was able to withdraw the garrison of the inner line.

At 3.25 the last guard on Walker's Ridge retired and at 3.30, with a minute's interval between the explosions, the two mines on The Nek—in Arnall's gallery and another—were fired. All over the dark waters, troops in crowded lighters moving out to larger craft, and on ferry steamers, transports and warships, saw the brilliant orange glow twice flush for a moment the underside of low angry clouds. A growing rattle of rifle fire spread along the Turkish line—a bullet from this stream hit a soldier in one of the boats causing one of the two Anzac casualties of that night. The last lighter left the North Beach about 4 a.m. The naval transport officer and his steamboat with the last of the Anzac staff waited ten minutes for stragglers, but there were none and at 4.10 they pushed off. Four miles to the north a fire broke out—the stores at Suvla were being burnt. At 5.10 the last party left Suvla, where also the casualties were negligible.

Till dawn the Turks were still sniping as on an ordinary night. At 6.45 they shelled the Anzac trenches and at 7.15 attacked—to find the position empty and the Anzacs gone. After a few shells which sent these Turks to earth, the covering British cruisers withdrew and left Anzac to the enemy.[9]

The part of the Anzacs in the Dardanelles campaign, though a major one, was only a part. The French casualties were nearly as great as theirs; and the British lost nearly three times as many. For all the forces there, and not least for the Turks, the struggle for those few square miles had been one of devoted endeavour; and this book has barely touched on any but the Australian and New Zealand share in it.

Yet for the withdrawing Anzacs Gallipoli had a special meaning. It was not merely that 7600 Australians and nearly 2500 New Zealanders had been killed or mortally wounded there, and 24,000 more (19,000 Australians and 5000 New Zealanders) had been wounded, while less than 100 were prisoners. But the standard set by the first companies at the first call—by the stretcher-bearers, the medical officers, the staffs, the company leaders, the privates, the defaulters on the water barges, the Light Horse at The Nek—this was already part of the tradition not only of Anzac but of the Australian and New Zealand peoples. By dawn on December 20th Anzac had faded into a dim blue line lost amid other hills on the horizon as the ships took their human freight to Imbros, Lemnos and Egypt. But Anzac stood, and still stands, for reckless valour in a good cause, for enterprise, resourcefulness, fidelity, comradeship, and endurance that will never own defeat.

On the night of 8th January 1916 the British withdrew from Cape Helles also with negligible loss. The

---

[9] For the sincere greetings—and also the traps—left for the Turks, and for the Turkish discovery of the evacuation, see *Vol. II, pp. 901-4.*

success of the whole evacuation went far to counteract the blow to British prestige.

During 1916 a British Royal Commission, of which Andrew Fisher was a member, inquired into the origin and conduct of the Dardanelles Campaign. The newspaper magnate, Lord Northcliffe, and others would have welcomed an outburst of dissatisfaction in Australia as giving them a lever to unseat Mr Asquith from the Prime Ministership. The Evacuation, it was thought, might provoke such a protest. But at such a time the Australian people was not disposed to question the higher leadership, as to which it knew itself to be in no position to judge. In the circumstances it could only trust leaders who were in contact with the events; criticism of them in Australia was felt to be futile and was sharply resented by the public. It accepted the whole incident as one of the inevitable "ups and downs" in a hard fight; and the *post mortem* examination was not strongly favoured unless it could be helpful in the conduct of the war.

One principle, vital to the content and efficiency of the A.I.F., and not fully settled when the Australians sailed in April for Gallipoli, had been practically assured by the time they left it: though the general operations in which they took part were directed by the British Command in whose Army they served, their promotion, organisation, training and discipline were determined by the A.I.F.'s own commander, who was responsible to the Australian Government. This responsibility (as well as the command of the 1st Division) lay with General Bridges until his death at Anzac. Thereafter—except for short intervals when it was held by Generals Legge and Godley—it was entrusted by the Australian Government to General Birdwood, who with Brudenell White as his adviser, received instructions direct from Melbourne. Of this system Neville Howse, who now became Director of Medical Services, was one of the strongest pillars.

CHAPTER XII

AUSTRALIA DOUBLES THE A.I.F.

THE Australians and New Zealanders who returned from Gallipoli to Egypt were a different force from the adventurous body that had left Egypt eight months before. They were a military force with strongly established, definite traditions. Not for anything, if he could avoid it, would an Australian now change his loose, faded tunic or battered hat for the smartest cloth or headgear of any other army. Men clung to their Australian uniforms till they were tattered to the limit of decency.

Each of the regimental numbers which eight months before had been merely numbers, now carried a poignant meaning for every man serving with the A.I.F., and to some extent even for the nation far away in Australia. The 1st, 2nd, 3rd and 4th Infantry Battalions—they had rushed Lone Pine; the 5th, 6th, 7th, 8th had made that swift advance at Helles; the 9th, 10th, 11th, 12th had stormed the Anzac heights; the 13th, 14th, 15th, 16th had first held Quinn's, Courtney's and Pope's; the battalion numbers of the 2nd Division were becoming equally famous—and so with the light horse, artillery, engineers, field ambulances, transport companies, and casualty clearing stations. Service on the Gallipoli beaches had given a fighting record even to British, Egyptian and Maltese labour units that normally would have served far behind the front.

The troops from Gallipoli were urgently desired by Kitchener for the defence of Egypt against the Turkish expedition that threatened to descend on it as soon as the Allies' evacuation had released the Turkish army

also. It was estimated that the Turks might concentrate
250,000 men for this purpose; and the plans announced
by the Germans might, Lord Kitchener feared, "set the
East in a blaze". His own proposal for countering this
threatened invasion by striking at Alexandretta had been
rejected by the British government, and he therefore
reluctantly fell back on the plan of the British War Office
for defending Egypt by holding the line of the Suez Canal.

Thither, then, the troops from Gallipoli and others
were directed, making a force of some twelve infantry
and two cavalry divisions for the defence of Egypt but
also as a reserve "for the whole Empire" against other
coming needs. General Sir Archibald Murray, hitherto
Chief of the General Staff at the War Office, was sent to
command it. Instead of "making the Canal defend him"
—a policy much criticised—he was to defend it by pushing
his garrison about eight miles east of it. The line they
were to fortify there was already being surveyed and was
guarded by a few isolated posts. The forces from Gallipoli
urgently needed their ranks to be filled, and also re-
equipment and reorganisation in accordance with the
new composition of British infantry divisions.

For these purposes the two Australian divisions, 1st
and 2nd, were sent to
a huge camp on the
site of Arabi Pasha's
old battlefield at Tel
el Kebir, on the desert
thirty miles west of
Ismailia and the Suez
Canal; the New Zea-
land and Australian
Division was sent to
Moascar Camp near
by, outside Ismailia.
The line east of the

Canal was still being surveyed, and the front along the

Canal was held by one English and one Indian division, the newly arrived 8th Australian Infantry Brigade, and some Indian troops. The nearest large body of Turks comprised 13,000 men at their railhead in southern Palestine at Beersheba, 120 miles away, on the other side of the Sinai Desert. Turkish forward troops were 70-100 miles away, making and guarding preparations for an advance through the desert against Egypt.[1]

The 8th Brigade was far from being the only Australian force found in Egypt by the troops returning from Gallipoli. In addition to the A.I.F. headquarters staff in Cairo, and the transport troops there and at Alexandria (the base of the Mediterranean Expeditionary Force), there were in the Australian training and convalescent depots very great numbers of sick and wounded and of reinforcements. Most of those who during recent months would normally have been shipped to Gallipoli had been stopped in Egypt by the decision to abandon the Peninsula. After the Evacuation over 10,000 joined their units in Lemnos. But the depots near Cairo still held at least 20,000, and more were arriving.

The chief reason for these numbers was the flood of recruiting in Australia. The plunge of the A.I.F. into Gallipoli, and the sudden, first, terrible casualty lists, had caused more Australians to offer. The sinking of the crowded liner *Lusitania* by a submarine without warning increased the bitterness against Germans; but the chief urge came from the realisation that, contrary to the optimistic communiqués, the war was going badly—with the repulse of all efforts to break the stalemate in France, and with the drive of the Germans into Russia. It is true that the entry of Italy on the side of the Allies showed that she expected them to win. But eager citizens demanded a properly organised recruiting campaign; and, in the energetic recruiting that followed, the enlist-

---

[1] During the Gallipoli Campaign Turkish spies and scouts had occasionally reached the Canal. A mine placed in it had sunk a British steamer.

ments rose from 6250 in April, 10,526 in May, and 12,505 in June, to 36,575 in July, 25,714 in August and 16,571 in September. The numbers in training camps in Australia swelled from 16,424 in June to 73,963 in October.

It happened that in October Australia experienced a change of Prime Ministers: Andrew Fisher, on whom the responsibilities of that position had borne heavily, was appointed to succeed Sir George Reid as High Commissioner for Australia in London, and William Morris Hughes, who already was the chief force in the Ministry, became Prime Minister in his place. At this juncture a War Census, which largely by the action of Mr Hughes had just been completed, showed that 244,000 single men of military age were still available for enlistment—according to the classification of the statisticians, not, of course, of the medical authorities. Australia was then maintaining overseas a force of some 60,000 men. The government thereupon decided that, in addition to the monthly quota of 9500 reinforcements, it would send, if desired by the British government, 50,000 fresh troops, organised as nine infantry brigades with attendant troops —in effect, three infantry divisions without artillery. This decision, announced on November 26th, would raise Australia's oversea force to about 110,000 men. The War Office subsequently indicated that it would prefer three divisions complete, but the Defence Department could not promise artillerymen, guns, or rifles.

A.I.F. headquarters at the front had been informed of this offer. At that time the A.I.F. was being administered by General Godley, commander of the New Zealand Expeditionary Force, who, during Birdwood's appointment to the Dardanelles Army, was commander of the Anzac Corps. On arrival in Egypt Godley—who was still holding these commands, with Brudenell White as chief of his staff—was faced by the problem of what to do with the 40,000 unallotted Australian and New Zealand reinforcements already there. He was most desirous of organising the New Zealand troops in Egypt into a division, the existing New Zealand Infantry Brigade being expanded with reinforcements to form two brigades, and the Rifle Brigade (then arriving from New Zealand) providing the third. The Australian reinforcements could similarly be used to expand the A.I.F. from two divisions into four divisions. These, and the New Zealand Division, officered and trained by experienced soldiers from Gallipoli, could then form two army corps. Later the 50,000 troops arriving from Australia would allow still another division to be formed besides providing reinforcements. Godley suggested that, for the period of the reorganisation, General Birdwood, with General White as chief-of-staff, should administer the whole Australian and New Zealand forces.

It was mid-January 1916, when Godley made this proposal to Sir Archibald Murray. Murray gave his approval against the advice of some of his staff, who had a very low estimate of the capacity of the Australian depot in Egypt for training officers and N.C.O.'s. Murray especially desired that the 30,000 Australian reinforcements, then unallotted at Cairo, and swarming in the streets and hotels, should be brought quickly into control and training in fighting units. Birdwood reaching Egypt on January 19th, enthusiastically developed the scheme, being particularly hopeful that, with two Anzac corps, the War Office might sanction the formation of an Australian and New Zealand Army. He suggested that the third new Australian division should be formed in Australia.

The War Office, though not yet prepared to sanction the grouping of the Anzacs into an "Army", passed on the rest of the proposal to the Australian and New Zealand governments, which presently agreed. Australia promised to send artillerymen with the third division—but it could not send guns or train their crews. This would ultimately give five Australian infantry divisions.

In addition there would be the New Zealand infantry division, and an Anzac mounted division, formed from the Light Horse and New Zealand Mounted Rifles Brigades, which had now returned from Anzac to their beloved horses.

Mounted troops were particularly needed for the defence of Egypt; even while the Light Horse were in Gallipoli, at the end of November 1915, a scratch regiment of them together with the horse transport of the 1st Australian Division had been sent as part of a composite force (Yeomanry, South African infantry, and armoured cars) into the Libyan Desert at Mersa Matruh. This expedition was now thrusting towards Sidi Barrani and Sollum to rescue some torpedoed British subjects held as prisoners by the Senussi Arabs.[2] Meanwhile part of the Light Horse immediately on returning from Gallipoli had been sent to guard the edge of the Nile valley farther south against the threatening Senussi. It was known that, even if the Anzac infantry divisions were ultimately, as their members hoped, sent to France, Murray counted on the mounted division to help in defending Egypt.

At this juncture reports that the Turks in Palestine were about to start marching across the Sinai Desert caused Murray to order his main defence forces to take up and fortify their intended position east of the Suez Canal. On January 23rd the Anzac Corps under General Godley began to move from Tel el Kebir to the central of the three sections of the Canal defences, east of Ismailia, and started to revet and wire a system of carefully sited posts along a thirty-mile front. Light Decauville railways took material to the line; and pipe-lines and endless strings of camels supplied water. In the camps among the sandhills, despite dust storms and fatigues, training was good; and for reserves camped by the Canal,

---

2 An account of this expedition over famous ground is given in *Vol. III*, pp. 959-64.

with frequent swimming, and with the passing ship traffic as a constant side-show, life was pleasant.

Meanwhile, working at Ismailia, Birdwood and White carried through the immense task of, within a few weeks, expanding the Anzac divisions from three to six. In this reorganisation, so far as the Australian troops were concerned, General Birdwood conceived the basic principle which thereafter gave a veteran character and a feeling of brotherhood to the whole force—namely that the new brigades and battalions should be formed by splitting in half the oldest ones, and then using reinforcements to expand each half into a whole. Though General White and many unit commanders feared a shock to regimental pride and tradition, General Birdwood with great wisdom, insisted.

The task was carried out through the issue of a succession of about fifty "circular memoranda", mainly the personal work of General White. Each of the sixteen oldest battalions was split into two "wings"—one to constitute the old battalion and one the new. The splitting was most fairly done—in some cases, when it was finished, the new commander was allowed to pick whichever half he chose. Between February 14th and March 7th the "second wing" of each battalion left its old unit and moved back to Tel el Kebir. The separation was a wrench, but ever afterwards the new and old battalions, however far apart, were bound together by the strongest feeling. Each wing at once organised itself into a skeleton battalion, and some two days later its reinforcements, arriving from Cairo, expanded it—at Tel el Kebir or at the Canal line—to a battalion of full strength. Most of the reinforcements were very raw, but coming thus into veteran units they quickly assimilated discipline and training.

By this means the 1st-16th Battalions (of the 1st-4th Brigades) at the Canal created the 45th-60th Battalions (of the 12th-15th Brigades) at Tel el Kebir. Two brigades

—the 8th, lately arrived from Australia, and the 4th
(Monash's) released from the now disbanded N.Z. and
A. Division—were brought to Tel el Kebir to complete
there the infantry of the two new Australian divisions.

This expansion meant a splendid field for promotion
of tried leaders and men throughout the force, and,
coming on top of the rapid promotions following the
heavy casualties of Gallipoli, it brought to the front a
quota of leaders—some of them very young—whose
quality, in general, has probably never been surpassed.
It was at this stage that William Glasgow, Duncan Glasfurd, John Gellibrand, and H. E. ("Pompey") Elliott
became brigadiers, Raymond Leane, W. E. H. Cass, H.
G. Bennett, Humphrey Scott (twenty-four years old), and
Owen Howell-Price (twenty-five years) battalion commanders, and so on in lower ranks. For the new divisional
commanders Birdwood tried to seize the chance of getting
two outstanding British leaders, the dour, capable Anglo-
Indian H. V. Cox, and H. A. Lawrence (afterwards chief
of the British General Staff in France). The Australian
government, however, most justifiably insisted that the
Gallipoli Campaign must have produced Australians
capable of command, and urged consideration of White,
Monash and M'Cay. Birdwood felt that White could not
be spared from the staff, but he now selected M'Cay for
one new division at Tel el Kebir, and held Monash in
view for the division to be raised in Australia. The other
division at Tel el Kebir, and temporary charge of the
whole force there, he gave to Cox. The Anzac Mounted
Division was allotted to Brig.-General Chauvel of the
1st Light Horse Brigade.

Ever since the concentration in Egypt had been
ordered the influence of the Turco-German threat to the
Canal had been dwindling; the divisions under Murray
were increasingly regarded as reinforcements for the
Western Front, where for the first time (although the
fact could, of course, only be guessed at by the troops

and the public at home) the Allies were approaching the day when they might undertake a formidable combined offensive. Lord Kitchener had long awaited the hour when the New British Army, raised by him, would be in France and Belgium in sufficient strength to make possible a combined Anglo-French blow on such a scale as to give reasonable hope of breaking the German front in the west. For this great trial Britain would need on the Western Front every division she could muster, and the force in Egypt must be an important source of these.

Though only headquarters had any certain knowledge of this plan, the Anzac troops guessed that their prospect of soon reaching the Western Front was daily increasing. A possible impediment to this—how serious is still, and may always be, undisclosed—lay in General Murray's views as to the discipline of the Australians. In a draft letter from himself to the new Chief of the Imperial General Staff in London, General Robertson, he spoke of this in the most damning terms. Murray sent a copy of this draft to Generals Birdwood and White. White protested that the letter, if sent, should be repeated to the Australian government, which would have the opportunity to consider whether troops held to be so valueless should not be withdrawn from France. Whether the draft was modified is not known, but it is known that, whereas the Anzac divisions had originally been placed first on the list for transfer to France, Murray presently placed them fourth, as being "most backward in training and discipline"—a not unnatural condition in view of their extraordinary expansion. The chief result was an intense "grooming up" of the divisions by their officers, even including some not very successful "saluting drill"—most of which, however, was a useful corrective to any tendency to be slack or slovenly.[3]

At this juncture there suddenly arrived news that

---

[3] For this interesting episode see *Vol. III, pp. 56-62.*

changed the face of affairs. The Germans in France had taken the wind from the Allies' sails by attacking months before the Allies could be ready: on February 21st they struck at the north-eastern bastion of the French front, the fortress of Verdun. The most urgent need of the Allies now was to take the weight off the French. Robertson telegraphed to Murray that in withdrawing troops for France some risk to the defence of Egypt must, if necessary, be accepted. As to the Anzacs, Robertson said, three of their divisions in France in April might "be worth six at a later date". On 29th February 1916 Murray warned Birdwood that the I Anzac Corps (to be composed of the 1st and 2nd Australian and the New Zealand Divisions, under General Birdwood himself) would begin moving to France in a fortnight. The II Anzac Corps (comprising the new 4th and 5th Australian Divisions, under General Godley) would for the present remain in Egypt.

This sudden order brought to the staffs of the A.I.F. probably the most difficult problem in organisation that ever faced them. The Anzac divisions had never yet been provided with artillery on the normal scale. Until the end of the Gallipoli Campaign an Australian infantry division had only nine 4-gun batteries whereas at that time the standard for the corresponding British divisions was fifteen batteries (including howitzer batteries of which the A.I.F. had none). When the divisions had to be suddenly expanded from two to four, Birdwood and White had felt that, for the moment, the most that could be undertaken was to double the Australian artillery on its existing scale. Accordingly they had arranged for each of the older Australian divisions to give up one brigade to each of the new divisions, while from reinforcements and large transfers of officers and N.C.O.'s there would be created one brigade for each older division and two for each new one.

This expansion of the Australian artillery from

eighteen batteries to thirty-six had begun on February 18th. But now, with the move to France in immediate prospect, General Murray gave the decision—obviously a right one—that the divisions going to France must have their artillery at full scale. This meant expansion to sixty batteries in all. With notice so short, the divisions going to France could be supplied only by robbing the two new divisions which were to be left temporarily in Egypt. This was accordingly done; the 4th and 5th Divisions would have to raise their artillery almost entirely from untrained officers and men. How they met this difficulty will be told in due course.

Meanwhile on March 5th the older divisions began marching from the desert to embark, handing over their section of the front to the mounted troops who were presently formed into the Anzac Mounted Division. The 4th and 5th Australian Divisions were to take over the section almost immediately. The I Anzac Corps began to sail from Egypt to France on March 13th. The reorganisation of the A.I.F. was then practically complete. In addition to the doubling of the divisions, three entirely new kinds of unit—pioneer battalions, machine-gun companies and trench-mortar batteries—had been created in each division, and part of a camel corps under British command. The whole process had been enormously helped by those commanders who, like John Gellibrand, regularly furnished their best men so as to give the best possible start to these infant units, but was equally hampered by some leaders who shortsightedly did the reverse. But the leader mainly responsible for the brilliant accomplishment of this big task was Brudenell White. General Monash, then a brigadier, after seeing these arrangements and those of the Evacuation of Anzac, described him as "far and away the ablest soldier Australia has ever turned out". White now went to France as chief-of-staff on Birdwood's corps (I Anzac).

The troopships reached Marseilles without any

14—os

sinkings, though German submarines were active. On March 19th the first transports, with men of the 2nd Division, moved past the Ile d'If into the crowded harbour. The regimental bands, resuscitated after Gallipoli, played the Marseillaise; the troops whistled it, cheered, stared (as at some strange animals) at the German prisoners working under guard of French territorials on the quays. The local British staff at this juncture was prepared against two expected contingencies—that the Australians might break out in riot into Marseilles, and that disease from Egypt might slip into France with these troops. But the Anzacs had by then been more thoroughly vaccinated, inoculated and disinfected by their own authorities than even the British troops (for whom vaccination was not compulsory). Strangely enough, an Australian hospital, kept for some time at Marseilles as a quarantine depot for any discovered cases, did intercept cases of typhus, but all among the troops of British divisions coming from Egypt.[4] Partly through the fine control of the Australian officers, the fear as to "riots" proved equally groundless; the Marseilles authorities afterwards told Birdwood's staff that no troops had ever given less trouble. Later, when the 5th Division passed through, the British commandant at Marseilles wrote to its commander: "Not a single case of misbehaviour or lack of discipline has been brought to my notice." This, he added, was "a record".

Actually the troops were too interested to give trouble and too eager to reach the Western Front. Day after day as their transports arrived, they marched at intervals through Marseilles to the troop trains that would carry them to the British zone, 130 miles north of Paris. Their journey up the Rhone valley—with the orchards in blossom, and, beyond, the winding blue river and the distant

---

[4] For this "dramatic" experience of typhus, see *Official Medical History, Vol. II, pp. 543-5.* The Defence Department in Australia was, however, badly behindhand in the inoculation of its troops against paratyphoid.

Alps—was like a plunge into fairyland. The halts were thronged by friendly, welcoming French people. From the moment the Australians set foot in France their confident approach and breezy friendliness evoked an outstanding response from the French. Long before they had given any evidence of their quality on the Western Front, the population had them marked as "des bons soldats"; that confidence was never lost and led to some astonishing scenes in the last stage of the war.

The weather became wet, cold, and even snowy as the troops neared Paris. After Versailles, within sight of the Eiffel Tower, their trains, to the mild disappointment of the troops, bypassed the city and made for Calais, 140 miles to the north. There they headed inland again towards detraining points at or near several small towns and straggling villages amid the flat, green, tree- and hedge-enclosed fields of French Flanders. Here British soldiers were seen on some of the stations or drilling in the fields, and British transport, a picture of neatness, on the roads. The chief towns in the area in which the journey ended were the old boroughs of Aire and St Omer, and the large country town and railway junction of Hazebrouck.

But few of the detraining troops caught more than a glimpse of these. They marched along tree-lined highways, over cobbles covered with a thin smear of mud, or down macadamised side roads deeper in mud, past, at intervals, convoys of twenty or thirty hooded motor lorries, to their billets in and around villages. Most officers were given rooms in the village houses or farmhouses, most of the other ranks slept in their blankets in the barns—big, straw-filled buildings with walls of wattle-and-daub, whitewashed. Many friendships sprang up with "Madame", the mother of the household; but of the kind of dallying that the cinema afterwards portrayed there was singularly little, the Flemish people being in the main hard-working folk, without thought of, or time for, "style" in ways or appearance, and the soldiers fully occupied in settling down and training in these rest areas twelve miles or so behind the line.

For, as with other British and Dominion troops sent to the Western Front, the I Anzac Corps was first brought to this quiet sector—generally known as "the nursery"—for a quiet introduction, in training for harsher experiences to come. The British held most of the northern section of the Allies' front in France; and here, in the northern third of the British zone, there lay just within the lines the considerable French manufacturing town of Armentières (about 30,000 people) on the Lys River near the Belgian border. South-east of Armentières the big French manufacturing city of Lille lay a few miles behind the German line, though screened from it by low hills. The British desired to avoid shelling Lille; and, possibly because this quiet was convenient for the German staffs and troops, the Germans reciprocated by seldom shelling the main part of Armentières. Moreover the Lys, running diagonally through the region, provided an obstacle to any important attacks.

Nevertheless, from the moment when the Australians detrained, their expectant ears caught the "bump, bump" of distant guns, and, as night fell, trees, hedges and houses to eastward were constantly outlined against the swift flicker of gun flashes and the pale, quivering halo of the white flares by which each side illuminated the no-man's-land between the lines. For two and a half years to come those sights and sounds were never to be absent.

CHAPTER XIII

THE WESTERN FRONT, 1916

THE British Expeditionary Force, at the date when the Australians reinforced it, had been in France and Belgium for nearly twenty months, having reached France on 12th August 1914. The old British Army—except its cavalry divisions—had practically ceased to exist after the First Battle of Ypres. Its divisions had been so reduced that, when filled up again with reinforcements, they were to a large extent new formations. These, and many newer ones, were still fighting on the north-western flank of the French, where the old army had helped to stop and then drive back the vast German turning movement in 1914. For only the first two months of the war had there been freedom to manoeuvre; since October 1914 the opposing armies on the Western Front had extended continuously for nearly 500 miles from the Swiss border to the North Sea. Since the First Battle of Ypres in November 1914, when the Germans failed in a final attempt to break through the Allies' northern flank, there had been a deadlock on the whole front.

At the time when the Anzacs arrived, much the greater part of the Allies' Western Front—370 miles of it—was held by the French (with 111 divisions in line and reserve). But Kitchener's measures for expanding the British Army had, since the middle of 1915, resulted in the growth of the British Expeditionary Force (usually known as the "B.E.F.") from 10 infantry and 5 cavalry divisions (2 of each being Indian) in October 1914 to 44 infantry and 5 cavalry divisions in April 1916. The British sector now extended for eighty miles, as far south as the Somme River, south of Albert (near Amiens), and as far north as Ypres; beyond this some twenty miles were held by the Belgians, with one French Army Corps on the extreme left touching the North Sea at Nieuport.

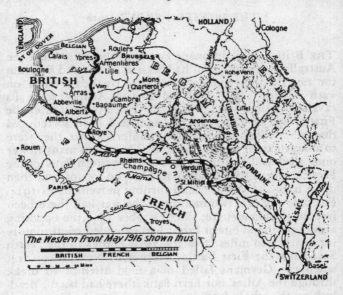

The Western Front May 1916 shown thus
BRITISH   FRENCH   BELGIAN

The B.E.F. was now organised in four armies each holding a section of the British front. Like the rest of the Allied troops on the Western Front and the 120 German divisions facing them, these troops spent by far the greater part of their time in the stationary siege-warfare of the trenches, or in training and resting in the quiet reserve areas behind the lines. At the end of April 1916 the B.E.F., including non-combatant troops, contained 1,263,000 men and was increasing at the rate of 100,000 monthly; it then included 40,000 Australians and 18,500 New Zealanders, nearly all, of course, combatant troops—their ordnance, munitions, food were all British, Australia paying so much per man for this supply. By July the Australians had risen to over 90,000; another 90,000 were in England (including base troops) and 25,000 in the Middle East.

In November 1914, when the German effort of First Ypres ended, the Allies had expected to be able quite soon to drive their enemy back. But though the Germans then withdrew large forces in order to pursue the campaign against Russia, the efforts made by French and British in December 1914 utterly failed; and the apparent half-heartedness of the British action at that time tended to cause General Joffre and the French staff to believe that, though stubborn in defence, the British Army, now consisting largely of reinforcements, was incapable of carrying out an offensive.[1] Nevertheless, as his armies grew with the gradual addition of Territorial and "New Army" troops, the British commander-in-chief, then Sir John French, was determined that they must take the offensive in collaboration with the French or without them, and this they had done on a number of occasions. Each of these efforts had been launched with high hopes, and two of them with big strategic aims—to at least endanger the enemy's supply lines to the big "bulge".

The first such effort began on 10th March 1915 at Neuve Chapelle, eight miles south of Armentières. It was hoped that it would lead to the seizing of the Aubers "Ridge", a gentle rise extending across the lowlands south of Lille. In this it failed; only the first of three stages was completed. But this attack, though made by only three divisions, had been important because for the first time the British used, on a narrow front, a concentration of artillery fire hitherto impossible for them, and had found that by this means they could shatter and seize a section of the enemy's front line. British commanders and their

[1] See the British Official History, 1915, Vol. I, pp. 17, 73.

troops felt this to be encouraging evidence of what the British Army would be able to do when it would have ample artillery and ammunition.

The preparation for a second offensive in the same region—this time in co-operation with the French at Arras—had been interrupted by the Germans' attacking on April 22nd (three days before the Gallipoli Landing) at Ypres. Characteristically the Germans achieved surprise mainly by breaking a treaty—their engagement not to use poison gas. Two French divisions north of Ypres, against whom the attack was directly made, were shattered; but the 1st Canadian Division, brought to France two months before and now happening to be posted next to the French, held on although the Germans drove far behind its flank. The line around Ypres was adjusted; the Allies had lost the main ridge there at Broodseinde hamlet and Polygon Wood, but still held a salient farther back on the flats and low ridges nearer to the town.[2]

The attack previously planned by the Allies, and thus interrupted, was undertaken in May 1915—the French using 20 divisions and 1400 guns in an effort to gain Vimy Ridge, and the British employing a small force at Festubert. Both failed disastrously. It was not till September 1915 that the British undertook the second important offensive. In a big attempt by the Allies against both sides of the great bulge, some ground was gained by the French in Champagne and at Vimy, and by the British beside them at Loos; but everywhere the attempt to push farther brought immense losses. The British command at Loos attributed the failure there to having the reserve divisions too far back to take advantage of the early success, and the staff bore this circumstance in mind when planning future offensives. The regimental officers

---

2 The Germans did not expect, or attempt, to break through. They launched a second gas cloud, this time against the Canadians, on April 24th, and others against the British on May 1st and 2nd. The troops had only improvised respirators—the Canadians only wet rags; but with great bravery all these attacks were held.

and men on the other hand, both French and British, were beginning to feel that, in the conditions of that war on the Western Front, neither side could break through the other. At the end of 1915 the British commander-in-chief, Sir John French, was replaced by the dour, hard-hitting General Haig.

These events were still fresh in memory in March-April 1916 when the Australians and New Zealanders arrived on the Western Front. The Germans attacking at Verdun in February seemed for the moment to have hit on a possible solution for the deadlock—erasing a section of defences by bombardment of unheard-of intensity, and then occupying the devastated ground and repeating the process against the next section of defences. But in that smoking cauldron the Germans were still advancing only by slow stages, and the conditions were really no exception to the general stalemate. In Flanders for two or three weeks the Anzacs were given the usual training—with lectures on the methods of billeting, of relieving trench-garrisons, of preventing frost-bite, of bathing and disinfection in the military baths. Most of the troops passed in gas helmets through a trench filled with chlorine gas; many saw an exhibition of flame projectors, then being used by Germans in some attacks. A number of selected officers and men were sent to trench-mortar, sniping, bombing and other training schools.[3]

On April 1st parties began to visit the line on reconnaissance, and numbers of artillerymen were attached to the British batteries covering the line. Within the next week advanced parties and specialists went up to the line and on the night of April 7th the 2nd Division, whose brigades had been marching up for three days, began to take over a sector. By the end of the following week the 1st Division was entering the line south of the 2nd. On April 13th the I Anzac Corps took over from the

---

[3] As in Roman, and even Persian, times the efficiency of armies largely depended upon elaborate schooling.

II British Corps the command south-east of Armentières. A month later the New Zealand Division also was brought into the line, north of the 2nd, on the eastern outskirts of Armentières.

The three months, May-July 1916, were, for most Australian soldiers, their outstanding experience of trench warfare in its most settled form. About half the troops had learnt trench warfare in Gallipoli, but here in Flanders it was less tense and more comfortable. Food, brought up on the tramways by nightly ration parties, was more varied; water was "laid on" through pipes. Instead of steep, dusty paths leading almost immediately down to the sea

lapping the shingles, there was an approach through mile-long communication trenches, winding through green fields and hedgerows. Behind these were country roads, farms and villages to which the battalions and brigades were regularly withdrawn for rest. There were shops in the villages, and *estaminets* selling Flemish beer and cheap wine—at least one of them within 800 yards of the firing line;[4] men hopped out of a communication trench to go across the fields to it. Farther back were excellent British canteens, reading and writing rooms, army baths where underclothing was periodically freed from fleas and lice. Many of the townspeople still lived in Armentières, and the cold weather and the presence of women, seconding the efforts of the staff here and in Egypt, resulted in the disappearance of

---

4 "Spy Farm", see *Vol. III, p. 136 and plate facing p. 108.*

the "Anzac uniform", and an increased tidiness in the
troops' dress which, if seldom rivalling the tight smartness
of the British uniforms, became noted as the most workmanlike on the front. Despite the training in Egypt, no
regulations or explanations could induce Australians to
salute all officers met, at least when off duty: their sense
taught them the much modified practice which has since
been generally adopted.

A further advantage, unheard of in Gallipoli, was
that of periodical leave—at about yearly intervals—to
Great Britain. This home of most of their ancestors, to
which nearly all Australians had longed to make pil-
grimage, was now only seventy miles behind them. Many
of their wounded had been sent thither from Gallipoli.
The administrative headquarters of the A.I.F. was now
being moved thither from Egypt; a Wesleyan Methodist
Training College in Horseferry Road, Westminster, had
already been taken over for offices, and the training
depots were being established on Salisbury Plain, with
an admirable system of a training battalion for the new
reinforcements of each infantry brigade, and four convalescent depots (known as "Command Depots") for the
return to Australia, or to the front, of men from hospital.
Later was added the "Overseas Training Brigade", in
which those men from the convalescent depots who were
fit for return to the front were given a final hardening-
up—largely a matter of morale after the comparative slackness of convalescence. Separate from all these troops the
new 3rd Australian Division, raised in Australia, began
to arrive in July at Salisbury Plain for training under its
own staff.

With these resources—much closer, fuller, and better
organised than previously in Egypt—the Australians also
had better weapons available than in Gallipoli. The
machine-guns and their crews had, in Egypt, been taken
away from the infantry battalions and organised in companies, one to each infantry brigade; but four Lewis

guns—weapons new to the Anzacs—had been allotted to each infantry battalion (one per company) instead. Trench mortars of three types, light, medium and heavy, had been allotted to batteries specially raised from the infantry, the light mortar being the newly invented "Stokes Gun", then still a jealously guarded "secret weapon". Each division's artillery had, in addition to its twelve batteries of 18-pounder field-guns, three batteries of 4.5-inch howitzers, though the Australian gunners had to be trained for these after arrival in France.

Moreover the troops had been equipped with steel helmets of the oval, saucer-like British pattern; and during the next three months their cloth gas-helmets were replaced by "small box-respirators"—an admirable invention following closely, though independent of, one made earlier at Melbourne University. But perhaps actually the most important change from Gallipoli warfare was that over their heads there now frequently hummed aeroplanes, British or German, followed by the fleecy puffs of anti-aircraft guns by day, and occasionally by searchlight beams at night.

The troops were conscious that they were now face to face with a much more formidable opponent than in Gallipoli, and they expected a kind of warfare more sophisticated than at Anzac. Yet there were several surprises. In that wet country the "trenches", though to anyone passing through them they

A communication "trench".

might in many parts appear to be true trenches, were

actually breastworks built of sandbags above ground
level—any excavated trench was at once waterfilled. Partly
for this reason, but partly because concrete construction
was hardly yet attempted in the British zone, where fortification had been less vigorous than at Anzac, there
existed in the whole area no safe shelter against even
medium high-explosive shells. Sniping was not nearly so
keen as on Gallipoli, nor did anything approaching the
tension of Anzac exist. Mining was done by special companies of tunneliers with whose work the infantry had
nothing like the intimacy that reigned at Anzac. The fire
of the supporting artillery was at this time—for reasons
then unknown to the troops—restricted to three rounds
daily for each field gun, except in emergencies. The German gunners at that stage fired much more freely.

Yet there were some signs that this was likely to be a
tougher campaign than any at Anzac. Little was seen of
the Germans—occasionally a grey-clad figure or two were
detected through an observer's telescope, passing down
some distant path overlooked from one of the houses or
other high points behind our line; sometimes at night
dark figures were silhouetted for a moment in no-man's-
land. But the Australians—always, in that war, over-
careless in exposing themselves to view—came by many
bitter experiences at last to realise that their own movements were patiently watched and methodically noted.

The day after a company of the 9th Battalion had
relieved some British infantry in a farmhouse two miles
behind the front, a shell whizzed down and burst in the
road near by; other shells quickly followed, the fourth
bursting in a doorway. Next a wall was brought down,
injuring fifty men. Within a few minutes 2 officers and
72 men had been killed or wounded. In the next few days
first one farmhouse then another, crammed with Australians, was as suddenly smashed. The troops looked for
spies—and in one case reported to the French police a

man whose movements during the shelling they considered "suspicious". He proved to be a worthy citizen, his excited movements being apparently due to the fact that it was his house that was being demolished.

It was not till they had lost several hundred men in this way that the Australians realised that the eyes watching them were not those of spies—who indeed in that war were rarely, if ever, found in or near the trench area. The eyes that noted the movement of the troops were in far-off trees behind the German lines, or were on the low hills that formed the horizon, or in some captive balloon that, like a fat garden grub, hung tethered in the sky above both trees and hills. It was the troops who betrayed themselves, by hanging out their washing on the side of the farm exposed to the enemy's view, or themselves lounging there, or lighting fires which smoked, or crowding on to the skyline to watch an aeroplane dodge the enemy's shells. Indeed it was not till 1917 that the Australian soldier thoroughly learnt that, although spies —often women or "commercial travellers"—did exist in the towns behind the line and the current talk of the back areas of each side normally reached the other side via neutral countries within a week, yet by far the most abundant and important information secured by each side was obtained by its forward troops, patiently watching their opponent, and when possible capturing one of him for cross-questioning.

The troops gradually realised that the German intelligence organisation was a most formidable machine, unlike anything they had known in Gallipoli. They also at once found to their cost that the German sniper, though less active than their own, was a deadly marksman. A tussle at once ensued; but though the Germans noted (as some of their histories show) that their opponents now shot terribly straight, and caused sharp losses, the German sniper's efficiency was always formidable. In the nightly patrolling of no-man's-land—usually a tangled, dishevelled meadow some 200 yards wide—although the Dominion troops prided themselves on clever and vigorous scouting, the Germans at this time were well trained, bold and persistent. On each side many an outstanding intelligence officer and scout was killed in these nightly expeditions along ditches and through tussocks towards the opponent's wire.

Active fighting by the Anzacs was at first confined to this patrolling and to sniping. It is true that at intervals there came down the line at night—often from some sector far to north or south—a sudden clangour of gas-gongs, hooting of sirens and blowing of horns—the alarm for a gas attack. On the first occasion this was due to a shelling of nearby British battery-positions with tear gas. On the second occasion, with even less justification, some-one fired a gas-alarm rocket and caused part of the 2nd Division's artillery to put down its first "barrage" on the German front line, a spectacle that gave much confidence to the infantry. On the night of June 16th the Germans ten miles north, at Messines, attacked the opposing British with cloud gas. The cloud was calmly met though 400 British soldiers were gassed. A few Australians who happened to be there were unhurt. The gas, chlorine and phosgene, then floated gradually across the Australian back area, nipping the crops and, according to one report, killing two young French children, but harming no Aus-tralians except one cyclist who had forgotten to carry his helmet and rode in haste to find it. This was the only time that the A.I.F. had to face cloud gas, which, as shell gas became more effective, the Germans gradually ceased to use.

By then, however, the Anzacs had experienced a much sharper incident of regular trench warfare, of a kind also unknown in Gallipoli though then common in France. At nightfall on May 5th there suddenly descended on a prominent bend of the Australian line, known as the Bridoux Salient, a deluge of German shells and trench-mortar bombs, a concentration of fire such as Australian troops had never known—and probably as severe while it lasted as any they afterwards suffered. The enemy had shelled and trench-mortared this place in the previous few days, and a couple of the new Stokes mortars had been sent up there and had replied. For two hours there arrived no news from the area under the bombardment—that of the 20th Battalion; all telephone lines had been cut and no messenger came through. Two rockets, however, had gone up from it—these were the "SOS" call for an artillery barrage, which was at once laid on the enemy's parapet; and reports arrived from the Australian battalions on each flank that they had seen Germans crossing no-man's-land.

At the end of two hours the uproar subsided almost as quickly as it had arisen. The "trenches" were a shambles —a mass of tumbled sandbags and other debris; but the survivors of the garrison appeared to be still among them though about 100 had been killed or wounded. It was only next morning that the finding of some German grenades amid the debris, and the reports from some of the men, proved that their trenches must have been entered by the enemy. Next the German wireless announced that the Germans had captured "some prisoners, two machine-guns and two trench mortars". The commander of the British 2nd Army at once inquired of I Anzac Corps whether this was true; and only then was it ascertained that, besides some men, the two precious Stokes mortars—Britain's secret weapon—were missing. By order from G.H.Q. they should have been brought back on the previous day, after their shoot; but an officer, unaware of the order, had most carelessly left them in the front line for further use.

It was long before the Australian infantry in France lived down the results of this incident, all the more mortifying because some British newspapers were making "copy" out of heroics concerning the Anzacs, who them-

selves were most conscious of being over-publicised at
a time when they were still really untried on this front.
The Anzac staff also was moved to severe measures against
the battalion command, which it believed to be responsible for allowing the enemy to enter the line. The staff
soon came to learn that, after such bombardment, no
army could prevent its line being entered, and that blame
rather attached to itself for crowding its front line with
troops instead of holding it very lightly and relying on
reserves in depth. In justice to the staff it must be said
that they fully accepted this principle, which indeed
G.H.Q. had enjoined, but that they considered the state
of the wire and trenches so bad that defence in depth
could not safely be adopted until the drastic improve-
ments, with which they were most vigorously pressing on,
had been completed.

Early on the night of 30th May a similar bombardment suddenly descended on a salient farther south, near
Cordonnerie Farm, in the sector of the 11th Battalion
(1st Division). Here mining had been in progress, and
the recently arrived 2nd Australian Tunnelling Company had just relieved some British miners. The deluge
of shell and mortar fire was, if anything, even heavier
than before, and the defences were thoroughly smashed.
Here, too, it was discovered that there were 110 of the
garrison killed or wounded among the debris, and 6 were
missing. The Germans had tried ineffectually to blow
up a mine-shaft.

Many interesting facts about these raids—as about
much else in this history—were unknown to Australians
until German records became available during the years
after the war. These show that in both the raids here
mentioned the Australians fought back, inflicting in
the first raid 20 casualties. As to the secret of the Stokes
mortars, a special study of those records made by an
officer of the German archives disclosed the astonishing
fact that, although both the captured mortars were carried

13-os

into the German lines, no special importance was attached to them nor is there any sign that they were ever recognised as Stokes guns.

The Australians had by then already begun to plan their own raids on the enemy. What force had first invented "trench raids" may probably never be certain. Their chief object was to secure information, which was best achieved by visiting the enemy lines and securing prisoners for cross-examination. Early in the war, and so long as patrols in their normal prowlings could capture prisoners, the need for specially planned raids did not exist. But as the campaign had become restricted by continuous trench-lines, and patrols were confined to a narrow and dangerous no-man's-land, the capture of prisoners by patrols had become rare. The surest method for doing so was now actually to enter the enemy trench or at least one of the advanced listening-posts which were pushed out like a fringe into no-man's-land.

Such entry was sometimes achieved by sheer surprise—a method in which the Canadians were reputed to have had success. But it had been found that, by sufficiently bombarding the enemy trench, breaking down his wire and cowing his garrison, and then placing the artillery fire as a "box barrage" around the point to be raided, cutting off the enemy's access and exit, his line could be entered and prisoners taken almost at will. The raiders often had to face the enemy's shell or machine-gun fire, at least on their return; and where the bombardment was insufficient these small affairs were often costly. Nevertheless the identification of the troops holding the opposing line was vital; and as these operations (which the Germans called "patrol enterprises") gave experience in planning and fighting, remedied the tendency to slackness and stagnation in siege warfare, and, when successful, gave confidence to the troops, they were being increasingly ordered by the command on both sides. The German

staff, however, usually allotted ammunition for a far
heavier bombardment than did the British.

The first Australian raid was made on the night of
June 5th at the south-eastern outskirts of Armentières,
the raiding party of the 7th Brigade being under Captain
Maitland Foss, a Western Australian farmer. The raid
had been carefully practised and each man and section
knew their particular work. The trenches were entered.
Foss flashing his torch round a box-shelter in the German
breastwork saw a frightened boy, pulled him out, and
swung him over the parapet to the waiting scouts. The
trenches were blocked and searched, and more Germans
taken and a few killed, before, on Foss's signal, the raiders
withdrew. About 30 Australians were hit, mostly in their
own trenches, by the reply of the German artillery.

This raid raised the confidence of the Anzac troops.
Their own men had been in the German trenches and
their artillery had dealt with the enemy as it pleased. The
raid was quickly followed by several others, each Australian brigade having prepared one or more, and the
New Zealand Division, now in line on the left of the 1st
and 2nd Australian, having done the same. By the time
the third had been undertaken a much more crowded
programme of them—already foreshadowed by an order
from the commander-in-chief, Sir Douglas Haig, on
May 28th—was put into operation. As many raids as possible were to be carried out between June 20th and 30th.

The reason for this, known only to the higher commanders, was that the great Anglo-French offensive, for
which all possible troops and ammunition had been con-
served since the failure of those in September and October
1915, was about to be launched. The new British Army
had now arrived in strength in France and been tested in
trench warfare. With the help of American manufacture,
Britain's programme of gun, machine-gun, bomb and
ammunition supply was at last approaching the stage that
would place her previously ill-supported infantry on an

almost equal footing with the French and Germans. In December 1915 the Allies had renewed the decision not to strike again until the British were ready, but then to strike together from all sides. On the Western Front the

THE INTENDED ALLIED OFFENSIVES FOR 1916
The arrows show the intended attacks.

French and British under Marshal Joffre and General Haig were to attack where their lines joined, that is, in front of Amiens astride of the Somme River. The French would attack with 39 divisions on a thirty-mile front south of the river, the British with, possibly, 25 divisions north of it. At the request of Joffre, to whom, by agreement between the two governments, was left the direction of the main strategy on the Western Front, the British were first to make a wearing-out attack on some other part of the front and to engage in vigorous raiding. As the Russians were not expected to be ready before June

the main Franco-British attack had, as long ago as
February 14th, been fixed for July 1st.

But the German offensive at Verdun had forced the
Allies greatly to modify this plan. The Germans had
turned against the French in the belief that Hindenburg
in his victorious offensives on the eastern front in 1915
had so shaken the Russians that they could not return
to the offensive, especially as the coming revolution in
Russia was already foreseen. With that great opponent
apparently so crippled and Serbia defeated, the chief
of the German General Staff, General von Falkenhayn
had no fears as to the east; in the south the Italian
army had been outmatched by the Austrian. Falkenhayn
believed that there had now returned a chance to force
his main opponents—England and France—out of the war.
The German Navy told him that he could not reach
England with his troops; and he believed that the defeat
of Italy would "make no serious impression on England".
But if he crushed France, "England's best sword would
be struck out of her hand". With that intention he had
attacked Verdun. It was also intended to attack England
directly by an "unrestricted" submarine campaign—that
is, by sinking without warning any ships met with in the
approaches to the British Isles.

Towards his object of "bleeding France to death" at
Verdun, Falkenhayn achieved much success; the battle
gradually absorbed most of the troops whom Joffre had
intended to employ in the French offensive south of the
Somme. General Pétain maintained the spirit of the Verdun defence by letting each division know that, after it
had achieved its task, it would immediately be relieved.
This was designed to prevent the complete exhaustion of
any division, but it also resulted in the number of French
divisions available for the Somme falling by mid-June to
16, all of them previously used but not exhausted.
The great offensive would now be predominantly British;
and, as the British also had to help the defence of Verdun

by taking over a sector held by the French at Arras, General Haig decided not to deliver any preliminary thrust but to use all his available reserve for the main stroke. The French, who since February had been bearing the whole brunt of the enemy's effort at Verdun, naturally wanted early action by the British. To Haig's proposal to postpone the main attack until August Joffre objected that if there were any such delay Verdun would certainly fall.

The Russians had, most loyally and against the German expectation, attacked the Germans on the north-eastern front in March. The attack was unskilful and unsuccessful, but, under Brusiloff, early in June they also attacked the south-eastern front and drove through the Austrian flanks. The Austrians, without informing the Germans beforehand, had used their best troops in launching a "private" offensive against the Italians. The situation was dangerous for Germany, especially as Rumania was clearly about to join the Allies. In this crisis the Germans sent help to Austria, but only on condition that the control of strategy should henceforth lie with the German high command. Against these conditions, generally favourable to the Allies, there weighed the fact that a large Franco-British force lay quite uselessly in the Salonica region, and in Mesopotamia the Turks had cut off and, on 29th April 1916, captured the Anglo-Indian striking force at Kut el Amara on the Tigris. Another Turkish force was about to attack the Suez Canal.

By June the plan for the Somme offensive had dwindled to an attack by 13 British divisions and 6 French ones on a front of twenty-three miles, with 6 more British divisions and perhaps 10 French ones in support. The attack was to be preceded by a bombardment far heavier than any before known to the British Army, lasting for five days and covering the German line for several miles in depth. But the only preliminary operations now envisaged by Haig would be the raids, great and small, on all parts of the British front.

Before the arrival of I Anzac in France its three divisions had been included in the troops intended for use in the Somme offensive; but a report from General Murray that part of their artillery was untrained had caused this decision to be altered. When, however, a preliminary British offensive was planned, and seemed likely to take the form of an attack on Messines (where the German line north of Armentières bent forward to enclose an important ridge) the commander of 2nd Army, General Plumer, asked for the I Anzac Corps to be allotted to him as part of the attacking force; he had commanded Australians and New Zealanders in South Africa. This was ordered, and on June 17th a brigade of the 2nd Australian Division followed by one from the 1st took over the front opposite Messines. A plan of attack was submitted by Generals Birdwood and White, and preparations were made to move thither the whole corps. By this time, however, it was certain that the attack would not be undertaken as a preliminary to the main offensive; what Haig now envisaged was that, if the Germans by rushing all reserves from the north managed to bring to a halt the coming Allied thrust on the Somme, the main British effort might be transferred to Messines.

Meanwhile the preliminary trench raids were launched all along the British front. In the sector of I Anzac Corps five raids were undertaken between the night of June 25th and the launching of the great offensive on July 1st, and in the next two nights five more. The task was carried out with vigour. By keen sniping and shelling the liveliness of "the nursery" had already been much increased, but, in this week, from being one of the quietest areas on the front it became one of marked tension. The corps suffered 773 casualties as against an average of 563 for each of the four other corps of 2nd Army. The loss among the Germans was probably higher;

in eight raids of which German accounts are available the enemy lost 522 men, 144 of them killed and 46 missing (a few of these casualties may have been due to other operations). In all 59 German prisoners were taken, 21 of them in a famous raid by parties of the 9th Battalion under Captain Wilder-Neligan just north of the Sugar Loaf salient[5] at the southern end of the Anzac sector. A much bigger operation against that salient was suggested by the British commander there but was held over as a future possibility.

The German infantry in that area became noticeably nervous, never knowing where the next stroke would fall. Yet they were mainly good troops, Bavarians and Prussians, and they presently replied effectively by themselves raiding, and also by improving their preparedness with the result that the New Zealand Division, launching another series of raids in the following week, was, for all its bravery, sharply repulsed.

Just before the great offensive on the Somme, General Joffre appealed to Haig to allot additional troops to that offensive, so that it might be maintained with a vigour which would force the Germans to cease their attacks at Verdun. It was with this in view that Haig on June 30th warned 2nd Army that the I Anzac Corps, instead of being sent to Messines, might have to be called south at any moment. In any case I Anzac was now about to leave the "nursery" front, this being made possible by the arrival from Egypt of the II Anzac Corps under General Godley.

---

[5] See Vol. III, pp. 273 et seq.

CHAPTER XIV

THE START ON THE SOMME—AND FROMELLES

THE two new Australian infantry divisions, 4th and 5th, which had been formed at the end of February, but left in Egypt for three months to create their artillery, had received at the end of May the order to move to the Western Front. The creation of that artillery was a task unparalleled in British experience, and is the classic example of the speed with which Australians could be trained.

To instruct the 3000 artillery officers and men required by each division, some 150 trained officers and men from the older divisions were allotted to each. The rest were light horsemen and infantrymen together with a few hundred artillery reinforcements, mostly untrained, and a handful from the engineer and other services. The 4th Division had not one regular artillery officer. For instructing the 12th Field Artillery Brigade Lieut.-Colonel R. A. Rabett (who himself started in the war as a young militia officer) had 5 artillery officers—3 with Anzac experience and 2 reinforcements—and some 30 more or less experienced artillerymen. He had to select 17 officers from non-artillery units, and train them each morning from 4.30 to 6.30, when they in turn began teaching their men. Within a fortnight the new officers, themselves being lectured for four hours daily, and teaching their men for eight hours, were producing results. Only five guns were available, but these were used in relays. In April the artillery were sent to join their infantry on the Canal defences where instruction continued.

In the training of the infantry of these divisions there occurred the harshest experience that the A.I.F.'s instruction had ever included. When the older divisions were being moved from the Canal there occurred a shortage of trains to take the new divisions to the Canal. It was therefore decided that all except the leading troops (the 8th Brigade and a battalion of the 4th) should march thither across the desert. The distance was less than forty miles comprising two fifteen-mile stages and a shorter stage on the third day. It was decided to make the march a test, the men carrying full kit, packs, and ammunition.

But even in Monash's, Glasgow's and Glasfurd's brigades, which took the usual precautions for desert marching, the movement was accomplished only with great suffering on the part of the troops. In the 14th Brigade, however, possibly because men broke the ranks in order to drink the foul water of the "Sweet-water" Canal, which lay beside part of the route, the brigadier (who was afterwards removed for this mistake) insisted on their marching on through the midday hours. The process ended in an almost complete break-down; parched and exhausted men staggered into the New Zealanders' camp at Moascar on the second evening, leaving many to be picked up during the night by the ambulances and by the succouring New Zealanders. It was rumoured later that some men died through the results; a search of the records after the war did not confirm this, but it may nevertheless have been correct.

On arrival in France the 4th Division, in which the "outside" States—Queensland, S. and W. Australia and Tasmania—were much more strongly represented than in any other division,[1] began to enter the line towards the end of June, and by July 4th its artillerymen, who in March had been light horsemen and infantrymen, were responsible for covering their sector of the Western

---

[1] It was composed of three all-States brigades—Monash's 4th Bde, the 12th Bde (formed from the 4th), and the 13th (formed from the 3rd).

Front. This division had by then already raided the Germans, and it was itself raided while its artillery was relieving that of the 2nd Division. (Though the Germans captured a prisoner, their staff remained unaware that the 4th and 5th Australian Divisions had left Egypt.) By July 5th the 1st and 2nd Divisions had been relieved. General Godley and the staff of II Anzac became responsible for the sector, the New Zealand Division remaining there under them, with the 5th Australian Division from Egypt just arriving in the back area. The 1st and 2nd under Birdwood and the staff of I Anzac were moving into the sector opposite Messines when, on July 7th, orders arrived that by the 13th they must be in the Amiens area, sixty miles to the south, ready for a continuation of the Somme offensive. The project of a stroke against Messines had for the present been given up, and plans and maps for that scheme, then in preparation by I Anzac at Bailleul, were returned to the 2nd Army staff.

For the great Somme offensive was then in full swing. A week previously, on 1st July 1916, the British and French armies twenty miles east of Amiens had launched their attack astride that river. After a bombardment, which eventually was extended to seven days, the 4th British Army (General Sir Henry Rawlinson) together with part of the 3rd, and a group of French armies under General Foch, were to break the German line, striking in three stages towards Bapaume, ten miles away. If, as was hoped, in any of these stages a sufficient breach was made, a British "Reserve Army", chiefly of cavalry, under the cavalry leader, General Sir Hubert Gough, would try to push through to the Bapaume plateau and then, turning north, would "roll up" the German line north of the breach.

The bombardment (in which two siege batteries formed from the regular Australian garrison artillery took part) had since June 25th methodically smashed the German defences. At one time every gun and howitzer

would fire rapidly with high explosive for twelve minutes
on all the villages, following this fire with shrapnel to
catch any troops disturbed by this deluge. On other days
all German batteries known to the British intelligence
staff were shelled; or trenches of the first and second lines
were taken under fire and methodically battered down
from end to end; or a barrage, like that which would precede the infantry's advance, was laid on the enemy's front
line, and then lengthened, and then suddenly brought
back to catch the German infantry, who might be
manning the parapet in expectation of attack. The
"bump" of the guns could be heard in England, and
under the long drawn out strain the German garrison,
whose food, drink and ammunition parties sometimes
could not get through, lost in some parts its power of
resistance.

Thus, when the attack came, on the sector astride the
Somme, where Foch's armies for their six-mile front were
supported by no less than 900 heavy pieces of artillery,
two splendid French corps, the XX north of the Somme
and the I Colonial Corps south of the river, penetrated
so fast that the German command opposite to them hastily
withdrew its troops to a line close in front of Péronne
town, six miles away. The British right flank, immediately north of the French, advanced to the same depth,
reaching Montauban village, on the ridge on which lay
the second German defence system. It was only through
Sir Douglas Haig's insistence—against the view of the less
optimistic commander of the 4th Army, General Rawlinson—that the first British thrust had been designed to
go so deep.

But the British Army, though supported by artillery
and ammunition on a scale previously unknown to it,
was not yet gunned on a scale comparable with the
French. Behind its fifteen and a half miles of front were
some 400 heavy pieces, and the 12,776 tons of shells used
by them on the first day was only half of what the British

were able to throw at the Germans on the first day of
the Battle of Arras, nine months later. The deep German
dugouts were almost unaffected by the bombardment; at
the La Boisselle ruins, on the road from Albert to
Bapaume, a little north of the British penetration to
Montauban, the attacking troops, Tynesiders of the 34th
"New Army" Division, were, for all their devotion, held
up practically at the front line. Farther north, where the
3rd British Army attacked with less powerful artillery
support, the assault, though it went deep at several points,
was largely stopped at the front line, with tragic losses.
That day the 29th Division lost 5000 men and the 36th
(Ulster) Division, which, with part of the 32nd, had
pushed to and beyond Thiepval on the ridge that but-
tressed the northern flank of the Germans, lost 5500.

Despite such losses a tremendous blow had been
struck; and though the achievements did not approach
the stage at which Gough's Reserve Army could be used,
nevertheless decisive results seemed to Haig within reach.
He knew he must first widen the wedge driven into the
German line, and, to do this, must take Thiepval. Joffre
vigorously urged him to attack Thiepval again frontally,
but Haig was determined to drive farther on the southern
flank, where his success had been greatest, and then attack
Thiepval from there. He accordingly placed General
Gough in command of the front facing Thiepval, the
divisions there becoming the "Reserve Army". Gough
was ordered to hold the enemy while Rawlinson with the
4th Army continued to drive ahead.

In the hope of great success within the next few days
Haig ordered his other armies, even in Flanders, to be
ready to attack at favourable points. But instead it took
a week of costly, piecemeal fighting before parts of the
4th Army were far enough forward to prepare an attack
on the Germans' second defence system. Then, in a
second great attack, launched on July 14th after two
days' bombardment, the 4th Army, after approaching (by

Rawlinson's plan) at night and attacking at dawn, carried the British line across a central part of the ridge on which the German second line lay.

The breach now made in that line was only two miles wide—the III British Corps attempting to extend it had been prevented by the stubborn defence of Pozières village, a sort of advanced post of the second line— and Thiepval, two miles to the north-west, was thus safeguarded. But a few squadrons of British and Indian cavalry were actually brought up to the centre of the breach, at High Wood, and looked out over the next wide valley above the far side of

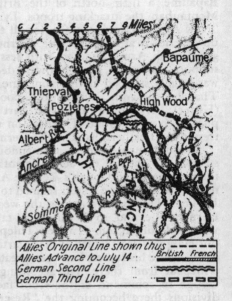

Allies' Original Line shown thus ----
Allies' Advance to July 14   British French
German Second Line
German Third Line

which lay Bapaume. There was never the least chance that this cavalry could be effectively used that day, even if two trench-lines and many other works had not still lain beyond.

Nevertheless again a heavy blow had been struck at the enemy; that his strongest defence lines could be pierced by the newly raised British armies had now been proved. Twenty-five British divisions had already been thrown in, and the cost was already approaching 100,000 men, killed, wounded or missing. But some of the exhausted divisions had already been sent to other parts of the front from which fresh divisions were brought down to replace them. However, the Germans were now found to have been doing likewise; on July 13th among the Germans on the Somme were found some just transported from Lille. The British staff at once thought of a recently suggested plan for a British attack south of Lille, which, if undertaken now, might pin the Germans to that front.

This project was to attack the Sugar Loaf salient, opposite the southern end of the II Anzac line south of Armentières. Lieut.-General Haking, the commander of the XI British Corps, which lay south of II Anzac, had been urging as a practicable operation a combined attack from his and the Anzac sectors, to cut off that salient and incorporate the ground permanently in the British 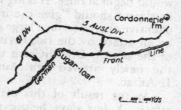 line. An advance here might seem to threaten the German possession of the Aubers Ridge, just south of Lille—where already, in 1915, the British had made two costly and unsuccessful attempts.[2]

On July 12th it had been decided that this project was unsuitable for the purpose then in view[3]; but now Haig's staff suggested that an artillery demonstration against the Sugar Loaf salient might deter the Germans from transferring more of their troops from that region to the Somme. Accordingly on July 13th staff officers from G.H.Q. hurried to discuss this project with the 1st Army commander (Sir Charles Monro, back from his Mediterranean command) and the staffs concerned. As

---

[2] See Vol. III, pp. 108-9.

[3] The original object of the proposed operation was to take advantage of any weakening of the German line in the north.

the Sugar Loaf lay opposite the boundary of two British armies, 1st and 2nd, each of them could contribute guns and ammunition for a strong artillery demonstration.

Haig's staff did not propose that the infantry should attack at all; but they found that Monro and the army staffs favoured General Haking's plan, which was an extensive one for employing three divisions (eventually reduced to two) and even, if possible, capturing the Aubers Ridge near where it was topped by the straggling village of Fromelles, a mile behind the German line. General Haking was to command the operation; and the bombardment, which was to last for about three days, would begin at once. Haking now proposed that his bombardment should "give the impression of an impending offensive operation on a large scale". It would be followed by an attack by the two divisions, one against each side of the salient. One division would be British, the other the newly arrived 5th Australian Division lent by II Anzac.

As the result of this conference Haig ordered the attack. A few days before this proposal G.H.Q. had decided, though with doubts, that the 4th Australian Division despite its having entered the Western Front line only a week before, should be sent with the 1st and 2nd to the Somme, leaving behind, however, its newly raised artillery. The British artillery normally serving the Lahore Division of the Indian Army would accompany it instead. Most of the 4th Division had been in the line only three days when, on July 10th and 11th, the still less experienced infantry of the 5th was hurried forward and relieved it. The half-fledged artillery of the 4th helped that of the 5th to acquaint itself with the Western Front, and was then attached to it for the coming "demonstration".

General Haking's conviction that the Sugar Loaf salient would be captured and held was apparently undiminished by the costly failure of a closely similar operation undertaken by him on June 29th against the Boar's Head salient four miles farther south. The present attack was to be made with much heavier artillery—258 field-guns and howitzers with 215,000 shells, and 64 medium and heavy pieces, mainly "60 pounders", with a due allowance of ammunition. There would be a field-gun or howitzer to every 15 yards of the 4000 yards front to be attacked, though the barrage would be less concentrated than that figure might imply. At several intervals during July 17th the artillery would lay half an hour's barrage on the German front trench system to be attacked, and would then suddenly lengthen range and throw its shells beyond. It was hoped that the Germans, assuming this to be the immediate prelude to attack, would man their parapets. The artillery would next suddenly bring its fire back to the front system in order to catch them there. It was hoped that after several such experiences the Germans would be shy of manning their trenches quickly. This might give our infantry—when, at dusk, it did attack after a strong barrage—the chance of crossing no-man's-land, in some parts 400 yards wide, before the Germans were ready to defend their trench. Further to help them to cross in time, opposite the Sugar Loaf, where no-man's-land was widest, the infantry would begin the crossing while the barrage was still falling.

Despite these and other precautions, Haig's staff was still highly doubtful about the project—one of them who visited the line with Brig.-General H. E. ("Pompey") Elliott formed the opinion that there was grave risk of disaster. On July 16th a leading officer of Haig's staff again went north to First Army, questioned the sufficiency of artillery and ammunition, and stated that the need for the operation was then no longer urgent. However, General Haking "was most emphatic" that the artillery was "ample"; and the commanders present said that the troops "were ready and anxious" to make the attack, and its cancellation would be bad for morale. They therefore urged that unless it would actually hamper the Somme operations, it should be carried out.

Notwithstanding the opinions of these commanders the troops were, in truth, far from ready. In the 5th Division the plans had been sprung on Maj.-General M'Cay on the night of July 12th on which he took over the line. Many of his troops had never yet been in a front line; and, when the day chosen for the attack (July 17th) actually dawned, in spite of their forced marches to the line and subsequent "side-slipping" on to the narrow front of attack—movements which kept many of them without sleep for most of two nights and two days—neither the infantry, artillery and trench mortars nor the ammunition were completely in position, nor were the necessary trench repairs finished. After the night-long approach through crowded communication "trenches", the weary infantry on reaching their proper bays dropped to the ground and fell asleep. The bombardment had begun the day before and was to continue during most of the morning.

But at this stage chance intervened. On the previous day the heavy artillery had been prevented by rain from registering its guns upon their targets, and now the country lay in thick mist. At 9 a.m. Haking asked for postponement of the attack and Monro agreed. The weary troops received the news with relief, and part of them were at once sent back to the reserve line and neighbouring villages to rest. General Monro now asked Haig if the project could be cancelled, but this time Haig, doubtless recalling the arguments of the previous day, insisted that it must be carried out as soon as possible— *if* Monro was satisfied that his artillery was sufficient and conditions favourable for the capture and holding of the Sugar Loaf. Haig had already ruled out Haking's proposal to push on to Aubers Ridge if opportunity occurred. It was decided to attack at 6 p.m. on July 19th, the final seven hours' bombardment beginning at 11 a.m. Down at the Somme Birdwood and White were acutely anxious as to the whole project but had no power to intervene.

However the troops of the 5th Australian and 61st British Divisions, which were to attack respectively the northern and western sides of the salient, were given at least one welcome day in which to rest and finish their preparations. Each division would attack with all its three brigades in line, but each brigade would use only two battalions for actual fighting; half of the third would carry ammunition and stores to the attacking troops—the other half would garrison the front system. The fourth battalion would be held in reserve.

July 19th was a bright summer's day, and during the bombardment, which began with mere registration but gradually increased in density, the infantry and other attacking troops from the rear moved gradually to the front line. Although the attacking troops were not aware that they were seen, signs of this movement—and of many preparations before it—were clearly visible to German observers a mile back among the trees and roofs on Aubers Ridge; in any case the bombardment since July 16th had warned the enemy that attack was probable. Early in the afternoon, therefore, the German guns began to shell heavily the area of the assembly. Half an hour before the attack the communication "trenches" had been so blown down or blocked that the 14th Australian Infantry Brigade sent the third and fourth waves of its attack formations over the open country to the front line. At the same time some of the troops opposite the Sugar Loaf began to move out into the very wide no-man's-land.

The Australians were in great fettle and were cheered to see the German parapets leaping into the air in shreds under the bombardment. The Germans were shelling no-man's-land, but their guns—73 light and 29 heavy—were insufficient to break up the two attacking divisions; and at 6 p.m., with three and a half hours of daylight still ahead, the general advance began.

In front of the left (8th) and centre (14th) brigades of the 5th Australian Division, no-man's-land was only 150-250 yards wide, and they quickly crossed it. The trenches of the 8th Brigade, on the left flank of the whole front of attack, had been so long and heavily shelled that several hundred Australians had been killed or wounded while waiting to advance. The fringe of their own artillery's barrage also caught them throughout the operation; and, when they leapt on to their parapet and walked down it into no-man's-land and towards the opposing breastwork, the Germans farther north, who were not being attacked, stubbornly manned their parapet despite hot fire from an English brigade which was to keep them quiet, and shot into the Australian flank. An Australian mine, which was fired there at "zero hour" in order that the thrown up earth might shelter the left flank, also announced the moment for the attack.

The men of the 8th Brigade had had no front-line experience until the last few days. But the brigade was well trained, and determined to show itself equal to the rest. Many men and leaders fell, but as the lines neared the German breastwork most of the enemy fled and the Australians, clambering up the sandbagged slope, fired from the top at men running away through neighbouring breastworks—alleys and dugouts—on to the flat, tousled grassland beyond. The left flank battalion, the 32nd, from Western Australia, seized and blocked the front line on that flank and also a long German communication trench, which led far to the enemy's rear past the stump of Delangré Farm. Leaving their first wave, as planned, to clear the front line, the second, third and fourth waves of the 31st (Queensland and Victoria) and 32nd pushed on as ordered to the grassland in search of the third and last line of the German front trench system which, they had been told, lay 150 yards beyond.

The two battalions of the 14th (New South Wales) Brigade on the right of the 8th had crossed no-man's-land

more easily, and found many of the garrison crouched
behind the breastworks or in concrete shelters built into
these. The front trench was quickly taken, but many
leaders were shot as they moved among Germans scattered
amid the breastworks just beyond. However, here too the
first wave was left to clear the front line; and the second,
third and fourth waves pushed on, through alleys between
the breastworks, and out into the meadows, where they
fired at Germans fleeing towards the higher ground sometimes visible in the distance through the haze of shell
smoke.

But here, all along the line, the scattered parties of
infantry and their leaders who emerged—mostly out of
touch or even sight of all other parties in the smoke haze—
were puzzled by the absence of any sign of the "third
trench" which they were to seize and hold as their front
line. They strolled on through the grass, like sportsmen
after quail, occasionally shooting at Germans who had
settled in shellholes and who now started up to run
farther. After crossing one or two watery ditches the
surviving leaders everywhere realised that some mistake
had been made; either the third trench shown on the map
did not exist, or one of these ditches must represent it.
Accordingly they gradually settled their men along the
ditches, in some sectors in the first ditch, in others in the
second. The troops began to fill their sandbags with mud
and made the best they could of the drains, though the
water in these was well over their boots and in parts
deeper.

Although actually the forward troops of 14th and 8th
Brigades thus formed a thin line of posts in the intended
position, the dust and smoke from their own barrage,
close ahead—and from enemy shells and exploding dumps
and, here and there, burning farms and villages—rendered
it difficult to see clearly, and few of the posts were aware
even of the general position of the others; and Colonel
Toll of the 31st, who with part of his troops had gone a

quarter of a mile or more before turning back, found no
recognisable "trench" except the old German front line,
and at sunset he withdrew most of his men to that
position.

The front line was thus disjointed. Nevertheless, in
the sector of these two brigades there was, at nightfall,
a fairly strong line in the position intended. The battalion commanders had established their headquarters in
the old German front line in various dugouts, some of
which were deep and well furnished. The carrying
parties were arriving with ammunition and stores; other parties
were digging trenches across the old no-man's-land; and
a number of messages reaching the brigadiers and Maj.-
General M'Cay gave an accurate account of this situation.

Unfortunately, in the sector of the right brigade (15th)
opposite the Sugar Loaf, where no-man's-land was widest,
the result feared by the staff officer from G.H.Q. had
happened. It is true that the bombardment had appeared
to be thorough. "Boys, you won't find a German when
you get there," Brig.-General "Pompey" Elliott had told
his men as he watched it. Yet even during the bombardment some German machine-guns had fired at the lines
of men beginning to leave the Australian trench; and
within two minutes of the bombardment's ending the fire
was fierce and rapidly swelling. Here no-man's-land
extended to a quarter of a mile in width, and from the
Australian trench it was difficult to see what happened.
At 6.15 the German fire died away and, judging from this
and other signs, Elliott at 6.30 reported that the attack
appeared to have succeeded.

Actually fire had ceased because the attack had been
shot to earth. The men of the 6th Bavarian Reserve
Division had managed to survive the shelling and to man
their machine-guns immediately the bombardment ceased.
And the Victorians of the 15th Brigade on emerging
from the remains of an old orchard, half-way across, had

met such a tempest of machine-gun and rifle fire that line after line, its leaders shot and its ranks decimated, was forced to shelter in ditches and furrows in the unkempt grass. The wide ditch known as the River Laies, crossing no-man's-land obliquely, became a death-trap down which swept fire from the German breastwork. The later lines, trudging across no-man's-land looking for their predecessors who, they imagined, must be lying ready for the final rush, met the same fire and found only dead and wounded and a few survivors in shellholes and the Bavarians lining the parapets, 150 yards away, firing at everything that moved, "and looking," as a survivor said, "as if they were wondering what was coming next". Of the two Victorian battalions here attacking 35 officers were hit, more than half of them mortally.

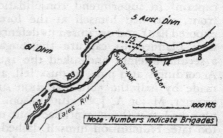

The extreme right flank of the 14th Brigade had been caught in the same manner and lay in no-man's-land next to the 15th. And the three brigades of the 61st British Division, which had attacked the other face of the salient, had been caught by German artillery and machine-guns during their assembly and in crossing no-man's-land. Except on the extreme right, where one British battalion seized, and for a short time held, a section of trench, they reached the German line only at isolated points, from which they were quickly driven back. Near the Sugar Loaf, though they were pinned down like the 15th Brigade, some troops were at first believed to have entered the enemy trench. Actually the only material success on the battlefield was that of the 8th and 14th

Australian Brigades which had captured 1000 yards of the enemy's front system.

By the non-success of the 15th Brigade the flank of the 14th was from the first exposed to the Germans who still held the Sugar Loaf. All senior officers of the 53rd Battalion having been killed or wounded, this section was under a young Duntroon graduate, Captain C. Arblaster of the 53rd Battalion, who, leaving a junior captain[4] to superintend consolidation and defence in front, stationed himself at the foremost angle of the exposed flank and organised its defence. The 61st Division now planned to capture the Sugar Loaf salient by a second attempt and asked the 15th Brigade to help. Accordingly at 9 p.m., as dusk fell, a brave attempt was made by half the 58th Battalion under another Duntrooner, Major A. J. S. Hutchinson. The 61st Division's plan had then been cancelled, but news of this arrived too late. Hutchinson himself dashed on, even when his men stopped, and was killed at the German wire, but the attempt was hopeless from the start. As the 61st Division was then being bombed out of its last foothold in the German line, Haking decided to withdraw all its troops to their old front line for a renewed attempt next day.

Meanwhile, about dusk, the reserve companies of the Bavarian battalions that had been driven from the line tried, with help from the neighbouring German regiments and the supports, to recapture from both flanks the Australian line. On the left they were seen assembling and the 8th Brigade with help of artillery (though at first it shot too short) repelled them. But on the right flank the situation was more dangerous. Part of the old German front trench there had been left empty by the Australians—according to the plan the troops there were to move forward when the trench was cleared. The

---

[4] Captain J. J. Murray, a major-general in World War II.

Bavarians from the Sugar Loaf worked along this, and, to his amazement, young Arblaster in the advanced line suddenly saw their spiked helmets along the parapet of the old German front trench, between his position and the Australian line. He organised a fierce counter-attack on them, as did part of the 55th Battalion which was sent up to reinforce. In constant fighting at this point the intruders were stopped, but not driven out.

It was now dark. All night the forward parties worked to turn their ditches into trenches, while others from the rear reinforced them. The inexperience—and the eagerness—of the troops was shown in the way in which most carrying parties, arriving with their first loads, stayed to join in the fight instead of returning for more supplies. As the call for reinforcements continued, the brigadiers were allowed to use their reserves; and thus, except for a thin garrison in its old front line, almost the whole 5th Division was gradually drawn in. The command of the forward troops of the 14th Brigade was now being exercised by the commander of the 54th Battalion, Lieut.-Colonel Cass (of Krithia fame); but not until after 2 a.m. was he aware that his right flank in the enemy's line was exposed. Till then the fact that some of the 15th Brigade had entered the German trench on the flank of the 14th had led him and others to suppose that the 15th was duly holding the flank.

But shortly after 2 o'clock it was realised that the Bavarians were again attacking and had forced their way farther behind Arblaster's trench. Where that youngster held out, the din of bombing, which for a time had lessened, again became continuous, and white flares, blurred by dust and smoke, constantly curved through the air. From that corner the call for bombers never ceased; and, as it came, Captain Murray, farther along the front, would nod to one of his officers after another to move off with their men into the inferno. Of every ten men who went barely one came back. Troops firing to their front were being shot from the rear. Bombs ran short, ammunition began to fail. Finally, having held the Germans till early morning, Arblaster decided that the only remaining chance of saving the position was to face to the rear and charge the portion of the Germans who were holding their old front line. He lined his men out, distributed bombs, gave the signal, and then led the charge. Heavy fire immediately broke out. Arblaster was mortally wounded, and the line fell back to its trench.

The right flank was now almost cut off; and shortly before dawn the left and left centre also were attacked. Germans appearing out of the mist eventually managed to thrust, both from the gap between the two brigades and also from the left flank, into the old front line behind part of the 8th Brigade, whose advanced troops still held out in the big communication trench and the ditches. By 3.45 most of these Australians on the left, under the leaders who had directed them all night, had to face the desperate task of charging back through the enemy to the old Australian trench.[5] Notwithstanding the terrible fire laid by the Germans on no-man's-land, a large number got through. By 5.45 on July 20th the last of the 8th Brigade had been forced out of the German line.

At that hour General Haking was holding a conference to consider the renewal of the 61st Division's attack, which, despite his repeated order had, fortunately, not been again attempted, the 61st having been unable to get its companies into position. The army commander was present when news arrived that the 8th Brigade had been driven out and the position of the 14th was desperate. Orders were at once sent to prepare to withdraw the 14th Brigade. In the old German front line Colonel Cass arranged for a rearguard under a particularly fine leader, Captain Norman Gibbins of the 55th Battalion, to hold

_____
[5] See Vol. III, pp. 424-5.

part of the captured line to the last, while the troops withdrew through a communication trench dug across no-man's-land during the night.

Gibbins, a Queensland bank manager, of great height and strength, magnificently performed this duty. Already, largely under his direction, parties of the 55th had greatly eased the position by vehement bombing attacks from both flanks of the 14th Brigade, driving the Germans back along their old front line. Now, though for some reason unknown the final order to withdraw was not received till nearly 8 a.m.—and some of the troops even then would not believe it genuine—the difficult task was carried out successfully. Though hard pressed, Gibbins and his party held off the Germans till the brigade had withdrawn. He himself, the last to leave, on nearing the Australian line, left the communication trench in order to avoid crushing the wounded with whom it was clogged, and as he walked over the Australian parapet a German bullet killed him. Behind the German lines other Australian parties, hopelessly cut off, fought on till 9.20 a.m.

The scene in the Australian trenches, packed with wounded and dying, was unexampled in the history of the A.I.F. In one night and the hours preceding it the 5th Division had lost 5533 men, of whom 400 were prisoners. Very many wounded lay in no-man's-land, especially opposite the Sugar Loaf. Here an Australian batman, searching for his dead officer right up to the German wire, was challenged by a Bavarian officer, whose humanity now made possible an informal truce to which many Australians owe their lives.[6] The loss of the 61st Division in this battle was 1547 and that of the Germans apparently 1500. Two years later, when the German defences here came into British possession, the present writer examining the battlefield found that the supposed "third line", which the Australians were set to reach,

---

[6] For details of this episode see *Vol. III, p. 439.*

though then indistinguishable from ordinary field drains, was apparently the remains of old trenches begun by the Germans a year before the Fromelles attack, but abandoned on becoming waterlogged.

Within a few hours of its delivery, the infantry attack at Fromelles had achieved precisely the opposite effect to that intended. An artillery demonstration, as suggested by Haig's staff, might have avoided all this loss and have led the Germans to apprehend that a bigger attack was being prepared. But now they knew the operation to be a mere feint, and if they had previously any doubts as to the wisdom of "milking" that front for reserves for the Somme, the fight had actually dispelled those doubts.

The episode had another unintended effect. The 61st Division had previously, while in England, been used as a second-line division, and constantly robbed of some of its best elements to feed other divisions. It was under strength, and the orders and counter-orders of its staff during the night, though possibly inevitable in the conditions, did not make it a satisfactory partner in a desperate offensive. The impression already created in the A.I.F., that the new British armies lacked something in fighting capacity, was noticeably strengthened by this episode.

CHAPTER XV

1916—POZIÈRES, AND MOUQUET FARM

THE fight at Fromelles was a short, sharp incident—
G.H.Q., most unwisely, reported it as "some important
raids" (140 Germans had been captured), and thereby, as
often happened in that war, deceived its own people, not
the Germans; and shook the faith of its soldiers in the
British communiqués—faith which might have been of
great value. The battle put out of offensive action for
many months the 5th Australian Division.

But of all the great battles of the next two and a half
years, the fight that now lay a few days ahead of the
1st, 2nd and 4th Divisions, then just marching up to
the Somme Battle, was in several ways the hardest
experienced by the First A.I.F.

This narrative left the British and French armies of
the Somme at the stage at which the great first and second
blows, struck on July 1st and 14th, though driving fairly
deep into the German line, had still not led to the break-
through for which General Haig hoped, and the small
intermediate attacks, to round off the positions first
gained, had achieved slow progress at great cost. A closely
similar result was occurring in the small attacks following
the 4th Army's second stroke, of July 14th; it was being
followed by difficult operations in which the 9th (Scottish) Division, including the South African Infantry
Brigade, had taken—and was fighting to hold—Delville
Wood, on the 4th Army's centre, while that army's left
had tried to seize Pozières village which protected the
Germans' still unbroken flank at Thiepval farther north.

Pozières hemmed in the 4th Army's flank. But south

of that place the army had thrust over the ridge on which the German second line lay. Pozières village could therefore be attacked from two sides—frontally from the west, and in flank from the south; its capture would greatly improve the 4th Army's chance of pushing eastwards. But the British ammunition supply did not allow Haig to strike continuously along his whole front. He was still determined to thrust farther where the 4th Army had already succeeded—Pozières and Thiepval would then, he believed, automatically fall. Accordingly he ordered the 4th Army to continue striking eastwards to the ruined villages of Ginchy and Guillemont, while the left flank made "a steady, methodical, step-by-step advance as already ordered".

Actually the "steady, methodical advance" as practised was no more than a succession of piecemeal attacks on narrow fronts, which were proving neither successful nor inexpensive. Between July 13th and July 17th four attacks were made by British infantry against Pozières, first by patrols, later after heavy bombardment which reduced the village to heaps of rubble standing out behind a fringe of broken, shredded tree-stumps. But though the loop trench around the village was twice entered, there was little to show for the effort except the crumpled bodies of British soldiers left hanging in the German wire entanglement. Efforts had been made to help the attack by bombing up the second German defence line, an immensely strong system comprising two parallel trenches (and many long approaches), which ran along the actual crest 500 yards behind the village. South-east of Pozières this line lay on ground seized by 4th Army on July 14th, and from that foothold the bombing squads attacked north-westwards. At that time, however, the Germans were generally better at bombing than any of their opponents—especially in the range of their grenades and the support of their bombers by machine-guns—and these attacks also had been held up.

Meanwhile Haig had decided to withdraw the 4th Army's most forward troops from the most advanced positions beyond the crest, at High Wood, preparatory to delivering a third great blow. The main object in this offensive was to seize Guillemont; but on the extreme left Pozières also would be attacked.[1] This part in the coming attack, however, was now transferred from 4th Army to Reserve Army (afterwards renamed 5th Army) under General Gough.

On July 18th, when the 1st Division of I Anzac was marching through Picardy to the Albert area, close behind the battlefield, its commander, Maj.-General Walker, was sent for by Gough, whose first words were: "I want you to go into the line and attack Pozières to-morrow night!" Probably Gough believed that great results were still within reach if Haig could strike again soon, although the Germans, fully aware of their danger, were now steadily bringing down reserves to avert it. The Anzac leaders, however, felt that such haste meant the scamping of preparation; and they succeeded in having the attack postponed for several days. The 2nd and 4th Divisions were to remain at present in support and reserve.

On the night of July 19th the leading brigades of the 1st Division filed through the cobbled streets of Albert past the half-ruined cathedral, from whose tower the gilded statue of the Virgin hung precariously above the town square; and thence over the grassy nearer slopes, and rounded spurs of the battlefield, pocked with craters in the gleaming chalk; up a shallow valley (Sausage Gully) crowded with guns and with reserves living in old German trenches and shelters; through shallow trenches in chalk and clay, to the newly dug, narrow front line—most like a ditch just prepared for drain-pipes—from which the British were to have made their next attack.

---

[1] Previously it had been intended to make yet another isolated effort against this village.

As the battalions filed up in the dark there fell around them some small shells which exploded with a mere "pat"; they were thought to be "duds", until a few men were gassed by the phosgene fumes.

With morning the orchards, hedges and ruins of Pozières could be seen, close ahead. The village was

THE PLAN OF ATTACK ON POZIÈRES, 23rd JULY 1916

strung out along a main road (the old Roman highway from Amiens to Bapaume), and served as an outlier in front of the second German defence system along the crest, 500 yards beyond the village. The extreme right of the Australians took over the nearest captured section of that second line. From there leftwards the line ran in a loop round the south of the village, the Australian left resting on the Roman road west of the place. The

Germans held an inner loop ("K" and Pozières trenches) 300-800 yards away, behind which were the shattered orchards and other hedged enclosures. The 1st Australian Division was to attack from the south and advance in three stages to the road through the centre of Pozières. On the left the 48th British Division would attack some communication trenches still held by the Germans west of the village. A preliminary attempt by the 9th Battalion in the early hours of July 22nd to get closer to Pozières by another bomb-attack along the two trenches of the German second line failed.

The British command was determined to make a certainty of Pozières this time, if thorough bombardment could do it. The village and the old German second line (known as the "O.G. Lines") were pounded methodically for several days, the few broken pink and white walls that still stood in the village becoming more visible as their screen of trees was stripped. Barely once or twice a day the sight of some figure moving in that tortured area gave evidence that a garrison was still there. At dusk on July 22nd the guns of 4th Army began the final bombardment for the attack farther to the east, and three hours later those of Reserve Army increased their fire on and around Pozières. Three miles away, men of the 2nd Division, just arrived near Albert, watched from the hills there the glare and flash of that famous bombardment. The Germans answered with all kinds of shell, including phosgene and tear gas.

Half an hour after midnight, at 12.30 a.m. on Sunday, July 23rd, the 3rd and 1st Brigades of the 1st Australian Division attacked. The field artillery had fired for two minutes as fast as it could load, and the infantry, who had crept as near as possible to the front German position, seized it as soon as the artillery lengthened range. The advance was renewed, at half-hour intervals, over two succeeding stages, the second bringing the troops to the back hedges of Pozières, and the third to the main road

17—os

through the village. Many of the German garrison (117th Division) were killed or captured; others fled or withdrew to the northern end of the village or to communication trenches beyond it, and many more were chased by a number of Australians to the strong O.G. Lines on the crest. A counter-attack by a German battalion at dawn was shot to pieces by Lewis and machine-gun fire.

The only part of the objective not taken was in the O.G. Lines. These were to have been seized on the right, by bombing, as far as the main road; but here the Australians met a condition new to them, these trenches and the area surrounding them having been so cratered by shellfire that it was very difficult for troops to be sure where was their objective or what point they had reached. The whole surface of the ground was like that of a choppy sea; and the two trenches (the front line known as "O.G.1", and the support line 100-200 yards east of it as "O.G.2") were in some places untraceable, in others merely a depression detected with difficulty among the holes and mounds. But among these the deep German dugouts were held by brave garrisons, skilled at bomb-fighting, and covered by the support of watchful and terribly efficient machine-gunners in neighbouring shelters in the craterfield. The German stick bombs were unequal in effect to the deadly British Mills bomb, but were accurately thrown, and the small German egg bomb could be flung farther than any British hand-grenade. It was only by a drawn-out struggle, in which two Victoria Crosses[2] were won, that the first objective in O.G.1 was captured and held; O.G.2 could not be found.

The Germans still holding the O.G. Lines beyond this point were thus able to fire into the open flank of the Australians attacking the eastern end of Pozières, and, for the time being, the extreme right flank had to be bent back. During that day, July 23rd, while most of the

---

[2] By Pte John Leak and Lieut. A. S. Blackburn. The latter made seven very gallant attacks (*Vol. III, pp. 511-13*).

forward troops deepened their new trenches, parties of them pushed out, "prospecting" through parts of the village north of the road, capturing a number of Germans, and, at the western end, seizing by attack from its rear a concrete blockhouse (called by the troops "Gibraltar") with two deep dugouts beneath it. That night a reinforcing battalion, the 8th (of the 2nd Brigade), pushed through and secured most of the remainder of the village. For some time the German command remained unaware of its loss.

The Australian troops, as they smoked German cigars, or donned the shiny, black, spiked German helmets while they dug, were aware that they had achieved a striking success. A main buttress of the German line on that battlefield had been broken. Except on the extreme right in the O.G. Lines they had cleanly achieved their three objectives, and had dug in on each precisely as planned. The 48th British Division on their left had also taken part of the communication trenches west of the village. But the 4th Army on its whole front of attack east of the Australians gained no ground; the initial advances of its divisions were all eventually repelled. Haig's third big effort on the Somme had—except in the Pozières region—failed completely; and the situation on July 23rd had two important results:

First, the British commander-in-chief was forced to realise what in fact had been true throughout—that in the Somme offensive a break through the German lines was not within early reach. The offensive was, it is true, producing vital results in forcing the Germans to diminish their attacks on Verdun; and the German army's strength was being materially worn down. Haig knew the Germans were being strained, and his bulldog spirit led him to cling to the enemy's throat, whatever the cost to his own army. In some later attack, he felt sure, the German front would break beneath the strain. Before very long he would be supplied with a secret British weapon, not yet quite ready for his use, which might provide the instrument. For the present he would give up the attempt to break through, but would keep the Germans under strain by constant local assaults on such points as each army corps desired to secure in preparation for the next big offensive. For that offensive reserves of troops and ammunition were now to be built up in the back areas. Meanwhile the southernmost British corps would attack Delville Wood; the next High Wood; the next—near the Australians—the German communication trenches behind the O.G. Lines. Next in the line, I Anzac would make the "methodical, step-by-step" advance already enjoined on Gough and his army. The first such step, the taking of the rest of Pozières, north of the road, had already been arranged to begin that afternoon.

But the battle of the 23rd had a second important result. Pozières being a key position, the German staff was determined that it should be regained. Three early attempts failed—partly through the watchfulness of the Australians and partly through the dreadful conditions of the approach by night through the British artillery fire, and the difficulty of finding the way on that devastated crest. It was accordingly decided to make sure of success, as the British had done, by bombardment, and at 7 a.m. on July 24th, as soon as the loss of the village was certain, the Australian position was methodically bombarded. As the Pozières area was the only one in which ground had been gained on the seven-mile front of Haig's last offensive, the IV German Army Corps, in the western half of whose front Pozières lay, switched a great part of its artillery on to that crest.

The German bombardment was, at first, methodical rather than intense. One battery of 5.9-inch howitzers, for example, firing directly along a deep trench just dug by the Australians on the southern side of the Roman road, pounded it systematically with about four shells a minute, breaking down its sides and burying men whose comrades, working with furious zeal, constantly dug them out alive or dead. By evening parts of that trench could not even be found by the relieving companies. The south-west entrance of the village, near "Gibraltar", was most heavily and continuously pounded, and the main approach route there was so lined with dead that it came to be called Dead Man's Road.

All the while, General Gough pressed the Australian leaders for early action. He explained, in an order, that

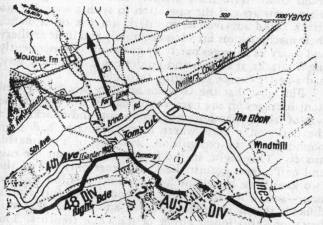

THE OPERATIONS INTENDED BY GOUGH AT POZIÈRES
JULY-AUGUST 1916
The arrows show the (1) earlier and (2) later advances proposed.
(British line, after the attacks of July 24th-25th, black, German white.)

his intention was, after seizing Pozières, to capture the O.G. Lines, and then to push north-westwards along that crest past Mouquet Farm—a mile from Pozières—to where the ridge dipped northwards to the river Ancre. He believed that there were few Germans at present on this ridge except in the O.G. Lines, and that, if the move could be quickly made, the Germans at Thiepval might be cut off.

The first step, to be taken that night, was to drive the Germans from parts of two trench systems which they still held, "K" trench, along the western edge of Pozières, and the O.G. Lines east of the village (these to be attacked only up to the Bapaume road). Throughout this piecemeal, local fighting it was thought best to attack at night. If the Germans could actually see the assault they could concentrate their artillery and machine-guns on the narrow area of the operation in such a way that no attack could survive. In the dark, on the other hand, their machine-guns fired less accurately and their artillery had to lay its barrages partly by guesswork. Consequently night attacks, if officers and guides could find their way, had a better chance of getting through.

But, now that the German artillery was laying constant barrages on the narrow approaches to Pozières, the task of troops marching up, lining out, and attacking in the dark, on a crest where most landmarks had been pounded out of recognition, was one of nightmarish anxiety. This night, in the frontal attack from the east end of Pozières against the O.G. Lines only one of the two assaulting battalions had got into position by zero hour—and, when the troops attacked, it was only after a difficult search in wild confusion and uproar that this battalion (5th) found either of the O.G. trenches. The British 1st Division, which in the same conditions made a local assault immediately east of the O.G. Lines failed; and the 5th Australian battalion, though it seized its sector of the O.G. Lines, was counter-attacked by part of the 18th German Reserve Division, just brought up there to make the German counter-attack on Pozières. There followed a titanic bombfight—the bringing up (as one Australian wrote) of "bombs at the double—machine-guns at the double—carriers at the double—more bombs at the double—strings of men going up" to feed the mêlée.[3] Parts of the 10th and 7th Battalions were ultimately drawn into this, but only a portion of the trenches thus captured could be retained. On the western side of the village, however, the 4th and 8th Battalions in a brilliant advance in the grey dawn of July 25th seized "K" trench and Pozières cemetery, where the 48th British Division from the left linked with them on the following night.

This day, July 25th, the German bombardment on Pozières increased in weight. The shelling was really preparation for the final attempt by the Germans to retake the village. Their attack was to be launched at 4.30 p.m. and German artillery from far around was able to take part, since here alone on the whole battlefield was the British line progressing. The long trail of smoke and dust from that summit, as salvo after salvo hit Pozières or flung the powdered earth in clouds into the air, was the spectacle for both armies. Fortunately, for the moment, many of the Australians were ahead of the German barrage line, or else sheltered in the deep dugouts left by the Germans.

This furious bombardment aroused sure expectation of a counter-attack, and when, at 4.30 p.m., men were seen moving on the skyline beyond the village the British barrage also descended. Actually, the Germans did not counter-attack. The unexpected fight that morning in the O.G. Lines, the repeated changes of orders by the German staff, the dreadful approaches under artillery fire, and the strain of the last three days, had worn out even the fresh German regiment brought up for the main thrust. After many reports that the task was hopeless General von Boehn of the IX German Army Corps (which had just taken over that front) had countermanded the attempt. The safety of the German front would have to be assured by holding the O.G. Lines.

---

[3] For this Herculean bombfight, see *Vol. III, pp. 564-6.*

These were, of course, the next objective of the Australians, and the Germans realised it. But the earlier intention of the British and Anzac commanders, that the 1st Australian Division should carry out this attack, was now seen to be impossible of fulfilment. During July 26th, while the division was trying to establish posts and trenches facing the O.G. Lines in readiness for the assault, the German artillery deluged the whole area with shell, working up at 5 p.m. to such intensity that all commanders in the village thought the Germans were about to attack; at 6.45 from the midst of this inferno an appeal at last got through to the artillery to shell the O.G. Lines in which the enemy's troops might be assembling. By 7.5 p.m. Australian and British artillery was replying with all its might. The Germans, on their part, mistaking this as preparation for a new Australian attack laid their fire again with great intensity on the village. On the British side the guns of the two neighbouring corps assisted. Not till nearly midnight did the uproar finally die out.

It was followed by a merciful silence in which troops and ration and ammunition parties could move into and out of Pozières almost safely. But the staff and commanders knew that the 1st Australian Division was at the end of its tether. The last three days' bombardment was an experience such as Australians had never before suffered —it was typical of the Verdun and First Somme battles, and on no part of the front in France were such bombardments more severe than at Pozières. The 1st Division had lost 5285 officers and men, and was already being relieved by the 2nd Division. The 5th Brigade, lent to the 1st Division, had come into the line the night before, and at dawn two companies of the 20th Battalion had made a fourth unsuccessful attempt to seize—this time by surprise—the section of the O.G. Lines south of the Bapaume road. No further attempt would now be made until the 2nd Australian Division had taken over the line from the 1st.

Only those who saw the troops come out from such experiences could realise their exhaustion. "They looked," wrote a sergeant (E. J. Rule) of the 4th Division, which watched the 1st pass into a rest area, "like men who had been in Hell . . . drawn and haggard and so dazed that they appeared to be walking in a dream and their eyes looked glassy and starey".[4] When they reached bivouac in Vadencourt Wood, and had washed, shaved and rested, they were strangely quiet, far different from the Australian soldiers of tradition. They resembled rather boys emerging from long illness, many lying quietly apart in their blankets, reading books, smoking, or writing home letters.

Meanwhile the men of the 2nd Division had by July 27th taken over the whole front at Pozières. The 2nd, though it had served on Gallipoli and in the evacuation of the Peninsula, had never yet fought a pitched battle; but its infantry had not been drawn on for creating the 4th and 5th Divisions, and most of them, therefore, were old hands. Its commander, Maj.-General Legge, and his staff had no experience of operations on the scale that now faced them—a fact which was a disadvantage in view of the pressure consistently placed on them by the anxiety of General Gough to hasten the date of their attacks.

The O.G. Lines could be seen from the eastern edge of Pozières village; the chalky parapet of O.G.1, with the iron stakes of the first belt of wire-entanglement before it, rimmed the horizon 500-700 yards away to north and east. The German observers there looked down, across the gently falling crest whose turnip fields were thickly pitted with shellholes, to the broken skeletons of the village hedges near which the Australians were dug in.

---

[4] For some of the personal experiences, see *Vol. III, pp. 597-8*; also Captain Rule's book, *Jacka's Mob*.

Hedges, village and fields were by this time little more than an expanse of desert, the village area itself being so pounded by shell-burst after shell-burst that the powdered debris of houses and earth was spread like ashes six feet deep over the surface,[5] as featureless as the Sahara, and level except for the shell-craters which lay edge to edge—like the scratchings of gigantic hens in an endless ash heap. Each fresh salvo flung up rolling clouds of this dust and rearranged the craters. Except for two fragments of German concrete every vestige of building above earth level eventually vanished. Visitors shocked by the destruction of other Somme villages were unimpressed at Pozières because it had simply become an open space, marked vaguely by tree-stumps, but with no other sign that a village had been there.

General Legge was confident that by the night of July 28th his artillery would have battered down the wire before the O.G. Lines sufficiently for the 2nd Division to attack. Gough was eager for speed. For once, General White, chief of Birdwood's staff, allowed his own doubts to be overborne, and the attack was accordingly ordered for 12.15 a.m. on the 29th. But meanwhile several strongly adverse conditions arose. First, on the afternoon of July 26th the right brigade (5th) of the division, in and next to the O.G. Lines, had been drawn into another titanic bombfight in voluntary support of the 23rd British Division, which was attacking an old German communication trench, Munster Alley. In this fight, lasting all the afternoon and night, all bombers of the 5th Brigade were eventually used and some 15,000 bombs spent by the British and Australians who finally gained a few yards near O.G.2. On the rest of the Australian area on July 27th the German artillery fire had

---

[5] A sandbag-ful of this from the centre of the village is in the Australian War Memorial, as are several of the old tree stumps. A description of this extraordinary area, set down by the present writer immediately after going round it on July 31st, is in *Vol. III, pp. 615-17.*

been almost as heavy as on the 26th. A German observer
had reported that trenches evidently in preparation for a
new offensive were being dug in front of Pozières, and
throughout the day these and other known trenches
around Pozières were systematically pounded. In one
heavy concentration part of the 24th Battalion, sitting in
"K" trench in support, was annihilated, and the front
trenches were so shovelled-in by shellfire that there
vanished any chance of digging a regular "jumping-off
trench" for the attack. The day-long dust of this shelling
prevented Australian artillery officers from accurately
observing their own fire on the German entanglements.
Nevertheless forward posts were put out by the infantry
along the jumping-off line; and, in default of a trench,
the assaulting troops were to line out on an old light-rail-
way track that skirted the far side of the village.

At dusk on July 28th the 7th Brigade—which was to
come in between its two sisters, 5th and 6th, and form the
centre of the attacking force—moved up from a rear area.
That night the supporting artillery was not to lay down
any special bombardment until three minutes before the
assault, when it would vehemently shell the enemy trench
for three minutes and then throw its fire beyond.[6] The
Germans were equally quiet, and most of the troops duly
reached the broken line of the old railway and lay down
there. It had been realised that this position was too far
back for the actual start; the attacking battalions would
have to move forward from it about midnight to reach
the previously intended starting line at 12.14 a.m.

Unfortunately the 7th Brigade thus had to move forward for twelve minutes before the barrage, descending
at 12.12, forced the Germans to shelter. Enemy sentries
detected its advance, and the 5th Brigade, attacking south

---

[6] Here a "creeping barrage" was first deliberately used by Australians.
As the Germans were believed to have machine-guns behind O.G.2, the
barrage would there gradually advance 50 yards every two minutes till it
lay 150 yards ahead of O.G.2.

of the Bapaume road, had been perceived even before.
The German machine-gunners in the O.G. Lines were
ready and their fire was terrific. The 5th Brigade was
pinned to the ground. In the 7th Brigade the 28th Battalion, just north of the main road, was faced by uncut
entanglement. Some men tried to cut the wire, others
wrenched at the stakes, many fell dead upon the wire.
Farther north the centre and left of the brigade penetrated parts of O.G.1, and some went on towards O.G.2.
On the extreme left the 23rd Battalion (6th Brigade),
advancing northwards, far overran its objective—a road
so shattered by shellfire that it was at first unrecognised.
The troops were quickly driven out of all their foot-
holds in the O.G. Lines, but the 6th Brigade managed
to hold part of the ground won on the northern flank,
and here the neighbouring British infantry duly pushed
forward and gained touch. This was the sole gain in the
battle which, together with the days of preparation, cost
the 2nd Division some 3500 men. The 7th Brigade was
temporarily withdrawn to close reserve.

General Haig felt that the failure was due to lack of
preparation. "You're not fighting Bashi-Bazouks now,"
he said to White and Birdwood at Corps Headquarters.
Actually, though serious mistakes had been made, they
were not the ones that Haig supposed, as White, ignoring
a warning look from Haig's staff, at once pointed out
to him. "I dare say you're right, young man," said the
commander-in-chief laying a hand on White's shoulder.
However, a lesson had been bloodily learned; and White
and Birdwood, as well as Legge (who rightly asked that
despite its heavy loss his division might attack again
rather than be withdrawn after failure) were determined
that this time careful forethought should exploit every
possible means for success.

One of the greatest difficulties in these terrible night-
attacks had been to be certain that each part of the force
took and kept its right direction. This doubt and diffi-

culty—in the uproar, confusion, and blackness—was dreaded by all officers and most of the men. Legge accordingly decided this time to attack at 9.15 p.m., just before dark, when the O.G. Lines would still be clearly visible. The low mound of the tumbled windmill, and the faint trace of the main road leading to it, would be good directing signs.

But to attack at dusk would mean assembling by daylight. For this, deep approach-trenches would have to be made for each of the three brigades, and each brigade would also have to dig itself a jumping-off trench in which to deploy undetected before the attack. Provision was made for digging these systematically each night, and a most careful scheme of bombardment, to continue several days, was arranged. But the experience of the first two nights showed that the German bombardments regularly answering our own made it impossible for the battalions of the 7th Brigade to reach the line on which they were to dig. By taking aeroplane photographs it was ascertained that, after two nights of preparation, the 7th Brigade's jumping-off trench was still almost completely undug. General Legge was forced to postpone the attack from August 2nd to August 3rd, and later General White, on careful inquiry, telephoned to Gough's headquarters that it must be delayed until the 4th. "You can order them to attack if you like," he told Gough's staff, "but I tell you . . ." and he cited one matter after another in which the preparation was dangerously incomplete. Gough agreed to the postponement although certain operations on other fronts, which were to have taken place on the same night, could not be postponed.

The task of digging was now driven through as a battle operation. On the nights of the 2nd and 3rd the Germans apparently saw the digging parties and mistook them for troops assembling for attack. The area was furiously shelled. But the communication trenches (including the famous Centre Way) and nearly the whole of the intended jumping-off trench were eventually dug. The task was one of the most terrible undertaken by the A.I.F. Men were buried as they worked, were dug out, and buried again. Trenches disappeared, were dug again, rubbed out, and again dug. The casualties amounted to those of battle—in ten days the 4th Pioneers lost 8 officers and 222 men mainly in keeping open one section of communication trench; and the strain was intense—many officers and men broke down temporarily with what was really intolerable overstrain, but was termed by the troops (and by medical officers, till its true nature was determined) "shell-shock".[7]

The three brigades were thus able to assemble most of their attacking troops before dusk on August 4th without the enemy's detecting them. At 9.15, again after three minutes' intense bombardment, O.G.1 was rushed and at 9.30 O.G.2. The 7th Brigade advanced almost in its own barrage, leaving the Germans insufficient time to mount machine-guns, or, in most cases, to leave their dugouts. The one danger of failure occurred where, in a heavy German barrage during the assembly, part of the 7th Brigade marching up crossed the route of the 6th, making a battalion of each late for their task. In the 6th Brigade the resulting danger was met by Major Murdoch Mackay of the 22nd Battalion, a young Victorian barrister, who at once guided his men by another route, through the German barrage, and then, arriving at his jumping-off trench twenty-five minutes late, led them straight on to attack in spite of the decision of a senior officer who had temporarily held back the troops there. Attacking late, Mackay met machine-gun fire and was killed, but his men seized the objective. His determination thus saved the left flank and, probably, the whole operation. In the 7th Brigade, Major Currie, seeing that the rear waves of his battalion (26th) were late at O.G.1, took his own

7 The famous letters of Lieut. J. A. Raws who, with his brother, was killed in this battle are quoted in *Vol. III, pp. 658-60.*

wave forward instead and seized the battalion's objective in O.G.2.

Part of O.G.2, near the mound of the old Windmill, could not be traced; men at first went beyond it both there and south of the Bapaume road. South of the road it was presently identified by the half-buried steel posts of the old entanglement. North of the road Captain Cherry with the 7th Machine-gun Company covered it by spacing his guns along the corresponding part of O.G.1.

The Pozières crest and the old German second line along it had been firmly seized; the Germans had known that an attack must be impending, but were swept away by the vigour of the stroke after four days' of dreadful bombardment. In the grey of dawn on August 5th a line of them was detected advancing north of the Windmill, just where the Australian line was thinnest. A German officer led them most bravely but Cherry's machine-guns sufficed to shatter the counter-attack.[8] Two reinforcing companies from Pozières led by Captain Maitland Foss now found and occupied O.G.2 about the Windmill.

From this crest the Australian infantry at last looked over the wide, shallow valley behind the German second line, with the treetops and roofs of Courcelette, a welcome picture, close in front, and the woods about Bapaume five and a half miles away on the farther side. This was the same valley on which the British had looked out from High Wood on July 14th. German guns and convoys could be seen and many moving troops. Naturally the German army commander was greatly disturbed by the loss of the heights and ordered their immediate recapture.

The Australians at this stage might possibly have pressed a little farther eastwards. But General Gough's orders were to endeavour at the earliest moment to push, not eastwards, but north to Mouquet Farm and on be-

---

[8] The meeting of Cherry, who later won the V.C., with this brave man, who was mortally wounded, is described in *Vol. III, p. 694n.*

hind Thiepval. Before dawn Brig.-General John Gelli-brand, commanding the northern (6th) brigade, had to ascertain for Gough whether an immediate thrust to the north was possible. The barrage on Pozières that night was intense, but, by going up himself, Gellibrand found that immediate advance was out of the question. His brigade was accordingly ordered to attack northwards on the following night instead.

But the 2nd Australian Division was now more ex-hausted than the 1st had been. It had carried out its great task at heavier cost, heavier indeed than any other Australian division (though not quite any British one) ever suffered in one tour in the line; and it was now again under an intense bombardment laid by the Ger-mans on its new and old positions preparatory to another attempt to recapture them. "At any price," ran the Ger-man order, "Hill 160 (the Pozières plateau) must be recovered." At last General Holmes of the 5th Brigade asked that his troops, who in eleven days had engaged in four heavy attacks, should be relieved. The 4th Australian Division was close behind, and it was ordered to replace first Holmes's brigade and then the others, and carry the attack northwards.

But before the relief was complete—by the night of August 6th—the Australians on Pozières heights had suf-fered the crowning bombardment of the whole series. In Haig's piecemeal offensive the Australians had gradually pushed a big bulge into the German lines; and this now permitted the enemy artillery to shell them from the rear, Thiepval way, as well as from front and both flanks. A great part of their front line was now completely enfiladed by German batteries and the loss was heavy. At the Windmill the 2nd Division troops were withdrawn a short way but the incoming 4th Division placed a post there under Sergeant Twining. On the morning of August 6th the Germans tried to counter-attack, but stopped at a distance when fired on, and merely "ruled off" the gap in their line. The bombardment, however, continued that day and the following night; but during a comparatively quiet interval at dusk most of the remaining infantry of the 2nd Division was relieved by that of the 4th. A few who could not evade the barrage stayed in the line.

On the night of August 6th the bombardment was so heavy that the garrison of the 4th Division was largely kept in the old German deep dugouts as the only means of survival. Most of the shelling missed O.G.2, but that trench was now held chiefly by small light posts. At 4 o'clock on the 7th, in the dim dawn, the enemy attacked, and passed through most of the now barely-held O.G.2, and over several of the deep dugouts in O.G.1, capturing some of the garrison, and down the slope towards Pozières on a front of about 400 yards.

At that moment the Australians on the flanks saw a party of eight Australians, an officer leading, leap from a fold in the ground behind the Germans and charge them in rear. It was Albert Jacka (of Anzac fame), now Lieutenant, whose platoon, waiting in a deep dugout, had been surprised by the attack. The enemy had bombed the dugout and left a sentry over the stairway. Jacka, firing his revolver from below, had rushed up the stairway followed by his surviving men, lined them out, and then sprung on the Germans from behind, fighting like a wild cat. Not far away, men of the 48th Battalion were resisting; and now they, and other Australians scattered across the slope and on the flanks, joined in. There was a wild mêlée; Jacka was very badly wounded, but supports were coming up. The tables were turned. Most of the captured Australians were freed, many Germans captured, and the lost ground, and more, was taken. Thus the attempt by von Boehn and his subordinates to retake Pozières heights utterly failed. It was not repeated.

But the cost of all this fighting to the Australian infantry had been tremendous. The 2nd Division in its

18—os

twelve day tour lost 6848 officers and men; five of its battalions each lost between 600 and 700 men. Even in the 4th Division in the last two days the 48th Battalion lost some 600, and the 45th 350.

The thrust had now immediately to be directed northwards, I Anzac fighting its way along the ridge (on which the O.G. trenches still continued northwards), while on its left the British II Corps kept pace by seizing, one after another, the old communication trenches running between the old German front and second lines. The first step was taken on the night of August 8th by Monash's old brigade (4th), now under Brig.-General C. H. Brand, Monash having been sent to England to train and command the 3rd Division. In this attack, made at dusk, the 15th Battalion advanced behind a creeping barrage which moved slowly ahead of the troops. The next German trench to the north (Park Lane) was seized, and indeed was passed by the right flank, the troops crossing it without recognising it, and seizing another trench 150 yards ahead. The line was thus disjointed. The British troops who were to advance on the left, in and west of "K" trench, were swept away in front of a German strongpoint. As the Germans still held "K", the Australians were withdrawn before daylight. On the following night they attacked again. This time the task in "K" trench also was given to them, and they captured the same trenches as before, and also the strongpoint. The Germans answered with very heavy shelling, but on the right the Australians were farther ahead than either their own staff or the enemy yet realised. The forward troops thus escaped the German bombardment but came into danger from their own.

These were only the beginnings of the extraordinary task set by Gough for his troops. In planning to drive a comparatively narrow salient of his own behind the salient held by the Germans at Thiepval he can hardly have foreseen the difficulty. The only way by which Australian troops could reach their front—except in ones or twos—was by a long route up to Pozières and then north-wards by one of the dreadfully bombarded trenches along the ridge. This led over two undulations whose crests were in sight of the Germans, who barraged these trenches on every sign of movement or assembly, and could enfilade the northern ends of them with machine-guns.

The German shells came from front, flank, and rear. Yet by this route food, water and stores had to come up. Trenches changed their shape under bombardment. The whole area was flayed and pounded into a veritable sea of shell-craters. In rain, which fortunately fell only once or twice—the area became a bog. Often neither the attacking troops nor their leaders could recognise the landmarks that they reached; at one time, when the heavy artil-lery was about to bombard a trench, the 3rd Battalion staff felt sure its men were in that trench, the brigade staff felt sure they were 200 yards behind it, and the divisional staff felt sure they were in a third position. The battalion commander, 26-year-old Lieut.-Colonel Owen Howell-Price, then sought out and stood on the only identifiable object, a powdered depression recog-nised by him as a particular road cutting, and so proved that in this case the battalion was right; but his message could not be got through in time to prevent the heavies from shelling him and his men.

In such conditions the 4th Division pressed on with Gough's plan. On the night of August 10th patrols pushed out and established posts in the valley south of the mound of rubble which appeared to be all that re-mained of Mouquet Farm, and at a sunken road east of the farm. Next day the Germans twice counter-attacked—in this sector their XIX (Saxon) Corps had just relieved the IX; but the newly planted Australian posts, eager in the opportunity to pay back the sufferings of their bat-talions in the bombardments, swept them away with Lewis-gun fire. On the night of August 12th, after pre-

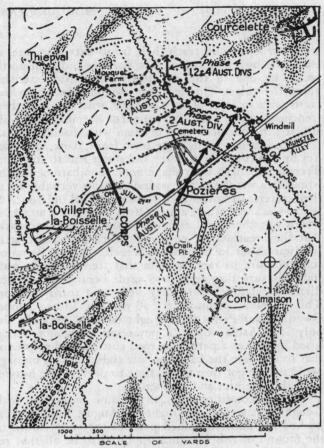

THE POZIÈRES POSITION
(Shaded portions are valleys.)

This shows the British line on 21st July 1916, and phases of the subsequent offensive to outflank Thiepval, 23rd July-5th September 1916.

Adapted from map in "The Empire at War" (10 metre contours).

parations of dreadful difficulty, a formal attack was made, bringing the Australians and the II Corps on their left to a line directly facing the German position running through Mouquet Farm. For the night of the 13th, in face of equal difficulties, an attack on the Farm itself and the high ground east of it was prepared.

That day the Germans recaptured the gain just made by the British II Corps. The 4th Australian Division, however, attacked a modified objective. The Germans by now had rightly guessed General Gough's plan and daily expecting a further thrust, treated every detected movement as an attack. The bombardment became so heavy that on August 14th Lieut.-Colonel Ross, a British officer commanding the 51st Battalion, wrote to his brigadier (General Glasgow): "It is my genuine (not depressed) opinion that it would be a mistake to press the offensive further locally in this salient."

The attack, however, was made. A quarry near the Farm was captured and a company under Captain Harry Murray seized part of the German "Fabeck trench", north-east of the Farm. Here Murray and his men were outflanked by the Germans, who had been ordered by their corps commander not to permit the British plan to develop. But this former miner, who was to become known as a most famous fighting leader, fought his way back with his men in one of the most ably conducted actions in Australian experience.[9]

Colonel Ross was undoubtedly right. Although, in accordance with Gough's orders, the attempt to drive the salient deeper was continued in attack after attack for another month, its ultimate achievement was to secure no more than part of the Fabeck trench reached by Murray's company that night.

Upon the 4th Division's being relieved after a loss of 4649 men, the 1st Australian Division, with its battalions

---

[9] See Vol. III, pp. 766-8.

brought up by reinforcements to two-thirds of their full strength, was put in again. The approach routes were improved so far as shelling permitted. Each brigade now made its attack with comparatively light forces, but with these each could hold on to only a very small part of its initial gains.[10] By August 22nd, when this process pursued under constant barrages had cost another 2650 men, the 2nd Division took up the task and tried with larger forces to seize Mouquet Farm, which was by then realised to contain very large and deep dugouts. On August 26th, making, for once, a dawn attack, the 6th Brigade, preceded, as now was usual, by a "creeping barrage", reached the Farm but could not hold it—the German Guard Reserve Corps was now defending the place.

The 4th Australian Division was next brought back[11] and on the nights of August 27th and 29th delivered attacks, in the second of which the 4th Brigade, fighting desperately, occupied most of the objective including the Farm—but with attacking forces too thin to cope with the counter-attacks. Yet almost every assault had gained some small patch of ground; the Farm was now half surrounded, and on September 3rd the 13th Brigade, attacking at dawn and at the same time as the 4th Army some miles to the south-east, again captured most of the Farm and neighbouring trenches. After fierce fighting both above ground and in the deep passages below the Farm, it was thrown out of the Farm itself; but north-east of the Farm it clung to part of Fabeck trench and other posts. Lieutenant Duncan Maxwell—whose fine company commander, Captain Littler, of Anzac fame, was killed in this attack—held on to the most exposed corner under a bombardment that shattered most of his troops, and

10 On the night of August 18th the 1st Bde attacked northwards while the 2nd separately tried to advance eastwards from part of the O.G. Lines. On the night of the 21st Mouquet Farm was first reached and bombed by the 3rd Bde.

11 The 2nd Division in its second tour had lost 1268.

with the rest was still in position when the Canadian Corps, which had been relieving I Anzac on the Pozières front, got a full company under Captain J. H. Lovett through to reinforce him.[12] After fighting beside the Canadians for two more terrible days Maxwell (afterwards a brigadier of the Second A.I.F.), and the Australians surviving in these positions, came out. One who saw them come through Pozières wrote at the time in his diary: "The way was absolutely open (to shellfire), and others were bending low and running hurriedly. Our men were walking as if they were in Pitt Street, erect, not hurrying, each man carrying himself as proudly and carelessly as a British officer."

That was how the tradition of Anzac Beach, then only sixteen months old, worked at Mouquet Farm. And here also was where Gough's strategy of slowly pushing a salient behind an enemy salient came to a full stop. At the cost of another 2409 casualties the 4th Division had driven that salient as far as it ever went. On September 15th, ten days after the Australians had left the Somme, Haig, having received his new "secret weapon"[13] in sufficient quantity, returned to the plan of trying to break through the German line by a great offensive on a wide front. From the old Windmill stump at Pozières and from other points along the line, land-battleships, secretly manufactured during the previous year under the deceptive title of "tanks", heaved their monstrous shapes forward among British, Canadian and New Zealand infantry, who succeeded in driving the enemy almost to the bottom of the valley on which the Aus-

---

[12] The story of this fight has been told in *Vol. III, pp. 848-58.*

[13] The "tanks"—the name chosen to help the secrecy of their manufacture. In 1912 an Australian, L. E. de Mole, had placed before the War Office (in the words of a British Royal Commission) "a brilliant invention which anticipated, and in some respects surpassed, that actually put into use in the year 1916". But his invention, of which a model is in the Australian War Memorial, had been forgotten and the tank was re-invented by two British inventors in 1915-16. (See *Vol. XI, pp. 249-53* for this and other inventions of that war.)

tralians had looked out. Even then Mouquet Farm did not fall—the Canadians seized it next day, but it was not cleared and was lost again. It was not until September 26th that, in a wide advance, Gough's army seized Thiepval and Zollern Redoubt, and swept far past Mouquet Farm, where the German garrison still held out in the dugouts for the greater part of a day.

The eight weeks of piecemeal attacks—the dreadful link by which Haig connected his big early offensives with these later ones—was past. During that "piecemeal" period there had been only one sector in which the British forces on the Somme steadily pushed ahead—on Pozières ridge—and on that sector the German artillery was free to concentrate as its commanders desired. At Bullecourt, Messines, Ypres and elsewhere Australian infantry afterwards suffered intense bombardment, but never anything comparable in duration or effect with this. On that crowded mile of summit the three Australian divisions engaged lost 23,000 officers and men in less than seven weeks. The Windmill site, bought later by the Australian War Memorial Board—with the old mound still there—marks a ridge more densely sown with Australian sacrifice than any other place on earth.

In those forty-five days Australians had launched nineteen attacks—all except two being on a narrow front, and sixteen at night. They knew their constant advance during a time of deadlock would compare with any other achievement on the Somme. Under bombardment, of intensity and duration probably unsurpassed, they had held every trench once firmly captured. But they felt little confidence in the high tactics and strategy of it all. Indeed not a few British and oversea divisions that served there under Gough dreaded ever again to experience the results of his optimistic tactical aims and his urgency when caution was needed.

For the frequent shallow thrusts on narrow fronts Haig's policy was largely responsible. He looked on this

as a "wearing down" phase of the struggle. His intelligence staff knew that Germans had constantly to withdraw divisions, and apparently assumed that these had
suffered loss commensurate to that of the British divisions similarly withdrawn. But this was not so. Haig was
certainly wearing down his enemy; but he did not realise
that he was even more quickly wearing down the numbers—though not morale—of his own army. Apparently
no effort was made to devise special methods of attack
which would bring greater loss to the enemy than to the
British. That I Anzac, immediately after its three divisions had lost 17,000 men in their first tour, was again
charged with an impossible attempt to drive further the
wedge behind Thiepval, was a grave mistake; it cost
6300 casualties, achieved no useful result, and embittered
the troops who knew they were mishandled. For a short
time Birdwood's popularity waned; the men felt he
could have saved them this experience—and so perhaps
he could at the risk of asking that they should be
treated differently from other divisions of the British
Expeditionary Force.

During the September offensive (in which the New
Zealand Division, fighting beside the Guards in the XIV
Corps made itself a great name) I Anzac was in the temporarily quiet line at Ypres, raiding the enemy, and
digging what it believed to be its trench lines for the
coming winter. The Somme Battle again came to a standstill near the bottom of the valley below Bapaume
heights. Haig abandoned the hope that the Allies might
break through that year. But Joffre wanted a spectacular
achievement to encourage the French people, who were
becoming highly critical of his leadership and of Somme
tactics. Haig also wished to get his army out of the lowlands on to Bapaume heights before winter. Accordingly
fresh troops were summoned to renew the thrust, and,
after seeing one British division after another recalled
to the Somme, the I Anzac divisions learnt on October

9th, with a shock, that it was their turn: the British staff had a list of divisions fitted for this task, and they were next upon it. An onlooker who on October 12th saw them leaving Flanders noted how grim they looked, "but not the least buoyancy about them".

This time the 5th Australian Division from Armentières joined them. By the time they reached the Somme the autumn rains had set in and the whole battlefield had become a vast slough of mud. This was inevitable in these great "battles of material" in which the massed artillery in breaking the enemy also ploughed up the ground over which its own infantry must pass. The broken ground was easily traversed in dry weather, but in wet it became a bog. In the pressure of the offensive the staff had had no time or man-power to prepare against these conditions; both the trenches and the tracks leading to them were in many parts almost

INTENDED ATTACKS, OCTOBER 1916

impassable. Next, the roads up which timber and road metal should be arriving to repair this situation gave way under the vast traffic of heavy lorries with munitions for

the offensive. On the paths across the cratered fields troops
sank at every step, and the strain of pulling out each foot
from the suction of the mud caused a journey of six miles
to occupy between nine and twelve hours. Battalions came
through dazed with exhaustion. In the morass of the
trenches first-rate care and discipline were required to
avoid losing toes or feet through frost-bite. Putties
wrapped round the shins dangerously restricted the circu-
lation. It took five or six relays of stretcher-bearers, each
team six or eight strong, many hours to get a wounded
man from front line to the ambulance, a few miles back:
Brig.-General Glasfurd, mortally wounded, was ten hours
on the journey.

In these conditions—the worst ever known to the
First A.I.F.—two attempts were made to carry forward
the line. On November 5th two attacks were launched;
one near Gueudecourt during the small hours, in rain
which made the attempt a nightmare;[14] the other near
Flers in mid-morning. In the first attack the troops for
the assault reached their front line half-exhausted after
a terrible journey over the mud, some of them late. The
1st Battalion was seen and shelled and, being therefore
unable to assemble in no-man's-land, the men of its
leading waves had to bridge with their bodies the top of
the trench while the supports crawled in to assemble
beneath them. In the drizzle the troops advanced in good
order; but, slithering over shellholes, they could not
nearly keep pace with the creeping barrage.

In both operations portion of the assaulting forces
entered the enemy trenches, and held parts of them
for some hours until the impossibility of keeping the
partial gains was realised. The effort near Flers was
repeated on November 14th when portion of the objective was seized and held for two days. At the same time,
miles away on the high ground near Thiepval, Gough's

---

[14] For this, the most difficult fight of the 1st A.I.F., see *Vol. III, pp. 904-9.*

army made a vigorous and largely successful attack at
Beaumont Hamel. This confirmed Haig's belief in
Gough's leadership; and the ease with which Germans
surrendered showed that their morale had undoubtedly
been effected by the strain of the Somme Battle.

But the clogging of attack after attack in the mud
of the Somme had now convinced Haig that all his
troops could do for the remainder of the winter was, as
far as possible, to keep up this strain on the Germans by
means of small attacks and raids.

So the First Somme Battle ended. The Germans had
been hard tried but not broken. The armies had taken each
other's measure—the British, if not yet fully trained, were
at least a growing danger to their opponents and both sides
now knew it. But the battle was also the hardest and
bloodiest fought by the British in that war, and its cost
to them and the French was almost certainly greater than
to the Germans. The British loss of about 415,000 included
the flower of the British youth in the New Army.[15] Yet
the Allies could afford loss better than their opponents;
and, in the terrible determination with which Haig wore
his enemy down, the Germans really faced the beginning
of the end.

On 16th November 1916 a conference of the Allies
at Chantilly in France decided to strike at the enemy
from all directions—east, west, south and south-east—in
the coming spring. So far as the Western Front was concerned Joffre and Haig could think of nothing better
than to take up the Somme offensive, as soon as possible,
at the point where it had been left off.

During the winter, both Allies and Germans on the
Somme found their time and powers fully occupied in
battling against mud, rain, and frost-bite. Little by little,
railways, motors and waggons brought up the stone and
timber to repair roads seven miles back, over which more
stone and timber could be brought to repair the next

---

[15] The British official historian gives the Allied loss at over 600,000, the
German being almost as great.

mile of road; over that again came material to repair the
next mile—and finally tracks and material reached the
trenches and the dreaded conditions of that front were
slowly improved. Perhaps for Australians the experience
was really no harsher than for their mates of the splendid
15th Scottish Division at Le Sars on their left[16] or for the
Guards Division at Le Transloy on their right. Lord
Cavan, commanding the XIV Corps (including the
Guards Division) had written to the higher command:
"The conditions are far worse than in the First Battle of
Ypres; all my general and staff officers agree that they
are the worst they have seen"—and it was partly his repre-
sentation that stopped the offensive. For the Germans
there were green fields and better roads close behind the
front, but they now had to endure heavier shelling than
the Allies and frequent bombing from the air.

Finally thousands of duckboards were laid on long
tracks across the morass and there began to arrive at the
trenches duckboards for dry standing, frames, dugout
timbers, hot food containers, leather waistcoats, thigh
boots, worsted gloves, "Tommy Cookers", dry socks. In
the nearer camps, largely through the ceaseless care of
General White, came better huts, comfort stalls, even
cinema material. A strong appeal by Birdwood to officers
to place their men's comfort above their own caused
great offence—and did great good. From mid-January
1917, four weeks of colder, brighter weather froze the
land and water hard, temporarily banished the mud, and
covered northern France with snow.

Inch by inch, day by day, determined that no one
should hold them a whit inferior to those around them,
the Australians victoriously emerged from the dreadful
shadow of that experience, their spirit gradually regaining
its old elasticity, their sector one of the best furnished
on the battlefield, and their corps recognised as one of
the finest fighting instruments on the Western Front.

---

[16] Even before this the Australians fraternised in a marked degree with
the Scots. The independent and democratic outlook of both peoples gave
them a strong affinity, and many Australians spent their leave in Scotland.

CHAPTER XVI

THE DEFENCE OF EGYPT

WHILE the soldiers of this new nation were thus pulling their full weight in the vast, swaying struggle in which the Allies were trying to overturn the main German incubus on the Western Front, in the Middle East the war against the Turks had again suddenly flared up.

When, by March 1916, the cool season in Egypt had ended without the Turks' having made any attempt to advance across Sinai from Palestine, it had become certain that the danger of any overwhelming attack upon the Canal was over for the year. But attacks in moderate strength were possible. On April 7th Murray pushed out a British Mounted (Yeomanry) Brigade from the Canal defence line to Romani, Katia, Oghratina and Mageibra, fifteen to twenty miles out along the old caravan route to Palestine, skirting the Mediterranean Sea. A fortnight later, in the misty morning of April 23rd, a strong body of Turks surprised and overwhelmed the Oghratina and Katia camps (which had been studied from the air by German pilots), killed or captured several squadrons of Yeomanry, and drove in the whole brigade. They even tried to raid the Canal defence line at Dueidar, but here Scottish infantry beat them back.

The Anzac Mounted Division had then been only partly formed—its 1st Light Horse Brigade was still in the Libyan Desert. But the 2nd and 3rd Brigades had relieved the 1st Australian Division at the Canal and had made two small successful raids into Sinai: to reconnoitre the Wadi Muksheib—down which early in the previous year the Turks had made their first thrust at the Canal

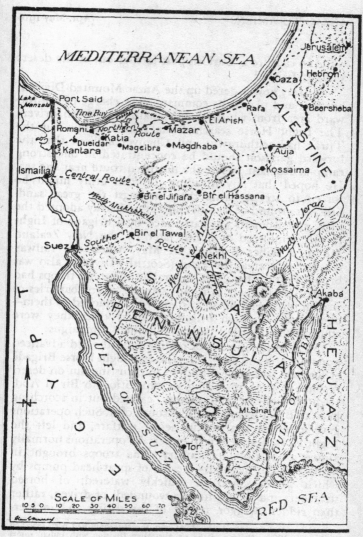

THE SCENE OF OPERATIONS IN SINAI, 1916-17

—and to capture a Turkish post farther out at the desert wells at Jifjafa.[1]

Murray now ordered up the Anzac Mounted Division hot foot and placed its commander in charge of the forward area from which the Yeomanry had been driven. The Light Horse searched the raided camps but the Turks had withdrawn; and Chauvel advised that the forward garrison should be concentrated in one strong camp at Romani, beside the northern route near the sea. He hoped that any invading Turkish army might be forced to accept battle there amongst the great sand-hills, on ground of British choosing. Murray adopted the plan, and Romani was garrisoned by a brigade of Light Horse, reinforced a month later by the New Zealand Mounted Rifles Brigade. In May, when the railway reached that area, the 52nd (Scottish) Division also was brought up thither. The Australian mounted troops had no artillery of their own, but some excellent batteries of British territorial horse artillery were attached to them— one battery to each brigade; and by these they were admirably supported throughout their campaigns.

Meanwhile, instead of maintaining the old advanced posts at Katia and elsewhere, the 2nd Light Horse Brigade at Romani had been employed in thrusting out on desert reconnaissances, including an expedition to Bir el Abd, twenty miles east, and another, carried out in scorching heat, to Bir el Bayud six miles south of it. Such operations gave excellent practice in desert warfare, and left the Light Horse competent to undertake operations normally almost impossible for cavalry. The troops brought in many unusual methods—the use of spear-head pumps by which horses could be quickly watered; of horsed stretchers and sleighs for the wounded; of driven, rather than ridden, waggon teams; of the sifting and inciner-

---

[1] A month before the Light Horse raid, the Muksheib had been searched by Captain Wilder-Neligan of the 1st Australian Division with Indian camel troops, some Light Horse supporting them (*Vol. III, p. 28*).

ation of all refuse, to keep down the flies; even of mounted dental units (a New Zealand improvisation) to deal with dental plates and simple troubles. Several of these innovations—pumps, driving of waggons, dentists— were at first stoutly resisted by Murray's regular Army staff. The necessary material was therefore bought from Anzac funds until the staff swung round and authorised the changes and, in some cases, ordered their adoption in the British Army. The "pedrail", however, with which guns were fitted to cross the desert, was a British invention of great importance.

General Murray, himself, was quick to appreciate the work now being done by his Anzac mounted troops. Writing to the War Office after he had sent most of his infantry to France, "I am assuming," he said, "that you are leaving the three Australian Light Horse Brigades and the New Zealand Brigade with me. Otherwise I shall be deprived of the only really reliable mounted troops that I have." After the terrible experience of the raid to Bayud, he wrote that he did not think "any other troops could have undertaken the operation successfully in the present weather". And at the end of May: "any work entrusted to these excellent troops is invariably well executed".

Provided that he had troops who could work in the desert, Murray's policy of going out to fight the Turks on the narrow approach to Egypt was far more economical than the earlier British plan of meeting them on the Canal line, which could thus safely be held much more lightly than a few months earlier. To render difficult the central route across the Sinai Desert he sent out in June part of the 3rd Light Horse Brigade to spill a large supply of water which, through a sudden storm, had collected in the old wells and pools of the Wadi Muksheib. Actually this rare flood had come down while the Light Horse were out there on the earlier raid to Jifjafa. The water was pumped out, and the wells sealed; it was there-

19—os

fore now most probable that any Turkish invading force would use the northern route, and meet the defenders of Egypt at Romani.

Air reconnaissances were difficult for Murray's force. Of his two British air squadrons one had just been relieved by the 1st Australian, but this was divided between Suez, Upper Egypt, and Kantara, and the aeroplanes, B.E.2.c's, were much inferior to the German-piloted Fokker scouts and Aviatiks which served the Turks. German airmen could reconnoitre Murray's positions at will, since he was given no anti-aircraft guns. In June they bombed the horse-lines at Romani killing a number of men and horses. Bedouin Arabs also constantly informed the Turks of British movements and positions. Although the Arabs of the Hejaz in southern Arabia began in June 1916 their remarkable campaign of revolt against the Turks, the Bedouin, larrikins of the desert, served as the spies of both sides but especially of the Turks.

Murray's whole infantry now comprised only four weak territorial divisions. For mounted work, he wrote, "I rely entirely on my Anzac Mounted Division". At this stage, on July 18th, Brig.-General Chaytor of the N.Z.M.R. Brigade, reconnoitring by aeroplane over the northern route towards Palestine, noted that four large bodies of Turks with camel transport had suddenly appeared a day or two's march beyond the British posts. Evidently they came from El Arish in the borderlands near Palestine. The total forces seen were estimated at some 8000 men, and presumably they had one of two objects—either to attack the British, as Murray hoped, at Romani, or to seize and fortify the Katia-Oghratina oasis area, and so establish a standing danger to the British on the Canal.

Murray kept touch with these Turks by sending out every day one of his Light Horse brigades to watch and harass them. For the moment, the enemy troops dug

themselves in at Oghratına. The Light Horse—1st and
2nd Brigades alternating—would ride out in the small
hours to Katia (where a dummy camp was maintained to
deceive the Turks) and then at dawn would advance,
pressing back any forward Turkish posts until resistance
stiffened. Occasionally a Turkish post, or a scout, was cut
off, captured and sent back for examination. Sometimes
the Turks counter-attacked the thin Light Horse screen—
there occurred even hand-to-hand fighting and at least
one exciting dash on horseback through the Turkish outposts. The midsummer heat was intense and after a fortnight of this work the Light Horse, animals and men,
were becoming seriously worn.

At this stage the War Office changed its previous
defensive policy. Although in Mesopotamia, as already
noted, the Anglo-Indian force, that had been thrust up
the Tigris, had been surrounded late in 1915 at Kut el
Amara, and had been forced to surrender in April 1916,[2]
prospects both there and in Europe now seemed better.
Murray was urged to attack. But, before he could arrange
to do so, on the night of August 2nd the Turks advanced
to Katia. It seemed probable that they were marching
straight into Murray's trap. The expectation was that the
enemy would try to envelop the southern end of the
Romani defences and then to seize the camp and railway
behind them.

Accordingly on the following night General Chauvel
placed his "resting" Light Horse Brigade, the 1st, as
already planned, extending southwards the line held by
the 52nd Infantry Division at Romani. Two regiments
(2nd and 3rd—about 500 rifles) were lined out very
widely south of the camp, in small posts reaching across
three miles of hummocky sand, with the main line
of lofty sandhills, south-west of the Romani defences, in
rear of them. The 1st Regiment was in reserve; the

---

[2] Part of the 1st Australian Half-Flight was captured there (*Vol. VIII*,
p. 25).

2nd Light Horse Brigade was out on reconnaissance in touch with the Turks; the 3rd Brigade, attached to the central section of Canal defences, had been ordered to move up towards the Romani area. The New Zealand Mounted Rifles Brigade was in reserve ten miles away with the special duty of falling upon the southern flank of the Turks when they attacked. The 3rd Light Horse Brigade would be available for the same purpose farther south; and southernmost of all was a column of mixed Light Horse and Camel Corps under Lieut.-Colonel C. L. Smith, which would have the same duty.

These forces should be able to envelop any Turkish force which itself tried to envelop the Romani position. They might even have a chance to capture or kill all Turks engaged in the expedition. In order to improve this chance Murray directed Chauvel not to call on the reserves too early, but to hold on with his already much-tried brigades until the Turks had committed their reserve to the fight, and were thoroughly involved in the attack on the camp. Chauvel, therefore, planned, not to hold the Turks on his present line, but to swing slowly back, when necessary, across the big sandhills, towards the camp at Etmaler behind Romani, his left flank pivoting on the 52nd Division's southern post at the high sandhill of Katib Gannit. The sand through which the Turks would here advance would make very heavy going, and so anxious were Chauvel and Murray for the enemy to take this route that the Light Horse screen was not allowed to fortify its outposts lest the sight of the defences might cause the Turks to choose another line of advance.

As expected, the Turks who had advanced to Katia on August 3rd, were presently detected in a further advance: during the following night the Light Horse outposts saw men moving at certain points over the starlit sand. At 1 a.m. on the 4th, a sudden wild babble of "Allah! Allah!" heralded a creeping attack against the Australian screen. The Turks had meant to move past

the British flank to a long sandhill (Wellington Ridge)
flanking the camps and railway behind the British, and
then at dawn to rush these and attack the 52nd Division
from rear and front. The existence of the Light Horse
screen, posted that night, was until now unknown to
them. Each side fired at the other's rifle flashes while the
Turks crept up towards charging distance.

The British and Australians had some 10,000 rifles in
their firing line and supports this night, and the Turks,
perhaps, 12,000 to 14,000—not a great preponderance
with which to attack a strongly fortified position. But the
main part of the British strength, some 7000 rifles of the
52nd Division, was to the north, in the Romani defences,
which were not seriously attacked, while the real Turkish
thrust was faced by the 1600 rifles of Chauvel's two Light
Horse Brigades,[3] of which only two regiments, comprising some 500 rifles, were holding the three-mile line
of the screen. In various parts, when the Turks were close

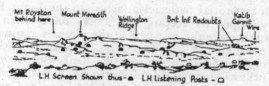

Position of the screen, seen from the Turkish side.

enough actually to rush and kill one or two posts, the
Light Horse mounted and galloped back to the next
position, where despite that most trying experience—
galloping away from the enemy—they instantly turned
and resumed the fight. Before dawn the Turks—estimated
at 8000—rushed an overtowering sandhill in the centre,
Mount Meredith, and were also seen to be obviously

---

[3] One man in every four was a horse-holder, sent to shelter with the
horses. Moreover the brigades, after their hard work, were not at full
strength.

trying to outflank the Light Horse line by making for a similar dune to the south-west, Mount Royston. The 1st Light Horse Brigade had retired gradually to Wellington Ridge, south of the camps; but, following the plan laid down, it was not till this outflanking movement became urgent that Chauvel, at 4.30 a.m., ordered up his 2nd Light Horse Brigade on to the right flank of the 1st.[4]

From then onwards there raged a long, intense, difficult struggle, the Turks trying to feel their way round this extending flank, the Light Horse, constantly withdrawn from the left and tacked on to the right of the line, trying to extend the flank still farther and bar their way. The 52nd Division spontaneously helped by taking over the left of the Australian line. The great leader of the fight on the threatened flank was the South African, Brig.-General J. R. Royston, temporarily commanding the 2nd Brigade, who galloped from one threatened point to another, putting in reinforcements, cheering the men, and keeping Chauvel informed of the situation. The British territorial batteries attached to the Light Horse greatly helped by keeping the Turks under their fire; and at this stage the first part of the reserves, a squadron of Gloucestershire Yeomanry, was put in to assist in meeting the threat to the extreme flank. But by 7 a.m. the Turks had occupied Wellington Ridge and the Light Horse line was pressed almost against Etmaler Camp.

Now at last, with the Turks fully extended and growing tired, was the time for the reserves to strike their flank and rear. But here was found the weak point in the British plans. All troops in the area, except those coming from the central section of the Canal Defences, were under control of Maj.-General Hon. H. A. Lawrence, commander of the Northern Section of those defences,[5] whose headquarters were at the Canal at Kantara.

---

[4] The Wellington Mounted Rifles were with the 2nd Bde, in exchange for the 5th L.H. Regt, attached to the N.Z.M.R. Bde.

[5] Afterwards Chief of the General Staff of Haig on the Western Front.

Murray had suggested to Lawrence that his control was centred too far back, and that he should either move up his headquarters or delegate command to someone in the forward area. On the other hand Lawrence feared, what Murray did not, that the Turks might bypass Romani and strike at the Canal, and he accordingly maintained his existing arrangements. But the direct telegraph line to his headquarters was broken in the battle. Communication became very slow, and the battlefront and reserves were in fact under three separate commanders with no machinery for combining their action.

Very late Chauvel managed to inform Lawrence of the position. Lawrence had by then discovered, through despatching the 5th Light Horse Regiment on reconnaissance the night before, that the Turks were not making for the Canal. He now, therefore sent forward the New Zealand and 5th Yeomanry Brigades; and though the orders to the New Zealanders were twice changed, about noon the tired battle troops, holding up 2000 Turks at Mount Royston on the exposed flank, caught sight of a distant body of cavalry. It was the approaching New Zealanders. Early in the afternoon they and the 5th Yeomanry Brigade attacked the Turkish flank—which in its turn became exposed—at Mount Royston. A brigade of Lawrence's reserve infantry division, the 42nd (Lancashire) was marching up to help; but the sand made heavy going, and though the stubbornness of the Turks caused the fight to last throughout the afternoon, this infantry had not arrived at 6 p.m., by which time the dismounted New Zealanders and Yeomanry had gradually pushed close enough to be almost within charging distance. The Turks then put up the white flag and began to surrender in large numbers.

Meanwhile other Turks, who had been massing farther east behind Wellington Ridge, had again tried to advance over its crest but were shelled off by the territorial batteries. The Light Horse began to advance, cap-

turing many of the enemy. But an intended assault by
part of the 52nd Division in that sector had not developed;
and the 3rd Light Horse Brigade coming up from the
south-west had not received its orders in time to reach the
Turkish flank during the battle. As night was now falling
and his Light Horse brigades were exceedingly tired
Chauvel held them back till dawn; and Lawrence, who,
incidentally, was under the mistaken impression that the
52nd Division in the Romani defences had been strongly
attacked, did not believe that even on the southern flank
a bold encircling movement had much chance of success.

Horses had to be watered and wounded cleared.[6] A
brigade of the 42nd Infantry Division arrived and took
over the right flank from the New Zealanders and
Yeomanry. The forward troops of both sides rested in
the positions reached in the battle. As it was clear that
the Turks must be exhausted, Murray and Lawrence
ordered their infantry and cavalry to move forward as
soon as possible. At 4 a.m. on August 5th the 1st and 2nd
Light Horse Brigades, together with the nearest infantry,
advanced with the bayonet. Only in the centre of the
southern front on Wellington Ridge did the Turks resist
strongly, and there too they were eventually rushed and
surrendered. The Turkish flank having gone, Lawrence
at 6.30 placed Chauvel in charge of all mounted troops
with orders to pursue keenly; the 3rd Light Horse Brigade
was to outflank the Turks on the south and Smith's camel
force to operate still farther inland.

The New Zealand, Yeomanry and 3rd Light Horse
Brigades were still watering, but by 10 a.m. all had moved.
By 4 p.m. the 3rd Brigade had boldly rushed the southern
flank of the Turks south of Katia, capturing 425 men and
7 machine-guns, just as the rest of the mounted troops
approached Katia from the front. But as the 3rd Brigade

---

[6] There were great defects in the clearance of wounded in the rear areas,
almost matching some of the incidents in Gallipoli and Mesopotamia. The
system was afterwards amended.

now came under shellfire their brigadier withdrew tnem and the possible chance of striking decisively was lost. The rest of the mounted troops, after taking many prisoners and much booty, approached Katia and set their horses to the charge. The Anzacs, who had no swords, carried their bayonets, but after racing across a salt-pan the horses plunged into swamp. The troops dismounted but could not reach the Turkish line, which also was protected by heavier artillery than the mounted troops possessed.

The mounted troops could not take Katia and had to retire. The infantry of the 52nd Division had advanced much too late to take part, and that of the 42nd Division, new to desert marching, broke down with heat, weariness and thirst. At one time Murray thought his mounted troops, also, disappointingly slow. But at this stage he realised that three weeks of continuous hard reconnaissance and fighting had largely exhausted the Anzac horsemen, and the horses also. The Turks had not been completely destroyed as planned.

Nevertheless the threat of Turkish invasion had been dispelled. While the British that night fell back from Katia on the one side, the Turks were hurriedly abandoning it on the other. The 3000 mounted troops followed them, and on August 9th attacked the Turkish remnant, about 6000 strong, at Bir el Abd. The enemy eventually held them and at dusk they had to be withdrawn, carrying their 210 wounded. Again the Turks had been left in position, but two days later they again withdrew—to Salmana; and, when on August 13th the Anzac Mounted Division and its British artillery lightly attacked them there, they finally fell back to El Arish, fifty miles away on the coastal approaches to Palestine.

In truth the Turk had learnt to fear the operations of these horsemen; and possibly he did not fully realise how difficult they found it to come to grips with his infantry when it was strongly posted. At all events

Romani, though fought by comparatively few troops, was one of the decisive battles of the war. In the five days' fighting—and mainly south of Romani—the Turks lost half their force; some 5250 are believed to have been killed or wounded and nearly 4000 were captured. The British loss between August 5th and 9th was 1130, all but a few hundred being among the 5000 Anzacs. Very few of these were prisoners; with the Light Horse it was (says their historian)[7] "a voluntary and unwritten law that no sound man should allow himself to be taken prisoner, and no wounded man should be permitted to fall into enemy hands". In the two and a half years of these campaigns only 73 light horsemen—and not one of their officers—were captured by the Turks. In the same time they captured over 40,000 Turks.

More than for any other leader, including even Royston, Romani was a personal triumph for Chauvel. Fought on the very days on which the 2nd Australian Infantry Division in France was capturing and consolidating its hold on Pozières ridge, it completely changed the outlook of the campaign in the Middle East. Now, even more keenly than before, Murray urged upon the vacillating British government that the best defence of Egypt was to advance, at least to El Arish; and, in the hope of eventually receiving more support, he now began to plan to drive the Turks from Palestine.

But across the waterless stretch from Bir el Abd to El Arish the British infantry could go only as fast as their railhead and line of water pipe. As the engineers and Egyptian labourers gradually extended these, the mounted troops occasionally thrust ahead on some foray. Smith's camel force together with some Yeomanry and Light Horse had, during the Romani operations, been striking at Turkish posts on the inland flank, at Aweidia, Hilu, and Bayud. Henceforth one condition of the fighting

---

[7] Sir Henry Gullett, *Vol. VII, p. 185.*

improved. The 1st Squadron, Australian Flying Corps,[8] was now concentrated at Kantara, and with the 14th British Squadron it constantly reconnoitred the ground ahead and bombed the Turkish camps. In mid-September three Light Horse brigades together with camel companies and artillery, and with vast provision for watering, tried to surround and seize the next Turkish post at Mazar, half-way to El Arish; and in mid-October a mixed force, with greater provision for watering, made a four days' expedition to cut out a Turkish garrison at Maghara, twenty-five miles away to the south-east in the Sinai Hills. Each of these attempts seemed to be meeting with some success when, to the great disappointment of his troops, their commander withdrew them in accordance with an overruling order that, if the first attack did not succeed, he was to consider the operation a reconnaissance and pull back his force. The Turks, however, abandoned Mazar two days after the attack.

In November Chauvel, then at Mazar, was ordered to prepare for the advance to El Arish, and on the night of December 20th the Light Horse to their delight finally marched clear of the loose sand of the dunes on to the hard plain bordering the Wadi el Arish. By dawn the village was surrounded by Light Horse, New Zealanders, and the camel brigade. The squalid place—which to troops so long in the desert appeared "a pleasant, civilised town"—had been rightly reported to have been abandoned by the Turks; and the Arab populace and chief sheikh came out to welcome the strangers with a demonstration of excited welcome.

Murray's railway was still thirty miles short of El Arish, but the British Navy could here land stores and supplies on the beach and immediately began to do so.[9] The 52nd Division came up to hold the town. And then

---

[8] Flying B.E.2.c's, Martinsydes, and R.E.8's. *See Vol. VIII, pp. 31-3, and 47.*
[9] The Royal Australian Naval Bridging Train made a pier.

at last, on the firmer ground, the mounted troops had the
chance of operations more suited to themselves and their
horses. Two routes led from El Arish to Palestine, one
along the beach past Rafa to Gaza; the other south-south-
east past Magdhaba to El Auja, near the head of the railway which the enemy was building into Sinai. To block
each route the Turkish rearguard from El Arish had split
in two and posted itself at Rafa and Magdhaba, each
about twenty-five miles away, and about thirty miles
apart. As will later be explained, a change had been made
in the organisation of Murray's army; being responsible
for the defence of Egypt, which was showing signs of
unrest, he had removed his own headquarters from
Ismailia to Cairo, and had obtained from the Cameroons
Lieut.-General Sir Charles Dobell to command the force
in Sinai, and from the Western Front a cavalry leader,
Sir Philip Chetwode, to control his advanced troops (now
known as the Desert Column). Chetwode, arriving at
El Arish by sea on December 22nd, decided at once to
seize these two advanced enemy posts.

The expedition against the inland one, Magdhaba,
began that night, Chauvel and the Anzac Mounted
Division forming the striking force, but with the 2nd
L.H. Brigade absent and the new Imperial Camel Corps
Brigade, under Lieut.-Colonel C. L. Smith, and its
mountain battery (from Hong Kong and Singapore) attached instead. This camel brigade had been raised mainly
from the Gallipoli infantry after the Evacuation and comprised 2½ battalions of Australians, ½ battalion of New
Zealanders, and 1 battalion of British troops. Its strength
was about 2500, roughly twice that of a Light Horse
brigade, and its men, like their British brigadier, were
tough fighters.

The march to Magdhaba was made along the east
side of the Wadi el Arish, and by night. In the small hours
the Turkish campfires were seen, and, when their flicker
was apparently close, the troops were halted and break-

fasted. As soon as the Turkish dispositions were clearly known, through aeroplanes flying low after dawn, Chauvel distributed his force, the camel brigade going straight for the nearest Turkish redoubt, east of the wadi, the other brigades making detours round the position, mainly on the hard plain east of the wadi, where horses could go fast. The New Zealanders worked round to the Turkish flank, and the 10th L.H. Regiment, by a long detour, to the enemy's rear.

A hard fight now developed in which the Camels, and part of the Light Horse had to advance over the open under heavy fire. Progress was slow. The horses had been long without water, and efforts to find a supply had failed. The urgency of watering the horses daily was the ruling factor in cavalry work in the desert, and after consulting some of his leaders Chauvel reluctantly ordered his brigades to withdraw.

But already, without his knowledge the Camels and 1st Brigade were in position to rush the central redoubt. Brig.-General Cox laid aside the order to retire. This redoubt was taken. Other regiments rushed the remainder, the 10th Regiment actually galloped through and over one redoubt and then attacked it from the other side. Few Turks escaped; by 4.30 p.m. 1282 had been captured and, perhaps, 300 killed. The raiding force returned with its wounded and prisoners to El Arish.

The Turkish post at Rafa was attacked a fortnight later, on 9th January 1917. Murray's airmen had clearly mapped the Turkish dispositions, and the Anzac Mounted Division, after advancing during the night and seizing the Arab village of Sheikh Zowaaid, from which news would otherwise have reached the enemy, had the Turks and their redoubts completely surrounded before dawn. At once, however, the difficulty of the operation became obvious: the redoubts lay on two central heights with completely open slopes leading gently up for a mile on every side. The approach by the surrounding lines of men, though Chauvel's batteries tried to keep the Turkish heads down, was extraordinarily difficult; and though the reserves—3rd Light Horse and 5th Yeomanry Brigades—were put into gaps in the cordon, the prospect of reaching the redoubts seemed precarious. Ammunition was short; and at 4.25 p.m., when two forces of Turks were reported to be approaching from west and north-west, Chetwode, after consulting Chauvel, ordered the troops to withdraw, and the nearest brigade, the Yeomanry, actually began to carry this out.

But again some of the troops were then so near to victory that the order was ignored. The New Zealanders on the north and the camel brigade on the south, by long advances, rushed their redoubts. The other troops joined the attack, the Yeomanry turning back to do so. The 1800 Turks in the posts were all killed or captured. The force returned to El Arish. The approaching Turkish reinforcements withdrew; part of them next day attacked a force of the 3rd Light Horse Brigade, left behind to cover the bringing in of the wounded, and were beaten off. The total British casualties had been 486.

A month later, in mid-February 1917, two small expeditions farther south into Sinai, one to Nekhl under Lieut.-Colonel W. Grant with the 11th L.H. Regiment and some camel troops, the other made by the British camel battalion to Hassana, eliminated the remaining Turkish garrisons from the interior of Sinai. The task of clearing that difficult peninsula had fallen almost entirely on the mounted troops, of whom four-fifths were Anzacs. About that time, on hearing that Birdwood, after Pozières, wanted the Light Horse reinforcements in Egypt to be sent to France for the infantry, Murray wrote: "I cannot spare a single man from these reinforcements. These Anzac troops are the keystone of the defence of Egypt."

The way was now clear for an advance against the Turks in Palestine.

CHAPTER XVII

THE HOME FRONT, 1916-17

POZIÈRES had many results beside the direct one of shaking the Germans from a key position in the First Battle of the Somme. It brought the main Australian forces into the whitest heat of modern war. All the Australian divisions in France were afterwards classed by the British command there as among those tried British and Dominion divisions on which any responsibility could be placed; Sir Douglas Haig surprised Queen Victoria's son, the old Duke of Connaught, by telling him that the Australians were among the best disciplined troops in France: "When they are ordered to attack they always do so," he said.

But it was also a result of Pozières that afterwards, possibly, shook Haig's opinion. Hitherto the supreme punishment in the A.I.F. had been to be discharged from the force in disgrace. After the dreadful, long drawn out bombardments of Pozières that punishment had, for some types of men in the force, very little effect. Return to Australia—to which, till September 1918, there was no return on leave—was no longer any deterrent for the persistent deserter. Absence without leave increased. At times of strain, or before a great battle—the very time when the average Australian refused to go sick or, not infrequently, broke away from convalescence to get back to his mates in the line—a certain section persistently "went absent". In almost every other army such desertion could be punished by death. But by the Australian Defence Act this punishment was restricted to cases of mutiny and of desertion to the enemy. The restriction was fully supported, both in Australia and in the services; the general feeling was steadily against the infliction of a death penalty on men who had volunteered to fight in a cause not primarily their own (or at least not realised as being such). Consequently the A.I.F. had to rely increasingly on the leadership and example of its officers and N.C.O.'s, the tone and *esprit de corps* of its men, and the substitution of other penalties—including, ultimately, the publication of lists of offenders in the Australian newspapers.

Another result of the immense casualties of Pozières was that the Australian reinforcement depots in Europe had not troops sufficient to replace them. The camps at Salisbury Plain were quickly drained dry. The British Army Council decided that the 3rd Australian Division, then training under General Monash at Salisbury Plain, should either be broken up to reinforce the other divisions, or, at least, lend enough troops to bring them up to strength. Without consulting Birdwood, Colonel R. McC. Anderson, who was in charge of A.I.F. Headquarters in London and in touch with the War Office, cabled this decision to the Australian government.

Birdwood and White were strongly against this course; rightly or wrongly, they suspected that the Army Council was really using this decision as pressure to induce Australia to adopt conscription for its army. Great Britain had introduced conscription seven months before, on 24th January 1916, and New Zealand in August. Canada did so a year later. Birdwood and White felt that, instead of the use of something bordering on a threat, Australia should have been given the opportunity to supply the men desired. They therefore drew up their estimate of the numbers required and urged that the Australian government should be asked if it could supply them.

The experience of full-dress modern offensives on the Western Front was then very new, and Birdwood and

White, like the War Office, based their calculations on the assumption that operations such as those on the Somme would be an almost constant factor. The numbers estimated by them to be necessary were, first, in addition to the monthly reinforcement (11,790), a special draft of 20,000 to bring all five divisions to strength; and then, for each of the three next monthly reinforcement drafts, an increase to 16,500.

These numbers—over 80,000 in four months—would certainly refill the units and the depots against future heavy fighting. But, for the Australian government, the demand was staggering. It is true that Australian recruiting in June-September 1915 enlisted over 90,000 men, and in the first three months of 1916 rose to numbers not much lower. But the reservoir of enthusiastic or willing men had by then been largely spent; and the government, whose efforts were now bringing in not much more than half the normal monthly reinforcement, was suddenly required to raise this great excess.

A considerable part of the Australian people felt that their nation was "falling down" in its due share of the Allied war effort, and this feeling was intensified by the realisation that, in spite of the misleading optimism and evasions of the Allies' communiqués and newspaper reports, the war was not going altogether well for the Allies; at least signs of victory for the Allies seemed no clearer than those for the Central Powers. In 1915 the Russians had been driven back with tremendous blows. They seriously lacked transport and munitions, and their counter-blows in 1916, though cheering, were far from decisive. The Allies had failed at Gallipoli; and on the Western Front and at Salonica, despite their losses, had made little progress. But it was the reverses on the Russian front in 1915 that had first generated in many thinking people in Australia an urgent desire to see their nation's shoulder bent more closely to the wheel. Whether voluntary enlistment would give enough recruits had long

20—os

been doubted by some leaders—as early as 16th April and 9th June 1915 the question of compulsion had been raised in the Senate, on the latter occasion by a Labour senator from Western Australia, P. J. Lynch. Mr W. A. Holman, Labour Premier of New South Wales, and the Roman Catholic Archbishop of Sydney, Dr Kelly, were among those who supported the idea. Trades union leaders, however, generally were against it, and on 24th September 1915 the then Prime Minister, Andrew Fisher, told them that he was "irrevocably opposed to it". Senator Pearce, Minister for Defence, had pointed out that obviously such a step was not yet necessary in Australia—a truth then not open to dispute.

But Mr W. M. Hughes, who on 26th October 1915 succeeded Mr Fisher as Prime Minister, had in pre-war years been one of the most influential among those who established compulsion for home service in Australia; and in the first year of his prime ministership conditions of recruiting entirely changed. The voluntary system under-went its first heavy strain when, after the consideration of the "War Census" figures[1] in November 1915, an additional force of 50,000 (over and above reinforcements) had been decided on. A systematic campaign by "War Councils" in each State, with local recruiting committees to help them, was begun. Local authorities co-operated. Special methods aided the appeal—particularly the marches of recruits from country towns to the capitals, gathering more men as they went—the first being that of the "Cooees" from Gilgandra, starting with 30 men and ending in Sydney, 320 miles away, with 263. The large enlistments from January to March 1916—totalling 56,206—were the result.

But this time in trades union circles there was some active opposition to the methods employed, especially to an appeal asking every man whether he was prepared to

---

[1] See p. 186.

enlist and, if not, why. Trades union circles themselves
were divided, but feeling rose fairly high when an official
of the Clerks' Union who led the opposition to this inquiry was tarred and feathered by returned soldiers. This
kind of division quickly led to a general taking of sides,
and the arousing of bitterness. Even the sentiment "Australia has done enough" began to be heard. In the middle
of 1916 the monthly enlistment dropped to 6170, lower
than ever before. To those whose sons, fathers and brothers
were at that moment bearing the terrible brunt at
Pozières, the system by which the willing were killed and
maimed, and the unwilling remained at home enjoying
high wages and comfortable living, seemed intolerably
unfair.

A very strong movement for compulsion had thus
been growing before the huge demands consequent on
Pozières reached Australia. Mr Hughes had been away
from Australia, the British government having at the end
of 1915 invited Dominion Prime Ministers to England
for the purpose of informing them more confidentially
on the war situation. This visit developed rather as a
personal triumph for Mr Hughes. His intense concentration upon ensuring vigorous action—especially upon
fighting Germany in the economic and commercial as
well as the military field—led to his sweeping through the
Mother Country on a fiery crusade, in which a large part
of the British press and people vehemently supported
him. At times this popular approval tended to carry the
British Prime Minister, Mr Asquith, and his Cabinet off
their feet. Mr Hughes was invited many times, though
not regularly, to take part in British Cabinet meetings,
and popular insistence forced the government to send
him to the Economic Conference of the Allies in Paris.
In Cabinet he was shocked by the apparent lack of set
policy and the rather fortuitous manner in which war
issues were determined; and this led to his decision to act
for himself in some important matters—as will be seen

later. He visited the Australian troops then still in the "nursery" sector, and obtained from Haig a promise—afterwards faithfully observed—to keep them together as far as possible.

On 31st July 1916 Mr Hughes returned to Australia. During his stay in England conscription for the Army had been adopted there; and a considerable part of the Australian people were hanging on his return, believing that he had only to say the word and it would be adopted in Australia also. But for a month he made no decisive statement. His difficulty was that he knew the issue would split his Labour party; and though, by the Opposition's help, conscription would be carried in the House of Representatives, the Labour vote would certainly reject it in the Senate.[2] For a month he tried to convert the Labour objectors in Cabinet and caucus. During this time he received the colossal demand of the Army Council for making good the losses of Pozières and replenishing the depots. Obviously this could not be met from volunteers. The only practicable way remaining for him was to refer the question from Parliament to the Australian people, for decision by referendum.

Even this method was opposed by some of his party in both houses, but in September the bill for holding a referendum was passed; and with this began the most violent struggle in Australian political history. Its bitterness was natural. A great part of one side—men and women—felt that its dearest friends were being sacrificed through the lack of courage and patriotism of their opponents; a great part of the other side felt that the advocates of conscription were largely ineligible people—too old, or possibly "indispensable" at home—who were trying to force sons from mothers without themselves offering even the sacrifice of their own wealth. The details

---

2 If he obtained a dissolution of Parliament, only half the Senate would be sent to the electors; the other half—entirely Labour—would remain, necessitating further delay and a "double dissolution".

of that campaign—in some ways perhaps as tragic as those of Flanders—have been vividly described in Sir Ernest Scott's volume (XI) of the Australian official history. It must suffice here to say that undoubtedly the Celtic fire and vehemence of Mr Hughes on the one hand, and of the Roman Catholic coadjutor-archbishop of Melbourne, Dr Mannix, on the other, accentuated the bitterness. Mr Hughes at this juncture made a great tactical mistake by using the government's powers under the Defence Act to call up *for home service* all men between twenty-one and thirty-five. His object was that they should be in camp ready for entry to the A.I.F. when, and if, conscription for oversea service was enacted. But the many difficulties, appeals, interruption of work and so forth, probably lost more votes in the referendum—and recruits for the A.I.F.—than they gained.[3]

Actually—though it is hard even now to realise it—there was no issue of principle between most of the protagonists of the two sides. A high-minded leader who was the heart and soul of the fight against compulsion, Mr H. E. Boote, editor of *The Worker*, told the present writer long afterwards: "If Australia had really been in danger *of invasion*, there would have been no need to conscript me—I would have fought there myself!" The true issue was whether Australia was in imminent danger, and the vote really hung upon whether the majority of her people in their hearts felt the nation's existence or liberty to be immediately endangered or did not feel it.

Inevitably many side issues swayed the people. A vital

---

[3] The medical historian, however, notes that this call-up furnished one valuable source of information about the general fitness of Australians: 191,610 reported, 180,715 were examined, 114,322 found fit, 49,138 found unfit, 36,923 went into training, and 4810 joined the A.I.F. He also notes that, whereas under the voluntary recruiting system medical officers had to keep constant watch for unfit men trying to pass into the army, in this call-up that experience was suddenly reversed—the watch then was to prevent fit men from getting themselves classed as unfit; 46 per cent lodged applications for exemption. See *Official History of the Aust. Med. Services, Vol. III, pp. 888-9.*

one was a reflection of the strife between Great Britain and Southern Ireland which had flared out in Easter 1916; citizens of Irish birth or descent in Australia had always been highly sensitive to these divisions. Irish allegiance was the mainspring of Archbishop Mannix's opposition, and with him went a great part—though by no means the whole—of the Irish Roman Catholic vote. In the poll taken on Saturday, 28th October 1916, conscription was defeated by 72,476 out of 2,247,590 formal votes. The States—from which a majority vote was also needed if "yes" was to be carried—were equally divided, Victoria, Tasmania and Western Australia being for conscription and the others against. The soldiers' vote, which, in France, was taken when the divisions were returning in autumn to the Somme, gave 72,399 for and 58,894 against: after Pozières many were not inclined to force a man into the service against his will.

The result was a staggering blow to many supporters of conscription, who felt that it meant a determination not to put Australia's full effort into the support of her own troops or of the Allied cause. Actually it meant something very different—that, in a conflict so remote, and in danger that seemed to many hypothetical, the average citizen would not impose on himself the degree of sacrifice that he would be inclined to make if he felt himself faced by the immediate loss of his country or of its liberty. Twenty-five years later, in the Second World War, it was proved again and again that, with danger of national extinction undoubtedly impending, nation after nation was incapable of supreme effort until directly and physically attacked or in imminent danger of it.

In the First World War Australia unquestionably stood in danger; defeat of the Allies meant the certain extinction of the British Navy—and that the Australian nation could have survived the post-war years without that Navy's protection is almost unbelievable. But this danger was too remote to have the driving force of a threat of immediate invasion. Most people did not believe their danger sufficient to make conscription necessary, and no argument as to its fairness would compel them. Mr F. G. Tudor, Minister for Trade and Customs—a man whose devotion to the Allied cause was never in doubt—resigned from the Hughes government in this crisis, as did several other ministers. In London Mr Andrew Fisher, whose devotion to the war effort was equally marked, said to a friend: "I am not blind to the fact that conscription is logical. It is economical and saves lots of waste—of putting the wrong men in the wrong places. . . . But men are not logical, and you cannot rule them by logic. I never believed that, if conscription were carried in Australia, you could enforce it. I think you would have had terrible trouble. . . . I don't believe it was worth it, to get the few men extra who might have been raised by conscription." Actually, this internal campaign gravely hindered recruiting which soon fell to 4000, 3000, and even 2000 enlistments monthly.

In this struggle the Labour party, since 1914 most powerful in Australia, was utterly split. Mr Hughes had now only three of his nine original ministers left with him; and on 14th November 1916, seeing defeat in caucus inevitable, he and Senator Pearce walked out of the party room at Parliament House, Melbourne, twenty-two other members following and forty-two remaining. He found sufficient ability among his followers (known as the "National Labour Party") to form a new government, and for three months carried on with the support of the Liberals under Mr Joseph Cook, the Australian Labour party led by Mr Tudor becoming the opposition. In January 1917 the Hughes party and Liberals formed a joint "Nationalist" (or "Win the War") party, which on February 17th took office with Mr Hughes as Prime Minister, Mr Cook as Minister for the Navy, Senator

Pearce as Minister for Defence, and Sir John Forrest as Treasurer.

But despite the continuance of stable government, and the sincere support given by Mr Tudor and some other Opposition leaders to the war effort, the bitterness engendered by the conscription struggle now underlay almost every activity in Australia. It had exalted the issue to one not merely of principle—which, for most people, it was not—but almost of a fundamental religious belief. In extreme cases, as such quarrels will do, it had driven men and women, who at first were merely anti-compulsion, to become anti-British, and finally to oppose the continuation of the war. The divisions thus unfortunately raised were far from healed a generation later, and were one of the conditions by which leaders of all Australian parties—including Mr Hughes himself—had to guide their action in the Second World War.

In other respects life in Australia differed comparatively little from that of peace-time. The raising of voluntary funds was probably the chief war activity on the home front. The voluntary giving in Australia was immense. From one collection day in New South Wales alone—"Australia Day", held on 30th July 1915, after "Belgian Day" and several similar efforts—no less than £839,550 accrued. Throughout the war the work of all classes and ages, including children, in making comforts and raising money was enthusiastic and devoted—that of the women above all. The Junior Red Cross—afterwards a world organisation—started its existence in Australia. When the sick and wounded from Gallipoli flooded the Egyptian hospitals, it was found necessary to send thither special commissioners representing the Australian Red Cross and the combined comforts funds, and to distinguish between the Red Cross effort—protected by international law and confined to sick, wounded and prisoners of war—and the effort to provide "comforts" for the fighting troops. Henceforth each organisation maintained a staff overseas.[4]

Another war activity on the home front was the raising of loans to finance the war effort and public works. The war expenditure of Australia (stated in millions of pounds) rose from 15 in 1914-15 to 41 in 1915-16, 62 (1916-17), 67 (1917-18), and 81 (1918-19) then declining to 68 (1919-20) and 57 (1920-1). The aggregate total for the crucial years 1914-20, including £43 million advanced by the British government in the form of pay, goods and services for Australian troops, was £376 million. Of this, £70 million was paid from Federal revenue, now including succession duty, income tax, entertainment tax and a war-time profit tax,[5] and the rest (including the British advance just mentioned) from loan. As already stated, the British government agreed to the States' borrowing in London only to complete works already begun or to renew existing loans when they fell due, but the restrictions did not remotely approach those of the Second World War. The total "national" debt of the six States (as distinct from the Federation) before the war was £318 million. In these years 1914-20 they increased it by £100 million, partly lent by the Federal government from its notes fund.

The Federal government found that in 1915 the British government could lend it only £6½ million. It was therefore forced, late in that year, to raise its first Australian loan. It appealed for £5 million at 4½ per cent interest. The response exceeded £13 million. In all, seven loans were thus raised during the war—generally two in each year, each of about £20 million—and four in the five years after the war; and loan money was increased by the sale of war savings certificates and stamps. The Commonwealth Bank greatly helped to reduce costs.

---

[4] For an account of the patriotic funds see *Vol. XI, pp. 697-738.*
[5] This tax was on the amount by which the profit in the war years (from 1915) exceeded the average profits of certain years, or exceeded 10 per cent. For 1915-16 the tax was 50 per cent, for the later years 75 per cent.

Although, in consonance with British practice in that war, the rates of interest were attractive, eventually reaching 5 per cent,* and although pageantry and propaganda were freely used in floating loans, the amounts raised were considered extreme for Australia, and, in October 1918, on the launching of the last war-time loan for £40 million, the Nationalist Treasurer, Mr Watt, brought in a bill by which, if necessary, sub-scription could be compelled. The ending of the war caused the bill to be dropped, and the loan was over-subscribed. In all, £274,378,624 of loan money was raised by the Federal government in 1915-24. The note issue also increased from £9,573,738 in 1914 to £56,949,030 in 1920; £23,658,092 of gold reserve was held against this; but gold, hitherto common coin in Australia, dis-appeared from the people's pockets. From a variety of causes, by 1920 the price index had risen from 100 to 247.

Australian industry was flourishing. In the early part of the war this was due to the daughter nation's serving—as expected and intended in any such crisis—as a source of raw material for the mother nation, and, so far as British requests permitted, for allies and neutrals also. Australian meat and wool were always wanted; fearing to be at the mercy of Argentine companies the British government early in 1915 arranged to buy all surplus meat from Queensland and other exporting Australian States, and soon afterwards met the Argentine threat by securing the insulated (i.e. refrigerated) space in prac-tically all steamers in the South American meat trade.

In the wool trade, at the British government's request, sales to other countries were from time to time banned. But in October 1916, when it was found that South Africa would not so ban them, Australian woolgrowers became very dissatisfied. Mr Hughes during his visit to England had discussed the possible purchase of the whole Aus-tralian wool-clip by the British government—which was then buying the whole British clip. Now, in November

* Two years after the war a loan was floated at 6 per cent.

1916, Britain offered to buy the Australian and New Zealand clip during the rest of the war at 55 per cent above pre-war values. The wool and meat industries were thus maintained in full activity at a price fair to both Britain and Australia.

In wheat, the Australian crop of 1914-15 failed and for a time wheat had actually to be imported. But the next year's crop, of 1915-16, was a record one and, if it could be exported to Britain, the whole of it would certainly be sold at prices advantageous for both nations. But here, in mid-1915, there began to appear the difficulty which henceforth controlled this trade. By that time British and Allied shipping was becoming extremely scarce. This was due less to sinkings by enemy submarines and raiders, heavy though these sometimes were, than to the need for ships to transport and supply the British expeditionary forces, in France, Gallipoli, Mesopotamia, Salonica and Egypt—as well as to supply Britain's allies. With so immense a demand for ships, freights had risen prodigiously. In Australia the Federal and State governments conferred, and, to avoid competing against each other, entrusted to two leading firms—Elder Smith and Antony Gibbs—the task of chartering the 2 million tons of shipping necessary to carry the Australian grain. But by December 1915, barely half the necessary shipping had been secured. Mr Hughes pleaded with the British government to requisition for him fifty ships.

But the British government was itself in such need that it was forced to economise by using its food ships on the short runs to North and South America, on which each could make two or three voyages in the time required for one voyage to Australia. In January 1916 the British people's outcry over profiteering in freights also compelled the British government to establish a central Shipping Control to requisition, buy and build ships. And a main and necessary part of the Control's policy—though this was not realised in Australia—was to transfer

299

every obtainable ship from the long Antipodean route to the much shorter American journeys.

Mr Hughes on his visit to England petitioned Admiralty, Shipping Control, and Mr Asquith for ships, without making any headway—Asquith merely sympathised and then referred him to the other two, who shook their heads. The Australian government had necessarily promised its farmers to make advances on all wheat delivered at railway stations. In despair Mr Hughes now played his last card. Drawing on a credit of £3½ million already given to him by his government for the purchase, if necessary, of twenty-five ships, he quietly bought fifteen—tramp steamers mostly of 4400 tons, all that the agents could obtain. The Shipping Control protested in Cabinet, but here Mr Asquith at last stepped in—Mr Hughes agreed to buy no more ships if allowed to keep these.[6] He sailed for Australia, but while at sea learnt that Mr Runciman (the Shipping Controller) had threatened to commandeer his ships as soon as they reached a British port. Mr Hughes, in retort, threatened to return to England at once. Mr Runciman chose the lesser evil.

So was founded the Australian Commonwealth Line; but these few ships could have done little to meet the wheat difficulty.[7] Actually it was solved by a mere chance. Mr Hughes had returned to Australia when, in August 1916, the British government was suddenly informed by its advisers that a serious shortage would occur in the wheat harvest of North America. It was therefore suddenly decided to buy 3½ million tons from Australia, and send shipping to carry it. The British Admiralty and Shipping Control persuaded their government to use this offer as a lever to induce Australia to refrain from

---

6 For details of this episode see *Vol. XI, pp. 614-18.*

7 As to the unjustified criticism of this Line by Mr Fayle in his generally admirable work, *Seaborne Trade* (British Official History), see *Vol. XI, pp. 626-7.*

chartering British ships even for troop transports, as it had consistently done hitherto. Henceforth the British authorities would provide transports.

So the wheat crop was bought; but this had no sooner been done than the estimate of American shortage was reversed. The British ships turned again to America, and the Australian wheat purchased by Britain accumulated in immense stacks at Australian railway sidings, where it eventually was attacked and largely spoiled by a great plague of mice and weevils. It was ultimately disposed of, satisfactorily in Victoria but amid angry accusations between local politicians in South Australia and New South Wales.

Australian butter and cheese were carried to Great Britain largely in the military transports so long as these were available. The War Office doubted the quality of Australian leather for British boot-soles and saddlery, but the reputation of the Australian soldier's boot eventually led to large exports of leather and boots to India; 120,000 horses also were supplied to India and to the A.I.F.

From the beginning of 1917 the acute shortage of shipping was quickly made worse by the German decision to instruct submarine commanders to sink, without examination, all ships found in the sea approaches of the Allies. All real danger from the German surface navy had ended with the Battle of Jutland (30th June 1916), which caused the German Admiralty to keep its main fleet in port for the rest of the war. An "unrestricted" submarine campaign had already been launched by the Germans early in 1916, but it necessarily involved the sinking of neutrals and had been quickly abandoned on the United States' protesting. It was now resumed with the knowledge that it would bring the United States into the war, but in reliance on the advice of the German naval and military leaders, that it would, by starvation, force Great Britain to make peace before American help could come into the scales.

And indeed the attack made immense inroads on British and other shipping. In April 1917 alone, 881,027 tons were sunk, and it seemed possible that, after allowing for new building, at the end of the year there would be barely enough ships left to carry food sufficient for the British people and the necessary troops and munitions. The British government met this threat not only by, ultimately, grouping ships in escorted convoys, and improving naval devices and weapons against submarines, but by every possible economy in shipping. By special loading and storing, ships were unloaded at single ports and returned much quicker than before. Since nearly all trade to Australia and India had to go by the long Cape or Panama routes, every possible ship was transferred to the short American run. The Australian trade was at the same time, most usefully, directed to the supply of India and Egypt.

In this crisis in 1917 shortage of butter in Great Britain caused the British government to buy the surplus of Australian butter and cheese; wheat went partly to America to replace the supply sent from there to England.[8] Britain was now forced to ban imported fruit as a luxury, but this blow to Australian orchardists was compensated for by the increased export of tinned fruit and jam. This trade again received a blow when tinplate from Britain was denied priority—later special arrangements were made. In August a repeated appeal from the British government led to the eventual withdrawal of some fifty Australian coastal liners and other ships from local Australian trade, to serve as transports and freighters in the Atlantic, Mediterranean and elsewhere. A well-known Australian coastal liner was the first transport to enter the Black Sea; another was sunk as a hospital ship in the English Channel.[9]

---

8 The British government bought 1½ million tons in 1919.

9 Many of the Australian merchant ships of that time, with particulars of their war service, are listed in *Vol. IX, pp. 478-501.*

The shortage of shipping of course, gave an unprecedented opportunity for local manufacture of many civilian goods. Of munitions only rifles and small-arm ammunition were made in quantity. The manufacture of shells for Great Britain was attempted in 1915-16, chiefly in the State railway workshops, but at such distance it was found impossible to keep pace with the constant changes in design. Only 15,000 shells had been produced when the immense expansion of the British industry rendered the effort futile. In munitions the main success was in the manufacture of steel in the new Broken Hill works at Newcastle, which produced 17,900 tons of munition steel to the satisfaction of the British authorities. Even more practical help was the sending to Britain of 6000 volunteer munition workers, including some prominent experts.

In civil manufacture at least 400 articles, never before normally made in Australia, now had to be manufactured there, including electrical batteries, dynamos and radiators, sheep dips, dyes, ether, weights and balances, typewriter ribbons, gas engines and even aeroplane engines. Many common articles were now scarce in Australia—not till then did most people realise that such things as braid, wadding, chalk, canvas and the like, were all imported. Linoleums, carpets, curtains, were eventually unprocurable, as, for a time, were wire netting and galvanised iron.

Mr Hughes eagerly fostered shipbuilding in Australia, but only after he had obtained trades union guarantees as to dilution of labour, continuity of work, and the adoption of piecework under certain conditions. The main difficulty was shortage of skilled labour. Except for the cruiser *Brisbane*, and destroyers *Swan*, *Huon* and *Torrens*, finished in 1916, big-ship building came late in the war. Twenty steel steamers of 5500 tons were undertaken and a number of smaller wooden freighters, intended to be unsinkable—the contracts for these were partly let in America and were afterwards largely cancelled or modified, partly owing to the unearthing of serious corruption. The plates for the steel ships built in Australia were imported, but not the frames, which were made at the B.H.P. works at less than the oversea cost. Some of the steel steamers, when completed, and three much larger ones built in England, together with eighteen of the twenty-seven German steamers seized in Australian waters, and Mr Hughes's purchased steamers, composed the Commonwealth Government Line. The line much more than paid for itself during the war, but afterwards lost heavily, and was sold in 1928 to the White Star Line for £1,900,000.

For economy and to help industry "daylight saving" was introduced for three months on 1st January 1917, but, through protests from the country industries, was not repeated. Further to help commerce and industry an Institute of Science and Industry and a Bureau of Commerce and Industry were established; the latter was only short lived, but the former developed into one of the most valuable institutions of Australia, the Council for Scientific and Industrial Research. Another step, to be of incalculable benefit in the Second World War—was the establishment, by advice of Dr J. H. L. Cumpston, of the Commonwealth Serum Laboratories.

In the First World War the prices of many goods in Australia eventually doubled themselves, while the average wage (for a man, £2 15s. a week in 1914) increased only by, roughly, a third. By 1919 metals, coal, textiles, and leather had about doubled in price, agricultural produce increased by five-eighths, dairy produce by a third, meat and groceries by nearly a half; and building material and chemicals rose to more than two and a half times the 1914 value. In Great Britain, as already noted, there was at times very strong feeling that shipowners, and some classes of manufacturers, distributors and financiers, were making great profits from the nation's need, and the old term "profiteer" came into frequent use. In Australia the Interstate Commission, charged in 1917 with investigating the cause of increases, found no sign of any deliberate organising to increase prices of butter, cheese, boots, or bread; but it reported that in New South Wales such organisation did exist in the wholesale meat industry and probably in the vegetable and fruit industry also. Rents had risen only slightly.

By 1916 the Federal government was forced to regulate prices—various attempts made by the States had generally failed. The action of New South Wales in buying wheat at a fixed price caused great controversy, farmers being eager to realise a higher price by consigning to Victoria. The High Court, however, upheld the State government's right.[10] In 1916 the Federal government, after first appointing a political Board, changed its mind and transferred the task to a Necessary Commodities Commission, with a Prices Commissioner in each State, the Victorian Commissioner, Mr W. H. Clarke, acting as chief. They were empowered to fix prices of food-stuffs, necessary commodities, and services. In practice the Commission is said to have aimed chiefly at seeing that *profits* were not unduly high. Sugar was exempted from its jurisdiction, the Federal government taking control of that industry in order to prevent sugar from leaving Australia to take advantage of the soaring prices abroad. The whole industry and its prices were regulated, from canefields to consumer, and, as sugar-growing was of great political importance in populating part of the north, the system continued after the war.

In the First World War, as in the Second, the industry most disturbed by disputes was that of coal mining. Most of the mines were in New South Wales, and there were many more industrial disputes in that State than in all

---

[10] In the case of *Farey v. Burvett*. Incidentally this judgment overruled a decision of—and eventually destroyed—the Interstate Commission, the High Court deciding that the Commission had not the powers of a court.

21—os

the rest of Australia. The coal-strike of 1916—in which the miners aimed at securing certain conditions, among them shorter hours—and the great railway strike of 1917, which began in protest against the introduction of the "time-card" system, were very serious disturbances. The railway strike quickly spread to coalminers, wharf-labourers and others. Even the Coaling Battalion, formed by the Sydney Coal Lumpers' Union early in 1916, joined in. Each strike happened at a time when the Australian government had great commitments for shipping—in 1916 for getting away the wheat crop, and in 1917 for its own line of steamers. But after the 1916 strike the government had built up big stocks of coal, and in the 1917 strike the New South Wales government took possession of all mines in that State, and the Victorian government, whose factories urgently needed coal, actually provided labour and police protection at two New South Wales mines. In the coal strike of 1916 the Commonwealth Arbitration Court under Mr Justice Higgins—great maker of Australian industrial precedent—refused to arbitrate while the men were not working, and Mr Hughes accordingly established a special tribunal under Mr Justice Edmunds for the coal industry. The tribunal raised wages, and improved conditions; and the price of coal was increased. The railway strike of 1917 failed.[11] Distribution of coal was now controlled by a board. A special tribunal was established in the shipbuilding industry also.

In the First World War, as in the Second, there were some strong interests that bound the Australian workers to the fighting services, and some that divided them. A great proportion of the A.I.F. were trades unionists—64 per cent were "tradesmen" or "labourers". The miners of Australia—from the coalfields, as well as the goldfields—provided some of the best soldiers of the A.I.F. But the

---

11 The shipping strike of 1919 which followed the war may be considered outside the scope of this book.

men from country callings, also, were outstanding, and
it was noticeable that the great Australian Workers'
Union—which was always largely connected with country
industries—was particularly free from disputes during
the war.

The degree of unrest in 1916-17 was probably influenced by the acute controversies over conscription.
Another factor, though probably it was credited with
much more trouble than it actually created, was the
Industrial Workers of the World, generally known as
"the I.W.W." This body originated in the United States;
its aim was revolution and its avowed policy to destroy
capitalism, partly by sabotage. In New South Wales in
1916 it was connected with a series of murders, bank-note
forgery, and fires in stores. Most of the men concerned
were natives of other countries. Of twelve convicted in
connection with the fires, ten were released in 1920 after
several years of protest by the editor of *The Worker*,
Mr H. E. Boote. In Western Australia nine men were
found guilty, but only of distributing sabotage propaganda, and were allowed to go free. The I.W.W. was
finally stamped out by an amended Unlawful Associations
Act of 1917.

CHAPTER XVIII

THE AUSTRALIAN NAVY, 1915-18

Most of the division, in industry and politics, that hampered the war effort of Australians was due to the difficulty already referred to—which events of 1939-40 showed to be common to nations in similar conditions— the difficulty of realising that their fate hung on a struggle of which they saw so little. Only the German Navy, in that war, could have brought the war closer to Australians; and of the two German merchant cruisers, which, we now know, were ordered to do this by raiding Australian sea traffic, the *Prinz Eitel Friedrich*, unable to get coal, had made for the Atlantic and been interned in March 1915 at Newport News, and in December 1914 the *Cormoran* had been similarly interned at the United States coaling station at Guam.

No part of the devastation of war physically and directly affected Australia until, on 6th July 1917, the large freighter *Cumberland* was sunk by an unexplained explosion ten miles off Gabo Island. In consequence of the absence of nearly all Australian warships in the general war effort in other seas, the Admiralty had already arranged with Japan for two cruisers to be sent to Australia. These were then at Jervis Bay, and, on one of them visiting the wreck, the damage was at first thought to be due to internal explosion. The I.W.W. again was suspected, and not for two months were minesweepers sent to the area.

Then an enemy minefield was at once discovered. Two other steamers, the *Port Kembla* and *Wimmera*, had been sunk by mines off New Zealand. A well-known passenger steamer, the *Matunga,* suddenly disappeared when about to reach New Guinea, on 6th August 1917. An intense search was carried out, largely by the cruiser *Encounter,* but no trace was found. In this case a German commerce raider, believed to be in the Pacific, was suspected; and on 15th January 1918 came secret news that a bottle had been found in the Celebes, thrown overboard by prisoners on the German raider *Wolf.* In the bottle was a message telling of her movements, minelayings, victims—including the *Matunga*—and giving her description. The *Matunga* had been captured through her own wireless signals. The *Wolf,* with this and many other crews aboard, eventually reached Germany safely in February 1918. Not till after the Armistice was it found, by a German disclosure to the British Admiralty, that the *Wolf* had laid another minefield off Cape Everard in Victoria. The area was then swept and a few mines were found. The German story that the *Wolf's* seaplane flew over Sydney has been proved untrue.[1]

One other German raider visited the Pacific in 1917, a much less powerful ship, the *Seeadler,* captained by Count Felix von Luckner. That adventurous character, who prided himself on being a descendant of one of Napoleon's marshals and a sportsman by nature, captured a number of prizes, mainly sailing ships, in the Atlantic and then came to the Pacific and was wrecked in the Society Islands. After escaping in a motor launch he was made prisoner in September 1917 in the Fiji Islands.

After the capture of New Guinea in 1914, and the transfer of the battle-cruiser *Australia* and the light cruisers *Sydney* and *Melbourne* to the Atlantic and eventually the North Sea, the Australian "little ships" were for about half of the war used as part of the net for foiling German plans of raising revolt in India. These plans had

---

[1] For the details see *Vol. IX, pp. 342-58;* also *The Amazing Cruise of the German Raider "Wolf",* by Capt. Donaldson, and *The Cruise of the "Wolf",* by Roy Alexander.

been made before the war, an Indian revolutionary organisation, known as "Ghadr", having touch with the German General Staff in Berlin. German staffs or agents in Persia, Java and Siam were to engineer the uprisings and supply arms and literature. Early in the war these staffs became active; the agents in Persia were met by still more effective British agents and by organising land forces to bar their penetration. Those in Siam, Java and Malaysia were unable to move owing to the constant British naval patrol. Some of the principal German staffs organising this campaign were in America and Shanghai; but three ships that were to bring arms or other help—the American sailing ship *Annie Larsen*, the American steamer *Maverick*, and the schooner *Henry S.*, were eventually forced into Dutch or American ports where their cargo was seized.

Nevertheless seventy-four German ships were in ports of the Dutch Indies, and at any time attempts might be made to sneak some of them out through the British patrol and arm them. In mid-1915 Australia sent, first, the small cruiser *Psyche* and sloop *Fantome* (two old British warships lent to the R.A.N.) to patrol together with some British ships the Bay of Bengal. Almost immediately afterwards the commander-in-chief of the British China Squadron telegraphed to the Australian Naval Board that the Germans had a munitions base near Java, Timor or

Celebes. He asked the Board to have Dilli visited, and to patrol Macassar Strait (eastward of Borneo) and the Aru Islands. Accordingly in October 1915 the three destroyers

Warrego, *Parramatta* and *Yarra* with the *Una* (the German government yacht *Komet*, captured in New Guinea[2]) began this patrol, working largely from Sandakan in Borneo. The larger cruiser, *Encounter*, after visiting Fanning and Christmas Islands, was sent there also, but early in 1916 was brought back to Australia, which was without naval protection, and the *Una* returned to New Guinea. But, under the C.-in-C. China Squadron, the three destroyers were sent early in 1916 to Bangkok and Saigon.

The Australian Naval Board now feared that the Germans might revert to the use of armed merchant raiders or minelayers. Four new ships built in Australia, the light cruiser *Brisbane* and destroyers *Huon*, *Swan* and *Torrens*, soon became available, and in August 1916 the new destroyers relieved the older ones, then working off the Philippines. Early in 1917 the older destroyers in their turn were about to relieve the newer ones when there came, first, an alarm as to a raider, and, in May, a request from the Admiralty (which, under the Australian offer of its fleet, had the right to send an order) that they be sent to counter the very grave submarine menace to Great Britain. They were at once refitted and sent to the Mediterranean, and were joined, at the Australian government's suggestion, by the three newer destroyers, refitted at Singapore. By August the six Australian destroyers were at Malta. Based there and at Brindisi until October 1918, they helped to carry out the blockade known as the "Otranto barrage", barring the exit from the Adriatic Sea against German and Austrian submarines.[3]

The *Fantome* and *Psyche* patrolled in Indian and

---

[2] The naval historian, Mr A. W. Jose, points out that she was renamed the *Una* evidently in commemoration of her being the first naval vessel captured by the R.A.N., but that the Latin for "first" is "*Prima*". Una means "the only one"—which, in fact, she was (*Vol. IX, p. 121*).

[3] The full story is told in *Vol. IX, pp. 310-27* (Black Sea, *pp. 328-30*).

Malayan waters for more than two years—a trying task, in very great heat. The entry of America into the war made possible their return to Australia in September 1917. Both badly needed refitting; their speed was very low. On the *Psyche's* way home she passed through the Karimata Strait between Sumatra and Borneo on the very night on which the German raider *Wolf* (much more heavily armed) passed through it in the opposite direction. The *Wolf* sighted a two-funnelled "English" cruiser against the gleaming moonlit water, and her gun and torpedo crews were ready at their positions and itching to fire, but were not allowed to do so, the raider's policy being to hide.[4] The *Psyche* saw nothing and her log places her slightly too far south for this encounter—but no other British cruiser was anywhere near.

The *Brisbane*, after being sent to Malta, and then searching the Indian Ocean for a raider, was returned by the Admiralty in June 1917 owing to the Australian Naval Board's fears of a raider. As has been seen two raiders did visit the south-west Pacific in the next few months. The destroyers had then been sent away, but the Admiralty had obtained two Japanese cruisers, and later obtained for a time the help of others. The *Psyche*, and, at times, *Encounter* were in Australian waters. The *Una* and the French cruiser *Kersaint* carried out a punitive expedition on Malekula in the New Hebrides in October, 1916, and the *Fantome* and a French party another in October, 1918.

But the main service of the Australian ships in that war was in the North Sea with the British Grand Fleet. From early 1915 the battle-cruiser *Australia*, and from the second half of 1916 the light cruisers *Sydney* and *Melbourne*, took their full share of the work and enterprises of the fleet. By an unlucky collision with the *New Zealand* (a British battle-cruiser, the gift of that Dominion)

---

[4] *See Vol. IX, pp. 349-50.*

the *Australia* missed the Battle of Jutland, and the only action of Australian ships with the enemy in those waters —except against submarines—was a fight on 4th May 1917 between the *Sydney* and a German airship, the *L43*, which tried to bomb her—apparently neither side received damage. In the last part of the war the ships were often employed covering the vital Scandinavian convoys. Both the *Sydney* and the *Melbourne* were at that stage fitted with launching platforms for aeroplanes, and on 1st June 1918 both their aeroplanes went into action against two German machines which tried to bomb the 1st Battle Cruiser Squadron.[5]

The first two batches of cadets from the naval college at Jervis Bay served with the Grand Fleet in 1917 and 1918.[6] Selected Australians represented their Navy in the famous raid on Zeebrugge. The *Australia*, as flagship of the 2nd Battle Cruiser Squadron led the port line of the British fleet escorting the surrendered German High Sea Fleet on 23rd November 1918. On 24th November 1924 she was voluntarily sunk outside Sydney Heads in accordance with the Washington agreement for the limitation of naval forces.

---

[5] For the fight with *L43* see *Vol. IX, pp. 294-6*. The *Sydney* (Captain J. S. Dumaresq) and *Dublin* and four destroyers were at the time engaging two submarines. For the action with aeroplanes see *Vol. IX, pp. 304-6*. For the fine summary of the Australian Navy's services, by its historian, Arthur W. Jose, see *Vol. IX, pp. 334-5*.

[6] For the outstanding successes of these and subsequent batches in the British naval schools—and of Australian soldiers at British army schools—see *Vol. VI, p. 23 (text, and footnote 25)*. High among the first batch were J. A. Collins and F. E. Getting—both to be distinguished in the 2nd World War.

CHAPTER XIX

1917 (1)—BULLECOURT

WITH Russia half defeated, 1916 had begun with the
Allies in a serious position. The Gallipoli Campaign had
failed, and the situation on the Western Front was believed by many to be an unbreakable stalemate. In 1916
the plan of the chief of the German General Staff, von
Falkenhayn, had been merely to hold the ground, 125-
250 miles deep, gained from Russia in 1915, and try to
drive France out of the war while the Navy's submarines
attacked British supplies. But the submarine campaign
had quickly been given up through the American protest,
and the Verdun attack, though it placed the French under
extreme strain, had been stopped by the Somme Battle.

Indeed in October and December 1916, by two brilliant strokes, the French general, Nivelle, had regained
a fair part of the ground originally lost at Verdun. And
though the immense cost of the Somme effort had shocked
the Allied peoples, nevertheless to the British, who had
borne its main burden, that battle gave hope for the
future: at least their new army was forcing the Germans
to give ground. The Russian part of the general attack on
Germany, begun in June, had, on the front south of the
Pripet marshes, regained about half of the area lost in
1915, but had not saved Rumania, which joined the
Allies in August but was crushed by December. The
Italians had been attacked by, and had attacked, the
Austrians, who were hard pressed by the Russians; but,
fighting on the difficult Alpine front, neither side achieved
much. The Salonica campaign made progress in October,
when the Serbs advanced thirty miles in Macedonia. The

Turks had failed in Sinai, and had not followed up their success at Kut. They were still wasting vast effort against Russia, whose Caspian oilfields they coveted.

Thus at the end of 1916, while neither side had succeeded in its plans for that year, the Allies' position seemed to have improved, though at great cost. The Germans had called off their first unrestricted submarine campaign, and had achieved little on land. They were now under intense strain, and the Allies' plan of great blows from every direction in the spring of 1917 seemed likely to test them to the utmost.

But in December the plan for the spring attack on the Western Front had suddenly been changed. The French Parliament and people were profoundly dissatisfied with Joffre and the Somme operations; and the Premier, Briand, was forced to replace "Father" Joffre by the hero who had re-won so much ground at Verdun, General Nivelle. There was a cry of "No more Sommes!" Nivelle believed he had devised the method for victory, and the French political party behind him believed that in his tactics they had a quick and cheap means to that end. He would make a whirlwind attack and drive deep—and he chose to attack the main German "bulge" not from where Joffre had intended, from the west beside the British, but from the south. Haig would still attack it from the west, between Arras and the Somme.

Haig at once agreed to the change, but also clung to a secondary part of the old plan to which he attached great importance—by which at a later stage the British were to strike the Germans in Flanders and drive them from the Belgian coast. Needing reserves for this, he refused to take over as much of the French line as Nivelle desired. Nivelle felt that his own stroke, destined (he believed) to decide the war would thus be imperilled. The French government appealed to the British and at a conference in London on January 15th-16th Nivelle so impressed Mr Lloyd George, the vital Welshman who in

December 1916 had forced his way to the prime ministership of Britain, that Haig was ordered to conform to
Nivelle's plan. The battle was to begin on April 1st. To
support the supreme effort of 1917 all the Dominions
were asked to supply additional troops; the request to
Australia, for a 6th Infantry Division, was agreed to by
the Australian government with some embarrassment,
and the division began to be formed in England from
men recovered from wounds.

Unknown, of course, to the Allies the German plan
had been even more fundamentally changed. In August
1916 General Falkenhayn had been superseded, and the
victorious German leaders on the Russian front had been
brought to the west, Hindenburg as commander and
Ludendorff as chief-of-staff. On reaching the Western
Front in August 1916 they decided that Germany could
no longer launch a land offensive there—she would need
her reserves for defence against the Allied attacks which
were certain to come. Ludendorff, who henceforth had
by far the most powerful influence in the German conduct of the war, agreed that the Navy should again return
to unrestricted submarine warfare in a final effort to
reduce Britain by starvation; meanwhile, an Austrian
suggestion, that a "peace offer" be made, was also agreed
to. The hopes of its supporters lay partly in the fact
that President Wilson of the United States, through
whom it was made, and who was known to be devoted to
peace, had just been re-elected for his second term. But
Ludendorff insisted that the "peace offer" should not
"give the impression of weakness". It did not. Indeed it
issued in terms so bombastic that it was almost laughed
out of serious consideration by the Allies. Neither then,
nor at any time, did Ludendorff offer to consider even
the return of Belgium to complete freedom, which necessarily was the first requirement of Britain and France.

As the "peace offer" failed, on 31st January 1917
Germany's notice of unrestricted submarine warfare was

published to neutrals—with one almost immediate result expected by its authors: on April 6th the Congress of the United States on the recommendation of President Wilson declared war.

Ludendorff's plan was defensive: he would hold fast on land while the submarines—in six months, according to the German naval staff—were to reduce Great Britain. One of the first orders given by Hindenburg and Ludendorff in September 1916, after surveying the Western Front, had been for the construction of a defence line in rear, across the "bulge" of the German front in France, from Arras to near Laon. By retiring, if necessary, to this much shorter line—which was called the "Siegfried"

system—the German Army could save a number of divisions. The local German "bulge", south of Arras, caused by the wedge driven farther south by the British and French in the First Somme Battle, offered a flank favourable for a British attack. But if the Germans retreated at the right moment to the Siegfried Line that offensive would have to be postponed. To avoid a battle,

and gain time for the U-boat campaign to have effect, was considered vital. Accordingly on February 4th Ludendorff ordered the withdrawal to begin on March 16th, and preparations for it on February 9th. If the British pressed, the retreat could begin earlier.

The British intelligence had heard from prisoners about the Siegfried defence line; it was referred to by the Allies as the "Hindenburg Line". It lay ten to thirty miles behind the German front, and airmen had sighted parts of it. Prisoners had spoken of its immense strength, particularly of its broad, boldly planned wire entanglements. It was assumed to be merely a new reserve line.

In the 5th British Army, under General Gough, the early spring offensive was already planned. All four divisions of the I Anzac Corps were now in line, having sideslipped slightly northwards in order to form the right of that army when it attacked. As a preparatory measure, the corps was ordered to place the enemy under strain by small assaults. One of these, at Stormy Trench, completely succeeded at the second attempt on February 4th, largely through the bold, untiring leadership of the same Captain Harry Murray who had distinguished himself at Mouquet Farm (and who now won the Victoria Cross). The ground here gained was being much extended by constant nibbling, when the month of bright freezing weather ended in thaw.

The battlefield had again become a scene of mud and fog when, on February 24th, all troops were electrified by news that German front trenches at the northern end of the old battlefield had been found abandoned; a prisoner there said that the Germans were retiring towards Cambrai—evidently to the Hindenburg Line which ran west of that town. Australians in some parts noted that the enemy flares on their front also rose farther back. Patrols sent into the fog presently found that the Germans were retiring on most of the I Anzac front also, leaving, however, a thin screen of small posts and patrols. Opposite the southern flank of I Anzac, and farther south, they held their positions for the time being unchanged.

It was conjectured that the prisoner was right, but that the Germans were retiring by stages. This would entirely dislocate the impending spring offensive of 5th Army, but not of 3rd Army, farther north at Arras. But the news had magic effect. The German Army was withdrawing! Already, in the improved condition of the trenches, the Australians had largely recovered their spirits; and now the winter depression lifted like vanishing fog. Who was winning now?

In bounding spirits—but careful to detect booby traps left for them—the troops followed the withdrawal, patrols pushing back the German screen as far as Warlencourt and near Le Barque at the foot of the Bapaume heights, where stronger German posts held up the advance. As the Germans would be saving divisions, the British, by Haig's order, did so too, the I Anzac Corps at once pulling out the 4th Division for a rest. On the night of the 26th the 3rd Brigade (1st Division) seized Le Barque and Ligny-Thilloy and it soon had posts around Thilloy village, close below Bapaume. Two attempts made by the 2nd Division to get on to the heights north-west of Bapaume, near Loupart Wood, were repulsed; but, after bringing up the artillery, the trench on this height (Malt Trench) was seized early on March 2nd by the 7th Brigade. While that fight was going on, in the morning fog parties of Germans tried to retake Le Barque-Thilloy, but after a mêlée with the Australian posts they completely failed. On the same night part of the 5th Division seized Sunray Trench at the southern end of the Australian sector, where the German retirement had till then hinged.

Another division, the 1st, was now also withdrawn. The remaining two—from left to right, 2nd and 5th—were now close to what was afterwards found to be, for the moment, the main German position (known to the Germans as the I Reserve Line). The Australians and the II British Corps on their left were about to attack it at Loupart Wood, and the bombardment of it had begun, when, early on the night of March 12th, the 2nd Division discovered that the Germans had left it. The Australians quickly occupied Grévillers village, little over a mile from Bapaume, the II Corps similarly advancing farther north. To avoid the attack the Germans in those sectors

had withdrawn to their II Reserve Line close in front
of that town.

In a dugout in Loupart Wood were discovered German orders for the retreat to the Hindenburg Line. The
dates at which it was to take place were not stated, but
by close reasoning March 15th was guessed as the day
for the main retirement, the rearguard withdrawing on
the 17th. The Australian staff and troops were intensely
keen to catch the enemy in the act of withdrawing and
the vigorous commanders of the 6th and 5th Brigades,
Gellibrand and R. Smith, pressed for leave to attack at
3 a.m. on the 17th; but, as earlier in the night the German
lines seemed to be normally held, General Nevill Smyth
(2nd Division) disallowed their provisional order. However, by 5.45 a.m. on the 17th their patrols were in the
German trenches, and by 7.45 in the northern outskirts
of Bapaume. Opposite Bapaume itself the 5th Division,
making a small attack at 3.40, had found the German
trenches empty. Bapaume was burning. The 30th Battalion moved through the smoking streets and emerged
into the almost untouched green country beyond just in
time to see Germans scampering away, and, in the distance, hooded waggons slowly withdrawing.

Rarely did Australian soldiers experience such exhilar-
ation as on that morning when, with the Somme morass
finally behind them, they skirmished across green fields
and found touch with the German screen a little beyond.
The "pursuing" force, already thin, was now further
reduced, each forward division providing an advanced
guard of an infantry brigade complete with other arms
(including light horse) to press the enemy. Haig wisely
feared that the German command might plan suddenly
to strike back at him, and therefore disposed his armies
in great depth. The main body for the present was to
hold a line through Bapaume and Péronne.

A great part of the German line was now retiring, in
front of the British 4th and 5th Armies and of the French

armies south of them. The original withdrawal opposite 5th Army had been no part of the plan of "Alberich" (the German code-name for the main withdrawal); it was a step asked for by the local German command in order to relieve the exhaustion of the 17th and 18th German Divisions opposite General Gough's army. The British II Corps had been attacking, and these divisions could stand no more. The Guard Reserve Corps, opposite the Australians, had better morale and strongly objected to the preliminary withdrawal, but had to fall in with it. The second preliminary withdrawal, on March 11th to the II Reserve Line, was made in order to avoid being attacked before March 17th. The II Reserve Line was fully held, opposite the Australians, until 1.30 a.m. on March 17th.

But then the German garrisons went back in one step to the Hindenburg Line having withdrawn nearly all movable stores, cut down all useful shelter trees, destroyed houses and railways, blown up cross-roads. They left a screen, besides strong entrenched garrisons at almost every village, in order to delay the approach to the Hindenburg Line which, despite enormous labour, was not nearly ready.

The two Australian advanced guards under Brig.-Generals John Gellibrand (left) and H. E. ("Pompey") Elliott (right) moved out at once, at daybreak on the 18th, on to the green plateau, passing north and south of Bapaume respectively. At first great difficulty was found in getting guns and supplies to Elliott's column, which had seven miles of Somme mud behind it—Gellibrand's was fed by the crowded Albert-Bapaume road, in which the large craters blown by the enemy were quickly bypassed by tracks made by the pioneers. That day, after some fighting, Elliott's column captured Frémicourt village and Delsaux Farm, where, on the dead body of a German officer who had fought with noticeable bravery, was found a copy of the rearguard's orders. On the 19th,

22—05

Elliott, directing his troops not to swing in against any opposing force but to bypass it, captured Lebucquière and Vélu villages and Vélu Wood, far ahead of the 4th Army's patrols on the right.

On the left Gellibrand's column had outdistanced all others. The three nearest villages it found deserted, and

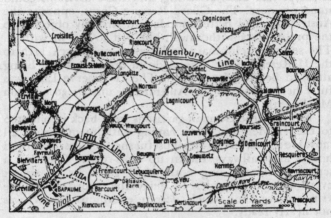

THE AREA BETWEEN BAPAUME AND THE HINDENBURG LINE

(Main German defences are indicated by white lines but all villages also were fortified. The boundaries shown are those of the Australian advanced guards.)

Vaulx-Vraucourt was occupied on the 18th with the last German party still in it—some of them were shaving when captured. The wide rusty-wire belts and white chalk parapets of the Hindenburg Line could now be seen crowning some of the rises three miles away. Haig's policy of caution had been communicated to the columns; but on the night of the 18th, on information that villages *beyond* the Hindenburg Line were burning—which suggested that the Germans might be withdrawing beyond that line, perhaps with a view to dislocating also the 3rd Army's coming offensive at Arras—Haig ordered the 3rd Army at Arras to raid for information, and Gough ordered the left flank of 5th Army to probe to the Hindenburg Line.

A number of fortified villages still lay between 5th Army and that line, but Gough visiting the front on the 19th was dissatisfied with progress. He was intensely and rightly eager that his army should reach the Hindenburg Line in time to help the 3rd Army's great offensive in April. Accordingly that night Gellibrand tried to capture one of the next villages, Noreuil, by surrounding it. The attempt made in the drizzling dawn of March 20th failed with loss, the approach in the dark being difficult and late, and the chain of German posts in and between the villages of Ecoust, Noreuil and Lagnicourt too strong.

Early on the same day the Light Horse of the southern column, Elliott's, had been heavily fired on from the two villages next ahead of it, Beaumetz and Morchies. The day was snowy but part of the 15th Brigade advancing on a wide front easily took Morchies. Field-guns had to be brought against Beaumetz. The Germans ran from it and by the morning of the 21st it was held by Australians.

As Elliott's column was now three miles ahead of its southern neighbour, the 4th Army, and as Haig had enjoined prudence, Maj.-General Hobbs of the 5th Division forbade Elliott to advance farther until ordered to do so. Actually the German garrison had retired before the German command was prepared to allow that movement, and at dawn on the 23rd the Germans counter-attacked, broke through the Australian posts, and nearly retook Beaumetz. The troops on the spot, however, though partly cut off, at once vehemently hit back, and within half an hour the village was fully retaken. Despite orders, Elliott was with difficulty restrained from pressing farther. At dawn on the 24th the Germans attempted another attack, but were beaten and were also cleared from some neighbouring posts.

The phase of comparatively rapid advance had now ended; other villages must be taken before the Hindenburg Line could be reached, and by March 20th Gough saw that they could not be rushed. Accordingly they were attacked in a series of open-warfare operations, limited only by the fact that the Hindenburg Line, immensely strong and fully garrisoned, was sited on well-chosen positions a few miles behind them. The advanced guard system was abandoned, but the 5th Army front was still very lightly held. The II British Corps was relieved, the V Corps sector being extended to the I Anzac boundary. The wide Anzac front—then about 13,000 yards—was held by two divisions each with only one brigade in the line.

The village attacks were to be as far as possible simultaneous along the 5th Army front; but the V Corps was delayed, and therefore the Australians made their next attack alone. The 2nd Division's advanced brigade (now the 7th, Brig.-General E. A. Wisdom) cleanly and cleverly captured Lagnicourt in a very hard enveloping fight, costing nearly 400 casualties,[1] the 15th Brigade (5th Division) swinging up its flank to keep touch. (That day Bapaume town hall and several other shelters, abandoned by the Germans nine days before, were blown up by delayed-action mines burying and killing some twenty-five men.)

Next, on April 2nd, a whole string of villages fringing the Hindenburg Line was seized by V and I Anzac Corps. On the northern flank of I Anzac, where the 4th Division had relieved the 2nd, its 13th Brigade at dawn seized Noreuil, in the valley north of Lagnicourt. This again was achieved mainly by envelopment, and in tough fighting at a cost of 600 casualties, 113 Germans being

---

[1] This rough and tumble tussle is described in *Vol. IV, pp. 195-6*. For the capture of Prince Frederick Charles of Prussia who, dying, told the Australians that he, too, was "a sport" see *Vol. IV. pp. 189-90*.

captured. At the same time several miles southward, on the 5th Division's front, the 14th Brigade also took Doignies and Louverval by a sharp night advance followed by a flanking thrust. In the southern sector the 1st Division now relieved the 5th.

Only one important village, Hermies, near the southern end of the Australian front remained to be taken. It was to be captured by April 9th when the main British spring offensive at Arras was due to start. Some hard fighting at a smaller village, Boursies, on April 8th and 9th, was used as a feint, to mislead the Germans as to the direction from which Hermies would be assaulted. In the small hours of the 9th Hermies was surrounded—for the first time an attack by Australian infantry went almost entirely according to an intricate plan. Hermies and a neighbouring hamlet, Demicourt, were captured by the 1st Brigade, over 200 prisoners being taken in Hermies at a cost of 253 casualties—the capture of the three villages cost 649.

That day, 9th April 1917, the British 3rd Army at Arras struck the first blow of the Allies' great offensive planned for that year. The relations between Haig and Nivelle had been difficult.[2] In this difficulty Lloyd George sympathised with Nivelle, and at the end of February the British government, without previously consulting its military leaders, placed Haig under Nivelle's orders. Nivelle's blow on the Aisne, from which so much had been expected, would be struck a week after the British offensive.

The 3rd Army's initial stroke in the Battle of Arras was one of the most effective in the war. After a great bombardment the Canadian corps seized Vimy Ridge and the British farther south[3] about Arras overran the German front. The enemy was deeply shocked and for a

---

[2] For details of their difference see *Vol. IV, pp. 9-12, 135-7.*

[3] The two Australian heavy batteries were with the British artillery here.

moment the chance of a real break-through seemed at
hand. General Allenby was afterwards criticised for not
having sufficiently elaborated his arrangements for following up his infantry's stroke—his transfer to the Palestine command soon afterwards undoubtedly provided
him with conditions more suitable to his temperament.
But events were to prove that no commander on either
side in that war was successful in breaking through on
the Western Front. The penetration that followed the
3rd Army's tremendous bombardment and impetuous
advance was checked at certain points before reaching
the third objective.

During this battle General Gough's 5th Army was
facing the Hindenburg Line behind the southern flank
of the Germans whom the 3rd Army attacked. Seven
miles in rear of those Germans was a "switch" line, newly
dug as a last reserve line in case the British at Arras broke
through, and known to the Germans as the Wotan Line.
It led northwards out of the Hindenburg Line near Riencourt, opposite the left Anzac division (now the 4th).
Gough had hoped that the V Corps (which had relieved
the II) and I Anzac would by April 9th be ready to attack
and seize the Hindenburg Line immediately west of this
switch, on either side of Bullecourt, a village incorporated
like a bastion in the Hindenburg Line. After seizing that
sector they would immediately wheel eastwards to capture the southern end of the switch behind the Germans.
Also, while Haig attempted to pass his cavalry corps
through any gap torn at Arras, Gough would try to put
the 4th Cavalry Division through any breach made at
Bullecourt. The division would then be operating in the
enemy's rear.

A company of the 13th Australian Brigade had on
April 5th rushed the Germans from a railway embankment and cutting—facing at 1000 yards the Hindenburg
Line west of Bullecourt. Engineers, pioneers and other
constructional troops—including the Anzac Light Rail-

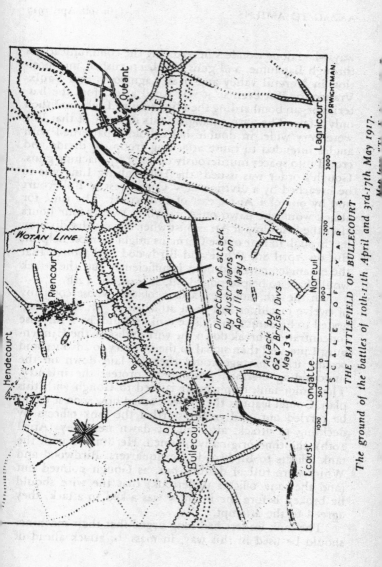

THE BATTLEFIELD OF BULLECOURT

The ground of the battles of 10th-11th April and 3rd-17th May 1917.

ways—had done wonders in restoring the communications through Bapaume, and guns had been rushed into position in Noreuil valley and near Lagnicourt and Vaulx-Vraucourt. But even so it was April 4th before the batteries began bombarding the Hindenburg Line—and then only a few. The wire entanglements in front of that line were very wide, in double belts, boldly patterned with angles intended to cause attacking troops to divide and crowd into spaces murderously covered by machine-guns. Gough's order was issued: the Hindenburg Line was to be breached by a division of V Corps west of Bullecourt and by one of I Anzac east of Bullecourt. The time for attack would be dawn on April 10th, twenty-four hours after the first blow at Arras, just when the cavalry division let through in rear of the Germans might be most helpful. But on April 8th White and Birdwood told Gough that the entanglements had been insufficiently cut; the attack would have to be postponed till, at least, the 12th.

On the 9th, however, a tank officer, whose company of twelve machines had been attached to 5th Army, suggested to his senior that these tanks should, by a surprise concentration, break down the wire and seize the Hindenburg Line, and then signal to the infantry to advance and occupy it. A barrage could then be laid down on the surrounding German position to protect the infantry. The senior tank commander rushed to Gough with this plan. Gough leapt at the project, asked how soon it could be carried out, and rather startled the tank officers by deciding to attack, after all, at dawn next day (April 10th), the time originally planned. He hurried with the tank officers to Birdwood's headquarters. Birdwood and White were full of doubts, but, as Gough pointed out (and the tank officers undertook) that the wire should be broken before the infantry was asked to attack, they agreed to the attempt.

The tank leaders had long urged that their machines should be used in this way, in mass, to attack ahead of the infantry rather than as part of it. Now was their opportunity. All twelve machines would advance ahead of the 4th Australian Division, east of Bullecourt. That division was to attack where the Hindenburg Line formed a deep gulf or re-entrant, with Bullecourt standing out on one side, and a gentle rise (on which a loop of the German line ran round Quéant) on the other. Neither Birdwood nor White liked attacking in this cavity. But it was arranged that the four tanks on the left on reaching the Hindenburg Line should turn westward along it, followed by an Australian battalion, and seize Bullecourt; on their firing signals to show that this had been done, the 62nd Division (V Corps) would advance and occupy the village and then, with these tanks, seize the Hindenburg Line west of it. After this both divisions would advance another mile to the villages of Riencourt and Hendecourt, west of the Wotan switch.

In extreme haste the two allotted brigades, 4th and 12th, of the 4th Australian Division were marched up, and before dawn were duly lying out in the dark, on the snow-covered grassland far ahead of the railway embankment and cutting, each brigade on a gentle rise along which it was to attack, with a shallow valley between them. General Gough had constantly been impressed by supposed evidence that the Germans were voluntarily retiring from the Hindenburg Line. During this night, by his order, patrols were sent to test whether this was happening. They found the German line as before, strongly held, and its wire very formidable. At 11 p.m., on hearing this, Birdwood telephoned to Gough saying with emphasis that he thought the operation very hazardous. A few minutes later came Gough's reply that the attack must take place as the commander-in-chief wished it. A little later, on news that the southern British flank at Arras had been driven back, General White renewed this protest but was told that there was all the more need for the attack.

However the infantry lying on the bleak, snowy pasture, eager to see for the first time tanks in action and to fight beside them, could hear or see no sign of any machine. The attack was postponed for half an hour. Finally just upon dawn an exhausted tank officer stumbled into a telephone office in Noreuil valley, a mile behind the railway embankment and told the 4th Division's headquarters that his machines had met blizzard weather and could not be in time. By a hasty message from Maj.-General Holmes the two infantry brigades were withdrawn in dawning light from under the muzzles of the enemy to the railway embankment and cutting. A passing snow-squall screened the retreat. Patrols of the 62nd Division, not being informed of the Australian withdrawal, tried to get into Bullecourt; they suffered heavily and brought bombardment on the Australians also.

At a conference later that morning (10th) General Gough told his corps commanders that the 3rd Army was then making another attempt to get its cavalry through, and the 5th Army's attempt with tanks must therefore be repeated at 4.30 a.m. on April 11th. Upon strong protests from Birdwood and White, General Gough telephoned to G.H.Q., and presently returned to say that Haig considered the attack to be urgently required. This settled the matter. The plan was slightly altered—in particular, as it was now known that the Hindenburg Line wire was partly cut, the infantry was to advance fifteen minutes after the tanks without waiting for signals. But there was barely time to get the order to the troops.

The two brigades, now very tired, again moved out and lay on the snow. But again until 3 a.m. no tank had arrived. By 4.30 only three had reached position in front of the right brigade (4th), and none had reached the left (12th). The three tanks started and, fifteen minutes later, the 4th Brigade advanced. In long lines extended with striking regularity the two leading battalions quickly reached the tanks, still some distance from the wire. The

Germans in the first line fired intensely at the slow monsters, whose shapes were outlined by the sparkling of bullets.

The infantry was now facing precisely the situation that the Anzac leaders had feared—being without artillery support in face of only half-cut wire. Hesitation would have been fatal, and their officers led magnificently. There now came to the front of the 16th Battalion one of the most famous fighting leaders of the A.I.F., Major Percy Black, formerly a gold prospector in Western Australia. "I mayn't come back," he had told his colonel, "but we'll get the Hindenburg Line." He led through the storm of bullets at the wire of the first trench. The Germans who were exceedingly good troops—Württembergers of the 27th Division—had been shaken by the appearance of tanks, and fled. The support trench was 200 yards farther, with a belt of intact wire between. Major Black found an opening, and was putting his men through it when he was killed. Elsewhere also, with similar leading, both trenches were taken by the 4th Brigade, and a start was made for Riencourt village before the advance was held.

The first tank for the 12th Brigade reached its infantry at 4.45, and at first fired into their trench, mistaking them for Germans. Here a confusion in orders, due to the haste in arrangements, caused the leading battalion to wait for the other tanks. Thus not till 5.15, with dawn breaking ahead, did the brigade advance. It was detected from Bullecourt and fired on, but it too seized part of both trenches.

The 4th Australian Division had thus taken most of its first objective. The tanks had failed—none reached the wire before the infantry; indeed only four reached it at all, and only one of these reached the first trench in the Australian sector.[4] The machines of that date were

---

[4] One later boldly attacked Bullecourt; one lost direction and reached the loop trench round Quéant, a mile to the east. For the position of each destroyed tank see *sketch in Vol. IV, p. 314.*

slower than walking men; their steel was too thin, and
some advanced German guns, whose flashes at the edge
of Riencourt Wood were plainly seen, were much too
deadly. By 7 a.m. the hulks of tanks were burning all
over the battlefield. At 7.15 a message accurately stating
the position came from Captain Harry Murray. It ended:
"With artillery support we can keep the position till the
cows come home."

But owing to mistaken reports, mainly from air and
artillery observers, all the higher staffs believed the attack
to be proceeding to its farther objectives with complete
success. Tanks leading Australian infantry were said to
have been seen far ahead, entering Hendecourt, and
Australian infantry was believed to have entered Bullecourt. These reports had two results. First, at 9.35, Gough
ordered the 4th Cavalry Division to pass through the
Hindenburg Line. A small dismounted party of it, trying
about that time to cut the wire behind the Australians,
was shot away; the 17th Lancers coming on to the rear
part of the battlefield were shelled and, at 10.30 a.m.,
withdrawn. The second result was that hour after hour,
despite the infantry's repeated appeals, the artillery was
not allowed to fire. The Germans on all sides were thus
able to move and shoot with impunity, except where the
infantry's Lewis guns held them. By 8 a.m. their fire
across the re-entrant behind the Australians practically
closed that route for supplies, reinforcements and
messages.

With bombs running out the effort of the two brigades
to join their inner flanks was stopped, and eventually the
German bombers made headway. The 4th Brigade, now
without bombs, was gradually driven back along the
trenches; and at 10.20, at a conference called by a senior
officer, Captain Gardiner, it was decided, if necessary, to
fall back into shellholes near by. By 11.30 it was clear
that the only useful course was to try to return to the
Australian lines. Terrible fire was sweeping the ground

but Murray told his men: "It is either capture, or go into that." Very many tried; Murray was among the comparatively few who got through.

The left brigade, 12th, had from the first been attacked chiefly by Germans from Bullecourt, bombing along the old German front trench. About 8 a.m. these Germans were fought to a standstill but shortly before noon another attack found the Australians in that trench

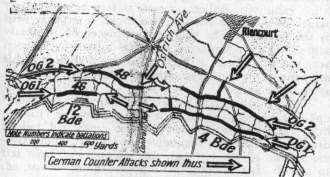

GERMAN COUNTER-ATTACKS, HINDENBURG LINE,
BULLECOURT, 11th APRIL 1917
(The hachured lines show the belts of barbed wire.)

almost without bombs and soon drove them out, leaving the 48th Battalion and part of the 47th in the old German support line, now the Australian front, completely cut off. The 48th was commanded by Lieut.-Colonel "Ray" Leane of Gaba Tepe fame. Many of its leaders were of his family; it was known as the Joan of Arc Battalion ("Made of All Leanes"), and his relatives used to expect, and were often given, any super-dangerous tasks. One splendid brother had shortly before been killed at the railway embankment.

A nephew, Captain A. E. Leane, commanded its troops in the Hindenburg Line. Under his lead the 48th now turned about and, in fierce fighting, retook the trench behind it. It then held both lines. At this stage, however, the supporting artillery, being at last allowed to fire, and being under the impression that these trenches had been lost, brought down its barrage upon them.

Then, at 12.25, a full hour after the other troops—with proud deliberation, under heavy fire, picking its way calmly through the wire, helping the walking wounded, its officers bringing up the rear—the 48th Battalion came out. Bullecourt was, at last, being shelled; patrols of the 62nd Division had found it strongly held by the Germans. The barrage now placed on it greatly helped the 48th. Captain Leane was missed by his men near the wire. Later it became known that he and his companion, the intelligence officer of the 48th, had been mortally wounded.

The 4th Australian Division had achieved a previously unbelievable feat—seized for a time part of the Hindenburg Line without a barrage. The tanks had indeed drawn much fire on themselves and scared many Germans; but, except for that, the infantry had been left to assault that famous fortification almost unassisted. Through the miscarriage of this hasty scheme the confidence of the Australian soldier in both the British command and the tanks had suffered a staggering blow. The tactics of Pozieres and Fromelles had shaken the faith of many intelligent men; and now an experiment of extreme rashness had been made, despite protests, with tanks and, in some cases, tank-crews, not nearly equal to the need. The 4th Brigade had 2339 casualties (out of 3000 men engaged) and the 12th 950. For more than a year afterwards few Australian infantrymen would place any reliance upon the help of tanks.

The 5th Army had been saving divisions in order to increase Haig's reserves. It was holding its front with only three. As the 4th Australian and 62nd Divisions had to concentrate on a 6750 yard front for the Bullecourt attack, the 1st Australian Division farther south had to cover more than 12,000 yards. This was held, by Haig's order, in great depth, with a light fringe of sentry groups in front, then platoon pickets, reserve platoons, reserve companies, reserve battalions, reserve brigade, and finally reserve division (with forward units at Bapaume). The commander of the XIV German Reserve Corps, opposite I Anzac, General von Moser, on being given at this stage a third division, the 3rd Guard, to defend his 11,000 yard front, suggested that the best defence was attack. Crown Prince Rupprecht of Bavaria, commanding all German armies on the British front, eagerly agreed—he wanted some counter-stroke to keep the British from transferring reserves to the main Arras thrust.

And here was his opportunity! This country was almost entirely open, and, to attack the Hindenburg Line, the Australian artillery had been pushed forward far down depressions leading towards it near Noreuil and Lagnicourt, where, incidentally, the crews came under fierce shelling, causing their heaviest losses, so far, in the war. On April 15th, an hour before dawn, some of the 1st Division's batteries close behind Lagnicourt heard heavy rifle fire in the infantry posts ahead of them, and then German infantry suddenly appeared near the guns and Australian infantry also fell back between them. Not knowing what troops were ahead, the batteries could not open fire. By order from artillery headquarters the gun crews withdrew, carrying their breech-blocks and dial sights.

The Germans using the greater part of four divisions —twenty-six battalions—had attacked nearly the whole thin fan-shaped outpost line of the 1st Australian Division and, at Noreuil, the extreme right of the 2nd, which had just relieved the 4th. Two nights earlier the 1st Division had still further extended its fan-shaped front by approaching 1000 yards closer to the Hindenburg Line, pushing its widely spaced posts over grassy slopes where men could not safely show themselves by day-time; they were now spread along 13,000 yards. The intention of the German command was to seize the seven nearest villages in or behind this weak front, capture or destroy the artillery and supplies around them, hold on for the day, and retire again at night. Most of the Australian posts were warned by the German bombardment; and though at several points near Boursies the enemy penetrated to and beyond the picket line, and captured a few posts, the line was barely dinted except at the extreme left, between Lagnicourt and Noreuil.

Here, contrary to Moser's orders, a Guards reserve division attacked without previous bombardment, with the result that some of its companies were marching between the widely spaced Australian pickets almost before these saw them. As already stated these Germans reached some of the batteries west of Lagnicourt. They overran that village, and at dawn were suddenly seen advancing over the rise close above Noreuil and the massed batteries farther up the valley. A Tasmanian company at Lagnicourt fought the Germans, front and rear; reserve companies held the intruders on both flanks, and at 7.10 a.m. two support battalions, 9th and 20th, counter-attacking drove the Germans in flight from Lagnicourt and from the guns. Though for two hours they had possession of 21 Australian guns the Germans damaged only 5; they had spent their time searching dugouts for food and souvenirs. The 43rd Battery, away near Ecoust, was intensely shelled but fired through the tornado till more than half its crews and guns were out of action.

This day a front line held by little over 4 Australian battalions had been attacked by 23 battalions; 4000 men attacked by 16,000. The Australians were driven back only from some of the dangerously advanced positions which they had occupied two nights earlier. Their casualties were 1010, some 300 (including only one officer) being prisoners. The Germans lost 2313, of whom

362 were captured.[5] German reports spoke much of the effect of the Lewis guns "cleverly emplaced and bravely fought", and urged the German need of a light machine-gun—just then beginning to be supplied.

On the day after this fight (known to Australians as "the Lagnicourt counter-attack") the great French offensive under General Nivelle was launched in the Aisne region. A new French government had lately come in; and though the Briand Ministry had once supported Nivelle with enthusiasm, this attitude had undergone an astonishing change. In the end it was only by threat of resigning that Nivelle brought the new French government, under Ribot and Painlevé, to allow the attack to be launched.[6] Though making some headway, it fell disastrously short of the deep penetration that Nivelle intended. As Haig had suspected, the Germans had long since learnt of the project—gossip in France was widespread. For several days Nivelle tried to continue the thrust as a "wearing down" battle, making some material advances—by Somme standards; but assurances of this coming from the leader who had stood for "No more Sommes!" inspired little confidence.

Yet the French and British governments each wanted the other to persist in its offensives at all costs, and at a conference on April 20th they temporarily agreed on this. The French were to strike on May 4th. The British at Arras renewed their attacks on April 23rd and 28th without great success; Ludendorff's system of defence—to keep back divisions earmarked for counter-stroke, and strike back with them immediately after each thrust—proved too effective. The next British effort was to be made on May 3rd by fourteen divisions on a front of six-

---

[5] For the action of the 43rd Battery see *Vol. IV, p. 388.* A report that huge loss (some said 3000) was caused by the Anzac artillery catching Germans retiring through the Hindenburg wire greatly pleased the defenders, and has passed into history. Actually the German troops so fired on numbered only 200, and their casualties were probably well under 100.

[6] For this episode see *Vol. IV, pp. 135-43.*

23-0\

teen miles, the widest attack undertaken till then by
British troops. The force, however, was not generally a
fresh one. On the extreme left the Canadians would
attack from beyond Vimy. On the extreme right I Anzac
and V Corps would assault their old objectives in the
Hindenburg Line about Bullecourt, and, if possible, go
on to seize the Wotan switch.

This time ample artillery and time were allotted to
5th Army for pounding the Hindenburg Line, and Bullecourt village quickly crumbled into heaps of rubbish.
British airmen flew over constantly, though Baron Richthofen with the better machines of his red-nosed squadron
frequently shot them down. Meanwhile the 2nd Australian and 62nd British Divisions each trained themselves carefully for the attack. Except that the troops
would advance to each successive objective behind a
creeping barrage, and that there would be no gap between the two brigades (5th and 6th) and no tanks, the
plan for the 2nd Division was very similar to that for
the 4th Division on April 11th. The 62nd Division would
be helped by ten tanks and Bullecourt village and the
Hindenburg Line west of it were part of its first objective.
As before, the Australians attacked east of the village, in
the re-entrant of the Hindenburg Line.

At 3.45 a.m. on May 3rd the great attack went in
under its barrage. On its extreme right flank the 2nd Australian Division advanced with its 5th and 6th Brigades.
About twenty minutes later anxious observers at the railway line thought that, among the German flares of all
colours rising and falling above the dust of the barrage,
they saw the success flares of both brigades, first of the
5th on the right, then of the 6th on the left.

The 6th Brigade was fired on from the left front and
from Bullecourt as its flank brushed past that village, and
part of it was thus pinned in the wire; but its right and
centre, partly sheltered by a half-sunken road that ran

between the two brigades, seized and cleared part of both
Hindenburg trenches, and, when the time came, part of
the 24th Battalion under
Captain Maxfield, went
on and seized the second
objective, the embank-
ment of a field railway
near Riencourt. But it
gradually became known
that the 5th Brigade had
not taken its first objective; met by a deadly
cross machine-gun fire at
the entanglement, it had
hesitated, thus missing
its chance of getting in.
A second effort made
soon after, without bar-
rage, proved hopeless. A
handful of its men on the
flank of the 6th Brigade had seized a few bays of the
Hindenburg trenches there.

On the other flank of the 6th Brigade the 62nd Division
had failed to take Bullecourt though some of its troops
seized the Hindenburg Line west of the village and a few
reached the second objective. Gellibrand, whose headquarters were at the railway embankment, could see this
situation, but reports from the 62nd Division's headquarters that it had taken Bullecourt were believed as
against his. When his reports proved true he was ordered,
against his own advice, to attack Bullecourt with a battalion (25th) from reserve. He did so, but on the first
platoons being immediately swept away he stopped the
attack.

The situation of the 6th Brigade, thrust out through
the Hindenburg Line on a narrow front, deep in the re-
entrant, and attacked on both flanks in every position,

might have seemed untenable; but it was held. Led by
Captain Gilchrist,[7] until he was killed, and then by others,
a furious bombing attack up the trenches won part of the
5th Brigade's objective. This was presently lost, but was
won again, part of the 5th and 7th Brigades being used.
This happened many times; but the enemy troops were
the same stubborn 27th (Württemberg) Division that had
held the sector against the 4th Division, and each time
they drove back the bombers. Out ahead, Maxfield was
killed; by 11.30 the remnant of his troops and those of
the 23rd, who had followed them with the duty of making
the next advance, were withdrawn to the Hindenburg
Line, where about 600 yards of the front and support
trenches was still held by the 6th Brigade and its
reinforcements.

Fortunately the central half-sunken road lying between the 5th and 6th Brigade areas gave some sheltered
communication back to the railway, and the pioneers
were making a trench along it. Early in the afternoon the
28th Battalion (7th Brigade) was sent up. In a fiery bomb-
attack it won 450 yards of the 5th Brigade's objective,
east of the road. Bombs then ran short, and the Australians were thrice beaten back to the central road. By
immense labour of carrying-parties new supplies came
and the 28th twice recaptured the trenches, trench-mortar
crews and rifle grenadiers assisting. Just before dusk the
6th Brigade won more room on the other flank, and thus
at dusk the 2nd Australian Division held most of its
original first objective.

But as night fell the almost exhausted 28th on the
right was again driven back. About the same time a heavy
German bombardment fell behind the Australians, and
against it could be seen figures closing in in rear of the
forward troops. The answering Australian bombardment

---

[7] A young engineer of Gellibrand's staff who with the signal officer
Lieut. Rentoul had rallied and led troops of the sister (5th) brigade. Both
fell before the efforts ended.

fell on part of the 6th Brigade trenches and some men left them. This caused a report that the enemy was threatening to cut the central road; and the commander of the 28th, a brave and hard fighter, believing that the 6th Brigade was retiring, ordered his battalion to do the same. The 28th accordingly came back.

But the 6th Brigade had not withdrawn; under the young leaders whom Gellibrand had trained—Captains Lloyd, Savige, and others—it was cheerfully holding on. A young company commander of the 28th Battalion, Captain Jack Roydhouse, had also served on Gellibrand's staff. Despite all that he heard and saw he refused to believe that the 6th was retiring; hurrying into their trenches, he found the young staff. Half crying with indignation he told them that his own battalion and all other troops had left them. The trenches on their right, and the road behind, were now open to the enemy. He himself had come to stay with them.

The youngsters instantly decided to hold on; if the worst happened and they were surrounded they would then cut their way through. Posts were placed in the abandoned trenches and road; and, with the barrages of the two sides thundering before, behind, and about them, the 6th Brigade held on, alone, in the night. The supposed enemy in rear was later discovered to have been part of the 5th Brigade leaving the old no-man's-land. At 1 a.m. on May 4th, troops of the 1st Australian Division, hurriedly brought forward to relieve the 6th Brigade, found it still steadily holding its line.

In all that day's great battle the only objectives reached and finally held were those of the Canadians in the extreme north, and of the 6th Australian Brigade in the extreme south. It will be remembered that the battle was intended to precede another great French attack, fixed for May 4th. But by May 4th French plans again had changed. As will be seen later, the French Ministry

by then suspected that its troops were for the present
unfit for big operations. The burden of fighting must
fall on the British. Accordingly Haig decided that, while
building up reserves for other offensives, he must continue to press with his already tired troops at Arras.

At this juncture, when it was desired that the declining
nature of his effort at Arras should be hidden for as long
as possible, the fighting that ensued at Bullecourt attained
a prominence most useful to the Allies. The Australians'
narrow foothold, like a mushroom on its stalk, deep in
enemy ground at the head of a single long track of communication, had little tactical value; but they would not
let go. On the contrary they daily kept on extending it,
and gave an opportunity to the British on their flank to
extend it still farther. The stubborn Württembergers of
the garrison, and other German troops after them, continually counter-attacked on both flanks, often with flame
throwers, but in the end were always thrown back.

General Birdwood from the first represented that the
Australians' position could not be maintained unless
Bullecourt, on their left rear, was seized by the British.
Till May 7th attempts, first by the 62nd and then by the
7th British Division, failed in this very difficult task; but
meanwhile the 1st Australian Brigade, by bombing, with
their trench mortars and rifle grenadiers firing over their
heads, had won 400 yards of the Hindenburg Line on the
right and 200 on the left. Part of the 3rd Brigade had
next to be brought in. Following this, at dawn on
May 6th, after some eighteen hours of intense methodical
shelling—the only bombardment ever justifiably described
by the Australians who suffered it as "perhaps worse than
Pozières"—the Germans made on both flanks their sixth
general counter-attack. Throwing against the Australian
right troops of the 3rd Guard Division headed by flame
throwers, they almost reached the central "Pioneers'
Trench", when an astonishing sally along the top of the
trenches by a corporal, G. J. Howell, and the stubborn

defence by others,[8] threw them back farther than their starting point.

Shortly before dawn the next day, May 7th, the 2nd Gordon Highlanders of the 7th British Division amid tremendous bombardment seized the eastern side of Bullecourt, meeting the 9th Australian Battalion which bombed down the Hindenburg Line to join them. At one time the sight of figures withdrawing from Bullecourt through the dust cloud of German shell-bursts caused a report that the 7th Division were retiring, but Australians who had seen them scouted the notion; the men seen would be a returning carrying-party—the "Jocks" would still be "in". And so it proved, although some of the remaining ruin heaps of Bullecourt resisted capture until May 17th.

By May 7th the Second Battle of Bullecourt, which, according to the original assumption, was to engage only one Australian division, had already drawn in most of two, 2nd and 1st; and now the 5th, about to hold its sports and horse-show at Albert, had to be warned for action. After their extreme trials, both in First Somme and through the "Somme Winter", the troops had long looked forward to a rest, and representations now made by General Hobbs to Birdwood and White, and by them, in writing, to Gough, led to a decision to rest the I Anzac Corps thoroughly when its fight at Bullecourt ended.

Meanwhile the 5th Division was brought up and put in. On May 12th its left brigade, like the 2nd Brigade before it, won more ground to the west, firmly linking with the 7th Division. This flank and the foothold in Bullecourt were now taken over by Londoners of the 58th Division. But at dawn on May 15th the 14th Australian Brigade, still holding the right, was—after nearly three hours' intense bombardment—attacked in front and

---

[8] In particular Lieut. A. W. L. MacNeil, D.S.O., and Captain Newland. V.C. Howell's action gained him the V.C. (*See Vol. IV, pp. 513-17.*) Capt. J. E. Newland (and Sgt. J. W. Whittle) had won it at Lagnicourt.

flank. The Germans thrust 200 yards into its trenches but were quickly driven out. Their attempt to retake Bulle-court from part of the 58th and 7th British Divisions also failed.

This was the Germans' most carefully planned and final effort. On its failure they decided to withdraw from Bullecourt. A British attack on May 17th caught some of the garrison before they were clear; and on May 20th part of the Hindenburg Line west of Bullecourt was also seized by the British, and the Battle of Arras flickered to its close. After the first stunning blow, it had achieved little except to engage attention on both sides at a time of crisis for the French—and for this the Bullecourt fighting was for a time almost solely responsible. On every day from May 5th to 17th, except one, the Bulle-court fighting was mentioned in the British bulletins, and it was often the chief item. As a French journalist once announced: "The Australians have again captured the British communiqué." The winning of their impos-sible position in the Hindenburg Line, and the holding of it despite seven general counter-attacks and a dozen minor ones, was, as Haig wrote, "among the great deeds of the war"; but its difficulty was due, as at Mouquet Farm, to Gough's clutching at valuable strategical ends by impossible tactics.

"Second Bullecourt" cost the A.I.F. 7000 casualties, and "First Bullecourt" 3000. The consequent drain on reinforcements helped to destroy the 6th Australian Division then forming in England. But Second Bulle court won for I Anzac a longer and happier rest than perhaps was ever given to another corps of the British armies in France.

CHAPTER XX

1917 (2)—MESSINES

WHEN the Prime Minister of Britain, Mr Lloyd George, and his naval and military staff, met the Premier of France, M. Ribot, with his clever war minister, M. Painlevé, and the French service leaders on 4th May 1917 in Paris, the whole effort of the British leaders was to make sure that the French maintained their part in the joint offensive of the Allies.

That great project, which had been envisaged as the possible turning point of the war, had been seriously threatened by a sudden revolution in Russia on 8th-16th March 1917, which overturned the Czar's government. It was uncertain whether the Provisional government there would proceed with Russia's rôle in the attack. As for Italy, her leaders were now hamstrung by apprehension that the Germans were concentrating against them. In France the great stroke from which governments had hoped so much, Nivelle's offensive, had already failed. At the Paris meeting, therefore, it was the British leaders who took the initiative, and Lloyd George, who so lately had placed Haig under Nivelle, now for once energetically supported the British commander.

Painlevé had already privately decided to supersede Nivelle by Pétain. It could hardly be done before this conference with the British, who had so lately been induced to put Haig under Nivelle's orders; but, along with Nivelle, the French ministers brought to the conference Pétain, who had just been made chief of the French General Staff. All agreed with the British commanders that a series of concerted attacks should be made by French and British. They were to be "step-by-step" offensives, that is, similar to the German attack on Verdun—a limited objective being set for each attack, and after that step, perhaps, another and another, each elaborately prepared for by the Allies' immense artillery, which now surpassed the German. The conference left it to the generals to determine the time, place and other details of the attacks. But it was understood that the main stroke would now be delivered by the British in Flanders. This had been urged by the British Admiralty, and had been agreed to by Joffre at Chantilly as one of the later phases of the great plan for 1917. The plan was cherished by Haig, but he was prepared to use his reserves earlier in a great Anglo-French attack near the Somme, suggested by Nivelle—if this eventuated. Haig doubted, however, whether Nivelle could stage it; but I Anzac, which was then expected to use only one division at Bullecourt, was to be pulled out and rested as part of the force for this attack.

As Haig apprehended, however, the French did not undertake that offensive. On May 15th Nivelle was superseded by Pétain. Though much of the truth was successfully hidden from both sides till after the war, on May 3rd there began in the French Army a series of sixteen mutinies which continued for five weeks and shook it to its foundations. Pétain, who had nursed that army during the Verdun offensive, was undoubtedly the man to restore its strength—after Nivelle's excessive demands it needed, for a time, nursing rather than leading. For many months no offensive, limited or unlimited, was launched by Pétain; the task of maintaining the initiative on the Western Front now fell solely on the British.

In this situation Haig turned at once to his plan of driving the Germans from the Belgian coast. This plan had one great merit. The Allied leaders knew that by heralding an attack with a sufficient bombardment, and then advancing their infantry—but never allowing them to go beyond the protection of their own guns—they could at most times seize almost any part of the German front, within certain limits of breadth and depth. By then moving up their artillery and repeating the process again and again they could, provided the advances were wide enough, gradually drive the Germans back, step by step, for many miles.

In most parts of the Western Front the Germans could be thrust back a dozen miles without suffering great disadvantage. But as their front neared the Belgian coast such an advance by the Allies would place the German garrison on the coast in danger of being smashed or cut off. In that region, therefore, the Germans must stand and take whatever battering the Allies' artillery could inflict. Yet, by using the step-by-step method against them, in spite of all their efforts they might be gradually driven back until they must consider abandoning the coast. Thus the offensive was designed both to wear the Germans down, and to bring a strategic success which might help Britain's defence against submarines and would at least cause great discouragement to the German nation. It now served the additional purpose of maintaining the Allied offensive in the west, partly relieving the French, and at least giving them time to recover.

The part of the German line at which Haig intended to strike was that which lay on or west of the low ridge around the battered Belgian town of Ypres. This ridge was sickle shaped; the handle, a few miles south of Ypres, was formed by the Messines-Wytschaete heights, held by the Germans; and the blade, curving around east of Ypres, formed part of the site of the original Ypres Salient. As already explained, Polygon Wood and Broodseinde, on that ridge four miles east of Ypres, had been lost by the British in the first German gas offensive in April-May 1915, and the salient had since been much smaller, the front running through Hooge and along low rises and flats two to three miles from the city. Haig meant to recapture the original salient and then push along the ridge northwards and north-eastwards through Passchendaele and down towards Roulers and Thourout. But first he must make safe his right flank by capturing the "handle", the Messines-Wytschaete ridge.

The preparations to capture Messines had begun, as we have seen, early in 1916. The whole front concerned was that of 2nd Army, and the main plans were those of the white-haired, cautious veteran, General Plumer, and his chief-of-staff, Maj.-General C. H. Harington. The deep mines, already well advanced when I Anzac had prepared to attack there in July 1916, were now complete; Plumer's provisional plan had been secretly issued in March 1917. The ridge was to be taken by three army corps, and

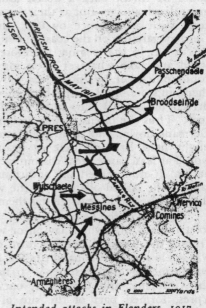

Intended attacks in Flanders, 1917.

of these the southernmost, which would capture Messines itself and then advance over the hill to the flats beyond, would be II Anzac. That corps, under General Godley,

348

had held the Armentières front throughout the winter, with three divisions—the New Zealand Division (back from the Somme); the 3rd Australian Division, which in December 1916 arrived from England under General Monash; and a British division. The 3rd Division had gained experience in a series of carefully planned and generally successful raids. The corps, including the 25th British Division, had already sideslipped gradually to the Messines front by April 27th; but the plans had been perfecting since March 18th.

Never had a big British operation been prepared in such detail; in the 3rd Division, in particular, Monash issued thirty-six successive circulars, one of them in seven parts. Points to be bombarded by artillery were carefully listed; 2nd Army staff designed an immense creeping barrage of artillery and machine-gun fire—to move in five tiers, nearly half a mile deep, ahead of the infantry. Huge models of the ground were built behind the lines and studied by the troops, especially in Monash's division.

On May 16th the three divisions of II Anzac were reinforced by the 4th Australian, which had been rested for nearly a month since its attack with tanks near Bullecourt. It was to carry out the final part of II Anzac's duty—the thrust to the plain after the 3rd, New Zealand and 25th Divisions (side by side, in that order from right to left) had captured (in two stages) the section of the summit facing that army corps.

To the 4th Division this transfer to Flanders while its sister divisions in the south were resting, came as a shock; but Australians had learnt by now to take philosophically their fate in war. The battle orders of its commander, General Holmes, were as short as those of Monash were long. The 4th Division now came among men of the 3rd, whom the rest of the A.I.F. had been waiting to see. The 4th was perhaps the toughest of all Australian divisions, the 3rd, without Gallipoli experi-

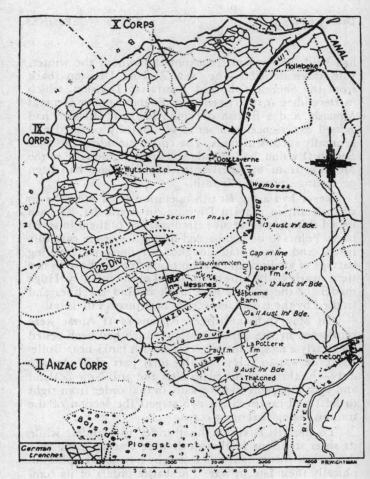

THE BATTLEFIELD OF MESSINES

*This shows the plan of attack, and the line seized
on 7th June 1917.*

Adapted from map in "The Empire at War".

ence,[1] the most "handled" and tractable, and there was keen interest to see how it shaped in and out of battle.

On May 31st the seven days' bombardment began. The area behind the British lines teemed with batteries and dumps, concentrated there in the past few weeks. The Germans had perceived all this, from ground and air, and under their heavy shelling several dumps and an ammunition train exploded. But they were completely unaware that nineteen immense mines had been tunnelled deep below their front trenches to be attacked. In the two years' tussle underground between the British and German tunnelling companies the British miners had outmanoeuvred and outfought their opponents.

At the oldest of these mines, at Hill 60[2] (at the southern end of the British "bulge" at Ypres, just where the German "bulge" round Messines began) the 1st Australian Tunnelling Company had been responsible for the workings since November 1916. Two deep galleries dug by British and Canadians had then already been driven below—and far behind—the German line, and filled with immense charges (50 and 70 thousand pounds of ammonal). The Australians had since driven a third gallery, lately at a rate of fourteen feet daily, but the offensive came too soon for its completion. Their main work was the tense fighting, explosion and counter-explosion in the network of tunnels at three different levels, to keep the enemy away from the deep mines.

How complicated was this contest may be judged from the experience of an Australian miner on duty "listening" on 24th April 1917, in a tunnel of the middle-deep system, when footsteps approached from the German direction. Thinking that the Germans must have dug through into the same tunnel farther on, the listener

---

[1] Except for some men who had re-enlisted in Australia. For a comparison of the troops see *Vol. IV, pp. 560-3, and 579-80.*

[2] Hill 60 was a low rise beside the Ypres-Comines Canal, its summit being heightened by part of the spoil from the canal.

blew out his light and prepared to act. The steps came very close—and then suddenly passed six feet overhead. The German miner was in some old German gallery, previously unknown to the Australians. They soon afterwards destroyed it.[3] Far above, on the surface, on 9th April 1917, a German raiding party discovered, in a British trench, clay of a kind which they knew must come from deep mines. They began to probe for them, and were very close to the "deeps" when Zero day and Zero hour (or "Z day" and "Z hour"), 3.10 a.m. on 7th June 1917, arrived.

The Germans had heard through a spy on April 29th that the British would strike at Messines a fortnight after ending the Arras offensive. Also, in all these huge "battles of material" it was impossible to hide preparations. The "Catacombs", a vast system of tunnels for housing two complete battalions in the bowels of Hill 63, opposite to Messines, had been dug by the 1st Australian Tunnelling Company in 1916. Roads, railways, dumps, assembly trenches had since to be made, hospitals set up, aerodromes prepared, artillery (at this stage of the war) ranged on to its targets. The Germans knew Messines would be attacked; and General von Kuhl (chief of Crown Prince Rupprecht's staff) suggested withdrawing to their third line through Oosttaverne village on the flats—the very line that the British intended to reach in the last phase of the attack. But the commanders of the German forward troops stoutly objected, and as a result their existing front was strongly held. As the day of battle obviously approached, the German artillery on several nights gassed with phosgene shell the ground through which British attacking troops might be approaching.

Thus all through the night of June 6th a rain of gas shells, with their shrill whine and low "pat", showered on Ploegsteert Wood through which the battalions of

3 For the full story of these underground battles see *Vol. IV, Appendix I* (p. 949).

the 3rd Australian Division, southernmost of the British attacking force, were then actually filing up, and also on the New Zealanders on Hill 63 north of them, looking out across the Douve valley at Messines hill. The approach of the 3rd Division through the gas-saturated wood was a task of nightmarish difficulty[4]—500 men were put temporarily out of action. Yet before dawn began to show behind that hill, this fine division was ready in its place— as were eight others north of it along the rest of the seven and a half mile front of attack. At 3.10 the hitherto intermittent artillery fire increased with a run; and then the trenches rocked, as nineteen great explosions tore immense craters at as many points of the front, and the powerful barrage thundered down, and the infantry went over.

The working out of 2nd Army's great plan was as smooth as that of previous British offensives had been confused. The explosion of the mines shattered German troops and morale in the forward area. Farther back there were tough fights about a few farm ruins and concrete block-houses—built like low boxes and about this time becoming known as "pillboxes". But the platoons could now outflank and capture these, under cover from their own Lewis gunners and rifle grenadiers. With well-trained, determined troops—such as the New Zealanders were and those of the 3rd Division now proved themselves to be—the advance went with a swing. The troops followed the barrage through both its first stages, and by 5.30 a.m. Messines had been captured by the New Zealand Division with the 3rd and 25th in their correct positions on its flanks.

The main heights had been taken along the whole battlefront—only in the extreme north, near Ypres, was there any serious hitch. The front line troops had been ordered to make sure of the objective thus far gained;

---

[4] See Vol. IV, pp. 589-91.

24—os

the Germans, under their system of holding special divisions ready for counter-attack, were sure to attempt its recapture. Against this certainty the troops quickly entrenched themselves. Meanwhile the forces for Plumer's afternoon attack were to move up. The long pause that now began was necessary because the central British Corps, the IX, had to come much farther than the two others (II Anzac and X), and had also to advance its artillery. Owing to the delay on the northern flank, the afternoon attack was at the last moment postponed by General Plumer from 1 to 3 p.m.

On the II Anzac front the afternoon attack was to be made by two brigades of the 4th Australian Division moving through the front taken by the 25th and New Zealand Divisions—the 3rd Division, farthest south, would merely use one of its own battalions (37th) to swing up the division's extreme left flank in conjunction with the advance of the 4th. Farther north fresh British troops would advance through the front reached by the IX and X Corps.

On the II Anzac front half the troops for the afternoon attack did not learn of the postponement until they had moved forward to assemble; the other half moved about 2 p.m. Each, passing Messines, was faced by a heavy barrage, which raised a pall of dust, but each went through this, though with casualties, including many leaders hit. Part of this fire was the bombardment preceding a counter-attack attempted by the German division held ready for that purpose opposite this sector. The tremendous British barrage descending broke up the movement of these Germans at the Oosttaverne Line; and, the time for the British afternoon attack now arriving, the guns simply passed to their duty of laying the barrage for it.

The infantry advanced; but here occurred the only serious hitch in the programme. While allotted troops of the southern and northern corps, II Anzac and X, started immediately, those of the centre corps were nowhere to be seen. Their orders had been late, and the march on that sweltering day had been too long for the allotted troops (33rd Brigade) to arrive in time. An Australian patrol found British troops of another brigade half a mile to the north. Seeing that a wide gap existed, the young officer now in charge of the Australian left flank company, Captain Arthur Maxwell,[5] at once led his company north-eastwards. Fortunately the Germans there had fled and the Australians occupied, though very thinly, the whole of the British brigade's objective in the Oosttaverne Line as well as their own. Later they found some tanks and a few British troops who helped to secure and extend this foothold.

The southern (12th) brigade of the 4th Division also, well assisted by a few tanks, had reached a section of the Oosttaverne Line; and so had part of the 37th Battalion, greatly helped by the bravery of Captain R. C. Grieve, who, throwing bombs ahead of him, managed, in successive rushes covered by the dust cloud and commotion, to reach and capture singlehanded an obstructing pillbox (he was awarded the Victoria Cross). The foothold here was temporarily lost through their own barrage falling on the troops, but despite German counter-attacks it was regained. A more serious difficulty was that, through the extension of the 4th Division's left flank (exactly half the battlefront being then held by Australian troops), a gap opened in the centre. The Oosttaverne Line here was not completely taken until after four days and nights of tense fighting.

Nevertheless, by the evening of the first day Plumer's army had scored an immense success. Confidence in his leadership became very high. A stunning blow had been struck, and the German salient south of Ypres eliminated. The way was open for the more important offensive from

---

[5] Like his brother (of the Mouquet Farm fight) he subsequently fought in Malaya with the 2nd A.I.F.

Ypres, now planned to be delivered in July. The losses of the two sides at Messines were practically equal. Of the 26,000 British casualties II Anzac (including the 25th British Division) suffered 13,900.

It was not intended to push deeply at Messines, but during the next six weeks the front there was gradually advanced, from farm to farm, towards the Warneton Line—the old third reserve line of the Germans, which had now become their front. On this ground east of Messines a new system of defences was dug by the 11th Brigade[6] in eighteen strenuous, dangerous days. IX Corps made similar efforts. During this time the fine leader of the 4th Division, General Holmes, while taking the Premier of New South Wales, Mr Holman, by a normally safe route to see the battlefield, was mortally wounded by a chance salvo.

---

[6] The other brigades (9th and 10th) of the 3rd Division also dug successive defence-lines in rear; but for the 11th and its fine engineer company the task was as dangerous as a battle—the loss included the whole staff of the 41st Battalion.

CHAPTER XXI

1917 (3)—THIRD YPRES (PASSCHENDAELE)

DURING the seven weeks following Messines the immense preparations for the attack from Ypres went on. On those open flats it was, of course, more than ever impossible to prevent their being seen by the Germans.

None of the chief Dominion forces were brought up for the first main attack, but the artillery of all our divisions except the 3rd (then in line at Messines) was concentrated with immense forces of other artillery to provide the great rolling barrage. The Australian heavy batteries also were present. Dug into the open plain near Zillebeke Lake, and therefore easily detected, the Australian field batteries during the long preparation suffered casualties such as had never been inflicted on them before, even in Noreuil Valley. German shelling not infrequently hid them from view with clouds of dust and smoke, but the flashes of their guns, and of British batteries near them, could be seen stabbing the dust clouds. The Germans now sometimes used mustard-gas shell, often firing it along with "sneezing gas" and high explosive—it was exceedingly effective though less often fatal than phosgene. The Australian artillery drivers were noted for the way in which they took up ammunition through the barrages laid on the tracks. Even more than most soldiers they seemed to realise that, by pushing straight through, the job would be better done and the loss lighter.

It was at this stage also that the Australian Flying Corps began its work in France; the fighter squadrons then forming in England sent over pilots to be attached to British squadrons for experience in "ground strafing", and in low flying in co-operation with attacking infantry.

During the preparation for the offensive the Germans made a surprise assault at the extremity of the Allied line, on the Belgian coast. Here, with a view to an attack from the sea if the Ypres offensive succeeded, the British took over a corps front previously—and afterwards—held by the French. Beside the seashore just beyond Nieuport, the Allies had a small bridgehead across the Yser River. The 2nd Australian Tunnelling Company had been sent thither to attempt mining in the sand-dunes, which the French had not tried. Using Australian methods the miners made deep dugouts, and tunnelled trenches. They were driving two galleries far under no-man's-land from the bridgehead, when on July 10th the Germans attacked, and seized that part of it; the fifty miners who happened to be working there were captured, excepting a few who were killed in fighting or who managed to cross the river.

While Haig's great attack was in preparation, the aspect of the war had further darkened. On July 1st the Russian Army, during the short-lived regime of Kerensky, undertook an unexpectedly successful offensive, chiefly against the Austrians. But when the German reserve counter-attacked, the Russian forces, eager for peace, melted like snow. On the wave of this longing for peace, the Bolshevik party came into power, and by the close of July the end of the Russian war effort had been reached. The Italians attacked in May, but were quickly stopped. In the French Army a project for a limited offensive on June 10th had to be cancelled, the spirit of the troops being too low; and not only Pétain but Foch and Clemenceau (not yet Premier) maintained that, for the French, the only safe course was to remain on the defensive until 1918, by which time the arrival of American forces, and the British and French output of tanks, should make victory certain. Meanwhile Pétain would in due course undertake two strictly limited offensives and provide a few divisions to attack beside the British at Ypres—from which co-operation he expected an improvement in his soldiers' morale.

The grim prospect now, therefore, was that the British Army, alone, would have to shoulder the weight of the whole Allied offensive against the Germans, and this changed the British government's attitude towards the projected Ypres offensive. Mr Lloyd George especially, though in May at Paris he had supported and advocated the general principle of step-by-step offensives on the Western Front, now objected strongly to Britain's undertaking them if France did not. Instead he henceforth tended to advocate the aiming of the Allies' strokes against what he conceived to be weaker parts of the enemy's front—in Italy, Macedonia, and Palestine. His policy now was to "knock away Germany's props". Haig on the other hand believed that his campaign in Flanders would shake the German Army. Also he believed that for the safety of Britain and France the offensive on the Western Front must be kept up; and Pétain, though not agreeing with his tactics, constantly impressed on him the urgency of maintaining the British offensive so as to prevent the French Army's recovery from being imperilled by a German attack.

Haig's staff were right in their belief that the German—and, more still, the Austrian—people and Army were war weary. The British also were feeling the strain, though less acutely. In Germany, early in July, the popular leaders demanded a more democratic form of government, and the Kaiser had to give way. The Chancellor, Bethmann Hollweg, fell, but was succeeded by Dr Michaelis, a puppet of the military leaders, who managed to avoid the consequences of a resolution of the German Reichstag favouring peace without annexations. The Pope at this juncture urged a return to pre-war boundaries. But the German military leaders had no intention of ever freeing Belgium; the French insisted on their claim to Alsace-Lorraine, which Lloyd George now had to support; and President Wilson of the United States had the Allies behind him in proclaiming that they could not make peace with the present autocratic government of Germany. The attitude then adopted by the Allies towards the making of peace was thereafter consistently maintained.

The British Cabinet, however, feared that Haig would involve the British Army not in a mere step-by-step offensive but in a single-handed, unlimited attempt to break through the strongest defences of the strongest enemy. Consequently it was not until the third week in July that it agreed to the launching of the attack—hitherto it had permitted only the preparations. By then the preliminary bombardment, to last a fortnight, had already begun. The Cabinet's fear was not baseless; Haig's conception of "step-by-step" differed from Pétain's and Rawlinson's. His mass of artillery, after crushing the enemy defences, would (on Zero day) lay a dense creeping barrage behind whose curtain the infantry would advance and occupy the ground, the artillery still protecting them from counter-attack. The guns would then be advanced and, as soon as possible, the process would be repeated, preferably with fresh troops. But, as in the Somme battle, Haig believed that under these attacks the Germans' morale would become so strained that at some stage—possibly even at the outset—there would occur the chance of breaking through. To miss this would be to throw away (as Haig believed the Germans had done on 31st October 1914, when fighting against him in the First Battle of Ypres) an advantage that might never recur. At this time General Gough agreed with this view. Possibly for that reason, he with his 5th Army staff was now given the force which would make the central thrust; those troops now therefore became known as 5th Army.

After a fortnight's bombardment[1] which strained the Germans to the utmost, so that one division even deserted its front, the great stroke of July 31st was delivered by three armies—2nd British on the right, 5th British in the centre, and 1st French on the left—with 17 divisions (of which 2 were French) on a seventeen-mile front. On this battlefield, where deep dugouts were almost impossible (though the Australian tunnellers made some) the German trenches were studded with "pillboxes" of concrete so strong that only direct hits with several heavy shells would crack them. But their rectangular shapes were detected in air photographs, and on the main front one by one they were pounded.

The 2nd Army (including the 3rd Australian and the New Zealand Divisions—the only Dominion infantry used at this stage) undertook that day little more than a demonstration. But on the flats north of Ypres, after the tremendous bombardment, most of Gough's army and the French reached the second and, on the left, even the third German lines. Gough's southern flank, however, attacking the vital sickle-shaped

The advance on 31st July 1917.

---

[1] The British had a gun to every 6 yards, the French one to every 2¼ yards. *See Vol. IV, p. 701.*

ridge, could seize only the first line; and at 4 p.m. down came the rain.

For days it poured, turning the battlefield into a quagmire like the bottom of an upheaved ocean. Haig insisted that this was the wrong time to relax pressure. Unfortunately the higher staffs knew too little of what was happening on the battlefield. The step-by-step method, as practised at Ypres and Messines, was effective only in fine weather. Then, with an immense artillery functioning at its best; with airmen spotting the targets; with guns, men and supplies moving across country on dry tracks; with nearly all shells bursting on the surface as intended, scattering fragments up to half a mile,[2] and raising a dust cloud (which was more helpful than a smoke screen, and rolled ahead of the infantry, who worked in the haze on its rear fringe)—in such conditions the infantry was almost certain to capture its objectives, no matter what the enemy attempted. But with the ground a slough; with guns and ammunition constantly bogged; with air observation difficult and uncertain; with the shells failing to explode in the soft mud or their bursts muffled and barely visible; with no dust or smoke, and the unscreened infantrymen often unable even to detect the barrage they were ordered to follow, and in any case unable to keep up with it across the sea of brimming shell-craters—in these conditions, though parts of the infantry often struggled through to sections of the objective, they could not link up, or receive supplies. With disastrous regularity their efforts failed and their losses rose—as did the spirits of the Germans beholding these failures.

For Gough be it said that it was now he who generally opposed the continuance of these attacks, and Plumer, whose men were not thus suffering, that favoured them. Gough finally represented that he could not take the vital ridge without more support from Plumer's army.

---

[2] Both sides now used "sensitive" fuses.

On August 26th Haig decided to make this ridge the centre of his attacks, transfer that sector to Plumer, and after a pause, attack in fine weather with fresh troops. The fresh troops for the spearhead of the drive upon the main ridge were the I Anzac Corps. They would attack, if possible, on September 20th.

The I Anzac Corps—after the Somme, Somme winter, and Bullecourt—had been enjoying perhaps the finest rest ever given to British Empire troops in France. Strangely enough it was at this stage that the Australian soldiers *generally* began to speak of themselves as "Diggers", a name already fairly general among the New Zealanders, and well satisfying their own conception of their job. During these happy months they were thoroughly trained—partly on the old Somme battle-field—in the new system of attack. In this each company, battalion and brigade, after a swift advance to escape the German barrage (with which the enemy would at first try to crush the attack), shook itself out into consecutive waves and followed the creeping barrage of its own artillery. In order to allow the advancing infantry time to subdue any block-houses that still held out, the barrage advanced very slowly—sometimes 100 yards in 8 minutes, instead of in 2 as on the Somme, and with several long pauses, each of up to an hour or more. Each of the sixteen platoons in a battalion now had its rifle grenadiers and Lewis gun to support the riflemen and bombers in attacks on such block-houses. A number of such fights always occurred, the infantry at those points often being held up, and unable closely to follow the barrage. But the rest of the line would go ahead, and the delayed platoons would catch up after overcoming the obstacle— sometimes a costly business and often a blood-thirsty one.

Australian troops in that war were probably at the zenith of their training when, at the end of July, they were moved north to rear areas in Flanders. On September 16th, after a night march through Ypres and out along the much-shelled roads across the flats, the 1st and 2nd Divisions took over the section of battlefront on the main ridge at Glencorse Wood and a low spur north of it, at Westhoek. The ground, except for the water-logged craterfield in each depression, was then dust dry. The battle was now planned to proceed in a succession of limited offensives, to follow one another, like blows of a sledge hammer at a few days' interval, the pauses being necessary for pushing forward the guns and ammunition—and the roads and railways, light and heavy, to carry them—over the shell-shattered wilderness, and for relieving the tired infantry by fresh troops.

Birdwood and White—to whom at this stage General Harington left the devising of the plan for attacking the ridge—chose first to strike along the "sickle" blade, as far as their southern flank could be protected by the X Corps thrusting across the eastern protuberances of the "handle" —that is, about a mile deep. To make sure of success after so much failure, they decided on much denser concentration of force than would have been used on less vital fronts—about 1000 yards of front to a division. The preparatory work on roads, railways and signals, and the making and marking of tracks, was greater than the A.I.F. had ever before undertaken. On moonlight nights the bombing of camps and horselines by German aircraft caused considerable loss but in no way disturbed the plans.

At dawn on 20th September 1917, after five days' bombardment,[3] eleven divisions of the 2nd and 5th Armies struck with almost complete success on a front of eight miles. Rain, falling during the night march to the assembly tapes, caused much anxiety, but it ceased in early morning. The two Australian divisions (with the 9th Scottish,[4] of 5th Army, on their left) formed the

[3] The Australians were supported by a gun to every 5 yards. For the density of guns in various offensives see *Vol. IV, pp. 701, 744, text and notes*.
[4] Including the splendid South African Infantry Brigade.

THE BATTLEFIELD EAST OF YPRES ON 19th SEPTEMBER 1917

The British front is shown in black and the main German defence lines in white. The arrows (with the divisional numbers attached) indicate the attacks subsequently made by divisions under I and II Anzac. In each case a number of British or other divisions, farther north or south, also attacked, but to avoid confusion only the advances by I and II Anzac are shown.

centre of the attacking force. Never before had two Australian divisions attacked side by side, and the "Diggers" were consequently elated with a confidence and enthusiasm which British leaders did not, at that time, understand.

During the assembly an officer of the 2nd Division, missing his way, was overpowered by a German patrol and an operation order was found on him despite his efforts to destroy it. The German command was consequently able to bombard the sector five minutes before the start.[5] This caused some loss but in no other way affected the attack. The Australian infantry closed up towards the front, and in a single line—all waves together—followed the great barrage half a mile to the first objective; then, after an hour's pause, followed it again 500 yards to the second; and, finally, after a further two hours' pause (during which, in Neligan's 10th Battalion, London newspapers were distributed to the troops), 200 yards to the third. Famous landmarks of earlier fighting—Glencorse Wood, Nonne Bosschen swamp, Black Watch Corner, and part of Polygon Wood, the shattered stubble of a young plantation—were retaken.

In the clear, fine day, after digging in, the troops waited in their successive defence lines for the German counter-attack divisions, so effectively used at Arras. But most of the waiting men saw no sign of these. Where and when they did so, front-line leaders fired the excellent firework then given to British infantry for their "S.O.S. signal", calling for the fire of their artillery—a rifle-grenade bursting into a string of three lights suspended from a parachute. The dense barrages thus called down broke up any counter-attack troops that got through the bombardments earlier called for by airmen. Only at two

---

[5] The start was at 5.40 a.m. As Dominion troops usually did, the Australians had favoured a slightly earlier start and quicker rate of advance than that desired by the British.

or three points could the Germans even approach the
British battlefront.

This "Battle of the Menin Road"—the first favourable
trial, after Messines, of the step-by-step attack—cost the
Australian divisions some 5000 casualties (the total
British loss was four or five times as great). These were
due mainly to German heavy artillery fire after the assault
(much of the German field artillery was destroyed by
shellfire). The plan had worked almost perfectly, and the
Australians came out from battle elated. The loss of the
German troops was, apparently, about equal but the
moral shock to them was great—as is stated in the German
official narrative.

As planned, the divisions that had attacked were
quickly relieved, the 5th Australian Division taking over
the right and the 4th—now again transferred to I Anzac—
the left. The most vital part of the effort at this stage, as
before and after every stage of this battle, was the intense
work put in by pioneers, engineers, tunnellers and transport drivers in extending the plank roads and the railways. It was this alone that enabled the next blow to be
struck on September
26th. The weather re-
mained gloriously fine,
but early on September
25th the normal sum-
mer haze was thickened
by dust from continu-
ous German bombard-
ment of the southern
flank. Later came word
that the Germans had
counter-attacked and
driven back the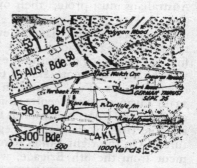
northern flank of X Corps in the Reutelbeek Valley, just
below the position from which the right of the Australian
line was to begin its further advance along the sickle ridge

at dawn next morning. This threatened the utmost danger to the attack.

Without hesitation Brig.-General "Pompey" Elliott, whose brigade, allotted for the advance at this point, was then in the line and in support, decided to help the British clear the flank. His forward battalion (58th) was already doing so. By a day's fighting under intense bombardment the Australian starting line was made secure, but the X Corps was unable to clear the Germans from the valley beside Elliott's right flank.

Elliott now was of opinion that the next day's attack was impossible. But, on being informed that many other divisions were involved and therefore the whole British assault must go forward, he assigned to his most trusted battalion commander, Norman Marshall of the 60th, always a hero for Australians,[6] the additional task of assembling his attacking force. As Elliott's own brigade had lost heavily, the 29th and 31st Battalions of the 8th Brigade (Tivey) were lent to seize the second and third objectives, their commanders being warned that the X Corps might not be able to attack, in which case the Australians must protect their own right flank.

At 5.50 a.m. on September 26th there descended the most perfect barrage that had ever protected Australian troops. Rolling ahead of them "like a Gippsland bush-fire" it raised a fog of dust in the edge of which the troops were by now sufficiently skilled to advance, fighting down enemy groups. Two Australian divisions (4th and 5th) again advanced as the centre, this time, of seven divisions on a six-mile front. Northwards from the Australian right all objectives, with slight exception, were quickly captured.[7] On the right Elliott's troops and their reinforcement from the 8th Brigade, with their southern flank

---

[6] He had started in 1914 as a private. He died as brigadier of the 2nd A.I.F. For an account of him see *Vol. IV, pp. 801-2.*

[7] As to Capt. H. B. Wanliss, a notable young leader of the A.I.F., who was killed here, see *Vol. IV, p. 828n.*

entirely open, managed, under Marshall's leadership, to fight their way not only to their own but to part of the X Corps' final objective, which was eventually captured. Farther north the rest of Polygon Wood, including the Butte (the mound of an old shooting range) at its eastern end, was seized by the 14th Brigade. On the low ground to the north the 4th Australian Division, in contact with the 3rd British at the edge of Zonnebeke, brought the line to the foot of the main ridge where the sickle swept northwards through Broodseinde towards Passchendaele. Again the German counter-attack divisions on attempting their task were crushed by bombardment and machine-gun fire.

This second clean, strong blow—in which the casualties of each side were again probably about equal[8]—advanced the front, as Haig intended, to a position from which to strike at the main (or Broodseinde) ridge. The I Anzac Corps was now sideslipped northwards into position to carry out the main attack on that ridge; and, to its extreme satisfaction, at this stage the II Anzac Corps was put in beside it. Owing to the risk of a break in the fine weather, road and railway construction were hurried forward by intense effort so that the attack might be launched on October 4th. This time twelve divisions would attack on an eight-mile front, four Anzac divisions forming the centre, the 1st, 2nd and 3rd Australian Divisions facing Broodseinde Ridge, and the New Zealand Division on their left facing Abraham Heights, which joined the main ridge at Broodseinde. Never before or since did four Anzac divisions attack side by side, and the already high spirit of these troops was greatly enhanced by this concentration.

On October 3rd rain fell, and the showery night resembled that of September 20th. The attack was to be at dawn—6 a.m. Forty minutes before that time, on lookers a mile in rear suddenly saw and heard the signs

---

[8] The two Australian divisions lost 5500.

that at such a moment they most dreaded. German flares, white and yellow, hazy in the drizzle, rose in sheaves on the Australian front, and presently the "crump crump" of a heavy German barrage in that direction could be heard. It seemed certain that the assembling troops had been detected and a barrage laid on them. And in fact at 5.30 a heavy trench-mortar barrage came down fairly on the troops of the 1st and 2nd Divisions lying in shell-holes along the white tapes marking the start-line. About one man in seven was hit, but there was nothing to do but wait. At 6 a.m., the noise of German shells was suddenly drowned in the roar of the British barrage. Falling in wet ground it raised no dust cloud—only smoke and steam. The I Anzac troops scrambled to their feet and were hurrying to catch up with it when, thirty yards ahead of them, they saw another line of troops, also rising from shellholes, and then waiting, as if disconcerted.

It was a German counter-attack timed for the same hour as the Australian attack. To gain elbow-room for the defence of Broodseinde Ridge the 212th German Regiment was being thrown through the garrison of the 4th Guard Division to attempt the recapture of some of the ground lost on September 26th, from Zonnebeke to near Polygon Wood.[9]

The Lewis gunners in the advancing Australian line opened fire; the Germans broke; the Australian lines rolled on over the remnant and up the slope. The rain stopped, the ground became drier. Below the top of the ridge there occurred the normal pause of about an hour in the advance. During this interval there was sharp fighting around pillboxes in which the staffs of the Prussian Guard regiments were awaiting news of the 212th Regiment's attack. Meanwhile the great British barrage wandered on deep into the German back area.

---

[9] The German barrage was the preparation for this attack. It is tru that the Germans saw some of the assembling Australians and apparentl sent the call for barrage; but the barrage for the attack was then due.

At the end of the pause the barrage came back, and the troops followed it over the ridge—indeed some Australians, and Gordon Highlanders of the X Corps, had already gone thither through their own barrage during the pause. Some German headquarters and their staffs fought hard, but the ridge was won. For the first time since May 1915 troops of the British side looked out on the green, tree-fringed Flemish lowlands beyond—and on the solitary Keiberg, an eastward extension of the ridge ahead of the Australian left. The 3rd Division, which had farthest to go, and which proved at least as skilled as the older ones beside it, fought cleverly on, astride the cutting of the Ypres-Roulers railway, to its objective. On the left the New Zealand Division, whose almost perfect alignment contrasted with the seemingly (but not actually) unorganised Australian advance, seized Abraham Heights, which was to be the starting position for an advance on Passchendaele in the next hammerblow. Along the British front to north and south practically the whole objective had been gained.

This day's success[10] was a very great one—indeed the most complete yet won by the British Army in France in that war. The two hammerblows of Menin Road and Polygon Wood (September 20th and 26th) had already shown the German command that its system of relying on counter-attack by divisions held close in rear was completely ineffectual against Haig's step-by-step tactics. The British never pushed beyond the range of their guns, and, when these divisions tried to approach, their advance was shattered by the barrage, through which they with difficulty reached even the retrenched front. Accordingly, on the advice of the local commanders and against his better judgment, Ludendorff had abandoned defence in depth and decided to bring up the counter-attack divisions to

---

[10] It cost the three Australian divisions 6500 casualties and the New Zealand Division 1700. The Germans this day lost 5000 prisoners, but, as usual, only a few advanced guns.

the forward area before each fight, packing them close behind the front-line troops, who themselves would be crowded closer to the front. By this means it was hoped to break up the British attack at an early stage. This change had been carried out just before the attack on Broodseinde. But that vigorous blow smashed the crowded troops in the front area, and a German attacking force as well, at one blow; and the counter-attack divisions were met, as before, by terrific barrages.

So evident was the day's success that some corps commanders urged General Plumer that the time had arrived to follow it up. Birdwood did not agree and the project was therefore dropped. Early in the afternoon rain began to fall and an effort made by Gough's army to probe farther failed. But—though after the failures of August Lloyd George and his ministers were opposed to Haig's strategy and sceptical as to his victories, and some were dreaming of offensives in the Middle East—there is no question that this third and greatest stroke within a fortnight had seriously shaken the German troops and command in Flanders. The German official account speaks of it as "the black day of October 4th". No army could go on suffering such blows without catastrophe.[11] According to Crown Prince Rupprecht reserves were short and the troops deteriorating. Ludendorff hurriedly reversed the new defence plan and reverted to a system of greater depth than ever before, with a "forward zone" lightly held, leaving all heavy attacks to be met at a "main line of resistance", perhaps 800 yards behind the front line.

Meanwhile Haig prepared to deliver the next blow. For a week he had thought that the chance of some breakthrough was approaching. Both Gough and Plumer thought that Haig exaggerated the enemy's confusion, considerable though it was; in this they were right, for

---

[11] For the very impressive situation at noon this day see *Vol. IV*, *pp. 875-7.*

fresh German troops were put in opposite the Anzacs on
October 5th. Nevertheless, despite the continuous rain,
which (as previously explained) changed all the vital conditions for success in "step-by-step" tactics, Haig decided
to attempt to break the German line.

Accordingly, over wet ground, an effort was made on
October 9th, on a front of 13,500 yards, to approach
Passchendaele—then a considerable village, with many
buildings and part of its red-brick church standing, visible
for miles around, on the next section of the main ridge.
From that day's objective an attempt would be made
a day or two later to thrust beyond Passchendaele. The
main objective was now opposite the II Anzac Corps,
which on October 9th employed two British divisions
one of which, the 66th, had only lately come to France.
On the lowlands to the north the French and 5th Army,
despite the rain, had considerable success; but on the
vital ridge—though progress was reported for a time—
none of the ground gained could be held. To protect the
southern flank the 2nd Australian Division (of I Anzac)
drove forward to the Keiberg but, being unsupported,
was driven back just as the 66th Division, long after the
proper hour, in conditions of mud and muddle that have
yet to be fully recorded,[12] made its brave, futile advance.

The strain on the infantry, pioneers, engineers, signallers, railway companies, supply and ammunition services, artillery, and stretcher-bearers was intense. However, on the strength of reports of October 9th, the higher
commanders believed that enough ground was gained to
justify the next attempt—to seize and pass Passchendaele—
on October 12th. Haig was determined to strike once more,
believing that the Germans had not recovered from the
shock of Broodseinde and that his army was now almost

---

[12] See Vol. IV, pp. 886 and 887. The 2nd Aust. Divn also seized part of
"Daisy" and "Dairy" Woods and the 10th Bn raided, with great loss, Celtic
Copse.

through the pillbox defences. The preparation was, therefore, shorter and the proposed advance deeper than before.

The attack was launched at dawn, the advance on Passchendaele itself being made by II Anzac with the 3rd Australian and the New Zealand Divisions, the 4th Australian of I Anzac supporting their right, and five British divisions attacking on their left. But heavy rainstorms had continued, and even in the few bright hours that morning the barrage was imperceptible. The New Zealanders were stopped by Germans firing from pillboxes with impunity; most of the 3rd Australian Division was bogged in the dreadful mud of the Ravebeek valley, below Passchendaele, Major L. F. Giblin (statistician, economist, and a most trusted fighting leader) forming with others in this chaos an organised advanced group. On the right, after a number of pillboxes had been captured largely through the devotion and skill of Captain C. S. Jeffries, a fragment of the 3rd Division reached the edge of Passchendaele,[18] and the 4th Division the Keiberg; but both had ultimately to fall back from the ground gained. The battle cost the 3rd and New Zealand Divisions 3000 casualties each, and the 4th Division 1000.

The fighting in the mud from October 9th onwards had, like that of August, resulted in no valuable gain; it caused German spirits to rise after the recent dangerous strain, and those of the attackers to sink. Haig now realised that he could not break through that year; but, partly to keep the Germans from attacking the French, partly to gain a better winter position, and partly to divert attention from another British stroke about to be made elsewhere, he brought in on October 18th another first-rate army corps, the Canadian, and set it to do in three stages what II Anzac had attempted to do in one. The Canadian Corps had lately been carrying out

---

[18] There were found there two or three survivors of the 66th Division's attack. Jeffries, who was killed, was awarded the Victoria Cross.

important diversion attacks at Lens;[14] and in five operations between October 26th and November 10th that splendid corps achieved its task of capturing the Passchendaele heights. I Anzac gave some support to the southern flank of the Canadians in the earlier of these operations. In this stage the German mustard-gas shelling was most severe; but by November 14th the last of the Australian divisions was withdrawn from the Ypres battlefield.

Meanwhile a serious reverse had occurred in Italy. The collapse of Russia had enabled Ludendorff, in spite of the heavy strain at Ypres, to send nine divisions to help the Austrians, and on October 24th in a sudden blow 180,000 Italians and 1500 guns were captured at Caporetto. Fortunately a limited French attack on the Aisne on October 22nd, and on November 20th a British stroke—Haig's first real use of surprise—with 324 tanks near Cambrai, largely offset this defeat. In the conditions of Ypres, tanks—though a few were employed—were almost completely useless. At Cambrai came their opportunity; but it was a brilliant flash in the pan. The cavalry—except the Canadian—missed the chance, if any existed, to follow up, and a week later the Germans, also by surprise, retook most of the ground. The 2nd Australian fighter squadron, first to reach France, made a fine name in this struggle under its splendid leader, Major Oswald Watt, and Australian siege artillery also took part. Despite its limited success, the Battle of Cambrai furnished a most useful lesson and a hard counter-blow for Caporetto.

But the great battle of 1917 had been Third Ypres. It had comprised eleven great attacks, for five of which—from the third to the seventh inclusive—the I or II Anzac Corps, or both, formed the spearhead, as did the Canadians for the final four. The first three attacks with the Anzac spearhead were the only ones delivered in

---

[14] The 3rd Australian Tunnelling Company had been constructing elaborate underground defences in the chalk there, and had some stiff underground fighting.

thoroughly suitable conditions, and German histories show that they placed an extreme strain on the German Army. In good conditions the Germans had no answer to the step-by-step method. Its defect was that it churned up the battlefield over which the attack must advance. In fine weather this mattered little; but by persisting when the weather was bad Haig gave advantage to the Germans, wore down his army with unnecessary hardship and casualties, and by mid-August finally lost the support of his own Prime Minister, Mr Lloyd George, who at first was not unattracted by the step-by-step method ("Pétain tactics", as some called it), but who now returned to his policy of "knocking away Germany's props".

The Third Ypres (or Passchendaele) offensive was far better planned and conducted than the First Battle of the Somme. Nearly every attack was made on a wide front; the British loss—400,000—was considerably less than on the Somme. The German loss perhaps equalled the British. But eight offensives in the mud made the name of this battle one to shudder at; and, as Lloyd George felt that his government was not strong enough to prevent Haig's committing his army to such battles in the next year, he decided to stop him by the characteristically indirect method of keeping him short of the necessary men.

For the two Anzac corps the three battles of Menin Road, Polygon Wood and Broodseinde were the cleanest and most decisive victories they had yet fought, even more so than Messines. The later fighting in the wet weather doubled the casualties, which mounted to 38,000 in the five Australian divisions in eight weeks, and left, for Australia, an insoluble problem of reinforcement.

Yet the verdict of the outstanding German authority on this episode, General von Kuhl, is: "English stubbornness bridged over the crisis in France. . . . The help which England brought was compensated by the result. The Flanders Battle," he adds, "wore down the German strength to a degree at which the damage could no longer be repaired."

CHAPTER XXII

A GREAT YEAR IN PALESTINE, 1917

ONE of Germany's props which Mr Lloyd George had been hoping to knock away was Turkey; for the campaign into Palestine had progressed greatly since the beginning of 1917.

It will be remembered that in January 1917 General Murray's advanced cavalry force (then known as the "Desert Column"), of which the Anzac horse and camel troops formed by far the greater part, had passed from Sinai on to the somewhat better country fringing Palestine. Murray, always favouring attack, had next planned to seize the strong Turkish position at Gaza, just across the Palestine border. The town lay two miles from the sea; and the Turkish line defending southern Palestine ran thence inland to Beersheba, some twenty-eight miles to the south-east.

Murray, though the War Office had left him only three infantry divisions (52nd, 53rd and 54th Territorial Divisions), and another (74th) was now forming from dismounted yeomanry, had troops enough for the task, and the railway and twelve-inch water-pipe line from Egypt were ready. As for the cavalry, the 4th Light Horse Brigade, formerly disbanded, had now been re-formed, and by redistributing his brigades Murray had two mounted divisions each of four brigades—Anzac Mounted Division (1st and 2nd Australian, one New Zealand, and 22nd Yeomanry Brigades) under Maj.-General Chauvel; and the Imperial Mounted Division (3rd and 4th Australian and 5th and 6th Yeomanry Brigades) under a sound British cavalry officer, Maj.-General H. W. Hodgson; as well as the Camel Brigade (two-thirds Anzac). Unfortunately for the contentment of the troops practically all positions on the staff and command of these last-formed forces were allotted by Murray to British officers, a condition that was partly remedied only after strong protest and long delay.[1] In the air Murray's pilots still had inferior machines, but the German bombing, though causing loss, did not affect the course of the campaign. Incidentally, it was noticeable that here, even more than on the Western Front, the relations between the opposing airmen in spite of their tense fighting were not merely chivalrous but cordial.[2]

The British government having approved the attempt, Murray decided to attack Gaza by surprise at dawn on March 26th. In front of the town and five miles from it ran the deep, wide, rough channel of the then easily fordable Wadi Ghuzze. Immediately east of the town from north to south ran the El Sire Ridge, covered with cactus hedges. West of the town were the sandhills bordering the sea.

In the small hours of the morning of March 26th the Anzac Mounted Division, led by General Ryrie's 2nd Light Horse Brigade, marched to the Wadi Ghuzze, crossed it, and in the morning fog, magnificently guided by their officers[3] so as to give Gaza a wide berth, swept past village after village six miles to the east of it, and then turning west, and galloping down any resisting Turks, made towards the sea on a line two miles beyond the town. The New Zealanders and Yeomanry followed, cutting off Gaza on the east, and facing inwards towards it. The Imperial Mounted Division, Camel Brigade, and a New Zealand light car patrol, made a wider circle and

[1] See Vol. VII, pp. 255-7.
[2] See the German Captain Felmy's letter, now in the Australian War Memorial (Vol. VIII, pp. 65n and 72-3).
[3] In particular by Capts S. A. Tooth and H. O. C. Maddrell, both former pastoralists.

faced outwards to prevent enemy reinforcements from approaching. With Gaza thus cut off the 53rd Infantry Division supported by the 54th was to attack it from south and south-west.

The 53rd Division was far more hampered by the fog than were the Light Horse. It was nearly noon before it attacked, which it did with great steadiness. Meanwhile, to help it and save time, the two mounted divisions were placed under Chauvel who, at 1 p.m., was ordered to make a dismounted attack on Gaza from flank and rear.

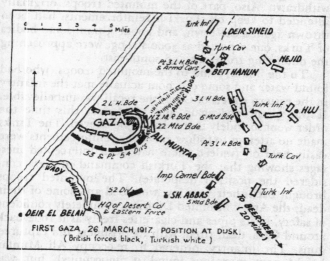

FIRST GAZA, 26 MARCH, 1917. POSITION AT DUSK.
(British forces black, Turkish white)

Men knew they were racing against time. At first progress was slow in both operations, but, as sunset drew near, the main heights at Ali Muntar, south-east of the town, were captured by the infantry, and those north of them by New Zealanders and Yeomanry, while the 2nd Light Horse Brigade, led by Major A. G. Bolingbroke and other daring spirits, pressed to the northern edge of Gaza. Men

thought that, as at Magdhaba and Rafa, the day was won.
A Turkish general and many men had been captured
behind the town; the defence seemed to be crumbling.

But at this stage, as before, there came to the apparently victorious troops the order to withdraw. This
time it came from General Dobell. The main difficulty
was the one that always hampered mounted operations in
this dry country—Dobell and Chetwode had decided that,
unless Gaza was taken by sunset, the mounted troops—
who might be without water for their horses—must be
withdrawn. Also, part of the mounted troops, originally
intended to keep off Turkish reinforcements, had been
thrown against the town, and about 5 p.m. some bodies
of Turks, one reported as 3000 strong, were approaching
the outer ring from east and south-east.

To the infantry and to the mounted troops (who had
found water and some of whom actually met the infantry
in the eastern streets of Gaza) the recall was unbelievable.
It was questioned again and again, but this time the
order went so widely that it had to be obeyed. The Turks
made no attempt to follow and their reinforcements were
easily held off (indeed there had been intercepted messages showing that the Turkish command in Gaza considered the position desperate). The mounted troops
brought back their very few wounded and some of their
dead; the Anzac Mounted Division, completely confident
of safety, lit its pipes and cigarettes freely as it rode back
around Gaza, dead tired, with its prisoners and captured
guns. The infantry, ordered to re-occupy Ali Muntar
height next morning, found it unoccupied, but was
driven off again before the position could be thoroughly
secured. For the whole battle the casualties of the
attacking side—mainly in the infantry—were about 4000.
The Turks lost 2500.

Murray now erred greatly in judgment by reporting
this battle to the War Office as "a most successful operation . . . it has filled our troops with enthusiasm".

Undoubtedly he and Dobell believed that a renewed attack—this time to be made with more preparation, and helped by 6 tanks and 2000 rounds of gas shell (never before used against the Turks)—would secure Gaza. On his advice, and in view of the good progress being made in the Mesopotamian campaign, the British government agreed. The attempt was made on April 19th—this time a straight-out frontal attack by the infantry, with the Camels and Imperial Mounted Division attacking dismounted further east, and the Anzac Mounted Division, still farther to the south-east, keeping away any threat to the inland flank.

The Turks were ready and stronger than before. The attack though continued all day completely failed. The Turks hardly noticed the gas shell—a German officer thought the fumes were those of high explosive. The British infantry barely reached the ridge south-east of Gaza. A handful of them with a larger party of Australians of the Camel Corps under Captain A. E. G. Campbell, bravely led by a tank, seized one Turkish redoubt. Other Australian camel troops, and Light Horse of the Imperial Mounted Division (which lost heavily), seized another. Far to the east a Turkish cavalry force was driven off by the Anzac Mounted Division. The whole attack cost some 6000 casualties, mainly in the infantry. The Turks were confirmed in their belief that they could hold southern Palestine, and accordingly strengthened their line there.

This second failure led to Murray's recall. Chetwode replaced Dobell in command of Eastern Force; command of the Desert Column (i.e. the mounted forces) which soon afterwards became the "Desert Mounted Corps", was given to Chauvel, who was raised to lieutenant-general; and in June General Allenby, sent from the Western Front after Arras, took command from Murray. The New Zealand leader, Maj.-General Chaytor, took over the Anzac Mounted Division.

Before Allenby's arrival Chetwode had worked out a plan for the capture of southern Palestine by striking with cavalry and infantry at the inland end of the Turkish line, at Beersheba, while keeping up the pretence of an intention to strike at Gaza. The plan would require seven divisions of infantry and three of mounted troops, and the main difficulty would lie in providing water for

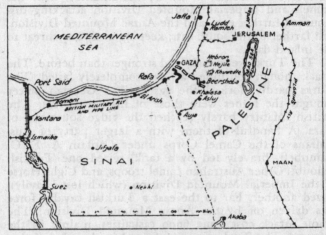

THE BRITISH AND TURKISH FRONTS BEFORE THE THIRD BATTLE OF GAZA, 31st OCTOBER 1917
(British line black, Turkish white.)

the striking force of *infantry* near Beersheba; the mounted troops would have to rely mainly on what water they could find in and beyond that town.

It happened that during these months it was decided to destroy the unfinished railway which the Turks had earlier built through Beersheba into the edge of the Sinai Desert at Auja. On the night of May 23rd two columns, one of Light Horse, the other of the Camel Brigade, with their flank protected by the Anzac and Imperial Mounted Divisions, made the long march and next day their engineers blew up seven large bridges and thirteen miles of line. On the way to Asluj lay Khalasa, site of the ancient city of Eleusa, of 60,000 people. Asluj also once held many inhabitants, and the engineers were therefore told to look for the water supply which must have existed at both places. The old cisterns were found, choked with earth and concrete, but the discovery proved valuable.

The arrival of Allenby was the turning point of the campaign. His task was easier than Murray's—he had not to concern himself with Salonica and Egypt. To the delight of the fighting troops he brusquely swept his headquarters staff from the all too comfortable Savoy Hotel in Cairo, and himself took command of the Palestine operations, with headquarters near Rafa. "Eastern Force" was abolished, Chetwode becoming commander of the XX Army Corps. Allenby constantly visited the troops in the field, who leapt to his vigorous change of touch. He adopted Chetwode's plan of attack. Of the troops required, the three mounted divisions were provided mainly by reconstructing the divisions with three brigades each instead of four. The Anzac Mounted Division (1st and 2nd Light Horse and the New Zealand Brigades), Australian Mounted Division (3rd and 4th Light Horse and 5th Yeomanry Brigades), and Yeomanry Division (6th, 8th and 22nd Yeomanry Brigades) were thus formed. The infantry divisions were increased to seven and, as so often happened, the government now poured in the long requested guns, ammunition, and aeroplanes in quantities unheard of before the recent failure. The railway from Egypt was largely duplicated, and, with the pipe-line, was extended as far towards Beersheba as could be done without arousing suspicion that this would be the direction of the new blow.

It was vital to strike before the winter rains. During

the last week in October the mounted brigades, the in
fantry of Chetwode's XX Corps, and great columns of
supplies, moved by night from the coast to the inland
flank. The old cisterns at Khalasa and Asluj were cleared—
Allenby visited the troops working there. By October
30th the Anzac and the Australian Mounted Divisions
were wholly assembled in this area for the long march
to attack Beersheba from east and south, and Chetwode's
XX Corps was within striking distance on the west—the
ground for its preliminary advance having been captured
by the Light Horse a few days earlier. For a week German
airmen had been kept away by Allenby's increased air
force, now partly provided with modern machines,[4] but
the Turks could not help detecting the eastward move
ment. They thought, however, that it merely foreshadowed
a raid by "one infantry and one cavalry division; the
main attack," said the Turkish command, "must be
expected on the Gaza front." The German commander
(Kress) had been led to this view partly through the capture of some faked notes in a pocket-book dropped by a
British staff officer who had purposely got himself chased
across no-man's-land by a Turkish cavalry patrol.[5]

At this time the Germans and Turks were at logger-
heads. It is true that the Germans, with their own dreams
of expansion to Baghdad, and seeing that Russia was no
longer dangerous, had agreed to help recapture Baghdad
which the British and Indian expeditionary force in Meso
potamia under General Maude had taken on March 11th
The German government lent General von Falkenhayn—
a most capable strategist—for the purpose; and Enver
Pasha, Turkish Minister for War and co-dictator, had
promised a special Turkish Yilderim (or Lightning)
Force to help carry out the plan. The Germans had also

---

[4] Bristol fighters. No. 1 Australian Squadron was still flying R.E.8's and
improved Martinsydes.

[5] See *British Official History, Egypt and Palestine*, by Captain Cyril
Falls, *Vol. II, pp. 31 and 43.*

widely advertised their intention of sending to Turkey's help an "Asia Corps".

But both Djemal Pasha, Governor of Syria and original defender of Palestine, and his former staff officer, the able Kress von Kressenstein, now commanding the 8th Army in southern Palestine, warned Enver that the British would shortly make a powerful attack on Palestine. Falkenhayn agreed with this view and desired to attack the British there from the inland flank. Djemal was bitterly opposed to Falkenhayn's coming to Palestine, but eventually it was so ruled. The 7th Army at Aleppo, waiting to move on Baghdad, was switched to help the 8th in southern Palestine. But only two divisions had arrived there by October 30th.

That night Allenby's cavalry and infantry, marching through the dark, made for Beersheba. At dawn the guns of Chetwode's corps bombarded the Turkish line west of the town; and having stormed the outer defences the 53rd, 60th and 74th British Divisions shortly after noon seized their objective there. Meanwhile the brigades of the Anzac Mounted Division had swept around the southeast and east of the town. Ryrie's 2nd Light Horse Brigade had seized the Hebron road far north of it. It had been hoped that Chetwode's attack would draw all the Turks to the western defences, but the eastern side, especially the hill of Tel el Saba, was strongly held. In spite of the bold support of their British batteries the 2000 men of the Anzac Mounted Division, attacking dismounted, could progress here only slowly. It was 3 p.m. before New Zealanders and Australians were close enough to rush this hill. Yet Beersheba had to be taken before nightfall—not only the probable approach of Turkish reinforcements but the watering of the horses made this essential.

Chauvel had the Australian Mounted Division in reserve. One brigade he had sent to help forward the

26—os

attack on Tel el Saba. Now he decided that the only way
to complete the task in time was to send one of the two
nearest brigades straight for the south of the town where
the remaining Turkish defences, he knew, were not protected by barbed wire as were those farther west. He gave
the task to the nearer brigade, the 4th Light Horse, under
Brig.-General Grant. The brigades were in scattered
formation—a disposition forced on them by German
bombing planes; and it was 4.30 before the two leading
regiments, 4th and 12th, with the 11th following, were
assembled behind rising ground four miles south-east of
Beersheba.

The light horsemen knew well that the fate of the
battle—and probably of the campaign—depended on this
charge; they also realised that, for the first time, Australian cavalry were to charge—for this time the Light
Horse were to act purely as cavalry though with only their
bayonets as shock weapons. They moved off at the trot,
deploying to five yards' interval and almost at once
quickening to a gallop. As they came over the top of the
ridge and looked down the long, gentle open slope to
Beersheba—somewhere in front of whose buildings the
Turkish trenches and their garrison lay—the Turkish
gunners saw them and opened with shrapnel.

But Australians had never ridden any race like this,
and the pace was too fast for the gunners. After two miles
Turkish machine-guns opened hotly from the flank, but
the watchful British batteries at once detected and
silenced them. Next came rifle fire from the Turkish
trenches, dangerous at first, but wild and high as the
Light Horse, who could now see the trenches, approached.

Next the foremost troops were over the front trench
and jumping the main one, dismounting, and turning
upon the Turks from rear with rifle and bayonet. The
bewildered garrison quickly surrendered. Other light
horsemen galloped ahead to the rear trenches, where

parties of fifty Turks surrendered to single men.[6] Other squadrons galloped straight into Beersheba.

The day was won. The 4th and 12th Light Horse had only 31 killed and 36 wounded; over 700 Turks were captured. But, above all, the eastern flank of the whole Turkish line was turned. It was found, later, that the Turks had just decided to make an orderly withdrawal after blowing up the wells upon which everything depended. The charge forestalled them; nearly all the wells were intact and a storm had filled the pools.

In the ensuing days the mounted troops and Chetwode's infantry followed up this advantage, thrusting into the steep hills of southern Palestine. On the flank of the mounted troops there had been acting, for the first time, a body of the Arab army. In July Lieut.-Colonel T. E. Lawrence—till then known to Australians in Egypt only as a young Oxford scholar working on the intelligence staff in Cairo—had led the Arabs in the capture of the port of Akaba;[7] and now a detachment under Lieut.-Colonel S. F. Newcombe, a British engineer previously with the Australians in Gallipoli and France, pressed ahead on the extreme right towards Hebron.

This, with the activity of Ryrie's brigade, apparently caused the Turks to think that Allenby would thrust northwards through Hebron, and they accordingly began to withdraw reserves from Gaza. Just then, on the night of November 1st, the XXI British Corps struck between Gaza and the sea and outflanked the town. The Turks still imagined the danger to lie on their inland flank and the attempt of the Desert Mounted Corps to strike for water at Nejile, in the hills twenty miles north of Beersheba, was stopped at Tel el Khuweilfe, a prominent

---

[6] Maj. C. M. Fetherstonhaugh of Coonamble had his horse wounded thirty yards from a Turkish trench. With his first revolver shot he put it out of pain, and then emptied the magazine into the Turks.

[7] At the end of the Ghor, the great desert valley continuing the Jordan-Dead Sea gorge southwards to this upper arm of the Red Sea.

height about half-way to Nejile. For a week this area was
the scene of tense fighting, the 53rd Division and Camel
Brigade reinforcing and relieving part of the Light Horse,
and, at times, being hard pressed to hold on. In the end,
on November 8th, as a climax to the stubbornness and
dash of the camel troops and 2nd Light-Horse Machine-
gun Squadron, the hill was seized by the 53rd Division.
Meanwhile on November 6th Chetwode's XX Corps had
captured a great part of the Turkish line between Beersheba and Gaza; and when, next day, the XXI Corps
attacked on both sides of Gaza, the resistance was feeble.
Gaza fell.

Allenby's intention was that Chetwode should now
create a breach, and the Desert Mounted Corps (which
had reassembled most of its two colonial divisions) should
strike through north-westwards to cut off the Turks
retreating from Gaza. Accordingly early on November
7th the 60th (London) Division—afterwards constant
comrades of the Light Horse—captured the main Turkish
position at Tel el Sheria, and the Anzac Mounted Division moved through a gap that opened to the east of this.
It galloped down the Turks at Ameidat railway station
four miles ahead, but was stopped by Turkish troops
beyond. A little farther south the Australian Mounted
Division, which also was to have passed through, was set
by General Chauvel to ride down a Turkish force which
had stopped the advance of the 60th (London) Division.
But when the 4th Brigade tried to charge it was met by
such fire that it was ordered to dismount. One troop
under Lieutenant A. R. Brierty, missing the signal, rode
right on. Some Turks held up their hands and the party
galloped over the trench and dismounted to attack. The
Turks however rallied and, despite a brave effort of
another troop, annihilated them.

Next day the advance continued. By 9 a.m. the
mounted troops could see the Turks, driven from Gaza,

retreating in long columns past their front; but the Turkish flank guards fought too stubbornly for the horsemen to get through, although the Warwickshire Yeomanry at great cost charged and shattered one column. All this while there was the utmost difficulty in watering horses and even men; horses sometimes went more than two days without a drink. On the 9th the mounted troops at last broke through to the coast at Esdud (the ancient Ashdod) to meet other cavalry advancing ahead of the victorious XXI Corps. A number of Turks, some guns, and much transport were captured—men and animals in dreadful condition. They were largely the weaklings straggling behind the Turkish army. The main forces had gone clear.

Allenby's drive against the retreating Turks was now transferred from his right flank to his left, the Yeomanry Mounted Division being brought round to help the Anzac Mounted Division and the infantry to drive up the Philistine plain, while the Australian Mounted Division remained in the Judaean hills to guard the right and to demonstrate against the Turks on the inland flank. The Turks, believing the threat still to be against this flank, strongly attacked and forced back the Australian Mounted Division on November 12th near Summeil. But Allenby's real thrust drove rapidly up the rolling hills and plain; through the modern Jewish settlements, at Wadi Hanein, Richon le Zion and elsewhere, with their vineyards and orchards; and so to Ramleh, Ludd and Jaffa. The Jewish settlers gave them an ecstatic welcome and many deep friendships were made with these, the first people of their own civilisation whom most of the troops had met since leaving home.

But water troubles still hampered the mounted troops. And though the seven infantry divisions for a time pooled nearly all their transport in order that two of them could keep up their speed; and the Yeomanry with their swords several times successfully charged the Turkish infantry—twice at high cost to themselves;[8] and forty light horsemen under Lieutenant W. H. James galloped down and captured a column of 300 Turks near Ludd—despite these and similar measures, the captured enemy were still only the belated elements or rearguard of the escaping Turks.

These successes caused the two retiring Turkish armies, 7th and 8th, to separate, the 7th having fallen back north-eastwards to cover Jerusalem, which lay in the terraced, rocky hills twenty-five miles east of Allenby's front, the 8th holding the line of the Nahr Auja, a stream running into the sea a few miles north of Jaffa. The railway to Jerusalem was only a branch of the main narrow-gauge line running near the coast, and the Turks had now lost the junction. The British government strongly desired the capture of Jerusalem. Its moral effect would be world-wide; but Allenby was warned that, to meet the future situation in France, his force might have to be reduced by the middle of 1918. In spite of this prospect he decided to strike—this time, from his right flank north-eastwards to cut off the Turks defending Jerusalem.

Accordingly, by directing the infantry on his left to force the passage of the Nahr Auja, Allenby led the Turks to believe that the coastal thrust was being continued, while with his right he advanced into the tangle of Judaean hills. At this stage the fighting was almost entirely for the infantry. The mounted troops scouted or covered the flanks and ran into several sharp fights, the heaviest perhaps being the vain attempt of a battalion of Turkish storm troops to break through the front of the 3rd Light Horse Brigade and some British infantry

---

[8] These tactics cost many casualties at Huj and El Mughar. The mounted dash at Tel Jezar was effective and less costly. (Two leading members of the Rothschild family were killed in these charges. *See Vol. VII, p. 489.*)

at El Burj. Near the coast the Turks drove Allenby's posts back again across the Nahr Auja, and Australian and New Zealand troops were involved in sharp fighting.

Activity in that area was what Allenby wanted in order to distract the Turks from his real purpose, of seizing Jerusalem; and though the weather now broke, and motor transport became almost impossible, and in the bitter cold and mud the troops had to rely on the amazing endurance of the Egyptian camel drivers and on donkey transport, his drive was maintained. Most of the Anzac Mounted Division was withdrawn to enjoy a hard-earned rest at the Jewish settlements in the south. The British infantry despite great hardship in the bitter conditions had, early in December, fought its way to a line threatening Jerusalem from west and south-west. On the 8th in pouring rain it drove the Turks from vital parts of this line (the 10th Light Horse Regiment and Worcestershire Yeomanry, attached to the infantry, took part). The Turks hurriedly left Jerusalem, and on December 9th General Shea of the 60th (London) Division was invited by the mayor to enter the Holy City. He was welcomed hysterically by Jews and Christians, coldly by the Arabs. Meanwhile the three British infantry divisions moved round the city—on its farther side they had to drive the Turks from the Mount of Olives. Bethlehem was occupied. The 10th Light Horse Regiment that night slept in Jerusalem—in houses for the first time since leaving Australia three years before. Next day they found touch with the Turks ten miles northward on the Nablus road. On the 12th Allenby, in marked contrast with the pomp of the Kaiser in 1908, entered the city on foot.[9]

The Turks stood fast beyond Jerusalem and on December 26th tried to drive the British back. But the British infantry, morally and physically elated, easily

---

[9] For the Kaiser a special entrance was driven through the old walls; Allenby entered by the side entrance at the old narrow Jaffa gate.

beat them and followed up the defeat. The front was drawn securely beyond Jerusalem; on the Mediterranean coast, too, Allenby's infantry, attacking by surprise, had again carried his line beyond the Nahr Auja so as to be ready for farther advance when the time should come. The Australian Mounted Division was withdrawn to rest south of Gaza. By the beginning of 1918 Allenby's brilliant victories in Palestine had for the time ended.

CHAPTER XXIII

LUDENDORFF STRIKES—MARCH 1918

As must have been clear to Allenby when the British government warned him that his army might have to be reduced in 1918, problems of the Middle East then hung on coming events on the Western Front.

There, when the fighting of 1917 ended in the impassable winter mud, the British commander-in-chief, Field-Marshal Haig, was still hoping to rest his troops during the wet months, and then to throw them again upon the Germans in Flanders.

The Australian divisions were among those intended to take part in this attack, and, for reasons presently to be stated, they were sent in mid-November to winter in a part of the front now likely to be specially quiet—on the ground won six months earlier, beyond Messines. But even before their arrival there any prospect of a great Allied offensive in the spring had faded from most minds except that of Haig. The Russian armies had simply dissolved; by the end of November the Bolshevik government had to ask for an armistice, and Ludendorff was transferring his forces from Russia to the Western Front at the rate of two divisions a week. It was evident that by the spring the Germans would have built up there an army strong enough to deliver a most formidable attack—the prospect of which, as weeks went on, became almost certain.

The lack of plan, or even of any real unity, with which the Allied governments and high commanders faced this tremendous threat would have been unbelievable to the troops holding that front, and also to the

Allied peoples, if these could have known the minds of
their leaders. Actually each Prime Minister and each
commander-in-chief believed in, and was working for,
a different plan. Haig, supported by the chief of the
Imperial General Staff, Sir William Robertson—an upright, cool-headed, stubborn soldier, risen from the
ranks—was for going on with the Flanders offensive as
soon as spring weather dried the ground. Lloyd George,
dreading and hating the prospect of another deadly and
(as he believed) entirely futile attempt to break the
Western Front, was all for remaining on the defensive in
the west, and "knocking away Germany's props" elsewhere. Lieut.-General Sir Henry Wilson—a brilliant,
ambitious, restless North of Ireland man, temporarily
in Britain without an appointment—had advised him
that troops, withdrawn before winter from the Western
Front, could be sent to Palestine to finish off the
Turks there during the winter, and be back in France
by the time that serious fighting on the Western Front
was possible again. General Pétain for his part, was determined to "wait for the Americans and the tanks" and
then, probably in August 1918, to strike on the Western
Front; meanwhile he nursed the French troops and
demanded that the British should take over more of the
French line. The clever French Minister for War, Painlevé, was intent on gradually bringing all armies on
the Western Front under French command. Haig was
strongly opposed to all this, seeing that it would mean
abandoning the Flanders offensive and (as he argued)
giving up the initiative to the Germans.

Each leader planned, so far as his control reached, for
the course that he believed best for the Allies, and urged
it on the others. The general "Council of the Allies"—
a body on which all of them, great and small, from
Russians to Siamese, had been represented—had proved
shockingly ineffective, a mere debating society; General
Smuts of South Africa described one of its meetings as

"the most futile exhibition of incompetence" that he had
ever seen. But a sharp turn in the war itself eventually
necessitated steps that led to at least some kind of method
and plan.

Haig's plan of an offensive in Flanders was check-
mated by Lloyd George. The Prime Minister had
not in 1917 been strong enough to bring to an early end
the "Passchendaele" offensive persisted in by Haig and
Robertson; and he now believed that Haig, if provided
with the troops, would continue in 1918 the same process
until all the troops, whatever their number, were spent
in uselessly snatching one "small, shattered village" after
another from the enemy's grip. He and War Cabinet,
therefore, deliberately decided to keep back in England
the men that Haig required. In addition, by agreeing to
the French demand that the British Army should take
over more of the line, Lloyd George further reduced
Haig's reserves; and still another reduction was brought
about when the French and British governments decided,
against Haig's and Robertson's wish, each to send six
divisions to help the Italians after their rout at Caporetto.

At one time it seemed possible that Caporetto might
be followed by the utter defeat of Italy. To decide on
the steps to meet that crisis the leaders of Britain, France
and Italy hurriedly met at Rapallo in the Riviera; and it
was this conference, early in November, that gave Lloyd
George the opportunity to initiate a most valuable step
suggested by General Wilson and Painlevé (then Premier
of France). This was the establishment of a supreme
authority above all the commanders-in-chief of the
Western Allies. The political leaders of the great powers
could form a Supreme War Council, and this Council
could have an Inter-Allied War Staff, whose head could
initiate the Allies' main strategy and determine to which
part of the front the final reserves of troops should be
sent. Lloyd George believed as strongly as Painlevé that
there should be a single commander of the armies of the

Western Allies—and so, probably, did most British soldiers except those of the regular army, although it was clear that such a commander would have to be French. But, especially since the fiasco with Nivelle, the Cabinet would not have attempted to put Haig under French command. The Supreme Council, however, would be advised by the Inter-Allied Staff. Lloyd George insisted that this staff must be independent of the national staffs; and, if he appointed General Wilson as the British representative, he would, by this typically circuitous method, be able to overrule Haig and Robertson.

The Supreme War Council was forthwith established, the United States, whose forces had begun to flow into France, agreeing to join with Britain, France and Italy on both Council and Staff. Lloyd George appointed Wilson, who duly went to Versailles where the Allied staff, like the Council, had its headquarters. The French appointed Foch, who was to be chairman of the Staff. Immediately after the Rapallo Conference, however, a defeat in the French Chamber of Deputies displaced Painlevé and brought to the French premiership the brilliant, stubborn, bitter old journalist and patriot, Georges Clemenceau, determined to spend his remaining years in ensuring and safeguarding the victory of France. He withdrew Foch from the Inter-Allied Staff to the French War Office, sending to Versailles as a substitute Foch's intimate assistant, General Weygand.

This left Wilson as the active spirit on the Versailles staff. His most important achievement in that rôle will be referred to presently; but it may be noted here that his proposal for putting Turkey out of the war was opposed by Clemenceau, who insisted that England should wait till after the coming attack in the West, and even then should use in the East only the troops already there. Also, Lloyd George's insistence on the independence of the Versailles staff, resulted in objection from General Robertson. In February Robertson was unseated, and the more imaginative, and perhaps less unbending, Wilson was called to London to become chief of the Imperial General Staff in his place.[1]

During Wilson's term at Versailles, on January 23rd, the Inter-Allied Staff produced its most vital proposal—for centralising the Allied command. It recommended that the main Western Allies, including Italy, should build up a common reserve of divisions—each national commander being asked to contribute a quota; and that this reserve should be controlled by the Inter-Allied Staff (acting as an "Executive War Board") with Foch as its Chairman. This was agreed to by the Supreme War Council, Clemenceau—though he would much have preferred the appointment of a generalissimo—permitting Foch to return to Versailles in this capacity. On February 9th Foch accordingly asked for 30 divisions for the reserve, 10 from the British Army, 13 from the French, 7 from the Italian. The intention of Painlevé, with whom this scheme had originated, had been to hold this reserve behind the junction of the French and British Armies, which was recognised as a crucial point.

Thus at last, after months of personal manoeuvres by generals and statesmen, there had emerged at least some system of united control and some definite plan to meet the supreme crisis known to be impending on the Western Front. But at this stage the two commanders-in-chief, Haig and Pétain, struck the whole plan dead. They disliked the higher control and mistrusted the efficiency of the staff committee. Two months earlier they had come to a mutual arrangement by which either would send reinforcements if the German offensive fell upon the other. Haig now said that it was too late to comply with the request of the Inter-Allied Staff for the reserve divisions. The Supreme Council, meeting on March 14th,

---

[1] General Rawlinson now became for a short time British representative on the Inter-Allied Staff at Versailles.

decided to postpone any drawing on Haig's or Pétain's forces; the Allies were left relying solely on the voluntary arrangement between Haig and Pétain—in which each would control his own action. A fortnight later the extreme need for the Inter-Allied reserve was to be demonstrated by events that threatened the Allies with the loss of the war.

The preparation of the German blow, the greatest offensive of that war, was a most difficult—indeed, at times, precarious—task; far more so than most people on the side of the Allies imagined. Although the collapse of Russia had given Ludendorff the chance of striking strongly in the west, the alliance of the Central Powers, on which any such blow was based, now showed many signs of falling to pieces. Austria-Hungary especially was in a bad way; and, when the Russian delegate, Trotsky, continually delayed the peace negotiations, and Ludendorff wished to break them off, the Austrian delegate, Count Czernin, said that, if this was done, his famine-threatened people might make a separate peace.

The urge for peace was indeed active in some section of almost every nation. In Great Britain a great shock had been given to Liberal and Labour circles by the publication by the Russians of secret treaties between the Allies for the partition of Turkey. Further, in England ever since the Somme Battle there had been those who doubted whether a continuance of such battles would bring any better peace than might now be had by negotiation. On 28th November 1917 a Conservative leader, Lord Lansdowne, published in the London press a plea to that effect which had been made by him in Cabinet a year before. The Russian revolutionary leader, Trotsky, invited all the Allies to come into the Russo-German peace negotiations, and on Christmas Day Count Czernin was allowed to announce, on behalf of the Central Powers, that they would agree to peace without indemnities or annexations if their opponents would immediately join in the negotiations on that basis.

The Allies rejected this offer. Any peace of compromise which left the Kaiser and Ludendorff in the saddle, with the German General Staff and the junkers behind them, would merely mean another war as soon as these could prepare it. But the offer had important results—it forced President Wilson and Mr Lloyd George to state their countries' war aims. President Wilson's statement laid down the famous Fourteen Points—foreshadowing open treaties, "freedom of navigation", equal trade conditions, reduction of armaments, government of colonies in the interest of the colonial peoples, evacuation by Germans of all occupied countries, self-determination for Russia, freedom for nations subject to the Turks, restoration of Alsace-Lorraine to France, re-establishment of Serbia and Poland with outlets to the sea, and other adjustments on national lines; and finally the formation of "a general association of nations" to guarantee security and independence. Lloyd George, after securing General Robertson's assurance that, if the Americans came quickly enough and the Navy coped with the submarines, the war could be won in the next two years, inspired new energy by several masterly statements: had the Allies abandoned their high aims? he asked. Victory could be ensured by holding on till American help was effective—was this the time for weakening? From Australia Mr Hughes protested against any suggestion of relaxation. On the opposite side both Czernin and the new German Chancellor, Count Hertling, rejected the terms as to territories. A crossfire of generalisations went on.

Ludendorff had already begun the transfer of force to the West, but before he struck he needed to be free of anxiety in the East. And though on February 13th he obtained leave to break off the dilatory negotiations with the Bolsheviks, and by March 3rd had forced the signing

of a robber's treaty at Brest-Litovsk,[2] he could not devote
all his attention to the Western Front. A large though
second-rate army had to be left to guard Germans against
Bolshevik infection. Although peace made with Rumania
on March 5th allowed the Germans to penetrate to the
Black Sea, the much needed food supply had to be protected from the raids of their Austrian allies, and coal
for the carriage of this food had to be fetched from the
far Donetz Basin. Caspian oil, needed by the Germans,
was coveted by the Turks who, instead of massing to
meet the grave danger represented by Allenby in Palestine, launched out south of the Caucasus to eventually
capture Baku.[3] In the Balkans the dissatisfied Bulgarians,
instead of bending their backs to help Germany's supreme
effort, were calling for more Germans to help them.

Yet, despite the onset of these anxieties, Ludendorff
quickly built up his great army in the West, and by
February German leaders and people, for all the talk of
negotiated peace, were hanging their hopes on a very
different means for peacemaking. Ludendorff, it is true,
no longer hoped for total victory. German manpower
was falling and the submarine campaign had failed to
starve Britain. But it might yet delay the transport of
Americans and so allow time for a military stroke against
the Western Allies before they were appreciably reinforced. He believed Britain to be the driving force of
his opponents. He estimated that his reinforcements from
Russia—35 divisions and 1000 heavy guns—would suffice
for one, but only one, offensive; therefore he would try,

---

[2] By which Germany controlled, through dummy governments, Esthonia
and Livonia, and occupied "independent" Poland (though giving part of
it to Ukraine). For the whole episode see *Vol. V, pp. 94-100.*

[3] A short account of the adventures of Australians in the selected
British detachment under General Dunsterville, which organised opposition
to the Germans throughout Persia and Kurdistan and on the Caspian
Sea, is given in *Vol. V, pp. 728-62.* The stories of Baku (*pp. 740-4*), and of
the rescue of 50,000 Assyrians in Kurdistan by the heroic work of an
American missionary and of a party under Capt. (now Lieut.-Genl.) Savige, are
of particular interest.

by a thrust against the right flank of the British, to separate their army from the French, and roll it up against the English Channel and there destroy it. He hoped by these means quickly to induce the Allies to negotiate a peace suitable to his views.

The Allies on the Western Front spent the winter in multiplying their defences, the British working with particular energy. Haig was, not unreasonably, forced to take over the French line to the Oise River (twenty-five miles south-east of Péronne); but at the same time he was denied the reinforcements for which he pressed. To economise men he was compelled to reorganise the whole B.E.F. with three battalions to each infantry brigade instead of four. All this resulted in his having too few troops for simultaneously reorganising and training, and constructing new defence lines behind the whole front.

The Australian forces, also, went through a manpower crisis; the toll of 1917—Bullecourt, Messines and Ypres—55,000 battle casualties in their five infantry divisions, 38,000 of these being incurred in the "Passchendaele" offensive—emptied their pool of trained men in England and left them 18,000 short. As the A.I.F. was almost entirely a front-line force, Surgeon-General Howse stubbornly and successfully opposed, from first to last, every attempt, even by the Australian government, materially to reduce the standard of its physique by employing less fit men in non-combatant duties in France.

The ranks in France had to be filled somehow. The half-formed 6th Division in England had already been disbanded to provide drafts, and the breaking-up of the much-tried—and therefore, numerically weakest—4th Division was proposed; but, by a happy suggestion to Haig, Birdwood avoided this. Mr Hughes and the Australian Cabinet had been pressing the British government to bring together all the Australian infantry divisions. Hitherto Haig had refused, considering a corps of five divisions too unwieldy. Birdwood and White now sug-

27—os

gested that instead of breaking up the 4th Division, Haig should allow it to be withdrawn into reserve as a "depot" division, to serve as a reservoir for the other four if necessary. These four could be combined in a single "Australian Corps". If it was possible to transfer them to a quiet sector, not only they but the "depot" division might be built up to strength; thus, when heavy fighting began, whichever division suffered the heaviest loss could change places with the 4th and become "depot" division for the time being. This would at least give the Australian people a chance of seeing whether, by increased recruiting, the disbandment of this famous division could be avoided.

To the delight of its authors, on November 1st Haig accepted the plan; and great was the pleasure of the Australian divisions, as they emerged from the Ypres battle-field and learnt that the 4th Division was temporarily saved; and that the other four were to take over, as one "Australian Corps", the comparatively quiet sector at Messines. Especial was the delight of the 3rd Division, which never before had been linked in a corps with the older divisions except the 4th. Meeting Australian wishes, Haig allotted to the Australian Corps as many of the Australian units as possible—including the 3rd Squadron Australian Flying Corps (flying R.E.8's for artillery work and observation) and the two Australian siege batteries. The motor transport of the corps now became practically all Australian.

So, too, did its staff and commanders. This development had already been almost completely carried out by Birdwood in I Anzac; at the request of the Australian government it was now brought to early completion. The average "Digger", though he felt the appointment of Australian officers to be wise and right, and much to his liking, was nevertheless deeply sorry to say good-bye to many who had led and served him exceedingly well—such as Generals "Hooky" Walker, Nevill Smyth (who afterwards emigrated to Australia) and W. B. Lesslie. Many others were no longer there, but lay among their dead Australian comrades at Anzac, Fromelles, and Polygon Wood. The parting from the New Zealand Infantry Division also was regretted; General Godley's II Anzac Corps, as it now contained no Australians except a few mounted troops, became the XXII British Corps.

The Australian Corps was not the "Australian Army" for the formation of which its government had several times pressed the War Office and Haig; its strength, though at times greater than that of some armies, would not have justified that "promotion".[4] Nevertheless it was, and remained, the strongest corps in France. Although—as will later be seen—the second proposal to introduce conscription in Australia was defeated at a referendum held in December 1917, the 4th Division was never broken up—which would have been felt by the A.I.F. as a disaster in view of its great traditions; indeed, even the decision to make it temporarily a "depot" division did not bring about its long-promised rest. No sooner had it reached the back area than the German counterstroke after Cambrai forced G.H.Q. to rush it into close reserve at Péronne. That battle ended without involving it; but early in January, on Haig's having to take over more front from the French, it was brought back into the front line on the left of the Australian Corps, south of Ypres. From that time till the war ended it continued its particularly active, hard-fighting career in the Australian Corps; if any units or formations had eventually to be disbanded through lack of recruits—as seemed certain—Birdwood and White now proposed to do this, at least in the first instance, by the method already adopted by the British Army but not by the Dominions—reducing to three the four battalions of each brigade.

---

[4] In May 1916 Mr Hughes had offered Haig a 6th Division if this was done. The War Office had written that it had always been the intention to form an Australian army. The Canadian Corps comprised four divisions. A fifth was formed in England but, like the 6th Australian, was disbanded.

Through shortage of recruits the Australian divisions were now, of necessity, built up largely by men gradually coming back from hospital through the "hardening" depots in England. To some, who had closely followed their record, it seemed unlikely that they would maintain the outstanding pitch of effectiveness which they had reached in 1917. The strain of battles like those of the Western Front tended to stretch a soldier's elasticity beyond the point of recovery; the old soldier, in such a war, was not always the best soldier; those who knew and dreaded the risks might be too clever to take them. An outstanding quality of the Australian soldier had been his readiness to take worth-while risks—"to give it a go", as he himself put it. Not without reason some observers wondered whether men who had been through Pozières, Bullecourt and Ypres would retain that quality undiminished. It seemed very possible that the A.I.F. had passed its zenith.

With some 117,000 troops in France, forming about one-eleventh of the total British and Dominion combat troops on the Western Front, the A.I.F. there played a quiet but active role during the winter of 1917-18, building or completing its part of Haig's three new or reorganised defence lines, with their camouflaged concrete blockhouses and strong wire entanglements. Haig intended to hold the enemy on the second line, two to three miles behind the thinly held outpost line, and itself one to two miles in "depth". In what time was left from digging, wiring and reorganising, the troops were rested and hurriedly trained.

For the Australians, by far the most useful exercise was the nightly patrolling in the wide moor- and marshland between the opposing lines in the Lys valley. Both sides constantly tried by thus probing, and by taking prisoners, to obtain information of the enemy garrison. The Germans, usually employing more formal methods than the Australians, made 54 recorded attempts, in which they obtained prisoners (or killed and identified their opponents) on 10 occasions, but lost prisoners (or were themselves identified) on 42 occasions. The Australians in 25 recorded attempts secured prisoners (or identifications) on 14 occasions and left them on 7.[5] One German regimental history states that the patrol enterprises of its regiment, though keen, "brought irreplaceable losses—the information obtained was often not in consonance with the great cost". Another says: "The enemy infantry was always on its guard.". Yet—as ever since Gallipoli days—the Australian infantry left the illumination of no-man's-land by flares almost entirely to their opponents, themselves usually preferring to keep watch in the dark.

On March 9th and 10th increased German shelling of the back area, and the night bombing of Bailleul by big Gotha aeroplanes, caused the moral atmosphere to become electric. The nervous strain on the troops—as always when daily expecting a great attack—was severe, but it was notable that there was no sign of lack of confidence among the Diggers. Far from it. Raids and patrols were ordered with a view to discovering the enemy's intention, and prisoners were frequently taken, but, from the signs, few Australians believed that the attack would come there, though many wished that it would.[6] Like Haig they believed that the Germans had little chance of breaking through, and that an attempt to do so would give the Allies a chance of "finishing" them.

The higher staffs were aware that the British air force and the intelligence staff had clearly detected preparations on two parts of the British front—the Arras-St Quentin sector, then held by the 3rd and 5th British Armies, next to the French, and the sector near the Lys

---

[5] Monash's 3rd Division on four occasions made big carefully planned raids at Warneton on the Lys, capturing many prisoners though at fairly heavy cost.

[6] This was the occasion of the posting of Capt. F. P. Bethune's famous order to his machine-gun section, quoted in *Vol. V, p. 110.*

south of Armentières, about the junction of the 1st and
2nd British Armies. The French also had seen preparations, near the Aisne north-east of Paris. The Allies'
reserves were evenly distributed, in good position to meet
these three clearly portended attacks. After several false
alarms, statements by Alsatian and Polish deserters on
March 18th and 19th made it certain that within two days
a very great attack would be launched against the Arras-
St Quentin sector.

Actually Ludendorff, after making thorough preparations on those three sectors and elsewhere—and so leading
Haig and Pétain
to believe that he
would spread his
forces in three or
more thrusts—had
in the last weeks,
by well-screened
night movements,
concentrated all
his available
strength for the
central one (to
which the Ger-
mans gave the
code-name of
"Michael").[7] At
dawn on March
21st, by throwing
it after sudden

*Arrows show attacks prepared by
Germans; but on March 21st only
"Michael" was launched.*

bombardment against the thinly spread 5th and 3rd
British Armies, he reaped the precious results of a great
surprise. The two Allied commanders-in-chief, Haig and
Pétain, who, as above related, had forced their governments to leave them in separate control of their respective

---

[7] Code names of other projected attacks were (as shown in the sketch)
George I and II, and Roland.

zones, had been outwitted; and the Inter-Allied reserve which Foch was to have built up, and which almost certainly would have been placed so as to strengthen the junction of the French and British zones, had—through their action—not been formed.

How Ludendorff's great attack, using the ancient method now called "pincers" tactics, and also "infiltration" (at which German infantry had been specially trained during the winter), caused the Allies within a few days to face a threat similar in some ways to that which Hitler presented to them in France twenty-two years later, must be read in other histories. Most foolishly the German leaders had despised the manufacture of tanks—"our attacks succeeded without them," says Ludendorff;[8] but they had immense quantities of guns and ammunition. The front attacked was nearly the whole of that to which the Allies had advanced a year before, facing the Hindenburg Line (at Bullecourt the British front line *was* the former Hindenburg Line). Owing to the thinness of the 5th British Army, which had only lately taken over from the French part of its new front about St Quentin, two crises quickly developed. One arose through the increasing threat to the French left flank. The second was caused by the separation of the 3rd British Army from the 5th.

The southern flank of the 3rd Army held the Flesquières "bulge"—the remnant of the ground gained in the recent battle of Cambrai. Part of the German plan was to cut this off by a pincers movement.[9] Haig had considered whether it might not be wise to withdraw beforehand from that salient—a step which, if he had carried it out, posterity might well have adjudged a master stroke.

---

[8] They had only eighteen rather clumsy German tanks and a small number of captured English ones. Of all these only one section was employed in this attack—in mopping up.

[9] *Volume V*, Australian official history, gives a short account of this in *pp. 112-14*, and *chapter X* ("The Truth about Fifth Army"), *pp. 236-97*.

Instead, the salient was held; and, when the southern German pincer struck swiftly through the thinly extended 5th Army farther south, and the troops of General Byng's 3rd Army in the tip of the salient found themselves but slightly attacked, these troops, who should have been withdrawn most quickly, actually retired most slowly.

Within two days they were almost cut off, and, though they escaped, a gap had opened between them and 5th Army, and it was only by a series of hurried, exhausting, nightmare withdrawals that they prevented the Germans from surrounding a great length of the line and so creating a breach that might not have been repaired. The British air force, and with it the 2nd and 4th Australian Squadrons, with bombs and machine-guns continuously attacked the Germans who advanced on the naked roads over the old Somme battlefield. Pilots returned again and again as fast as they could refuel and reload. In the gap that actually opened, the splendid South African Infantry Brigade, which (through non-receipt of an order) stood fast on March 24th north-west of Péronne, was surrounded and wiped out.

It was on this situation, which threatened a breach of his own front, that the British commander-in-chief, Haig, concentrated all his effort. As already mentioned he had arranged with Pétain that—instead of having Foch's "executive board" over them to send Allied reserves to the points of danger—they should mutually help each other. Haig had evidence that all the available German reserves were being used in the offensive against the British, and that no second offensive could be immediately launched against the French. Consequently he increasingly depended on Pétain to support the southern British army, the 5th, while he himself tried to stabilise the 3rd.

The Australians, sixty miles north in Flanders, had, like other British troops, heard with entire confidence of the German onslaught on March 21st. Let the Ger-

mans come, was the general feeling. The enemy would
only batter himself to bits! But by the 25th men read in
the communiqués with amazement the names of familiar
towns—Péronne, Bapaume, and—on later days—those of
the old villages whose ruins marked, though sometimes
only with a few heaps of rubble, the man-made wilderness of the old Somme battlefield. On March 25th it was
stated at the Press Headquarters in bomb-shaken Amiens
that there was possibly no British division between there
and the Germans, some twenty-eight miles away. Also
came word that some big German gun was shelling Paris
from a forest seventy miles distant.

In this crisis the Australian infantry divisions began
to strain on the leash which held them idle in the north.
"We all had the feeling," writes an infantry officer, "that
if we could only get down there it would be all right!"
On March 23rd there came to the youngest division, the
3rd, a warning order that sent its spirits bounding. By
March 25th the 3rd and 4th Divisions were on their way
to train or bus—their bands playing "Colonel Bogey" or
the men singing the old marching songs with a new
spirit. Many times they had fought hard, but in offensives
whose effect was, at the time, problematical. *This* time
they could see that every step led directly towards beating
the German. Here, at last, was the job they had come
for. "Australia," they felt, "is going to count for
something now!"

CHAPTER XXIV

SAVING AMIENS AND HAZEBROUCK

THE crisis changed rapidly even while these first Australians were moving south. As, on March 25th, the long string of motor lorries carrying the 4th Division's leading brigade, the 4th, rolled through clouds of white dust into St Pol, thirty-four miles north of Amiens, they were turned sharply to the left, into roads leading to the countryside south-west of Arras. The otherwise clear sky ahead was smudged by a distant pillar of smoke, probably rising from Bapaume, and in the villages old people were hastily loading their furniture on farm waggons. As lorry-load after lorry-load of cheerful, dust-covered Diggers bumped past, the old folk paused. No Australian infantry had ever been stationed there, but these were immediately recognised, and calling to one another, "Les Australiens", the old people began unloading their carts. "Pas nécessaire maintenant," said one, to an Australian who asked the reason. "Vous les tiendrez" ("Not necessary now—you'll hold them").

Next day, March 26th, the 4th Division was alarmed in its various villages and hurried to positions chosen for blocking a gap through which the Germans with tanks were reported to be heading; they would be only thirteen miles from the quiet old townlet of Doullens (seventeen miles north of Amiens) where at that moment, as will presently be told, there were meeting, in one of the crucial conferences of the war, the Prime Ministers and military leaders of France and Great Britain. Accordingly, the veteran 4th Brigade, marching up along roads past streams of retiring British troops and of villagers, hastened in the direction of the reported incursion, and at dusk pushed into the ruined village of Hébuterne on the nearer edge of the old Somme battlefield.

A scattered remnant of the 19th British Division was found there, completely exhausted—some men on being

The arrow shows the movement of Australians.

relieved broke down and wept. Most of the 4th Brigade saw none of them, but taking position around Hébuterne, and, driving back or capturing a few German scouts, took position beyond the village. By morning the place was firmly held. South of it was a gap in the British front, but the New Zealand Division, brought down from Flanders to Amiens, was reported to be already on the other side of this and thrusting northwards to close it. At daybreak

411

some skirmishers coming up over the open from the south-west proved to be New Zealanders.

The 4th Brigade eventually had to stay, apart from its division, at Hébuterne and repel several German attempts to break through; not till nearly a month later would the commander of the IV British Corps—as his messages made clear—entrust the position to the other available troops. The first of the German attacks was made as dawn broke on March 27th, disclosing to the brigade a spectacle such as it had never before seen. Around lay the Somme moorland, rumpled with old trenches like dug-out rabbit burrows in an Australian paddock, and covered with long grass on which the gusts played as on the flanks of a Shetland pony. But as the light grew the moorland eastward was seen to be alive with distant movement: German waggon lines on the distant slopes; a German battery blazing in the open. At 11 o'clock infantry came on, wave after wave. When shelled to ground by British batteries they still crept forward, by rushes from cover to cover. But neither then nor in their attempts on later days had they the least success. On the contrary, employing methods presently to be described, both Australians and New Zealanders began to bite into the German front.

Meanwhile in the exciting, fast-changing developments of the German offensive, the two other brigades of the 4th Division had not been left even for a night behind Hébuterne, in the support position to which they had been rushed. A new crisis had come into existence near Albert, a dozen miles south. Through some mistake among the senior commanders, a British division protecting Albert had been withdrawn. The 12th and 13th Australian Infantry Brigades were ordered thither at once and, after marching through the night across part of the German front, they reached at dawn some of the well-remembered villages north-west of Albert. Pozières, Mouquet Farm, Thiepval, Albert itself were in German

hands and the troops were in a rest area of 1916. The villagers had just fled and some of the tired but eager men
breakfasted in the cottages on wine and poultry. In a
quick march of seventeen miles not one straggler had
been left behind.

Meanwhile the division's commander, Maj.-General
MacLagan, had been ordered to report to Lieut.-General
Congreve of the VII British Corps, holding the southernmost sector of the 3rd Army's line. This sector began at
the western outskirts of Albert, passed across the Ancre
at Dernancourt, and thence extended over the high
triangle of open land between the Ancre and Somme
rivers, and ended at the Somme, where the 5th Army's
sector began. MacLagan found Congreve at Montigny
Chateau, in a bare, stately room, lit by a candle, with
the chief of the VII Corps staff, Brig.-General Hore-
Ruthven (afterwards Lord Gowrie, Governor-General of
Australia); and Maj.-General Monash of the 3rd Australian Division receiving Congreve's orders.[1]

It appeared that the withdrawal from south of Albert
could not be reversed; the main part of the British line
there—composed of remnants of the 9th (Scottish) and
35th Divisions—was withdrawing from the triangle between the Somme and Ancre and already taking up a new
line north of the Ancre; but an improvised screen—some
cavalry and a remnant of infantry—was still across the
triangle, and Monash was to place his division behind
them in a line of old French trenches, barring that
approach to Amiens. MacLagan was similarly to place
his brigades on the high ground farther north, behind
the 9th and 35th Divisions.

The 3rd Division had detrained at Doullens during
the vital conference there on March 26th, and in a rather
tense atmosphere part of its troops had been hurriedly
set to guard the town. During the following night it had

---

[1] With MacLagan and Monash were some of their own staff, Lieut.-Cols
Lavarack, Jess, and R. E. Jackson.

been carried from that area by motor-buses to the Amiens-Albert road—part of the Roman highway to Bapaume, here running along the high ground north of the Ancre. This road and every village along it were familiar places to all the Australian divisions except the 3rd, whose troops were eager to see the Somme country. Like all the

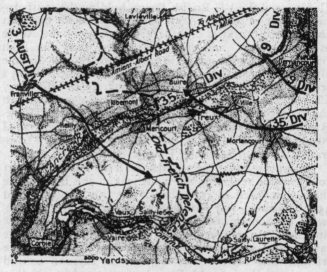

THE SITUATION BETWEEN THE ANCRE AND SOMME, ON NIGHT OF 26th MARCH 1918 AND FOLLOWING MORNING

Australian troops coming southward, they found themselves to be the only traffic heading towards the enemy. Villagers and British soldiers, including heavy artillery, streamed past, all in the other direction. "You're going the wrong way, Digger," shouted one. "Jerry'll souvenir you and your —— band too." "You Australians think you can do anything," said an artillery brigadier to Lieut.-Colonel Lavarack, chief of MacLagan's staff, "but you haven't a chance of holding them." "Will you stay and support us if we do?" was the reply—and this the brigadier very willingly did.

Again and again the Diggers were told by passers-by, "You can't hold them!" and some Australian leaders were a little anxious as to how all this advice and the depressing sights would affect their men. They need have had no worry; it was immediately evident—as was constantly found in the coming months—that the confidence of these troops was overflowing. Each man knew that every blow now counted; this, they felt, was what they had come from Australia for—and the sight of their cheerful, grim faces and confident gait put new heart into French and British alike. "They were the first cheerful stubborn people we had met in the retreat," said a British major of artillery. In the French villages whenever during those weeks these hearty, stalwart battalions marched in they were met by striking demonstrations of affection and trust—and this, too, reacted strongly on them. "Fini retreat, Madame," said a Digger to a village woman as he sat grimly cleaning his rifle while the 3rd Division halted in Heilly on its way to the triangle between Ancre and Somme. "Fini retreat—beaucoup Australiens ici."

It is true that men and officers were shocked by some of the scenes on the roads. Like all spectators in the rear of a great retreat, they saw the worst—the panic near Hébuterne; a car with "rattled" staff officers too hastily retiring; parties of men without arms; stragglers who had lost their units; senseless looting and destruction in villages on the Ancre. What they did not know was that a great part of the withdrawing troops were labour companies and heavy artillery, which, to clear the communications, had been ordered to back areas, largely west of Doullens.

By 11 a.m. on March 27th two battalions of the 3rd

Australian Division had relieved the few completely
exhausted British infantry (a few Scots at first refused to
be relieved) in the triangle between the rivers; and on
the other side of the Ancre, farther north and two miles
farther forward, two battalions of the 4th Division were
about then ordered to move up in close support of the
exhausted 9th Division which held the embankment and
cuttings of the Albert-Amiens railway curving round the
foot of the hills, near the village of Dernancourt and
the Ancre. The Australians—advancing along the open
hilltop astride the straight avenue of the Amiens-Albert
road, and looking down into Albert with its broken
cathedral tower, and the hills by Pozières (now three
miles behind the German lines)—were intensely shelled.
At dusk came an order to relieve the 9th Division at the
railway round the foot of the hill. Some Australian officers
did not expect to find the Scots there—but they were, in
niches along the top of the railway banks, exhausted, but
fighting as they had fought for seven days. "Thank God!"
they said. "You'll hold him"—and, waving good luck,
went off in the moonlight. Two miles to the south-west,
on the triangle between the rivers, the 3rd Division also
found itself holding the front line, the cavalry ahead
having been suddenly ordered to help the 5th Army
south of that river.

The situation of the 5th Army, under General Gough,
had, for a week, been the crux of one of the supreme crises
of the war. It has been seen that Haig looked to Pétain
to support this army while he himself supported the 3rd.
Pétain gave support, but the required help quickly
surpassed that previously arranged for by him and Haig,
and it was needed much sooner. French divisions had to
be thrown in piecemeal as they arrived, infantry sometimes without artillery—a most wasteful proceeding. On
top of all, despite Haig's assurances Pétain believed that
the main German attack had not yet been delivered, but
would descend at any moment on his own front.

It is now known that the German staff counted on the hesitation of the French Command—and rightly. When the 5th British Army continued to retreat beyond a line on which he and Haig only a few hours before had agreed that the Allies should stand, Pétain gave up hope of saving that army—indeed, always tending to pessimism, he believed it to be now practically non-existent. Visiting Haig at midnight on the 24th he intimated that he had decided to abandon the British flank and withdraw south-west to cover Paris.

To Haig this came as a thunderstroke. The one firm basis of Allied strategy, recognised in orders drawn by Kitchener, was that, whatever happened, the British and French Armies must remain united. It is true that Haig himself was contemplating a withdrawal of the 3rd Army north-westward—actually it was this withdrawal that the VII Corps mistakenly began to carry out on March 27th south of Albert. But Haig's purpose was to give Pétain time to reach out to him at Amiens (meanwhile, if the Germans thrust at Amiens, Haig planned to strike them from the flank, and it was for this purpose that the Australians and New Zealanders had originally been rushed to 3rd Army). Haig, receiving the whole first weight of the German blow, felt—and felt rightly—that he himself could not safely reinforce the 5th Army, but that Pétain could do so.

On hearing Pétain's decision Haig thought that his colleague's nerve had given way. He therefore at once took the only step likely to save disaster—telegraphed to London asking that "Foch, or some other determined general, who would fight, should be given supreme control of the operations in France", so that Pétain should be overruled.[2] The result was several hurried meetings culminating in the conference, in the critical hours of March 26th, at Doullens, at which Foch was given

---

[2] The details of the incident are described in *Vol. V, pp. 256-60.*

28—03

powers that quickly developed into supreme command of the Allies on the Western Front.[3] About this time there issued an order in a tone welcomed by most of the troops—there must be "NO withdrawal" except locally, and then only due westward—"NOT" so as to separate one army from the other. It was a bitter mischance that the first sequel to this was the mistaken retirement of the 3rd Army's flank south of Albert away from 5th Army's flank.

The effect of this retirement on the use of the Australian divisions, originally brought south for Haig's possible thrust against the German flank, has been seen. The 3rd and 4th were rushed into line to make sure of the 3rd Army's southern flank. But immediately south of this the 5th Army's northern flank, resting on the Somme near Méricourt, had been left wide open with three miles of unguarded river behind it. It is true that, far from being "non-existent", the 5th Army still managed to hold an unbroken line from that point southwards to the flank of the 1st French Army, under General Debeney; but the Germans north of the Somme were now free to cross the river and post themselves behind the tired British divisions, and on March 27th they began to do so. It was to meet this threat that the 1st Cavalry Division was hastily withdrawn that night from ahead of the 3rd Australian Division, and sent south of the river.

That night the two Australian divisions—with the remains of the 35th holding a short sector between them, astride the Ancre—became responsible for the 3rd Army's flank. Early next morning (March 28th) in the 4th Division's sector a scout of the 47th Battalion, Sergeant S. R. McDougall, posted to watch a level crossing on the railway overlooking the Ancre flats and Dernancourt village, heard through the dense mist the sound of

---

[3] The Belgians, however, under their Constitution, could accept only advice.

bayonet scabbards flapping on the thighs of marching troops. As he ran along the railway to alarm the nearest outpost, Germans emerged from the mist along the front as far as he could see; the nearest threw bombs over the embankment. One of these hit a Lewis-gun crew, but snatching up the gun McDougall shot the foremost Germans who were then crossing the rails, and then hosed those crouching along their side of the embankment. The attack quickly spread along the whole of the 12th Brigade's front, from Dernancourt to Albert; but after hard close fighting the Germans, whose supports could be seen pouring out from distant omnibuses, and throwing bridges over the Ancre, were completely beaten. The 50th Reserve Division, which made the attack, lost some 550 men. The few who had crossed the railway were captured by McDougall, whose actions won him the Victoria Cross.

On the same day (28th) the 3rd Division on the bare, high triangle between the Ancre and Somme was ordered to advance—Foch had been discussing with General Byng of 3rd Army a project of an offensive in this region, and more room was apparently wanted in preparation for it. Also the 5th Army, which was still ahead, south of the Somme (though with Germans behind its left flank), asked for that flank to be protected by the seizure of Sailly Laurette. Monash ordered an advance; but, on the crest, the 40th Battalion, set to advance in daylight, with little supporting artillery yet within range, soon ran into fire from distant Germans themselves advancing from the opposite direction. After costly progress, resumed after dark in drizzling rain, the 40th was stopped within close range of the Germans on the crest. On both slopes of the heights also Monash's battalions made ground, although that night on the southern slope the 44th was detected, and was caught in a deadly ambush by massed German machine-gunners as it slithered down one side of a gully to attack Sailly Laurette at the foot of the other side.

However, the 3rd Army's flank, down to the Somme, was now solidly held; but already the point of supreme interest was shifting beyond it. The Germans who on March 28th had tried in a vain, costly attack at Arras, to widen the front of their whole drive, henceforth directed their effort mainly south of the Somme, where the French were now hurrying to support and relieve the right of Gough's 5th Army. The harassed divisions of that army were till the night of the 27th still holding the line Foch had ordered them to hold on the 26th. But, with the Germans behind their left, Foch had to allow their withdrawal. The half-surrounded left managed to get clear, part of the 16th (Irish) Division actually crossing and recrossing the Somme behind the German lines, rushing the German picquets.

On March 28th the withdrawal was brought to a stop, largely by the 1st Cavalry Division, at the old French defence line, which ran in front of Hamel village on the Somme and two miles ahead of Villers-Bretonneux on the crest—a southerly continuation of the old trench-line held by the 3rd Division north of the Somme. Farther south, near the junction with the 1st French Army, this line was lost, and the 3rd Division's reserve brigade, the 9th, was next day hurried thither as a reserve for the 5th Army, which now comprised only one corps.

By this time the French were counter-attacking, the 3rd French Army (farther south than the 1st) having passed to the offensive. Only the spearhead of Ludendorff's armies, south of the Somme, was still advancing; and on March 30th it attacked here on a wide front, hoping to split the British from the French. On the extreme northern flank of this attack, north of the Somme, a fresh division tried to drive back the 3rd Australian, but suffered (as one of its regimental histories states) the "worst miscarriage" in its experience. The Germans could not take Hamel but the extreme point of the attack, now at the junction of French and British near the River Luce, drove closer to Amiens.

This was not far from where the 9th Australian Infantry Brigade lay in reserve, and, while British cavalry were used at the actual junction, on the hills just north of it the British commander threw in a battalion of the Australian brigade under Lieut.-Colonel Morshead. Without artillery, but with the help of the 12th Lancers, it was to re-establish the badly shaken line. Except for the 29th Division in Gallipoli, the British cavalry, whom the Australians watched with admiration throughout this campaign, were almost the only troops of the old pre-

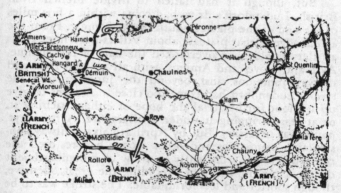

GERMAN ATTACKS ON 30th MARCH 1918
(The attacks are shown by white arrows.)

war British Army with whom the war brought them into contact, and the co-operation never failed to be enthusiastic. On this occasion, though most of the desired ground beyond "Lancer Wood" was not gained, the aggressiveness of the cavalry and Australians—like that of the French then attacking much farther south—helped to call the final halt to the German offensive.

We now know that a week earlier, by March 23rd,
Ludendorff had already seen that his original plan—to
swing north-west and crush the British armies—was likely
to fail, and he had therefore changed it to strike west
and south-west, where progress was easiest. By the end
of March he knew—and his opponents believed—that the
offensive had failed; in crossing the desolation of the old
Somme battlefield the Germans had outrun their communications. Guns and shells could not be brought up
in the quantities necessary for breaking down the new
Allied line, drawn around the wide salient made by this
thrust.

But, though it had failed to divide French from
British, Ludendorff's drive had come within a few miles
of the end of the plateau south of the Somme. From the
actual edge of that plateau, about Villers-Bretonneux, his
artillery could have overlooked the flats of the Somme,
Avre and Noye; and Amiens, with all its vital road and
railway junctions, just beyond the junction of those
rivers. Ludendorff had come too close to Amiens to give
up without further trial the hope of either reaching it,
or at least bringing it under artillery fire. A few days'
pause was necessary. But by April 4th sixty railway construction companies and other troops had restored the
communications sufficiently to allow of a bombardment
on the same lines as that preceding the great offensive,
though shorter and less formidable. The stroke was to be
towards Amiens and the railways south of it; but, if
successful, it would be followed by a chain of attacks
between the Somme and Arras also.

In the four days since March 30th the British 5th
Army had time to readjust its front. The remnants of
divisions, and the improvised forces, till then holding
its front, were relieved. Its centre ahead of Villers-
Bretonneux was temporarily taken over by one widely
extended Australian battalion, the 35th, of the 9th
Brigade, and the flanks to north and south, in front of

Hamel and of Lancer Wood, by two tired British divisions. These had previously been engaged farther south,
but had been relieved by the French, whose armies now
held the front up to Hangard village, north of the Luce
River, two miles south-west of Lancer Wood. The other
three battalions of the 9th Brigade were behind Villers-
Bretonneux in close reserve.

The second of the two incoming British divisions,
the 14th, had just taken over the front at Hamel from the
cavalry when, at dawn on April 4th, the German bombardment descended—not equally on the whole front, but
with particular force in certain sectors—including that
of the 14th Division. The Germans struck with fifteen
divisions on a front of twenty-one miles, two-thirds of it
facing the French and one-third the British. On the 5th
Army's northern flank they drove through the 14th
Division, captured Hamel, and forced the 35th Australian
Battalion to swing back to avoid being enveloped. The
18th British Division on the south stood fast, and the
northern thrust was eventually stopped by again calling
on the cavalry, together with the 33rd Australian Battalion. The Somme bridges on those flats were then being
guarded by the 15th Australian Infantry Brigade, under
Brig.-General "Pompey" Elliott—and some of its officers
and men crossing the river helped to rally the British
infantry and complete the line to the Somme.

The German advance on the 5th Army's front thus
seemed to have been held, when in the mid-afternoon the
Germans, attacking again, drove back part of the 18th
Division, south of the Australians. This time the 9th
Brigade's southern flank had to be swung back. The
whole line retired; the Germans reached the Monument
(of the 1870 war) on the outskirts of Villers-Bretonneux;
and the fate of the township appeared to be sealed.

But at that crucial moment the 36th Battalion, till
then waiting in a hollow beside the town, dashed forward
in a spectacular charge. A handful of British infantry

joined on its right, some of the 35th on its left, some Londoners in support—and, a little later, the cavalry farther left, beyond the Amiens-Péronne road. At the sight of the eager, swiftly approaching line with its flashing bayonets the Germans, then advancing from Monument Wood, first hesitated and then ran back to old trenches more than a mile from the town. On the left the 15th Brigade was brought across the Somme to hold, together with the cavalry, the vital heights (Hill 104) north of the town, and there the line stayed.[4]

But south of Villers-Bretonneux the Germans had seized Hangard Wood. Farther south they had captured Moreuil, and, between these places, had driven the French two miles beyond the Avre to Sénécat Wood, from which Amiens was visible. The German Command, hoping that the Allied front south of the Somme would crumble, had arranged also to strike next day at a number of points north of the Somme. One of these was south of Hébuterne. Here two German divisions attacking the New Zealanders and 4th Australian Brigade were, as before, thoroughly beaten. The Germans also attempted a farther advance just south of the Somme, which dwindled to a mere patrol action, described in a later chapter.

For the A.I.F., however, much the hardest fighting of April 5th fell on the 4th Division on the railway embankment and cuttings in the Dernancourt sector. Its 13th Brigade (Glasgow) had relieved the British 35th Division between Buire and Dernancourt, and the 12th Brigade (Gellibrand) held the left between Dernancourt and Albert. During the evening and night of April 4th word arrived that prisoners had disclosed that the Germans

---

4 This charge is described in *Vol. V, pp. 338-48.* The 9th Brigade was commanded by Brig.-Genl Rosenthal, but as he was held, by order, far behind the front, he gave the control of the forward troops this day to Lieut.-Col. H. A. Goddard (35th) in Villers-Bretonneux. It was Goddard who gave Lieut.-Col. Milne (36th) the order to charge.

were about to attack Amiens from this direction; but the front was quiet until after daylight on the 5th when artillery and trench-mortar fire suddenly fell on the 12th Brigade's outposts along most of the three-mile curve of the railway line between Dernancourt and Albert, and on the high, bare hill held by the supports behind them.

The fire on the outposts increased in intensity especially at the bridge in the high railway embankment immediately west of Dernancourt—the point where the

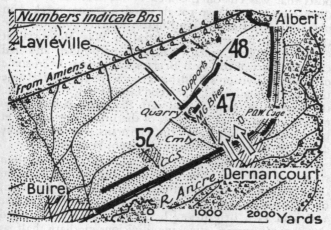

The arrows show the point of German penetration.

13th and 12th Brigades joined. After a fierce fight in the morning mist Germans forced their way under the bridge and took in flank and rear the neighbouring posts, which were lining the top of the embankment. In the supports and at headquarters the position was not known until the enemy had pushed far on up the hill from this point, attacking and outflanking the 12th Brigade's supports half-way to the top, and also establishing himself, with a field-gun, behind the outpost line of the 48th Battalion, which lined the railway farther north.

The 48th had been ordered to hold the front line at all costs; and not till shortly after noon, when the alternative was certainly complete envelopment, did the senior officer on the spot, Captain F. Anderson, give the order to withdraw. Then, as at Bullecourt, almost precisely a year before, that battalion came calmly and successfully out of an impossible position. At one of its posts that was cut off the men of the German infantry themselves erected two rough wooden crosses marked in pencil: "Here lies a brave English fighter" (one of these can be seen today in the Australian War Memorial at Canberra). The Germans had also surrounded and had captured part of the 12th Brigade's supports. Even some of the 4th Division's field batteries were thought at one time to be endangered, but stood fast. At last, at 5.15 p.m., the reserves of the 12th and 13th Brigades made a determined advance over the brow of the hill. They were met by intense fire but drove the Germans part of the way down the hillside, and there the front remained.

This was the strongest attack made against Australian troops in that war. The fight at Villers-Bretonneux on the previous day had cost the 9th Brigade (3rd Division) 660 casualties, and this battle at Dernancourt cost the 12th and 13th Brigades (4th Division) about 1100, and the three German attacking divisions perhaps half as many again.[5] The 4th Division was quickly relieved by the 2nd, just arrived from Messines.

On those two days, here and farther north and south, Ludendorff's primary and greatest offensive of 1918 really ended. But, as mentioned above, he had already given orders for the next blow. Most astutely, he would strike this time south of Armentières, using there the

[5] For certain very interesting experiences of prisoners this day see *Vol. V, footnote on pp. 395-7.*

preparations which had originally misled the British into expecting a triple offensive. The chances there were particularly favourable, since part of that front was held by the Portuguese Corps, which had been brought to France to help Portugal's allies, though most of its troops were conscious of no reason why they should be fighting the Germans. Indeed thirty of them, in the absence of their officer, had signalled to the Germans to come over, and then told them they were tired of the war.[6] Fear that the Portuguese would shortly be taken out of the line caused Ludendorff to hurry forward this offensive, and on April 9th he struck—just in time, for signs of the imminence of his attack had been noted, and the Portuguese were to have been replaced by British next day.

The Portuguese melted—why they should have been expected to fight so formidable an enemy in a cause of which they knew little is a question on which military and political leaders might well have pondered. They fled almost to the coast; fortunately, on the southern flank a stubborn North-English division, the 55th, completely defeated that wing of the attack; and though the British division north of the Portuguese was outflanked, the British reserves—two half-exhausted divisions who had been coming up from the Somme to relieve the

Portuguese—together with a few cyclists and cavalry were able at least to check the advance.

However the Germans had outflanked Armentieres, and when, next day, their offensive was extended by a blow north of that town, towards Messines, the whole northern front of the Allies was endangered. The 1st and 2nd Australian Divisions had in the last week been sent from Messines to the Somme, their places being taken by half-exhausted divisions just relieved from the Somme battle, including the 9th (Scottish) from Dernancourt. All these were at low strength, and even short of Lewis guns. The Germans, at first with greater ease than they themselves expected, drove through part of them, over the defences so carefully constructed in the winter at Messines. Armentieres was passed on both sides, and the Germans drove towards Hazebrouck twenty miles beyond—a railway centre almost as vital to the northern British front as Amiens was to the whole.

Upon Ludendorff's striking this second series of hammer blows against the British, Haig appealed to Foch, who was now accumulating his cherished reserve. But Foch was determined to use this precious force, if possible, for an Allied counter-stroke, and though he gradually moved two of his French reserve armies up to and north of Amiens, Haig still had to rely mainly on what divisions he could squeeze from his own front. At the moment the 1st Australian Division, from Messines, had just reached Amiens and was marching forward to the Australian Corps. Haig ordered that it should turn round and entrain for the north "to cover Hazebrouck". It was bombed and shelled while re-entraining at Amiens, but reached Hazebrouck on April 12th just in time to reinforce and relieve, that night and next day, part of the British troops, including the 4th Guards Brigade, driven far back and completely exhausted but with their line unbroken after the most intense fighting.[7]

The line was then (April 13th) some five miles east of Hazebrouck. As they had done near Amiens and Hébuterne, the Germans started boldly to continue their advance next day, but met on this sector—and farther south on that of the 5th British Division (just brought back from Italy)—such powerful blows that, in spite of personal urgings from Hindenburg and the Kaiser, Crown Prince Rupprecht, commander of the German armies facing the British, postponed the next punch in this offensive until he could support it with strong artillery bombardment.

Meanwhile a detachment of the French Army had been obtained from Foch, and came in north of the 1st Australian Division. It failed to drive the Germans back; but when, on April 17th, Crown Prince Rupprecht made, after bombardment, his postponed attack, the storms of rifle, machine-gun and artillery fire that met every visible movement caused the Germans finally to abandon their present attempt to reach Hazebrouck, and to confine their effort to seizing the chain of heights west of Messines, beginning with Mount Kemmel.

Deeply though the Germans had now driven into Flanders no high Allied Commander believed this to be a main offensive. Haig believed the principal blow would again be struck towards Amiens, and to make sure in that case of holding the northern gatepost, the Arras position, which the Germans must try to break, he constantly maintained there the Canadian Corps and the

---

[7] See Vol. V, pp. 453-63. With the British about Messines had been fighting several Australian units including the heavy batteries, and heavy trench-mortar company and, south of Armentières, some tunnellers under a heroic leader, Lieut. Neil Campbell, and the 12th Aust. Field Artillery Brigade, which, like its capable leader, Lieut-Col. H. W. Lloyd, succeeded in making an exciting escape from the German infantry (see Vol. V, pp. 439-42). The XXII Corps cavalry (partly 4th L.H.) fought near Kemmel.

Guards division, the forces that he most trusted for counter-attack.

By April 18th signs of a coming attack on Amiens were evident. The Australian dispositions there had changed considerably since the recent attacks on Villers-Bretonneux and Dernancourt. The 2nd Division had relieved the 4th opposite Dernancourt, with the 3rd next to it on the south, between Ancre and Somme, and the 5th brought in south of that again, astride the Somme. But in each case the reserve brigade of the division was detached and sent farther south to string out or support the imperilled line previously held by 5th Army—these extensions reaching as far as the boundary of the French Army.[8] On April 7th the southernmost of the brigades, 5th, was hastily ordered to retake the lost portion of Hangard Wood, but failed after a very gallant effort.

At this stage the whole of the 4th Army's line, from Hangard to the Somme and thence to Albert—about seventeen miles of front—was held by Australians. the southern half being temporarily under the staff of the III British Corps, the northern half under Birdwood and Australian Corps who had relieved the VII Corps. The Australians under III Corps were presently relieved by battle-worn British divisions, for which boy-recruits were now being poured across the Channel by Lloyd George's government which had previously withheld them. Haig directed that the Australian Corps should safeguard the Somme position by continuing to maintain its flank astride of that river, and should also keep one division in support near Corbie to retake Villers-Bretonneux if the Germans captured it.

On April 17th and 18th, the expected activity by the Germans at Villers-Bretonneux began, the enemy drenching with mustard gas the woods and gullies behind

---

[8] It will be recalled that the 4th Division, also, had its 4th Brigade detached at Hébuterne.

that township, thus putting out of action over 1000 Australian and other reserves. It was at this stage that the most famous German airman of the war, Captain Richthofen, was killed by a shot from the ground[9] while chasing a British airman low over the Australian positions near Corbie. At this stage also two battle-worn British divisions relieved the Australians, as arranged, on the III Corps front, from Villers-Bretonneux to the flank of the French at Hangard.

This change had just been made when, in the mist of dawn on April 24th, the Germans attacked with tanks—for the first time in the war, so far as was then known.[10] The attacking force had thirteen of these monsters, clumsier but, it is believed, a little faster than the British tanks. At two points—at Villers-Bretonneux and half a mile farther south—these suddenly bore down in the fog upon the young British infantry and broke through wherever they struck. The German infantry came out of the fog close behind them, and, though met by fire, followed the tanks through, and then rolled up the line to right and left. Before the III Corps staff heard of the attack, Villers-Bretonneux and the dense Abbey Wood behind it were lost, as were Hangard Wood and village, south-west of which the Germans reached the junction of the Avre and Luce.

All the morning the III Corps tried to organise a counter-attack with its British reserves; but except for an advanced battery, which hit back boldly, the most effective strokes were made by tanks. In the first duel that ever took place between these monsters, three British tanks came out and fought with three German ones, causing their final withdrawal from the field.[11] Shortly

---

[9] A summary of evidence which placed this disputed point beyond all reasonable doubt is given in *Vol. V, pp. 693-701.*

[10] As already mentioned a few had been used on March 21st in mopping up surrounded troops.

[11] See *Vol. V, pp. 564-5.* Two German tanks broke down and were later captured. One is now in Brisbane.

afterwards a charge of whippet tanks across the plateau also scattered some German infantry. Brig.-General "Pompey" Elliott's 15th Infantry Brigade, on the flats behind Villers-Bretonneux, stood ready all day to counter-attack, its tempestuous commander fuming and petitioning to be allowed to strike.

But till mid-afternoon no other vigorous step appeared to have been taken, though the Germans were digging in on the precious heights overlooking Amiens and through the difficult Abbey Wood. Then it became known that the III Corps would drive past either side of the township, but with two borrowed brigades—the 13th Brigade (4th Australian Division) under General Glasgow, hurried from north of the Somme, forming the southern pincer, and Elliott's 15th Australian Brigade the northern one. The two brigades would act under the commander and staff of the 8th British Division. On the southern flank a British composite brigade would retake the lost part of Hangard Wood, and British troops would also follow the Australians to mop up.

On the arrival of the Australian brigadiers the British divisional commander told Glasgow that the III Corps commander (Lieut.-General Butler) wished the attack to be made by daylight and from the south northwards; but fortunately Glasgow, like Elliott, was a very strong man.[12] "If God Almighty gave the order, we couldn't do it by daylight," he said; he insisted also that he must strike eastwards, not across the German front. He wished to attack by surprise, without previous bombardment, at 10.30 p.m. After the matter had been several times referred to the Corps Commander, Glasgow agreed to strike at 10.

That hour was too early. As the 13th Brigade assembled south of the woods, it was seen and fired on from

---

12 For this remarkable episode (and the photographs of these leaders) see *Vol. V, pp. 572-7.*

them; and as its advance swept past the woods there was
a crucial moment when, in the open under intense fire
from many machine-guns in the wood, its flank was
stopped. Next to the wood a sergeant, "Charlie" Stokes,
crawling to his platoon commander Lieutenant C. W. K.
Sadlier, urged him to deviate from the strict plan by

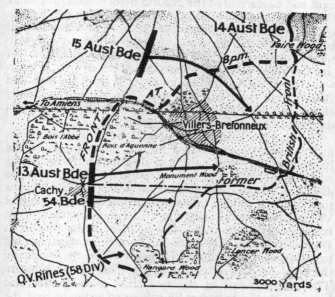

THE COUNTER-ATTACK AT VILLERS-BRETONNEUX,
24th APRIL 1918

entering the wood and bombing the machine-guns out.
Sadlier sent word to his commander and then carried this
out, most audaciously destroying six machine-gun posts
of the 4th German Guard Division,[18] and so quickly that

---

[18] Sadlier was given the Victoria Cross and Stokes, who also led, the
D.C.M.

the whole southern pincer was able to sweep forward in time. North of the township Elliott's pincer, attacking in the same manner though an hour late, swept with wild cheering in a swift onrush around the north of the town, a bright moon and a burning chateau in the township enabling both brigades to find their way, though the 13th had never visited the ground before. Reaching some German guns north of Monument Wood the 13th Brigade could not find the 15th east of the town and had to pull back slightly, leaving a gap, through which ran the railway cutting south of the town, an exit by which part of the Germans eventually escaped. After dawn the town was cleared by Australians entering it from the east and British from the north and west. The gap was gradually closed; and the Allied armies learnt with relief that a dangerous situation had been remedied.

Foch, ever since his appointment as generalissimo, had prudently accumulated French reserves behind the junction of the Allies, and had steadily reinforced Haig, who since March 21st had temporarily lost 9 of his 60 divisions, withdrawn unfit for service. The French now took over the British line almost to the southern edge of Villers-Bretonneux, using for this extension their most famous colonial divisions. On April 26th the Moroccan Division, perhaps the best in the French Army, attempted to recapture Hangard and Hangard Wood by advancing through the Australians in daylight across the plateau. The arrangements of the two allies as to guides and locations, however, were difficult to co-ordinate, and the advance was stopped with heavy loss, as was an Australian attack on May 3rd on Monument Wood.[14] Haig for his part—in order to ensure a firm junction with the French and make sure of Villers-Bretonneux—now caused the Australians and III Corps to change places, the Australians taking over the 4th Army's southern sector (which

---

[14] Here a German officer allowed a formal truce for picking up the wounded, see *Vol. V*, p. 653.

actually their troops now held) from Villers-Bretonneux to the Ancre, while III Corps took over north of the Ancre at Dernancourt.

The Australian infantry—except the 1st Division—was thus, at last, concentrated again under its own corps, now on the right of the British line in France. The troops were bursting with confidence, but—as anticipated—three brigades had, through losses, to be reduced like the British ones to three-battalion strength. Three battalions, formed in 1916 but long since famous—36th, 47th and 52nd—were disbanded to maintain their sister units.

CHAPTER XXV

HOME FRONT, 1917-18

THE breaking up of three battalions was of course due to the fall in recruiting in Australia.

Throughout the First World War recruiting was the paramount issue in Australian home affairs. A previous chapter has recorded how the great losses at Pozières led to the first serious proposal for conscription for the A.I.F., put by Mr W. M. Hughes to the people by referendum in October 1916, and rejected by a majority of 72,476 out of 2,308,603 votes. The Nationalist government, afterwards formed, accepted that result; and when in May 1917 that government faced the normal three-yearly election, Mr Hughes gave his pledge that a vote for his government would not mean conscription; if that was felt necessary, the question would again be put to the people by referendum.

The election was fought on the issue of support for the war effort; and, though the entire sincerity of Mr Tudor and many of his Labour colleagues in their promise to promote victory was unquestionable, the Nationalist government swept the polls. They captured all the 18 seats that were voted for in the Senate, and came back with a majority of 12 in that house and 33 in the House of Representatives.

But despite vigorous changes in the recruiting system—in particular the appointment of Mr Donald Mackinnon, a Victorian barrister high in the public esteem, as Director-General of Recruiting, and the establishment of hard-working State Recruiting Committees—enlistment flagged. The old methods were tried anew; for example, appeals for a "sportsman's thousand" were supported by returned soldiers (including one lately returned after wounds, Captain S. M. Bruce). It was now estimated that only 7000 recruits were required monthly. But, from 4000 in July 1917, enlistments dropped to 3274 in August and 2460 in September. It was estimated that 140,000 fit single men of military age had not enlisted. Mr Hughes repeated a promise given by Mr Fisher, that preference in employment in the Federal public service would be given to returned soldiers. It was also proposed that, if enough men were forthcoming, the original "Anzacs" in the A.I.F. should be given furlough to Australia; but the figure still fell. As a climax came news of the failure of Russia, of Italy's defeat at Caporetto, and of the special steps that had to be taken with the five Australian divisions after their 38,000 casualties at Third Ypres. The voting at the elections had caused many people to think that conscription would be carried, if put to the people again. On 7th November 1917 Mr Hughes announced that a referendum would be held: the people would be asked to vote for a limited scheme of compulsion.

The second Conscription Referendum campaign was as bitter as the first. Minor riots occurred in several towns, including Warwick (where Mr Hughes was hit by an egg—as the Queensland State police would not take action the Commonwealth government was ultimately led to appoint a few policemen of its own). The fiery Irish patriot, Dr Mannix, was foremost in the fight, though future students of this episode may wonder whether his concern was really with Australian interests. Alfred Deakin, then very ill, made, in writing, his last public appeal. On 20th December 1917 the vote was taken. It showed an increase of 94,112 in the "No" majority—and the State of Victoria also had swung to "No". The soldier vote again favoured conscription, but by a slightly reduced majority.

Mr Hughes had publicly stated that, unless the

government was given the power for which it asked in the referendum, he would decline responsibility for the conduct of public affairs. He now, therefore, tendered to the Governor-General his resignation. But as there was no chance of Mr Tudor's being able to carry on the government, and as the only likely and willing Nationalist candidate, Sir John Forrest,[1] was unacceptable to his colleagues, the Governor-General, Sir Ronald Munro-Ferguson, again commissioned Mr Hughes as Prime Minister.

The second referendum had placed conscription outside the pale in any event short of a supreme crisis. Actually, perhaps without many people outside the British government being aware of it, the most dangerous crisis of the war had occurred in April 1917 when the Germans were sinking Allied shipping so fast that the throttling of Britain's war effort within a year seemed possible. The vigorous British counter-measures—convoying, quicker turn-round of shipping, and anti-submarine devices—had overcome that danger. Nevertheless a very perilous position was suddenly presented when, in March and April 1918, Ludendorff almost separated the French Army from the British, and when Haig issued his famous appeal to his men—fighting "with our backs to the wall". No one, on the Western Front or elsewhere, knew what the next weeks or months would bring. While the Allies made their chief appeal to the United States, the British Prime Minister had on 1st April 1918 cabled to each Dominion referring to the extreme steps being taken in Great Britain, including the raising of the military age to 50. He strongly appealed to the Dominions to help by strengthening their forces.

It happened that an investigation by the Chief Justice of Australia, Sir Samuel Griffith, as royal commissioner,

---

[1] This fine old Australian explorer and politician was soon afterwards—flatly against the wish and tradition of Australians—raised to the peerage; he died on his way to England.

had just indicated that the A.I.F. overseas—then estimated at 110,517 in France, 16,908 in the Middle East, and 321 in Mesopotamia—could be maintained by recruiting 5400 men each month. The Governor-General now invited representatives of all sections of the Australian nation to meet at Government House, Melbourne, in conference over the British government's appeal.

The conference, which sat from 12th to 19th April 1918, was profoundly disappointing. It turned into a discussion of grievances, largely arising out of the referendum campaigns and recent industrial disturbances, and ended with a bare vague resolution to unite in securing the necessary volunteers. Recruiting figures rose from 1518 in March to 2781 in April and 4888 in May—doubtless a reflex of the war news, and then steadied at about half the minimum required.

Undoubtedly there was beginning to grow in Australia a section which, believing that the war could not be decisively won, and that in any case Australia was not as intimately concerned as Britain in the issue, favoured an early peace by negotiation. This section was strengthened by the reluctance of governments and economists alike to agree that the draft on private wealth should be made at least as painful as that upon manpower. The demand for "conscription of wealth" was, for once, treated a little seriously when Mr W. G. Higgs, the Federal Treasurer during the first conscription campaign, proposed to finance "Repatriation" by a "levy on wealth" of 1½ per cent on all estates of £500 or more. But the Nationalist government in 1917 dropped the proposal; and in general the argument for "conscripting wealth" was treated by the propertied classes as impracticable or even nonsensical (some contended that it was being achieved by the existing taxation) whereas at least half the public felt it to be well grounded.

The tendency to class war led the Sydney Labour Council in May 1918 to resolve that the greatest service to be rendered to soldiers and their families was to stop the war. As Mr Tudor, Mr Ryan, Premier of Queensland, and a number of other Labour leaders were helping the war effort, a further split in the Labour party now clearly threatened. To stave off this rupture there was held in June at Perth a conference, which tried to arrange a compromise to stave off this breach. (Among the Tasmanian delegates was the editor of the *Westralian Worker*, Mr John Curtin, then aged thirty-three.) The compromise, calling for a move towards peace, was to be voted on by the Labour party by November 1st. As will be seen later, long before that time arrived deep disagreement as to the proposed method had shown itself.

Internally, except for the bitter campaigns over conscription and for occasional turbulence in industry, Australia had come smoothly, indeed almost prosperously, through the war. The clean and able administration of Senator Pearce and the professional advisers brought the Service departments through with general credit. It is true that muddle and some dishonesty in Egypt during 1915 had to be remedied by sending a business man, Mr (later Brig.-General) R. M. McC. Anderson to reorganise part of the base there; and in Australia a case of grave defalcation in the Army Pay Department led to inquiry by Royal Commission, and to the appointment of an excellent Board of Business Administration under Mr George Swinburne; but no other major or even minor scandal of Army administration was revealed. The record of the naval staff and department was equally clear, but criticisms of financial transactions by politicians in the sale of a wireless station and the purchase of small ships forced the resignation of the Minister (Mr Jensen).[2]

In the stress of war the Australian Constitution had proved admirably elastic. The power of the Federal Parliament to control "defence" had for the time being

---

[2] *See Vol. XI, pp. 277-85.*

transferred to it supreme power in almost every sphere. By 1917 in all the most important activities of government and of the main industries, the war-time machinery was working in its finally developed form. The boards, commissions and other authorities were for the most part running smoothly; the real problems had largely been solved during the earlier stage by the committees and other makeshift organisations which had to face, explore, and grapple with them, generally without any precedent whatever to guide. Since Britain's purchase of the wool clip, the wool industry had, by War Precaution regulations, been working under the Central Wool Committee (Chairman, Sir John Higgins), which handled over 7 million bales, worth £160 million. By an admirable arrangement the wool-broking firms, with their great stores and many experts, handled the whole business of sale for the governments instead of for their clients— valuing, instead of selling; the purchase money from England was distributed according to their appraisements. The surplus of this wool, belonging to the British government when the contract expired in 1920, was sold by "Bawra" (the British-Australian Wool Realisation Association) by 1924; the profit (over and above the 15½d. per lb. already paid by Britain) was nearly £70 million which the British government justly but generously divided between itself and the growers.

In the wheat trade, when it became clear that, without shipping, a tragic deadlock would follow the huge harvest of 1915-16, the dilemma facing the States drove their governments to take action. They first proposed to the Federal government the setting up of a chartering organisation. Next, when it was seen that ships could not be obtained, they pressed for some authority to purchase the wheat. The Federal government agreed, and Federal and State Wheat Boards were set up. The Federal Board (Manager, Mr H. A. Pitt, of the Victorian Treasury), fixed the rate of advances, made all oversea sales, settled the prices to the millers, chartered ships and allotted them. The State Boards provided storages, paid growers and railway freights, sold to Australian millers, and made shipping arrangements. The sale of the 1916-17 crop to the British government, already mentioned, disposed of 3 million tons at 4s. 9d. a bushel f.o.b. Mr Hughes's subsequent efforts to sell to the British Wheat Commission the 1917-18 crop ended, in July 1919, with the sale to it of another 1½ million tons. The Australian wheat pool continued until after the marketing of the 1920-1 crop, and was followed by voluntary State pools organised by the growers on a co-operative basis.

The export of metals was controlled by the Federal government through the establishment, in September 1915, of the Australian Metal Exchange (Chairman, Mr W. L. Raws); shipping through the Commonwealth Shipping Board (Chairman, Mr H. B. G. Larkin); in the latter part of the war price-fixing was carried out (as explained in Chapter XVII) by a Necessary Commodities Commission under a Minister for Price-fixing.

The problem of rehabilitation of servicemen on return from overseas began during the Gallipoli Campaign. The first intention had been that, as after the South African War, invalids, after discharge from hospital, should be cared for by means of patriotic funds, voluntarily subscribed by the public. The Federal Parliament's War Committee first watched over the need for assisting soldiers in their rehabilitation, "War Councils" also being formed in every State to provide artificial limbs and vocational training, find work for those who could take it, help them to start or resume their occupations, and see that dependants were cared for. The former Labour Prime Minister, Mr J. C. Watson, was appointed organiser of this work with Mr D. J. Gilbert as secretary. As there were then at least twenty funds for the benefit of Australian soldiers, and much confusion as to the object of these funds, a special one was started for "repatriation" (a term that was generally and wrongly used in Australia for "rehabilitation"—a circumstance which led to some confusion and delay). To cap some very large private gifts, the Federal government contributed £250,000. It was understood that settlement of ex-soldiers on the land should remain the business of the States, the Federal government, however, contributing to the cost.

By the beginning of 1917 it was evident that the task of rehabilitation would be far too big to be left to private effort. Accordingly in April 1917 the Fund was closed and a Repatriation Commission established under one of the ablest ministers, Senator E. D. Millen, as Minister for Repatriation. Sir Nicholas Lockyer, one of the finest of Australian administrators, became Comptroller of "Repatriation". But, here as elsewhere, by the time the ultimate Commission was established the task was a fairly settled one. The State War Councils had grappled with many of the principal difficulties when they provided ex-soldiers or their dependants with the first "£80,085 for furniture and fittings, £15,802 for tools etc., £52,603 for establishing small businesses, £68,187 for general farming purposes, and £43,856 for the provision of homes".[3]

---

[3] See Vol. XI, p. 823. For the vagueness of the term "repatriation" see p. 834.

CHAPTER XXVI

A CRUCIAL SUMMER—THE DIGGER'S PART

On the Western Front the beginning of May 1918 found the British Army very heavily strained after sustaining on the Somme and Lys the main weight of the German offensive. Foch, like Haig, believed—and rightly—that Ludendorff's intention still was to destroy the B.E.F. One-sixth of its divisions had been so shattered that the task of reconstituting them had, for the moment at least, been given up; and another tremendous blow was certain to fall somewhere in the west as soon as the Germans could assemble the strength for it.

Haig's 51 effective infantry divisions (10 of them from the Dominions) had been reinforced by 13 French ones. On the much longer French front Pétain had 90 French divisions, reinforced by 1 British, 4 American and 2 Italian ones—but of these French divisions 34 were in the zone taken over since March 21st from the 5th British Army. (That is to say the French had helped the British with 47 divisions.) In the north were 12 Belgian divisions, making a total for the front of 173 Allied infantry divisions against 206 German ones. Of the Allied divisions 57 were at the moment in reserve; of the German—78; 4 other American divisions were assembling or training in France, and the advanced sections of 5 others were arriving.

Ludendorff's next stroke was almost daily expected; but at this stage, most disturbingly for Pétain, the French staff found itself almost entirely without information as to where was the bulk of the German reserves. Foch arranged that some tired British divisions should go to the quiet French front on the Aisne in return for French divisions placed on or behind the British front. Haig still kept the Canadians in the Arras region which he believed to be the crucial section of his line.

While the threat of the next offensive thus hung over the British and French Armies, the Australians and New Zealanders, after beating back the German attack wherever they had met it, were in overflowing spirits, and refused to leave the opposing Germans alone. This resulted in very interesting developments. Wherever the ground gave any freedom of movement, these Dominion troops began to pester the enemy, trying to waylay his patrols and cut out his posts—to wage, indeed, a ceaseless "private war" on the Germans opposed to them. This was supplemented by a series of set attacks, generally planned to capture sections of the new front line from the Germans before they had fully established it. Often, when the Germans tried to bridge with new trenches the gaps so made, these new trenches would be successively wrenched from them.

The artillery and air force also contrived to inflict bombardments and bombings intensely harassing to the Germans; and gas, in hundreds of drums bursting at one time, was frequently discharged in surprise operations by special companies of British engineers. But it was the "private war" of the infantry which, in the four months April-July, gave a strongly marked character to the campaign on the Australian and New Zealand fronts. Recalling the methods by which German industry before the war was "capturing" the trade of most British countries, the Diggers called these tactics "Peaceful Penetration". But before describing them in more detail the narrative must turn for a moment to the very great events that were their background.

At the middle of May the constantly awaited German attack had not yet been delivered, nor was there anywhere a clear sign of its imminence. On May 15th Foch expressed the opinion that "the enemy must be in some difficulty". Ever since becoming generalissimo, Foch had been eager for the moment when the reserve, which he had at once begun to build up, would enable the Allies to strike. He now arranged with Haig to plan a joint Anglo-French attack, to be launched from in front of Amiens, co-operating with a French thrust from the south—a plan which Foch himself had envisaged since early in April. The British drive would be launched from the Australian Corps front, the Canadian Corps being brought down from Arras and the two Dominion Corps then striking eastward, after which the northern French pincer would strike south from the ground thus gained. By Haig's direction a plan was very secretly worked out by Generals Birdwood and White (I Anzac) and their chief, General Rawlinson (4th Army). Foch meant to deliver this blow if the German delay allowed him; but before the 4th Army's plan reached Haig, Ludendorff had struck.

The blow fell on May 27th, most unexpectedly, against the French on the Aisne, and partly on the sector in which the tired British divisions were reinforcing them. The surprise was almost complete, and it caught the French ill-prepared. Pétain, always best on the defensive, had long before tried to dispose his armies in depth so as to meet any great attack at the second line. The German bombardment of the forward area would thus be largely wasted, and the attacking infantry, split by the French outposts, would be disordered before reaching the real line of resistance.

But the stubborn reluctance of a conservative army commander (General Duchêne) to give up any ground had thwarted this wise order, and it is said that this resistance was encouraged by the belief that Clemenceau also disapproved of Pétain's policy. When it was too late to insist, Pétain had had to give way. Consequently the French tried to hold their opponents at the forward system. The German bombardment shattered them there, and the advancing Germans in three days drove the thin remnants and the reserves thirty-two miles towards Paris, as far as the Marne River, fifty miles from the capital.

"This lamentable rout", as Clemenceau afterwards called it, came as a stunning shock to the French people and government; but in some respects it rendered easier the co-operation of Britain and France. Many of the more unthinking French people had been blaming the British for the disasters caused by the German offensive. The British seemed to them simply to have retired wherever hit. The attitude of the French populace was widely resentful. Villagers glowered, and even spat, as the "Tommies" passed by, and the French leaders became increasingly masterful in their dealings with their English colleagues. Foch and Clemenceau, who knew that Lloyd George had deliberately held back reinforcements from Haig during the past winter, suspected that the British government was

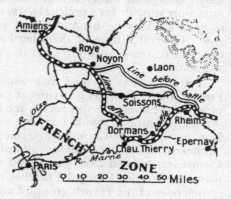

unwilling to bleed its people as white as the French government had been forced to do. "The British are trying for an excuse to escape efforts," Clemenceau told the French President, "and want us to do the same and leave to the Americans the burden of continuing the war. This also is to some extent the tendency of (the French) parliament." He was determined to fight any such tendency, if it existed; and he greatly irritated the

British leaders by probing into questions of British man-power. Lloyd George was stung into inviting him to send a representative to investigate British action on the spot. Foch and Clemenceau continually urged that the British should reconstitute the nine skeleton divisions, and eventually were assured that this would be done, though two of the divisions would have to be reinforced with "B" class men, unfit for hard fighting.

Many French people and some—though not all—of their generals had believed that the reverses suffered by the British could not have happened to the French. Consequently the shock of May 27th resulted in a marked change in their tone. Not that the tension disappeared. Lloyd George in conference sometimes replied with retorts more suitable for a political party room. Clemenceau complained that he became "more and more insufferable"; General Wilson on the other hand, warned Lloyd George that the French intended to "take us over, body and soul".[1]

French leaders resented that, without informing the French, Lloyd George's government provided extra shipping for the Americans in return for a promise that the infantry so shipped should carry out their training in the British zone; while Lloyd George complained that it was "unheard of" that, without consulting the British, Clemenceau should have transferred to the Allied command at Salonica General Franchet d'Espèrey, who, as commander of the French group of armies on the Aisne, had just "suffered the most serious defeat of the war".

The Aisne thrust—in which the Germans succeeded better than they had hoped—was, as Ludendorff and other German writers make clear, merely intended to draw thither the Allies' reserves and permit a final crushing blow against the British. Foch, with his respon-

---

[1] For these controversies see *Vol. VI, p. 449n*; and for the general problems of this critical time. *pp. 151-6, 163-83, and 442-54.*

sibility for the whole front, realised this; but Clemenceau, Pétain and most other Frenchmen, with the bias inevitable among allies, were now convinced that the supreme German stroke would be towards Paris. Their conviction was strengthened when on June 9th the Germans tried to broaden the western side of the Marne salient by thrusting from Noyon, a plan which the French had detected and now foiled after heavy fighting.

Later, when the Germans were found to be preparing still another great attack, farther east on both sides of Rheims, the idea that the enemy was aiming at Paris seemed to have been proved. On the other hand Foch knew that Ludendorff was also preparing, in Flanders, another offensive "in very great force". He was puzzled by the divergent direction of these two projected thrusts: why should Ludendorff launch two blows neither of which would help towards the strategic object of the other? He concluded that the stroke towards Paris had a political, not a strategic, intention. Clemenceau and Pétain thought him "hypnotised by the north", but he steadily refused to denude the British front of its reserves. His position with his own Prime Minister and government was for a time shaken by what they considered his wrong-headedness.

But, however the French, British and Italian leaders might differ between themselves, they all spoke with one voice when trying to get the forces of the United States into action without delay. Here the Americans were faced by a problem already encountered by Australians and Canadians. In order the earlier to obtain military assistance, the French and British leaders, military and political, naturally wanted the American troops, training or trained, to be put in the line beside their own experienced troops and under their experienced commanders. The American commander-in-chief, General Pershing, however, foresaw that, if he agreed to this, his army would

30—os

never be brought together. He also learnt by experience that, apart from any question of prestige, however well the citizens of different nations may have combined in certain gendarmeries or other truly international forces, it was an entirely different matter to place the soldiers of one national army, with different arms, organisation and training—and still more different loyalties and social and historical outlook—under the control of soldiers of another. Pershing wanted to train his divisions as self-contained American divisions and eventually send them to the line as such.

Nevertheless there was no doubt as to the need; and when the double blow of the great Michael attack and the Lys offensive had forced the British Army to place its back to the wall, President Wilson, on being directly appealed to over Pershing's head, agreed—within limits—to ship infantry without artillery and transport as fast as the British could provide the ships; and, though Pershing at first held out, the batteries of argument concentrated on him in the Supreme War Council (urging that "the war would be lost" if he did not agree) resulted in his concurring in a modified arrangement, which was afterwards extended for several months.

As a result, from May 1918 onwards American troops poured into France at a rate hitherto unknown. In January there had come 13,000, in February 17,000, in March 19,000; April brought 24,000, May 33,000, June 41,000, July 54,000, August 61,000, September 71,000. In May they began to appear behind the British front, and a company of the 6th Engineers was sent to help fortify the Villers-Bretonneux sector. The backs of some Australians bristled when these arrived, but the American fighting troops were not boastful. "Are you going to win the war for us?" asked a Digger in the back area. "Well," came the quick answer, "we hope we'll fight like the Australians." At this stage, when the A.I.F. and A.E.F.

met, their comradeship was marked. Brig.-General C. M. Wagstaff, who spent half the war with the Australians and the other half with the Americans, said

the two forces are the nearest thing possible to one another. Their discipline is founded on the personal influence of the officer over his men . . . and provided that they get the right class of officer there is no trouble whatever. . . .

On one principle the American leaders were especially definite (as they explained to the Australian war correspondents who visited them in February 1918): they did not wish to throw their troops into heavy fighting until thoroughly trained. They realised that their forces were inexperienced, and believed that premature employment of them would lead to confusion and much loss, which training could avert. Yet they recognised that a situation might arise when, in the interest of their side, it would be necessary to use half-trained troops and face those losses. That was, however, a situation which they particularly wished to avoid.

All this while, through all the German strokes, Foch had never ceased to plan his Allied counter-stroke. He had hoped that the Allied armies in Salonica and Italy would strike in co-operation with him. But when he and Clemenceau had succeeded in inducing the Italian commander, Diaz, to agree to attack the Austrians, the Austrians on June 14th struck first, across the Piave River; and though they were quickly defeated—the Piave descending in flood behind them—all chance of effective Italian co-operation vanished.

But Foch's plans for his own preliminary counterstroke were now well advanced. Early in June he issued to Pétain orders for the French part in it—now to be launched against the protruding German salient on the Marne. The plan was kept secret even from Haig and Pershing, but Foch asked Haig to prepare similar thrusts against the ground won by the German offensives on the Somme and Lys. Haig was eager to turn to the attack, but his response had to be conditional, because he was conscious, all the while, that Ludendorff was keeping a picked force of twenty-five to thirty divisions resting and training behind Crown Prince Rupprecht's front in Flanders, apparently with the intention of finally crushing the British Army as soon as British reserves were sent elsewhere.

At this stage there occurred a very puzzling development. On June 26th the German communiqué reported a speech in the Reichstag by the German Secretary of State for Foreign Affairs, Herr Kühlmann, in which he said: "Complete victory by force of arms is not possible to either side," and also blamed Russia rather than England for having caused the war. This speech was so inconsistent with the German attitude up to that moment that its true reason was suspected even by unskilled observers on the Australian front.[2] German accounts now make clear that Ludendorff was, for once, induced to resort to a method of attack which a generation later became a stock weapon of the Nazis—a "political offensive".

This had a typically German origin. One group of its sponsors comprised German liberals headed by Prince Max of Baden, who believed that Germany could never induce the Entente to make peace so long as Belgium was held as a vassal State. The German cause at this time seemed especially in need of moral foundation since a pamphlet written by Prince Lichnowsky, the former German ambassador in London—blaming Germany for the outbreak of the war and showing how Sir Edward Grey had striven to avoid it—reached the Allies and was published by them, with great effect on German morale. A promise to free Belgium would place the German war aims on a better foundation. But Ludendorff could be

[2] See Vol. VI, p. 444.

induced to offer justice to Belgium only on the understanding that the professed moderation was a sham, intended not to bring about peace but (so it was put to
Ludendorff) "to sap the enemy's determination and pre-
judice his war efforts". In other words it would be a
moral attack, aimed at weakening the Allies' home front,
and through this their fighting front, in preparation
for a physical attack. With that intention Ludendorff
authorised it. That it was well-timed the anti-war movements then on foot in Australia as well as other countries
showed. But it was abruptly and unskilfully initiated by
Kühlmann; Ludendorff in a rage immediately countermanded it, and every Allied soldier from Foch downwards was cheered by the evident German confusion.

Throughout these anxious months, while the French
now received blow after blow; while the exhausted
British—all too steadily for Ludendorff—recovered from
their early reverses; while the Americans, raw soldiers but
greatly inspiriting in their cheerfulness and their numbers, poured into the back areas—through all this time,
as was said at the beginning of this chapter, three sectors
of the British front were constantly in lively activity—
those held by the Australians and New Zealanders. From
the afternoon of April 5th, when a party of three Australians under a corporal saw and defeated the last German movement at First Villers-Bretonneux (and perhaps
the last in the whole Michael offensive) to the time in
July when this activity, together with that of General
Mangin's army on the French front, nonplussed several
German army commanders and forced a change of tactics
upon Ludendorff himself, the Anzac fronts provided a
quite extraordinary proportion of the news in the British
communiqués. In Australia, as in England, the general
impression was that these picturesque troops were receiving more than their due share of publicity; actually,
however, of the activities recorded during those months

they were responsible for a larger proportion than the communiqués themselves disclosed.

The first of the incidents referred to above is a good example of them all. When the Germans were stopped at Villers-Bretonneux on April 4th, their army commander ordered a continuance of the attack next day. The project was hopeless, but as part of it, at 2 p.m., a German officer with thirty men was sent to penetrate along the flats south of the Somme to Vaire, the next village beyond Hamel (which the Germans had taken on the 4th). On these flats was a post of three Victorian privates under a corporal (D. A. Sayers); they were protecting a machine-gun, which had been thrust out across the river during April 4th by Elliott's brigade on the urging of a machine-gun officer (Lieutenant H. G. Hanna) who saw the chance of taking the Germans that day in flank.

The four Australians watched the thirty Germans until the latter party perceived them and began to set up its own machine-gun. Sayers at once directed two of his men to fire from the front while he and the third man crept down a drain leading to the flank, with the intention of cutting off the party. On reaching a position commanding the rear of the Germans, Sayers and his companion opened rapid fire as did their two mates, and seven Germans were hit. Seeing the German officer now ordering his men to retreat to a sunken road, where the Australians could not have reached them, Sayers and his men charged. Sayers, firing from the hip, shot the officer. The surviving Germans fled, except two of the wounded who were brought in as prisoners.

This incident was one of the first of a string of similar enterprises which began to happen almost daily, and sometimes many times in a day, on the Anzac fronts at Amiens, Hébuterne and Hazebrouck. The activity broke out spontaneously, without the troops in any one of these sectors at first being aware that similar enterprises were occurring in the others. In early summer the most favourable ground for such sorties was that occupied by the 1st Australian Division between Strazeele and Merris in Flanders, where ditches and hedgerows gave the Australians a chance to creep around enemy posts almost at will. There in May and June German posts were taken almost daily. At the end of June the commander of the 4th Bavarian Division, Prince Franz of Bavaria, told his men that the state of affairs was a disgrace to the division; the climax there came on July 11th when, after that division had been relieved by the 13th Reserve, the Australians on a single morning cut out post after post until they had captured—without the higher authorities on their own side or the German knowing anything about it—over 1000 yards of the 13th Reserve Division's front line, taking 120 prisoners (including 3 officers) and 11 machine-guns.

On the Somme conditions were not at first so favourable to Peaceful Penetration, but the success was, in the end, even more important. It was here that, on the hot, drowsy morning of May 18th, guessing that the garrison of a certain troublesome German outpost was asleep, Lieutenant A. W. Irvine of the 18th Battalion quietly walked over with his scouts in broad daylight and brought back almost the whole garrison alive—21 men and an aspirant officer and their light machine-gun, without having an Australian hit, and without other German posts being aware of it until the company commander went his round that night and found this post gone. As the summer went on and tall crops covered the ground, the opportunities became excellent; and after the capture of Hamel, the tempo of Peaceful Penetration at Villers-Bretonneux so increased that, when Rawlinson and Haig set the Australian Corps the task of seizing a considerable part of the plateau east of the township, the required ground was actually captured by Peaceful Penetration before the day set for the operation. Here the 41st German Division reported to its troops:

At 11 a.m. on July 8th the enemy penetrated the forward zone of the 108th Division by means of large patrols without artillery preparation, and at 10 p.m. on the same day with artillery preparation. He occupied the trench where our most advanced outpost lay and apparently captured the occupants, comprising fifteen men. The larger part of the forward zone has been lost.

The German army commander stated that the removal of this outpost "was not even noticed" at the time by the other German troops. The German Command accordingly twice changed its method of holding the front, but it was still unable to stop this infiltration.[3] Both in north and south German infantry complained that these sectors, which their Army command had described as "quiet", were dreaded by the troops. More than one regiment records its relief when its "bloody tour" there "had found its end".

As already mentioned the activity on the Australian fronts was frequently increased by the carrying out of sharp, carefully planned attacks. On the Somme these began on May 4th-9th with thrusts by the 3rd Division along the high triangle between Somme and Ancre towards Morlancourt. At a cost of 260 casualties the new front line of the Germans, and 170 prisoners, were captured. The Germans hit back on May 14th, but after penetrating were cut off, losing 50 prisoners. On May 19th the 2nd Division, continuing the nibbling about Morlancourt, took the hamlet of Ville on the Ancre in a cleverly planned attack. Pincers struck from either side of Ville (the northern one bridging the river) and seized positions north and south of it. The village between them was then quickly cleared, largely through the dash of some men of the famous raiding party of the 23rd Battalion led by

---

3 For the details see *Vol. VI, pp. 376-81*; and for the details of July 11th and 12th, *pp. 411-22*.

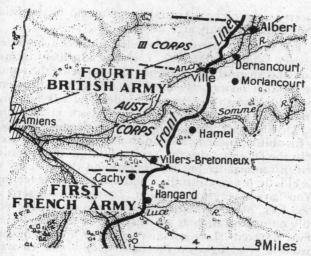

THE AMIENS FRONT, 1st MAY 1918

its keen signalling officer. The British armies being now
called on by Foch for a number of minor offensives,
General Birdwood decided to seize the new German forward system protecting Morlancourt.

While this blow was being prepared General Haig
decided to re-establish the 5th Army. Its former leader,
General Gough, had been relieved after the March offensive. Although his conduct of the Passchendaele campaign—which was fought largely against his advice—and
in the 5th Army's retreat in 1918 seems to have been
generally wise and spirited, glaring earlier mistakes had
robbed him of the Army's trust, and Haig was probably
right in dismissing him. Haig now offered the 5th Army
to Birdwood; and when Haig's chief-of-staff (Lawrence)
pointed out to Birdwood that if he remained with Australian Corps he would block the promotion of Australian

officers to the highest Australian command in the field,
Birdwood reluctantly accepted.

For the new corps commander Birdwood hesitated
between White and Monash. Each had a brilliant record,
marked with great successes; but Monash being the senior
the recommendation favoured him. Haig, also, had long
favoured Monash's promotion; indeed he was first and
foremost in doing so. From the first parade of Monash's
3rd Division in France, Haig had been deeply impressed
by his ability; indeed, most unusually for him, as he rode
from the field that day this seemingly cold, unexpressive
British commander put his arm around the shoulder of
the elderly Jewish-Australian, and said with some feeling:
"You have a very fine division; I wish you all sorts of
good luck, old man." From that impression—except possibly on one occasion at the very end of the war[4]—Haig
never wavered. His constant support of Monash indeed
throws a vivid light on the inaccuracy of the constant
implication since made by Lloyd George that Haig was
prejudiced against civilian soldiers and tended to suppress them.

Birdwood took with him to 5th Army General White
as chief of its general staff, Brig.-General T. A. Blamey
becoming chief of the corps staff under Monash. All the
main posts on that staff except two were already held by
Australians, and in this respect Monash made no change.
Then or soon after, when the War Office found positions
for the two last British divisional commanders in the
Australian Corps (Walker and Smyth),[*] Birdwood recommended for the vacancies three outstanding Australian
leaders: for the 1st Division, Glasgow, perhaps the
strongest commander in the force; for the 2nd, Rosenthal,
one of its most vigorous and loyal fighters; and for the
3rd Gellibrand, its finest trainer of young leaders. Bird-

wood, though transferred to 5th Army, remained administrative commander of the A.I.F.—a circumstance to which some influential Australians overseas raised strong objection.[5] He took with him besides White a small administrative headquarters of the A.I.F. including Brig.-General T. H. Dodds.

These changes did not interrupt the blows struck by Australian Corps. On June 10th, now under Monash, the 7th Brigade seized the latest German front system at Morlancourt capturing 325 prisoners at a cost of 400 Australian casualties. The German divisional commander informed the 2nd German Army that in a few minutes "a complete battalion had been wiped out as with a sponge"; he warned it that the same thing might happen again on a larger scale. And it did, perhaps more quickly than he expected.

Having advanced north of the Somme Monash was at this time particularly anxious to advance south of the river also, and seize Hamel; but it had been judged that the task would use up—for a time—one division, and General White had been anxious to keep the corps intact for more important tasks. Its strength was falling and an epidemic of influenza—though not of the deadly type that occurred three months later—was sweeping through all armies. It so happened that at this stage the new pattern "Mark V" tanks arrived in France. The commander of the Tank Corps, Brig.-General Hugh Elles, was very anxious to use these effectively before the Germans produced tanks to meet them. He knew that since the First Battle of Bullecourt the Australians had refused to rely on tanks, and he therefore invited Monash and Blamey to see the new machines in exercise.

On seeing the new tanks both Monash and Rawlinson conceived the thought: "Here is the means to lighten the

---

[5] They unsuccessfully tried to get Mr W. M. Hughes to make Monash administrative commander of the A.I.F., and White commander of the Corps. *See Vol. VI, pp. 194-7 and 212-14.*

loss in an attack on Hamel." At the same time, hearing that the 33rd American Division was to train with his army, Rawlinson leapt at another plan: here was the means of increasing Australian manpower for the operation. Monash welcomed the suggestion. The commanders of the II American Corps and the 33rd Division were thoroughly agreeable. It was arranged that a composite Australian division under General MacLagan (4th Division) should make the attack. Ten companies of Americans

would be attached by platoons to the Australian battalions for actual fighting experience. July 4th was the earliest day on which Monash could put in the brigades adjudged to be most suited for the task; and as it was also Independence Day it was chosen for the attack.

No less than sixty tanks were to be employed on a front of 7000 yards. Monash at first adopted the plan of Brig.-General A. Courage of the 5th Tank Brigade. By this the tanks would advance ahead of the infantry, virtually taking the place of the artillery barrage. The Australian infantry commanders, however, objected to this plan; they knew for certain that their troops could go through with the barrage, but of the tanks they were still uncertain. Accordingly Monash insisted that the tanks must advance immediately behind the barrage, with the first waves of infantry, and under general control of the higher infantry commanders.

At the last moment, on July 3rd, came news that by some misunderstanding the inclusion of the Americans had been arranged without the direct permission of General Pershing, and that six companies—if not the whole ten—were to be at once withdrawn.[6] The distress of the six companies themselves was so evident that they received sympathy from all sides. Eventually—because it was too late to recall any more—the last four were allowed to go forward.

This was Monash's first operational task as a corps commander—the attack on June 10th having been planned under his predecessor—and it was prepared for with the extreme thoroughness and elaborate care that characterised his command. In successive conferences at which every interest concerned was represented and every problem listed in Monash's agenda, the arrangements were discussed between those who must carry them out; Monash stood out, among all leaders met by the A.I.F., as a master of lucid explanation.

The attack was a brilliant success. The Australian infantry had been hurriedly trained with the tanks, and though at several points—one of them vital—the machines were late and the infantry had to go through without them, the general performance fulfilled the Diggers' highest expectations. The new tanks were slightly faster than the infantry, and could reverse, turn and manoeuvre quickly, and their crews never failed to take them where required. In addition the few carrier tanks, bringing up supplies behind the advancing line, did in a few minutes the work then ordinarily done by hundreds of infantry-men. The tank crews on their part particularly noted (to quote their commander) "the superb morale of the Australian troops, who never considered that the presence of

---

[6] The incident is described in *Vol. VI, pp. 277-9.*

tanks exonerated them from fighting, and took instant advantage of any opportunity created by the tanks". The infantry walked enthusiastically behind machines marked with the infantry's own battalion colours.

Within two hours the impression left by Bullecourt was reversed. From this time the British Tank Corps looked to the Australian Diggers above all other infantry in France, and the Diggers never ceased to welcome the chance of working with the tanks. Their only complaint, on this occasion, as constantly before, was: "Why did we stop before reaching his guns?"[7]

On the same day, by way of diversion, the 15th Brigade made a spirited advance beyond Ville. In the two actions the Australians suffered 1400 casualties (the Americans, who fought well though greatly hampered by inexperience[8] lost 176). Over 1600 Germans were captured and useful space gained. For the first time ammunition was dropped to Australian troops by parachute, the invention of Captain L. J. Wackett of the 3rd Squadron, Australian Flying Corps, which was constantly with the Australian infantry.

The Hamel success, coming at an anxious moment, was welcome news for the Supreme War Council, then sitting at Versailles, and brought the Australians a personal visit from the old "Tiger", Clemenceau;[9] Mr Hughes and Sir Joseph Cook had visited them a few days before. But the main result of Hamel was that Monash's careful arrangements furnished the model for almost every attack afterwards made by British infantry with tanks during the remainder of that war.

In the north, set attacks had been made by the Australians at Merris and—in co-operation with the British—

---

[7] The answer, of course, was that in attacking on a narrow front deep penetration was too dangerous.

[8] Pershing was right; the experiment, though valuable, was too like teaching a boy to swim by throwing him into the "deep end".

[9] He spoke to them in English (see Vol. VI, pp. 334-5).

at Meteren. They now culminated with a brilliant success in which Merris was surrounded, before the Germans knew it, by Lieut.-Colonel Wilder-Neligan's battalion, the 10th, advancing between two screens of artillery fire laid on and beyond the village. On the Somme the shaking of the enemy from his front lines at Hamel allowed Peaceful Penetration to proceed at a rate hitherto unknown. The Monument Farm, its orchard, and the plateau beyond Villers-Bretonneux were thus seized. These gains were rounded off by the capture, on July 17th, in a set attack, of the rest of the ground required there. Partly owing to these activities the enemy on this front was obviously deteriorating; but at this stage there issued sudden orders that Peaceful Penetration must, for the present, cease.

The reason was that on July 18th there came a great change in the war. On July 14th the Germans, as expected, attacked on both sides of Rheims. This time Pétain's prudent policy in defence had been better carried out. East of Rheims the Germans, after fighting their way through the French outposts, found that the real defence was much farther back. On reaching it they were disastrously repelled. West of Rheims where Petain's principle was less thoroughly followed,[10] the situation became tense. In this crisis, in his anxiety to obtain reserves, Pétain, who, under Foch, controlled the arrangements for Foch's coming counter-attack, began to modify them and sought a two days' postponement of it. Foch at once overruled him, and that night Pétain was able to assure him that the counter-blow would be delivered on July 18th as arranged.

Foch's counter-blow came as a stunning surprise to the German high command. The attack was made by 13 French and 4 American divisions (each of these with

[10] See Vol. VI, pp. 450-1. Some 4th L.H. (XXII Corps) were engaged here.

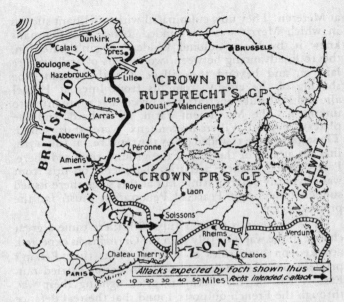

Attacks expected by Foch shown thus ⇒
Foch's intended c-attack ➡
0 10 20 30 40 50 Miles

nearly twice the infantry strength of a French division), covered by 2100 guns and closely followed by 325 French tanks. Towards the vital point, Soissons, the great French fighter, General Mangin, struck with the *élite* of the French Army, the Moroccan Division, flanked by the 1st and 2nd American and two good French divisions. Mangin's French troops had for weeks past been harassing the Germans with small set attacks, much like those of the Australians. The enemy had thus been overstrained, and by nightfall the French were within three miles of Soissons, through which town went the only railway into the big German salient on the Marne.

At that moment Ludendorff was in Flanders discussing the forthcoming main attack, on the British, for which the transfer of troops from the Aisne had already begun. This transfer, except of the heavy artillery, was at once stopped—Ludendorff now had to move divisions the other way. The plan of attacking the British was dropped. The Germans began to withdraw from the Marne salient. Their 1918 offensive had failed. Ludendorff, like Micawber, could only hope for something to turn up.

But Foch had steadily held to his plan of a double thrust against the enemy. Of late he had favoured Haig's striking in the north, to regain the Lys coalfields. But by July 16th Haig himself, after considering the several alternatives, strongly preferred the British stroke that Foch had previously suggested, along the Somme. Rawlinson and Monash also were pressing for an attack here, partly because the Villers-Bretonneux plateau was very suitable for tanks, but mainly because the ceaseless Peaceful Penetration by the Australian infantry had greatly strained the Germans there and apparently prevented them from thoroughly fortifying their front. Some Germans recognised this. Their 2nd Army commander, von Marwitz, urged upon his men there—

Troops must fight. They must not give way at every opportunity and seek to avoid fighting; otherwise they will get the feeling that the enemy is superior to them.[11]

That feeling, as he probably knew when writing this, existed among the Germans here; and through the numerous prisoners it was known to the British commanders. Accordingly the plan worked on by Rawlinson, Birdwood and White in May was resuscitated and expanded. In using it Haig aimed at surprise; probably Cambrai had opened his eyes to the possibilities of this. The Canadian Corps was secretly transported from Arras to the forward area close behind the 4th Australian Division, which had taken over some miles of French line south of the Australian Corps, and which remained there

---

[11] For some of the German accounts see *Vol. VI, pp. 482-3.*

31—os

till the small hours of August 8th holding the front line
as a screen for the Canadians. The 1st Australian Division
in Flanders was ordered south to strengthen Australian
Corps. Four hundred and thirty British fighting tanks
were assembled, to lead the three stages of the attack; and
all three divisions of British cavalry, to carry it beyond the

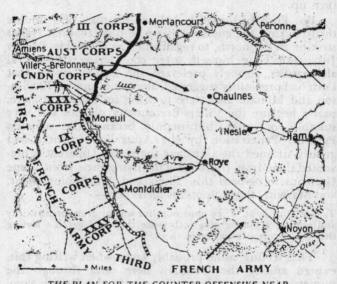

THE PLAN FOR THE COUNTER-OFFENSIVE NEAR
AMIENS, 8th AUGUST 1918

objectives if the infantry broke through. Three British
infantry divisions were available for Rawlinson's reserves.

The first stroke, six to seven miles eastwards, was to
be delivered by Rawlinson's 4th Army (Canadian, Australian, and III British Corps); but it was to be followed
immediately by a south-eastward thrust by the 1st French
Army, next on the south. To help the surprise, the British

466

would have no preliminary bombardment; this time only aeroplanes, flying low before dawn, would be relied on to drown the noise of the assembling tanks; the massed artillery would first break silence when the tanks and infantry attacked. But the 1st French Army (which was temporarily placed under Haig) had few tanks. It would, therefore, rely on preliminary bombardment but its guns would open only when the British infantry started. Even its left flank, therefore, would advance a little later than the British; its right would strike on the second day, and the 3rd French Army, farther south, probably on the third day, this army attacking north-eastwards. Both Foch and Haig insisted that their armies must try to break through—Rawlinson, Debeney and Monash had all, at first, favoured a limited advance. The methods for co-operation of tanks, aeroplanes and infantry were largely those worked out by Monash at Hamel.

This new Somme offensive, which was ordered by Foch at a conference of himself and the three national commanders, Pétain, Haig and Pershing, on July 24th, was not intended to be the final effort; he pictured it merely as beginning the Allied offensives by clearing important railways—others had been cleared on the Marne and would be cleared at St Mihiel near Verdun. Then, in the autumn, might come the supreme thrust from several sides; but no leader then believed the war would end before 1919.[12]

While Foch's first Allied offensive (as distinguished from his counter-offensive on July 18th) was thus preparing, there occurred several anxious moments. The first was on August 4th, when the leading Canadians had already arrived, and some posts of the 4th Division were raided by the Germans and several prisoners taken. The prisoners probably knew nothing of Haig's plans, but in any case—as German documents note—they were staunch,

---

[12] Haig, however, on July 18th told Rawlinson that it *might* do so. See Vol. VI, p. 1053n.

and divulged nothing of value. On August 6th a much more serious danger occurred in the capture of 282 British troops whose divisions had just relieved the 5th Australian Division in the triangle between the Ancre and Somme. Here the 5th Australian Division had on the night of July 29th captured yet another system of German defences at Morlancourt. The stroke was so clean, 128 Germans, 36 machine-guns and two trench-lines being taken, that the enemy did not strike back until he had brought up a fresh Württemberg division.[18] By then the Australians had been relieved by the III British Corps, which was to attack here north of the Somme on the northern flank of the Australians. Among the British now captured were some who knew of the plans, but the Germans learnt nothing, and most of the ground had been recaptured before dawn on August 8th when the great attack was to go forward.

The third incident occurred towards sunset on the 7th when a German shell set fire to a concentration of carrier tanks hidden on the northern edge of Villers-Bretonneux ready for the attack at dawn. Many tanks and their loads were burnt or blown up, but night fell without any sign that the enemy suspected the impending blow.

---

[18] In the Australian War Memorial at Canberra is a figure dressed in the uniform of a man of the 29th Battalion, still caked with the mud of this fight and torn by the barbed wire.

468

CHAPTER XXVII

THE CLIMAX—AUGUST TO OCTOBER, 1918

In the small hours of August 8th a dense fog gathered. The infantry, cavalry and tanks for the great attack were at the time going forward to their assembly positions,[1] with unseen aeroplanes droning above and bombing the German forward area to drown the noise of the tanks. At the boundary of the Canadian and Australian Corps, on the Amiens-Chaulnes railway skirting Villers-Bretonneux, a sharp German bombardment descended, and lasted for half an hour. Some men thought the enemy had heard the tanks, but actually the German guns were covering a raid, which, as it happened, entered some forward trenches just abandoned by the Australian infantry in straightening its line for the "jump-off". The fog was still dense when at 4.20 a.m. the secretly massed artillery opened its creeping barrage and the 18th and 58th British Divisions north of the Somme, the 2nd and 3rd Australian Divisions south of the river, and the infantry of the Canadian Corps on their right, south of the railway, advanced.

The first stage was carried out entirely in dense fog, made even denser by the inclusion of white smoke-shell in the barrage. Battalions, companies and tanks cleverly maintained for the most part their right direction, passing pockets of bewildered Germans, who sometimes fought but often surrendered at the first hint of attack from the rear. A British officer wrote in the 4th British Army's war diary that the Australian Corps had in the preceding months gained "a mastery over the enemy such as has

[1] For Monash's ingenious scheme of assembly see *Vol. VI, pp. 491-3*.

probably not been gained by our troops in any previous
period of the war".

In the fog this infantry had to do little more than find
its way. Two or three tanks ran upon mines, but there
were few mined patches and those insignificant; by 7.30
the German front system was completely broken and, for

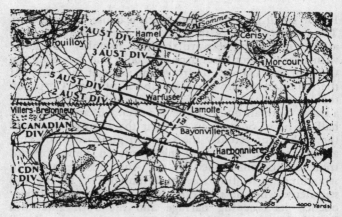

*THE ROLE OF THE AUSTRALIAN CORPS IN THE ATTACK
OF 8th AUGUST 1918*

*(The 1st and 2nd Canadian Divisions made a similar
advance, while the 3rd Canadian Division carried out
a difficult operation in crossing the Luce. The III British
Corps attacked north of the Somme.)*

the first time in Australian experience, most of the
enemy's field artillery had been overrun and captured.
The 2nd and 3rd Divisions dug in while the 5th and 4th
came up and assembled mainly in a valley close behind
them, ready to go forward to a second objective lying
generally beyond another valley two miles ahead.[2]

---

[2] Each Australian division attacked with two brigades. In the case of
the 2nd and 3rd these passed through their third brigades, which were
holding the old front line.

The artillery positions from which the barrage had so far been thrown were now almost out of range, and a proportion of the batteries had pulled out of them; through the fog came the jingle of trace-chains as the teams brought their guns forward to help the battalions and brigades in the second and third stages. Through the mist also were heard the panting engines and creak of the tanks earmarked for those stages. At 8 o'clock the fog began to thin; and at 8.20, when the 5th and 4th Divisions, and fresh Canadian brigades south of them, took up the advance, the sun began to come through.

A little later the mist suddenly cleared, and for a moment all eyes on the battlefield took in the astonishing scene: infantry in lines of hundreds of little section-columns all moving forward—with tanks, guns, battery after battery, the teams tossing their manes (among them the famous British Chestnut Troop, fast friends of the Diggers); from far in rear streams of cavalry and transport, all steadily pouring forward along the plateau south of the Somme where the German line had lain.

The sight brought one swift change. Many of those German gunners whose batteries had not yet been reached could now see the tanks and immediately blazed at them direct. Very many of these heavy machines were put out of action, but the infantry flowed on almost without check, and soon overran most of the guns. On the left flank, however, in the broken ground north of the Somme the British III Corps could not keep up with the time-table; and German gunners firing from the dense woods there, and from Chipilly Peninsula which jutted out from the northern side in a hairpin loop of the river, now shot with impunity into the flank of the 4th Division[3] streaming past on the exposed slopes south of the Somme. By one of the finest feats of the day the 4th Division, with only a brief check on the left, rushed the valley at Mor-

---

[3] For an account of this spectacle from the German side see *Vol. VI*, *pp. 572-3*. Chipilly was just across the Somme from Cérisy.

court, on the second objective, and there, among German bivouacs, stores and canteens, captured many hundreds of the enemy's support and reserve troops; and went on in good time with the third stage of the advance, although the Germans on the northern bank now swung their guns and machine-guns round and fired into its flank and rear.

The third stage was to have been carried out by infantry transported in huge passenger-carrying (Mark V Star) tanks. Most of these failed by reason of their unwieldy bulk and the exhaustion of passengers and crew.[4] But the infantry unaided reached the greater part of the intended line—the old outer line of the Amiens defence system, very little short of the old Somme battle-field of 1916.

By this time the cavalry had found its opening—first one brigade in the Australian sector at Harbonnières, and then two cavalry divisions on the Canadian front. They seized a considerable part of the old Amiens line, captured the 11-inch railway gun (now at Canberra) with which Amiens had so often been shelled;[5] and they scared the German troops at several villages beyond the objective and made many prisoners. But as they tried to scour the plateau they were quickly stopped by Germans rallying with machine-guns, and were soon held at, or forced back to, the Amiens defences. On the other hand one of the features of the day was the confusion caused by sixteen swift armoured cars which, breaking through before the infantry reached the second objective, raced eastwards along the Roman road towards Péronne and thence fanned out along side roads, firing into German head-quarters, billets and transport, spreading such panic and confusion that for several hours a great part of the foremost Australian front troops looked out over an apparently empty country.

---

4 For this most interesting experience see *Vol. VI, pp. 588-91.*

5 Its huge carriage was used for technical purposes in World War II.

The Canadian and French attacks had gone as well as the Australian—the co-operation of Australian and Canadian Corps being superb,[6] as was that with the cavalry, tanks and air force. Though the Allies' control of the air was never quite as complete as during the First Somme Battle, the German air force was for most of the day prevented from interfering or patrolling. By evening, when orders were given to continue the thrust next day, it was certain that a tremendous victory had been achieved, far beyond any previous success of the British Army in that war. For fifteen miles south of the Somme the German front had been swept away—in some parts about noon there seemed a possibility of breaking through towards Péronne. If such a chance existed the higher commanders were not aware of it till hours after it had passed—and the afternoon and night were spent in digging in.

Yet the blow struck had been a shattering one. The 4th Army had attacked with 7 infantry divisions in first line, and 3 in second, against 6 German front-line divisions, and had taken 13,000 prisoners and over 200 guns, and the French had taken 3500 prisoners.[7] Since Foch's stroke in the south Ludendorff had reorganised this front: two fresh divisions and some additional artillery had been put in. He had hoped to be able to hold and even to strike again somewhere. But, he says, "while still occupied with these thoughts the blow of the 8th of August fell upon me. . . . August 8th was the black day of the German Army in this war. . . . The 8th of August put the decline of that (German) fighting power beyond all doubt. . . . The war must be ended."[8]

The drive was next day continued to the south-east,

---

[6] See Vol. VI, pp. 532-3, 552, and (for next day) p. 629.

[7] The Allies had 2650 guns against some 500; 450 British tanks against none; and 1900 aeroplanes against 365.

[8] Ludendorff, My War Memories, 1914-1918, Vol. II, pp. 678, 679 and 684.

the cavalry and Canadians, with the French farther south, making the main advance, the Australians thrusting out a northern flank for them. In three days of difficult, and badly co-ordinated, advances, supported at first only by a few batteries some of which galloped into action as in Wellington's time, and by a dwindling number of tanks which, being totally unscreened, were hit like nine-pins by German guns on Lihons heights, the southernmost Australian troops (now 1st[9] and 2nd Divisions) thrust to and over those heights.

As the left was hampered by slow progress of the III Corps on the north bank of the Somme, Monash's command was extended thither, a composite division known as Liaison Force being formed by the 13th Australian Infantry Brigade and the 131st American Regiment.[10] On the night of August 10th General Monash attempted to win ground astride the Somme by sending out along two main roads, a few miles north and south of the river, two columns, which were then to close in as pincers. A few tanks accompanied them, these being intended to scare the already shaken enemy. The northern column, moving across country while two tanks raced clattering up and down the main road on its flank, was thoroughly successful, the overstrained Germans retiring in panic through Bray, and the Australians taking the Etinehem peninsula. The southern column, however, advancing with its tanks along the cobbled Roman road towards Péronne, ran into newly posted Germans. The leading tanks were literally outlined with the sparks of machine-gun bullets, and the thrust ended in sharp loss. Here it took two more days of difficult fighting by in-

---

[9] The 1st Division had arrived at the battlefield on August 8th, and was hurriedly thrown in on August 9th; as it arrived late Brig.-Genl Elliott, at a moment's notice, flung his 15th Brigade into the difficult task of supporting the Canadian flank (*Vol. VI, pp. 621-9*); the 8th gamely took Vauvillers.

[10] The story of the seizure of Chipilly spur there by an Australian patrol of only six men, co-operating with British and Americans, is told in *Vol. VI, pp. 650-3.*

fantry, with little artillery support, to secure the intended ground about the village of Proyart.

Meanwhile the 3rd French Army, striking from the south-west on August 10th, found the Germans already pulling out of the "Michael" salient. But there was never any break-through; and, as Ludendorff rushed reserves to the Somme region, the Allies found themselves pushing against constantly increasing resistance, especially when they began to reach the trenches of the old Somme battle-field. Thrusting among these the French and Canadians approached Roye, and the Australians and Canadians Chaulnes.

Haig now resolved not to waste opportunity by butting where the enemy was strong; by his stubbornness he succeeded in converting Foch and obtained his consent to a stroke farther north. The blow previously intended by Foch, and ordered for August 15th, was accordingly cancelled. For the next week, on part of the Australian front, Peaceful Penetration along the old Somme trenches superseded the set attacks. Since the first great stroke the Australian right and the Canadians had driven—by sheer infantry fighting—another five miles, making twelve to fourteen miles in all. The casualties of the five Australian divisions in the whole offensive were 6000, mainly incurred on August 9th-12th.

The Australian Corps was now up against a strong German front, lining the woods and folds bordering another long valley running south from the Somme through the villages of Chuignes and Herleville. The Canadian Corps, at the wish of its commander, Lieut.-General Sir A. W. Currie, returned north to the region so well known to it at Arras. The 4th Army was to be stationary for a week, until after August 21st, on which day the next big stroke would be delivered by the 3rd Army south of Arras. Next day the III Corps (of 4th

Army) at Albert would join in, as would the 3rd Australian Division, which had relieved Liaison Force north of the Somme. On August 23rd the rest of the Australian Corps south of the Somme would join the attack, and capture the valley and slopes ahead.

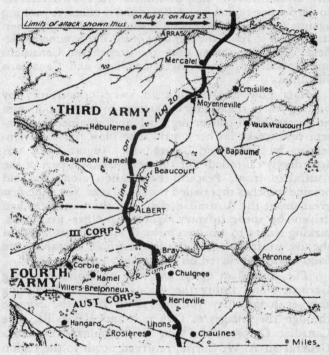

THE BATTLE OF ALBERT, 21st-23rd AUGUST 1918

(*The two short arrows mark the flanks of the first day's attack, and the longer arrows those of the third. The fight that day south of the Somme was known to Australians as the Battle of Chuignes [or Proyart].*)

During the quiet week preceding these blows General Monash, on August 18th, attempted to seize the new German front at Herleville by an attack with light forces, but it was too strong for such methods. For a few days the 17th British Division—and, after this attack, the 32nd—reinforced the Australian Corps front, and for one day a Canadian division also was under Monash's command, which at this time was larger than that of some armies.

The 3rd Army's stroke on August 21st reached most of its objective (on the northern edge of the old Somme field). Next day the 3rd Australian Division duly seized its objective north of Bray. Farther north the III Corps advanced well, but in the afternoon was driven far back, leaving the 3rd Australian Division with its flank unprotected, and with the Germans far behind it. But the 3rd Division guarded its own flank and held on.

The 1st Australian Division was thus enabled to carry out its full plan on the following day (August 23rd), striking hard south of the Somme with the 32nd British Division on its southern flank attacking Herleville. A few tanks helped. Despite stubborn opposition the difficult woods and valley at Chuignes and Herleville were overrun. Of 8000 prisoners taken by the 3rd and 4th Armies that day the 1st Australian Division captured 2000, itself suffering only some 1000 casualties. (This most successful blow is perhaps best known by two minor incidents—the capture in this valley of the 14-inch German naval gun, which became a famous relic of the fight; and the most effective single feat of Peaceful Penetration. In this, after the southernmost battalion of the 32nd British Division had been repelled by the enemy, Lieutenant L. D. McCarthy, whose company of the 16th Battalion was supporting the British flank, himself—followed by his sergeant and, later, by two British soldiers—attacked from the flank, killed a number of Germans, took forty prisoners, and handed over to the British 700 yards of captured trench.)[11]

Farther north the 3rd Army almost reached Bapaume, for the intended capture of which the New Zealand Division was now brought up.

Haig had decided that the time had come for commanders, in their plans, to take risks which would have been imprudent a month before. But he thought it unnecessary for the 4th Army yet to do so, since the thrust now being begun by the northern armies would automatically force the Germans on the Somme to retreat. Monash, however, felt that the capacity of the Australians for thrusting was being underrated, and (as he himself wrote) he seized on a phrase in the orders "to justify an aggressive policy". There followed a week in which, while the 3rd Army struck towards Bapaume and (on August 26th) the 1st Army farther north joined in the offensive, the Australians tried by Peaceful Penetration to force the Germans back across the old Somme field.

The 1st Division had been relieved by the 2nd and 5th when, early on August 29th, the Germans retired. The two divisions followed them, fast and hitting hard, right to the Somme where, near Péronne, the river comes in sharply with a right-angled bend from the south, forming with its stream and marshes an obstacle to the Australian advance. The Germans had been ordered to hold a line across the right-angle bend of the river but the 2nd Division rushed them off it and seized the whole of the western bank—a circumstance to which Ludendorff ascribes the events that followed. Meanwhile the 3rd Divi-

---

[11] See Vol. VI, pp. 742-3. McCarthy received the Victoria Cross.

sion day after day had forced its way along the slopes and valleys north of the river, seizing Bray, Susanne and Curlu.

The staff of the 38th Battalion, after seventy-one hours' continuous work was just settling to sleep when Brig.-General W. R. McNicoll arrived with the order to push on immediately to Cléry, at the actual river bend; after dark on the 29th, at the end of eighty-nine hours of almost continuous effort,[12] the battalion

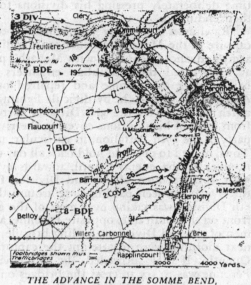

THE ADVANCE IN THE SOMME BEND,
29th AUGUST 1918

(The broken white line shows the German position across the angle. Mont St Quentin is at the north-east corner of the map.)

reached the eastern edge of that village.

Monash was thus enabled to make one of the few effective manoeuvres within Australian experience on the Western Front. He conceived that he might surprise the enemy by transferring his main strength to the northern side of the Somme, and then rushing the height of Mont St Quentin which, rising two miles beyond the river bend, and looking down on the old turreted, ram-

---

12 For details of this feat of endurance see *Vol. VI, pp. 791-5.*

parted and moated city of Péronne at its southern foot, was the recognised key of that position. He was at this time deliberately pressing his divisions to the limit of their endurance.

Rawlinson laughingly gave him leave to attempt the capture of the Mount, and changed the direction of the army's advance to conform with Monash's plan. Working at high speed the Australian engineers built several bridges over the Somme and repaired others. During August 29th and 30th, by difficult fighting on the hills north of the river, the 3rd Division thrust the enemy from most of his positions covering the river bend. One party of the 37th Battalion, in particular, under Captain Towl, helped to oust and hold back all day an astonishing number of the enemy[13] until, towards evening on the 30th, the first men of the 2nd Division from south of the river were seen passing close around the bend. The 5th Division was taking over most of the 2nd Division's front on the south side, opposite Péronne, and these were men of the 2nd Division's leading brigade (the 5th) who next morning were to attempt the capture of Mont St Quentin. If they succeeded, the 5th Division opposite Péronne was to try to cross the bridges on its front and work round the north and east of the city.

The 3rd Division drove the last Germans out of Cléry just in time to let the 2nd Division pass. But Germans in strength were holding the lower knuckle immediately beyond, from which tomorrow's attack was to be launched. With all their skill, the leading companies of the 20th Battalion (5th Brigade) after dark had to clear these trenches for a mile in depth, using bombs and rifles alone, before they could reach the starting point for next day. It was well into the night when, after capturing 120 prisoners and 11 machine-guns and routing out many more, they reached the starting line. A mile beyond the

---

13 See Vol. VI, pp. 797-802. At some previous stages, as often in March 1917, the 13th L.H. Regt (Aust. Corps Cavalry) had been used to keep touch.

intervening flats lay the famous Mount to be attacked
at dawn.

The troops, who had now been fighting for twelve
hours and moving for the greater part of two days and
nights, were, this time, given an issue of rum before
action—the usual Australian practice was to issue it after
action. Their number was few, most Australian battalions at this time
having only 300
men available for
action. The attack
was to be made by
two battalions
(17th and 20th)
going straight for
the hill and ignor-
ing on their right
the woods and
strong fortress of
Péronne (the two
other battalions
following in close
support and re-
serve). The troops
being so few, the

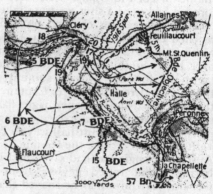

*Plan for capture of Mont
St Quentin.*

company leaders decided that the best chance lay in
making a noise as they attacked, "yelling", as Captain
E. T. Manefield urged, "like a lot of bushrangers".

At 5 a.m. on August 31st, as the grey sky began to
show behind the Mount, which was dimly visible across
a gentle dip, the Australian field artillery laid its fire
on certain targets ahead, in the first place along 2500
yards of one of the old trench-lines which, with their
belts of rusty wire, seamed the depression and the up-
slope beyond.[14] The cheering platoons at once ran

---

[14] The unfinished Nord Canal had not yet been dug across most of
this sector.

32—os

481

into crowds of Germans, who seemed bewildered and
quickly surrendered—indeed in many cases they were
simply pushed to the rear with their hands up, leaving
their machine-guns lying on the ground. They were from
one of the best divisions of the German Army, the 2nd
Guard, which had just been sent up to relieve the overstrained garrison. "It all happened like lightning," says
the history of the Guard Alexander Regiment, "and before we had fired a shot we were taken unawares."

The Australians charged on and, by the time they
reached the main trench-line in the dip, the face of the
Mount ahead of them was covered with Germans fleeing
over both shoulders of the hill. The Australians swept
on up the slope and over the summit, routing the German
supports and reserves there. Captain H. T. Allan seeing
that the woods on the open right flank, which were garrisoned, constituted an extreme danger, turned his company thither and thrust half-way to Péronne. In rear, the
19th Battalion crossed the Somme by Cléry bridge, which
Australian engineers had saved and had repaired despite
barrages that raised geysers from the marshes. And
General Rawlinson, as he shaved that morning, received
the astonishing news that the Mount had been captured.

The thin 5th Brigade could not keep its full gains;
part of the 2nd German Guard Division in reserve drove
back the scattered troops from Mont St Quentin village
on the crest. The history of the Guard Alexander Regiment cites one of its actions this day as proof "that even
good Australian troops were by no means invincible if
strongly attacked". But the Australians held on just below the summit. The 3rd Division had advanced near
Bouchavesnes farther north. Next day (September 1st)
the 6th Brigade, passing through the 5th, seized, at a
second attempt, the summit; and the 14th Brigade (5th
Division) which also had been brought round through
Cléry, captured the woods north of Péronne and, pressing
on during a short-lived German panic, crossed the moat

and took the main part of the town. An attempt to pass around the north of Péronne was stopped by withering fire from the ramparts. But on September 2nd the 7th Brigade (2nd Division) drove beyond the Mount, the 15th (5th Division) seized the rest of Péronne, and the 3rd Division made ground on the northern flank.

This brilliant action, in which, without tanks or creeping barrage,[15] the Australians at a cost of 3000 casualties dealt a stunning blow to five German divisions, coincided in time with a thrust by 3rd Army and the Canadians towards Cambrai, and gave Ludendorff additional cause for retiring from the line of the Somme below Péronne, where he had previously intended to hold on. He could now only retreat to the Hindenburg Line, which, however, also had been pierced by the British northern thrust (not far from Bullecourt). The 4th Army followed across the Somme, keeping an eye open for the usual booby traps. A new British Corps headquarters, of the IX Corps, now took over the southern part of the Australian line held by the 32nd British Division.

The German Command had decided to hold not only the Hindenburg Line but the three lines formerly constructed by the British to face it and captured by the Germans on 21st March 1918. By September 11th the Australians had won the first of these lines by Peaceful Penetration; but the second and third of the old British lines were too strong, and on September 13th Rawlinson obtained leave to prepare a full-dress attack on them. The British War Cabinet—owing to the London police strike and similar unrest—was anxious lest Haig might increase its troubles by incurring heavy loss in attacking the Hindenburg Line without success, and Haig had been warned of this. But he himself felt that now, if ever, was the time to overcome this

---

15 The artillery laid down heavy bombardment on points well ahead of the attack, and boldly thrust forward some of its batteries.

great obstacle. The coming action against the old British lines would test the German Army's morale and help to decide whether the true Hindenburg Line, beyond them, could be wisely attacked.

THE BRITISH FRONT AT THE START OF THE ADVANCE TO THE HINDENBURG LINE, 5th SEPTEMBER 1918

(*The old British lines, five miles deep, ran past Vermand and Hargicourt.*)

Very few tanks were available, but Monash had some dummy ones built by the pioneers and dragged to points where they could be seen. Over the first and second stages there would be a strong creeping barrage thickened with smoke-shell. But the infantry was asked to exploit any German disorganisation by thrusting farther and seizing the so-called "outpost" line of the actual Hindenburg defences—a very strongly wired line, constructed a mile west of the St Quentin Canal behind which the three main lines lay. This final task would involve, on the Australian right, a further advance of a mile, assisted only by a few detached guns. Monash doubted whether his troops could succeed in it but asked their commanders to make an "honest" attempt.

The attack was launched by 4th Army and part of the 3rd at dawn on September 18th. Heavy rain fell while the divisions were marching to their starting tapes, and dense fog arose. The rain caused intense anxiety to some of the headquarters staff, yet the attack was an overwhelming success. As on August 8th, in the first stage many Germans were passed and cut off in the fog; the main difficulty of the attacking infantry was to keep direction, but they were by now highly skilled in this; for such troops the fog was actually an assistance. In the second stage of the advance, which was covered by barrage and smoke-shell, but not by fog, the 1st Division, on the left, carried, in the rush of its well-handled groups, not only the second objective but the third. On the right, the infantry of the 4th Division, during most of that sunny day, worked its way across the open valleys up to the dense wire protecting the Hindenburg "Outpost" Line. The left of this division then worked round through the trenches captured by the 1st Division, and gradually bombed its way into its objective.

On the southern flank the 46th Battalion had been stopped by dense wire in front of a strongly held position. It was to resume the attack covered by a barrage at 11 p.m. Immediately before the barrage, a short, heavy rainstorm broke out. With this double assistance the two attacking companies of the 46th—160 men—got through the wire and seized their third objective, capturing 550 Germans and routing hundreds more. At the same time the 14th Battalion struck down these trenches from farther north. Dawn of the 19th found a great part of the Australian

line looking down on the St Quentin Canal and on the
Hindenburg Line beyond.

The attack had generally succeeded. The ten assaulting divisions had taken 12,000 prisoners and over
100 guns. But of these the two Australian divisions captured 4300 prisoners and 76 guns at a cost of 1260
casualties to themselves, and they had thrust far beyond
either of the corps on their flanks. In reporting the battle
to Haig, Rawlinson mentioned that captured German
officers had said that their men would not now face the
Australians.

The battle completely achieved one object—it showed
the German soldiers' morale as exceedingly low, certainly inadequate to resist a vigorous attack by skilful
troops. The 6800 Australian infantry engaged took 4300
prisoners. The attack on the Hindenburg Line was therefore authorised. The time had now come for those concerted allied offensives which Foch had envisaged
for the autumn. The Americans had already, on September 12th, eliminated the acute St Mihiel salient, near
Verdun. The 1st American and 4th French Armies 100
miles south-east of the Australians would now strike towards Sedan; the 2nd British Army and Belgians, 70 miles
to the n rth, would drive towards Ghent; and the 4th,
3rd and 1st British Armies, followed by the 1st French
Army, would attack between St Quentin and Douai. These
hammer-blows would begin on September 26th and follow daily, the 4th Army's attack on the Hindenburg
Line near St Quentin coming last, on September 29th.

In the 4th Army's attempt the Australian Corps would
be charged with what Haig called the "main attack",
that is, with thrusting through the Hindenburg Line at
the point where the St Quentin Canal ran in a tunnel
beneath the hills between Bellicourt and Vendhuille, and
therefore offered no obstacle (except possibly as a deep
shelter for reserves). The land here, in effect, formed a
bridge, three and a half miles wide, over the canal

obstacle, and here the Germans naturally expected attack, and had thickened their defences. As the certainty of their expectation ruled out most elements of surprise, a two days' bombardment to destroy the defences before attacking them could safely be planned.

But two difficulties remained. Most of the tunnel sector, to which the Australian Corps was to be transferred, lay farther north than the advantageous "jumping-off" position seized by the Australians on September 18th. The Hindenburg Outpost Line had not yet been captured there by the British III Corps; though many efforts had been made since September 18th,[16] the northern half of the British front there lay half a mile short of the intended starting line.

The second difficulty was that most of the Australian divisions were recognised as having, since March 1918, been worked to the limit. As already mentioned, many battalions after leaving behind their "nucleus" (a quota that had to be left out of every battle, to assist, if necessary, in reconstructing the unit) could put only 300 men into action. Monash had told his generals before Mont St Quentin that he intended so to work them, and he realised that he now had only two divisions—the 3rd and 5th—fit for action, with the 2nd perhaps becoming available a week later. Also, the Australian Prime Minister, Mr Hughes, feeling that it was inadvisable to allow the Australian Army to be whittled away before the peace settlement, had adopted for Australian ends a decision of Imperial War Cabinet, and insisted that, before Australian divisions were used in any important offensive, he must be consulted. Sir Henry Wilson apparently knew of his decision, but—probably for reasons of secrecy —it was ignored before August 8th. Hughes, however,

---

[16] One of these attempts, for which an Australian battalion, about to be relieved, was put back into the fight, occasioned in one company the only serious mutiny before action that occurred in the A.I.F. The rest of the battalion went in and carried out the battalion's whole part.

then intimated to Monash that he held him personally responsible for having the corps withdrawn to rest before the weather broke, at latest by October 15th.

The Australian strength had also suddenly been diminished by the "Anzac Leave" which Mr Hughes had managed at this stage to obtain for the original Gallipoli troops—two months' furlough in Australia. The shipping, on which this had been conditional, had been suddenly found by the British shipping control, and Birdwood insisted that the chance must not be missed. At the same time came another order from Birdwood that the battalion strength must be increased by breaking up a battalion in each of eight brigades to reinforce the sister battalions. This—which was an ordinary incident in the British Army, whose battalions in the field were associated with regiments at home—meant, for the A.I.F. battalions, extinction; throughout their services the men had lived for their battalions, and they now refused to disband.

There followed an extraordinary episode in which their officers left them but the N.C.O.'s and men for several days carried on, with specially strict discipline, the functions of their battalions in camp—except disbandment. They asked to go into the next fight, then impending, in their old units, and Monash obtained Rawlinson's agreement to this. One battalion, the 60th, had answered the appeal of its beloved brigadier, "Pompey" Elliott, and disbanded.[17]

. In any case, with only two divisions comparatively fresh, the corps was much too weak for so formidable a task as the breaking of the Hindenburg Line. But at this stage Rawlinson asked Monash whether he would undertake it if reinforced by two American divisions—27th and 30th—the only two which Foch and Pershing had now left in the British zone. Monash realised that

---

[17] The others were disbanded a fortnight later when the divisions were at rest. For the whole incident see *Vol. VI, pp. 935-40.*

these divisions were only recently trained; but he knew the Americans to be keen troops, and their divisions were probably at least three times as strong in infantry as his own.[18] Their numbers and vigour would, he believed, make up for their lack of experience, and he gladly accepted the offer. Maj.-General G. W. Read, commanding the II American Corps, of which these were the infantry, most generously agreed to Monash's taking, for the time being, the active command.

The 27th (New York) Division accordingly took over most of the British III Corps front (which now became the left sector of Australian Corps) and the 30th American Division took over the right sector. Two "missions" composed of experienced soldiers from the 1st and 4th Australian Divisions, 210 officers and men in all, were attached to assist them. Monash, in the most elaborate plan of his career—which at conferences he explained with the care and lucidity for which he was outstanding among leaders—arranged for them to attack both the main Hindenburg Line on the ground above the tunnel and the second, or le Catelet, line a mile beyond. There, after the usual pause for bringing up part of the artillery, the 5th and 3rd Australian divisions would pass through them. Monash counted on the skill of his own troops to carry the attack without creeping barrage another two or two and a half miles, through the third (or Beaurevoir) line of these defences—which was also the last complete German line (though the Hermann Line through Valenciennes and Le Cateau and an Antwerp-Meuse Line through Sedan were in preparation).

Tanks would support each division's thrust at each stage. The barrage would be thickened with smoke, especially on the flanks, so that troops and guns might safely pass over the tunnel sector, when it was captured,

---

[18] One American company sent up to train with the 24th Bn at Villers-Bretonneux in July had more men in the line than the whole Australian battalion (*Vol. VI, p. 510*).

and then fan out to seize the canal north and south of it. The southern corps (IX) would attempt to cross the canal, but Monash had not asked for this, and did not expect it to succeed. In the preliminary bombardment there would be used the first consignment of British mustard-gas shells to reach France—30,000 rounds.

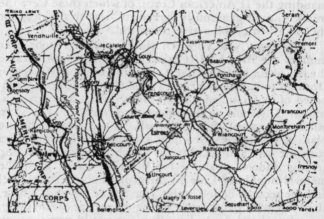

THE HINDENBURG LINE SYSTEM AT BELLICOURT BEFORE THE ATTACKS OF 27th AND 29th SEPTEMBER 1918
Showing the position of the British (and American) line.

The 27th American Division on arriving at the front was put to seize the intended starting line which the British had been unable to capture. In a preliminary attack on September 27th a regiment of this division managed in parts to reach this line but could not hold it. The usual reports—from air and ground—that many of its troops were still ahead, made its commanders reluctant to throw upon this ground the creeping barrage for the coming offensive. Consequently it was arranged that just before the main attack the 27th Division's infantry, without barrage but with the help of extra tanks, should try to reach the starting line—half a mile distant—in time to go on thence with the other divisions.

With this immense disadvantage, and in thick mist increased by smoke, the two American divisions attacked at dawn on September 29th. For years afterwards—until the histories of the 27th Division and of the Germans facing it were written—what then happened was unknown. Early reports said that an American battalion had been seen entering Gouy, a mile beyond the tunnel. But the Australian divisions, coming up at 9 a.m. to carry on the second stage, ran into German machine-guns firing through the fog—on the left this happened before even the Hindenburg Outpost Line was reached; on the right, just beyond Bellicourt. As the Americans were erroneously supposed to be somewhere beyond, the support of artillery was not at first allowed; and with Lewis guns and bombs the Diggers in three days' hard fighting had to make good the first stage of the advance.

It is now known that what happened on both September 27th and 29th was that many American companies, very strong in men but with half their officers detached at schools of instruction, could not find their way through the fog.[19] Some of the tanks, then and later, ran upon an old British minefield of which they should have been warned. Most of the all-too-few American officers were quickly killed or wounded; and the troops after having penetrated parts of the front enemy line—and in some cases on September 29th having gone well beyond it— were driven back or isolated and pinned down by German counter-attacks.

On the right, at Bellicourt, in the main offensive on September 29th, the 30th American Division seized the southern entrance of the tunnel, Bellicourt village, and

---

[19] Incidentally it should be stated that the previous capture of plans of the Hindenburg Line—a fine feat by a British armoured car commander on August 8th—had no recognisable influence on the result of this fight: the legend that it did so, which led to his reward by Lady Houston, was due to a "stunt" by a popular newspaper.

part of the Hindenburg Line and of the canal, but was then stopped. The right of the 5th Australian Division, pressing through with some of the tanks, struck out for miles to the south-east, meeting part of the IX British

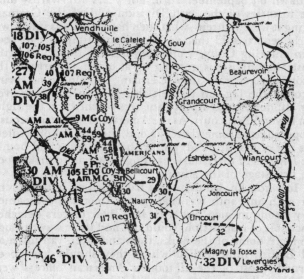

THE BATTLE OF THE HINDENBURG LINE,
29th SEPTEMBER 1918—POSITION AT 3 p.m.
The Australian battalions had then taken
up the attack through the Americans.

(*Where "Regt", "Regts", or "Eng. Coy" is printed, the units are American. Nos 29 to 59, standing alone, indicate Australian battalions.*)

Corps, which had brilliantly succeeded in crossing the canal and was pressing on to its distant objective.

By October 1st the Australian infantry in tough piece-meal fighting had completed the capture of all but the third system of the Hindenburg Line on its front. The American infantry, parts of which had fought among the Australians, had by that night been relieved; and now the 2nd Australian Division took the place of the 3rd and 5th, and on October 3rd broke through part of the third Hindenburg Line from Beaurevoir southwards—a feat already achieved by the British IX Corps at one point farther south. There being one Australian brigade, the 6th, still almost fresh, Monash put it in on October 5th to capture Montbrehain, a most brilliant but expensive, isolated action[20]—the last fought by Australian infantry in that war. That night the Australian infantry handed over the line to the II American Corps, now brought in again under its own commander, and was withdrawn almost to the sea coast for a rest which no one in France who knew its record begrudged.

While the infantry had thus throughout the year been building a great reputation, the Australian flying squadrons, few though they were, had done the same. After machine-gunning and bombing the German divisions while these advanced and consolidated in the Somme and Lys offensives, and later specialising for a time in attacks on German balloons, the two fighter squadrons had both been chosen for "circus" work—that is, offensive flying by groups of picked squadrons. In July 1918 the two squadrons—No. 2 flying S.E.5's and No. 4 Camels—joined the 80th Wing, which included also two British squadrons, at Reclinghem, and thenceforward played a prominent part in the British offensive. For a few days after the great attack of August 8th the two Australian squadrons were detached to fight over their fellow Australians in the 4th Army, where the corps squadron (No. 3) worked continuously with the Australian Corps. Nos. 2 and 4 then returned to their wing, and led it in two famous raids on August 16th and 17th with some sixty-five

[20] Some astonishing deeds were done, but many splendid leaders killed. See Vol. VI, pp. 1033-43.

machines against the German aerodromes at Lomme and
Haubourdin, on the outskirts of Lille. The British
squadrons kept guard while the Australian squadrons
went in to attack, Captain A. H. Cobby leading No. 4,
and Captain A. Murray Jones No. 2, the British wing-
commander, Lieut.-Colonel L. A. Strange, one of the
original air force in France, flying with No. 4. The
hangars and workshops were wrecked and fifty-four German machines were reported to have been destroyed on
the ground. Colonel Strange, in *Recollections of an
Airman*, wrote of these two squadrons:

Their records show that they were the finest material as an
attacking force in the air, just as their infantry divisions on the
ground were the best that the war produced on either side. It
became the practice for our Australian squadrons to lead the
80th Wing's bombing raids. When later in the year over a
hundred machines set out on one of them, the spearpoint was
always formed of Australian airmen led by an Australian.[21]

Such was the reputation attained after two and a half
years of intense warfare on the Western Front by the
force whose first trial was in the equally intense struggle
on Gallipoli. There is no question—although their own
home folk in Australia at first found this difficult to believe—that the spirit and skill of the Australian Imperial
Force, and particularly of the infantry, in this final year's
fighting in France materially affected the course of the
campaign there, as did that of the other Dominion forces.
And far away in the Middle East there broke out in
September a short, swift campaign (to which this narrative must now turn) in which the two divisions of
Anzac cavalry—and the notable 1st Squadron of the
A.F.C.—were equally prominent.

---

[21] This is the statement of a partial, but candid, English friend. For
others, see *Vol. III, p. 183n; Vol. IV, p. 711n; Vol. VIII, p. 146n.*

CHAPTER XXVIII

THE LAST CAMPAIGN IN PALESTINE

It will be remembered that at the time of the capture of Jerusalem (9th December 1917) Mr Lloyd George was most eager for the Allies to direct their blows not at Germany direct, on the apparently impenetrable Western Front, but at her "props" in the Balkans or Middle East. His adviser, General Wilson, while chief of the Joint Allied Staff at Versailles, secured the Supreme War Council's conditional approval of an offensive in Palestine.

But at that time Allenby, harassed by the winter rains, which broke down roads and railway, wanted to undertake for the present only a much smaller task—to adjust his northern front on the one hand; and on the other to strike out across the Jordan to co-operate with Lawrence's Arabs, who were harassing the Turkish garrisons in Arabia by constantly attacking the pilgrims' railway by which these garrisons were supplied. Lloyd George, however, wanted a much more extensive operation, a thrust northward to Aleppo in Syria; this, he assumed, would cause the Turks to abandon their allies. Allenby was accordingly asked what force he would require for it. His estimate was colossal; but General Smuts, being sent to Palestine to advise the War Cabinet, suggested that, as a thrust from Palestine to Aleppo would incidentally cut Turkish communications with Mesopotamia, the campaign in Mesopotamia should be relaxed and part of the Indian infantry and cavalry there brought to Palestine.

This was accordingly done; but by then the great German "Michael" offensive of March 1918 in France

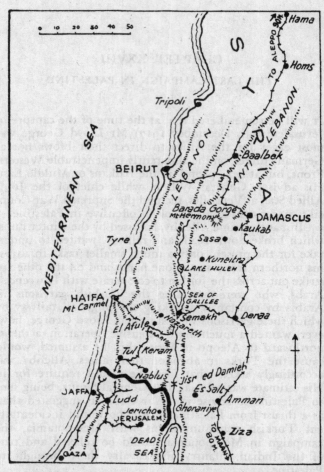

PALESTINE AND SYRIA, SHOWING THE BRITISH LINE
(BLACK) IN FEBRUARY 1918, BEFORE THE RAIDS ON
AMMAN AND ES SALT

had put an end to all plans for an early decision in Palestine. Instead 60,000 men—the 52nd and 74th Divisions and twenty-two British infantry battalions, as well as most of the Yeomanry (transformed to machine-gun companies), had to be sent from Palestine to France. Allenby had to reconstruct all his British divisions, cavalry and infantry, except the 54th, as Indian divisions, each with a British nucleus. Two new cavalry divisions, the 4th and 5th, were thus formed. The Australian Mounted Division was reorganised so as to become more completely Australian; the Imperial Camel Brigade was disbanded and its Australian members formed a new Light Horse brigade,[1] the 5th, under one of the finest Australian cavalry leaders, Brig.-General George Macarthur Onslow. The brigade (eventually completed by the attachment of a French colonial cavalry regiment) joined the Australian Mounted Division, which, differently from its sister division (the Anzac Mounted) was afterwards equipped with swords. In June a further call came from the War Office, for the 54th Division and half of the Australian Light Horse to be sent to France also—the Light Horse as infantry reinforcements. Allenby then made his first protest, and as some objection came also from Australian sources the proposal was fortunately dropped.

Meanwhile Allenby had begun his active co-operation with the Arabs. They were then harassing the Turkish garrison at Ma'an, sixty miles south of the Dead Sea, on the pilgrims' railway. He decided to destroy that railway where it passed along the high plateau east of the Jordan, at the squalid Arab town of Amman (once the flourishing Greco-Roman colony of Philadelphia).

In February the British front had been advanced eastwards through the desolate Judaean wilderness into the Jordan valley, nearly 4000 feet below, and to the western

---

[1] This occurred *after* the raids on Amman and Es Salt. The six British camel companies continued to serve as such in the Arabian Desert. Australians were given horses and became the 14th and 15th L.H. Regts.

shore of the Dead Sea. In this move the Anzac Mounted Division, working to the south of the infantry, had helped by outflanking the Turks, who thereupon withdrew from Jericho. The Light Horse had entered Jericho on February 21st, and the line had been established along the Jordan, whose normally dry, grim valley was just then blooming with its few weeks of spring flowers and greenery.

From this valley the raid on Amman was launched on March 22nd when some of the 6oth (London) Division and Anzac engineers managed, with great difficulty, to swim the river which was flooded by rain, and build a bridge at Hijla. After twenty-four hours' fighting the main crossing at Ghoraniye on the old road to Amman was also seized and bridged. By the morning of the 24th the 6oth Division and Anzac Mounted Division were pushing into the bare, precipitous hills rising to the plateau, 4000 feet high, on which Es Salt and Amman lay.

The force went by three tracks but at once found two of these impassable for any vehicle, and, in the rain which now recurred, almost impassable for camels despite the efforts of their Egyptian drivers. By the evening of the 25th Es Salt on the northern road was taken, and Ryrie's 2nd Light Horse Brigade and the New Zealand Mounted Rifles Brigade pushed up the other tracks straight for Amman. By the morning of the 27th the mounted troops were attacking that township, which lay in a dip before them, New Zealanders from south, Camel Brigade from west, Ryrie's brigade from north-west. The railway was cut and blown up north and south of the town, and in two days' stiff fighting the New Zealanders captured a commanding height (Hill 3039) on the south. But the Turks and a battalion of the German Asia Corps, firing across the valley from the old Roman citadel on the heights east of the town and from other positions, stopped the advance, the British infantry, when part of it came up, also being held.

After constant attempts, on March 30th the force was ordered to withdraw. Retirement was more difficult because many of the Christian and other inhabitants of Es Salt, who had eagerly welcomed the troops, now had to flee, escaping with the troops as best they could. With the Anzacs covering the rear, the movement back over

THE ES SALT-SHUNET NIMRIN ROAD
(The demolition in the distance was done by the Turks when retreating in September 1918.)

the Jordan ended on April 2nd. Only the Ghoraniye bridgehead was retained; the Turks attacked it on April 11th but were thoroughly beaten. A similar attack near the north-eastern shoulder of Allenby's front, where it turned westward from the Jordan valley along the Wady Mellahah, was twice repelled by the Camel Corps (not yet disbanded) on the same day.

The Arab forces, which were to have found touch with the British after the Amman raid, now could not do so. But farther south they pushed on with their attack from three directions against the pilgrims' railway at Ma'an, and in mid-April destroyed it so thoroughly that it could not be repaired. Allenby was still anxious to co-operate with them, and also to rob the Turks of the wheat-crop on the Moab plateau, then about to be reaped, and some local Arabs offered to co-operate.

Accordingly, after a strong demonstration at Ghoraniye bridgehead (an action later regretted) and two bold reconnaissances to the assembled Arabs, he launched a second big sortie—the objectives this time being the foothills at Shunet Nimrin, and Es Salt on the plateau above. Allenby hoped, if these were taken, to strike northwards to Deraa, a vital railway junction. Both Anzac and Australian Mounted Divisions took part, and the command in the Jordan valley passed to Lieut.-General Chauvel.

The attempt began on April 30th. While the 60th Division attacked the Turks in the foothills, the leading brigades of the Australian Mounted Division dashed fifteen miles northwards on the east side of the Jordan to near the Jisr ed Damieh bridge. Here, after leaving the 4th Light Horse Brigade to hold back any enemy from west of the river, the 3rd Light Horse Brigade (Wilson) scrambled up the mountains to Es Salt, and by most vigorous action seized the town that evening.[2] Two other brigades and headquarters came up a parallel track farther south. The plan was for two brigades—Ryrie's and 5th Yeomanry—to descend from there on the rear of the Turks facing the 60th Division.

But two projects miscarried. First, the 4th Light Horse Brigade guarding the Jordan crossing was driven

---

2 For this brilliant fight see *Vol. VII, pp. 610-13.*

back in hard fighting by Turks, some of whom then pressed on by that route towards Es Salt, in rear of the Australian Mounted Division—others pressed southwards, where a number of British guns, caught against the foothills, were lost. (The Turks were found to be also crossing by another bridge farther south.) Second, neither the 60th Division attacking repeatedly, nor the two mounted brigades, could dislodge the Turks in the foothills—the only chance had lain in surprise, which here failed. The Arabs—who, not unnaturally, considering how many of their people were at the mercy of the Turks, waited to see which side won—did nothing to help. On May 4th the troops had to be again withdrawn, many refugees from Es Salt again thronging the roads.

Of these two raids the unhappiest result, of which little has been recorded, was the fate of those villagers, Christians and others, who had welcomed the Allied troops but could not get away with them—a dreadful and ancient feature of war, but one which in 1914-18 was mainly confined to operations of the Middle East. But though generally unsuccessful, the raids had one result intended by Allenby. The new German commander (Liman von Sanders of Gallipoli fame, Falkenhayn having been recalled on March 1st) had his attention attracted to the inland flank, whereas Allenby intended, when the time was ripe, to break through near the sea. After an unsuccessful effort, on April 9th-11th, to improve the position there, the front was quiet throughout the summer while Allenby reorganised his divisions. During these most trying months the malarial Jordan valley—over 1000 feet below sea level—and its vital bridgeheads were held with as few troops as possible. To reduce numbers, mounted troops were used; and, as the British and Indian cavalry were then reorganising, this task—much the worst in that summer, as the

British Official Historian[8] states—fell mainly on the Anzac troops. For the Light Horse, despite full measures against malaria, this was the hardest service in the war.

In midsummer, on July 14th, occurred a night attack by a powerful German detachment upon the northern angle of the line in the Jordan valley at the prominent hills of Musallabeh and Abu Tellul. That corner was most difficult to defend, but these two hills were held as a protruding bastion, Musallabeh forming the front, and Abu Tellul behind it protecting the vital stream of the Auja. The attack was expected, and it was known that a determined enemy could penetrate between the flanking posts into the valley between the two hills. The Light Horse leaders, however, were confident that the posts would hold out even though surrounded, and Cox's 1st Light Horse Brigade, which held the bastion, would there overwhelm the enemy with its reserve regiment.

And so it happened, although the attacking troops proved to be German battalions of the Asia Corps. It was their only attack. The posts held to the last—one under Lieutenant W. K. King was annihilated; the Germans were swept from Abu Tellul by counter-attack, 358 being captured as well as 41 machine-guns. On the Mellahah a German side-stroke was upset by a handful of the 5th Light Horse Regiment who, under Lieutenant J. D. Macansh, twice cleverly worked out among the enemy and then, shooting right and left, killed, wounded or captured about 100 in all. This German enterprise was part of a plan to drive the British from the Jordan valley; the Turks failed to support it, and the German catastrophe had strong reactions in the Turkish Army and among the inhabitants of Palestine.

The three Turkish armies—8th, 7th and 4th—now facing Allenby were known to be in very bad shape.

---

[8] Captain Cyril Falls, *Egypt and Palestine*, Part II, p. 423.

Allenby estimated their strength at 26,000 "rifles", 3000 "sabres" and 370 guns, against which he had 57,000 rifles, 12,000 sabres and 540 guns. The "ration strength" of his three army corps was 140,000 against the Turkish 103,500. Captain Falls thinks the Turks were probably rather stronger than Allenby estimated; but their morale had sunk—in one week fifty-two deserters came in.

Allenby had long before decided that, in order to avoid the rains of November and December, he must deliver his great attack in September. By September 5th the Jordan valley was held only by General Chaytor of the Anzac Mounted Division with a light force of mixed troops of which his division was the backbone. As other cavalry was withdrawn to the coastal flank, lines of rough trestles resembling horses were erected to give to air observers the appearance of horse-lines. Sledges driven along the powdered tracks maintained the dust cloud that normally filled the stagnant air. When on September 16th General Chauvel moved to the coast, his conspicuous headquarters camp on the Jericho road was kept standing and lighted. An officers' hotel in Jerusalem was requisitioned ostensibly for Allenby's advanced headquarters. All real moves were made at night, and the air force—by then much superior to the German—kept away German pilots. The result was that, though by September 18th Allenby had massed the bulk of his army on the extreme left, the Turkish intelligence on September 15th reported only "some regrouping" of cavalry units there, "otherwise nothing unusual to report". Meanwhile the air force was mapping the Turkish dispositions almost at will, the 1st Australian Squadron being conspicuous in this work.[4]

At dawn on September 19th, after a bombardment

---

[4] The commander of the British Air Force in the Middle East, Air Vice-Marshal Sir J. Salmond, referred to this squadron as "perhaps the finest that ever took the air".

from air and ground, Allenby's infantry broke the
Turkish line at its coastal end. By 9 a.m. the cavalry of
the Desert Mounted Corps, commanded by Chauvel,
was picking its way over the old trenches and through
barbed wire cleared by its advanced parties, while
the infantry wheeled north-east towards the hills to

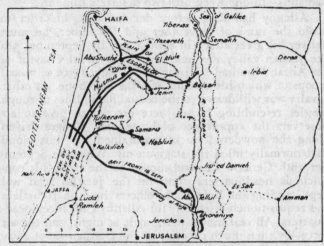

THE CAVALRY THRUSTS IN PALESTINE,
19th-21st SEPTEMBER 1918

*(The infantry thrusts which broke the line for these,
and then pressed the retreating Turks, are not here
shown. On September 23rd, after infantry action, the
Anzac Mounted Division began a similar thrust from
the Jordan Valley to Es Salt and Amman.)*

attack Tul Keram and other positions. The two Indian
cavalry divisions, going first, raced parallel along the
coast and then, crossing the Carmel range by two
passes, emerged before dawn of the 20th at Lejjun
(near Megiddo) and Abu Shushe on the plain of

Esdraelon some thirty miles behind the Turkish front,[5] just in time to stop some Turkish reserves from blocking the Musmus Pass.

The two divisions then raced eastwards for the vital points on the Turkish communications. They reached Nazareth that evening and almost captured General Liman von Sanders whose general headquarters was there, but who managed, with clerical staff, temporarily to fight off the attack.

The Australian Mounted Division was Chauvel's reserve in this drive. It had followed the more easterly cavalry division, the 4th, through the Carmel range, and then despatched one brigade (the 3rd, under General Wilson) south-east to Jenin, in order to catch in rear the main part of the retreating Turkish centre, which would there emerge from the hills. The brigade moving very fast reached the place by evening of the 20th, and swooped on it from the rear. Lieutenant P. W. K. Doig with his troop, seeing an outlying camp, instantly charged it, capturing nearly 2000 Turks and Germans. While the main body was seizing the town, the 10th Regiment went on southwards to encounter, in the night, the main force of retreating Turks. Actually the Turks were met by a troop under Lieutenant R. R. W. Patterson who, in the dark, struck the road farther south than others. On the suggestion of a Victorian trooper (T. B. George), Patterson opened fire and bluffed nearly 3000 Turks into surrender.

By morning 8000 Turkish prisoners were held by the 3rd Light Horse Brigade at Jenin. The 4th Cavalry Division seized Beisan through which Turkish communications led to the Jordan valley; the 5th captured Haifa, on the coast. Brig.-General Onslow's 5th Light Horse Brigade, attached to the British infantry at Tul Keram,

---

[5] Lieut.-Col. W. J. Foster (formerly A.D.C. to Genl Bridges but then G.S.O.1 of the 4th Cavalry Division) wore himself out that night in successful search for a brigade that had taken a wrong track through the range. He reported to his chief, Maj.-Genl G. de S. Barrow, who then went on alone and saved the situation.

working in most difficult country, destroyed the railway line north of Samaria, behind the Turkish centre.

This overwhelming sweep was vitally helped by the air force. Flying the only Handley-Page bomber in the Middle East, Captain Ross Smith, with other pilots, during the hours immediately before and after the main attack bombed the Turkish signal centres, which the Australian airmen had carefully mapped out, at Tul Keram and Nablus (8th and 7th Army Headquarters), El Afule and Nazareth; it was largely through this that the Turks had no news whatever from their western flank, and in most cases the first intimation of the catastrophe was the appearance of the cavalry at these vital centres in their rear. The retreating Turks were also terribly bombed on the narrow roads through the passes. Their 8th Army, nearest the coast, was completely destroyed; and the 7th (under Mustafa Kemal) next to it was routed. But the 4th Cavalry Division after its great ride had left a gap of twenty-five miles along the Jordan between Beisan and the bridge at Jisr ed Damieh (which the New Zealand Mounted Rifles, from the Jordan valley, and British West Indians seized on September 22nd). Across this a considerable part of the 7th Army and 700 Germans escaped before the gap was closed on September 23rd.

Liman von Sanders had now decided to defend Damascus by holding the Yarmuk Gorge, east of the southern end of Lake Tiberias, and the southern and western sides of that lake. But Chauvel forestalled him by sending the 4th Light Horse Brigade straight for Semakh at the southern end of the lake. Here the railway station was strongly held by 100 Germans and a larger number of Turks, and its buildings, looking out over two miles of plain, made it a difficult place to attack without artillery. But it was charged from the east before dawn on September 25th by the 11th Light Horse Regiment, while part of the 12th, and the 4th Machine-Gun Squadron, attacked farther west; nearly half their horses were hit, but by 5.30 the place had been taken. Most of the 100 enemy dead were Germans, and several hundred Turks were captured. A few hours later Tiberias, on the western side of the lake, was rushed by a joint attack through the hills and along the shore.

Von Sanders' intended defence line was thus broken. Moreover Semakh was less than forty miles from Deraa, the crucial junction on the pilgrims' railway, loss of which would cut off both the survivors of the 7th Army and all Turkish troops east of Jordan (now organised as the 4th Turkish Army).[6] The Arabs under Lawrence boldly blew up this railway both north and south of Deraa just before the offensive. By September 23rd there were signs that the 4th Army was retreating, and Chaytor's force now advanced from the Jordan valley to Es Salt and Amman. The Anzac Mounted Division seized Amman after a hot fight on September 25th, capturing the 4th Army's rear-guard, 2500 strong.

The main body had escaped the day before, but the remnant of the Turkish army from Arabia, 5000 strong, painfully toiling northwards, was now hopelessly cut off seventeen miles south of Amman. Here on the 28th their commander intimated to Lieut.-Colonel D. C. Cameron of the 5th Light Horse Regiment that he would surrender provided the Australians could protect his men against the Beni Sakr Arabs, who were circling about his force at Ziza station, shouting and firing into the air, and ready to loot and kill as soon as the chance offered. Eventually, on Brig.-General Ryrie's arrival at great speed with the 7th Regiment, the Australians and Turks, together, held the trenches through the night. At dawn, on the arrival of the New Zealand Brigade, the Turks (except a few retained for escort duty) gave up their arms to the Anzacs.

---

[6] This army was under Mohammed Djemal Pasha, but not the same Ahmed Djemal who originally commanded it in Syria and Palestine. On this point Vol. VII is in error.

In nine days Chaytor's force at a cost of 139 casualties had captured 10,300 prisoners and 57 guns.

Not till September 22nd, at Megiddo, did Allenby mention to Chauvel that he intended to continue the advance, to Damascus and Beirut. The task would be one for the cavalry, the Australian Mounted Division followed by the 5th Cavalry passing west of Lake Tiberias and thence across Jordan to Damascus, the 4th Cavalry pushing east of the lake to Deraa junction, and thence north along the pilgrims' railway to the same city. Colonel Lawrence with the Arab army from the country farther east would join in. The Germans had been hitting back at the Arabs with air raids which, however, ended when on September 22nd-23rd Ross Smith and other Australian pilots after visiting Lawrence's position shot down or smashed on the ground all the German machines at Deraa. The Arabs eventually sacked and looted Deraa, and hung on to the rearguard of the Turkish 4th Army, the 4th Cavalry Division, after several sharp fights, catching up with them near Damascus.

The Australian Mounted Division, converging from west of Lake Tiberias, struck a tough rearguard of German machine-gunners and Turks on September 28th at the Benat Yakub bridge over the Jordan south of Lake Huleh (The Waters of Merom). The plans to surround this rearguard failed, but it was driven back and was met again on the 29th at Sasa. Here again it was dislodged by the 3rd Brigade after a fight lasting till dawn. The 4th Brigade now (September 30th) taking the lead raced towards Damascus, cutting into Turkish and German parties as these streamed towards the city. At Kaukab a Turkish column, converging across the front, made a stand on a ridge. The 4th and 12th Light Horse Regiments under Lieut.-Colonel M. Bourchier charged them, while Onslow's 5th Brigade brushed past their western flank and bypassing Damascus, made for the steep Barada Gorge along which the railway and road for Beirut lead

out north-westwards from that city. The enemy at Kaukab, being shelled by the horse artillery and seeing the
conspicuous grey horses of the French cavalry with
Onslow's brigade moving to their rear, broke before the
charge of Bourchier's force.

The 5th Brigade skirting the garden groves of Damascus—that most wonderful of oases—reached the Barada
Gorge just as a column of Turks streamed along the
slender main road beside the railway and river, far below.
With heavy fire from the rocky heights the Australians,
presently joined by the 3rd Light Horse Brigade (Wilson),
turned the head of the column, which before dusk was
irretrievably jammed and cut to pieces in the narrow
passage. Meanwhile the rest of the cavalry and the Arabs
harried the Turks struggling into Damascus.

Brig.-General Wilson with the 3rd Light Horse
Brigade had been ordered to cross the Barada Gorge and
make his way over the farther heights to the Homs road,
leading north-east from Damascus, the only other escape-
route for the Turks. The country, however, was so rough
that he decided the quickest way to reach the Homs road
was to wait for morning, and dash to it through the enemy
in Damascus.

At 5 a.m. on October 1st, believing that Damascus
was still in Turkish hands, the 10th Regiment headed by
the brigade scouts and Major Olden, after making its
way through the terrible debris in the Gorge, galloped into
the great and ancient city. They were greeted by a fusillade of shots, but mainly from excited Arabs firing into
the air in friendly demonstration. Clattering over the
bridge they found a crowd at the Serai. Inside the
building was a gathering of Arab notables, who had taken
control of the city. It was with difficulty that the Australians disengaged themselves from the Arab welcome;
but, having obtained a guide to the Homs road, by 7 a.m.
Wilson and his brigade were soon clear of the cheering,
shooting crowd.

Though without sleep for two nights, and though the German machine-gunners always stoutly opposed them, Wilson's light horsemen clattered on, and overtook and captured two bodies of Turks and Germans, 750 in all, but just failed to cut off a column of 2000 before it reached the pass at Khan Ayash, fifteen miles from Damascus, into which the few Australians could not follow it. Early next day (October 2nd) the 9th Regiment, seeing another column of Turks making for this pass, cleverly outflanked and rushed them, capturing 1500 and the colours of the 46th Regiment. A little later eighty-five Turks under a German officer, while getting into action a machine-gun, were rushed into surrender by two Australian signallers (a jockey and a station foreman) who overpowered the officer and turned his revolver and machine-gun on his men.

These were the last actions of the Light Horse in the war. That afternoon Damascus—a city of 300,000—till then in ferment of looting and lawlessness, was quietened by Chauvel with the age-old method of an impressive parade of his battle-stained mounted troops through its streets. The shops reopened. But two dreadful legacies of war remained in the crowds of sick, dying and dead left behind in the appalling Turkish hospital, and in the onrush of malaria and pneumonic influenza that now mowed down the divisions of the Desert Mounted Corps. Their recent passage through areas swarming with infected mosquitoes and unequipped for prevention struck down a great part of the force. As for the Turks, Lieut.-Colonel T. J. Todd of the 10th Regiment, a sick man who himself died a few months later, was given charge of 16,000 Turkish sick organised in camp at Kaukab, and heroically fought for their lives against the apathy of the Arab authorities.

Meanwhile Chauvel, with the 5th Cavalry Division now in the lead, after conference with the Arab King Feisal, pushed on through Lebanon and Syria—past

Baalbek, Homs and Hama to Aleppo—the infantry marching up the sea coast to Beirut and Tripoli, and the Arabs making touch with the cavalry's right. Half the surviving Turkish Army had been destroyed at Damascus. Aleppo was abandoned by it on October 26th, the Arabs rushing in as the rearguard withdrew. An Australian armoured car detachment, in Ford cars, was the only fighting unit of the A.I.F. in this advance. But at Aleppo, through sickness in the other divisions, Chauvel had to wait for the Australian Mounted Division to come up from Damascus. It was nearing Homs on October 31st when its commander (Hodgson) received news that on the previous day Turkey had signed an armistice.

CHAPTER XXIX

THE WAR ENDS

TURKEY was not, however, the first of the Central Powers to collapse. The defeats of Germany on the Western Front had dispirited the Bulgarian Army. When attacked by the Allies from Salonica on September 15th, it was driven back and sought an armistice, which was signed on September 30th. It was this event combined with the defeats in Palestine that caused the Turkish government on October 20th to ask for an armistice.

The German and Austrian governments had already done so, by cable to President Wilson of the United States on the night of October 3rd. That step had been taken on the insistence of Ludendorff and Hindenburg. After the "black day" of August 8th they had arranged a conference at the Kaiser's headquarters at Spa, at which, on August 13th, they informed Wilhelm II and the government leaders that peace must be brought about by negotiation, the condition of the Army and Germany's allies being such that it could not now be brought about by force of German arms. The Kaiser then directed the Foreign Secretary to open peace negotiations.

But seven weeks followed in which nothing decisive was done; Hindenburg and Ludendorff, especially the former, inevitably spoke in such pompous terms of the German Army, and—when once they had thrown on the civilians the responsibility of making peace—so completely abstained from any part in that odious task themselves, that the ministers did not realise the urgency; instead they waited, as they thought was the common intention, for some temporary recovery by the Army

which would give a more favourable basis for opening
negotiations than if this were attempted during a series
of defeats.

But the defeats increased in frequency and gravity
until, in the crisis that followed the Allied blows along
the Western Front on September 26th-29th, the two
military leaders were seized by an acute fear that their
front might completely break at any hour. Ludendorff
would hardly wait for the appointment of Prince Max of
Baden, who at that moment was replacing Count von
Hertling as Chancellor, and who—in view of the previous
attitude of the High Commanders—found it hard to
believe that the risk of catastrophe was so immediate as
they now insisted. However, as they demanded, he sent
the request to President Wilson because he feared that
if he delayed longer they would send it themselves and
so betray to the world their opinion that the position of
their army was hopeless.

A few days later Ludendorff's anxiety about the front
had diminished, and as the politicians had by then taken
the responsibility of asking for an armistice, the military
leaders became less definite about the urgency. Ludendorff undoubtedly wanted an armistice that would give
his forces a chance to recover their breath, and he hoped
that if the Allies' terms for it were too severe the German
Army and people might be ready to make a last desperate
resistance. In that case, he believed, dissension might
arise among the Allies, sections of opinion in France,
England and America becoming discontented at the
"needless" prolongation of the war.

On October 28th, however, Austria, against which
the Italians had at last launched their offensive, sued for
a separate armistice; and in this crisis the German people
turned against its leaders, whom it felt to be the last
impediment to the longed-for peace. On October 26th
the Kaiser, on Prince Max's demand, dismissed Ludendorff. On October 29th and 30th the crews of German

warships at Kiel, being ordered without their government's knowledge to put to sea to fight the British, mutinied. Two reliable divisions (the first being the 2nd Guard Division that had been surprised by the Australians at Mont St Quentin) were rushed to prevent the mutiny from spreading, but were too late to do so. The Austrian Armistice was signed on November 3rd. On November 5th arrived President Wilson's note saying that the Allies were willing to make peace with Germany on the basis (requested by Prince Max) of Wilson's Fourteen Points with two modifications, and that General Foch was empowered to arrange an armistice.

Since the breaking of the Hindenburg Line the Allied armies in France had continued to advance, defeating the Germans in several great offensives—though none as bloody as the preceding ones—and forcing back the enemy twenty to sixty miles across France and Belgium to Ghent, Mons, Mezières and Sedan. The Australian air squadrons were with the British to the end, as was much of the A.I.F.'s artillery (with the II American and, later, the IX British Corps) until the great battle of Le Cateau on November 4th. The Australian infantry divisions, after their rest, had begun again to move up to take over part of the British line beyond Le Cateau preparatory to the final thrusts when, on November 9th, British airmen, flying over French and Belgian towns, reported they could find no enemy to shoot at. The streets were thronged with people, German soldiers mingling among them.

A revolution, though almost bloodless, had happened in Germany. The Social Democrats had insisted that the Kaiser and Crown Prince must go; the workers in Berlin rose, and the troops would not fire on them. The Kaiser at his headquarters wavered; but Prince Max, receiving a message that Wilhelm II intended to abdicate, authorised an announcement that he had done so. Max himself handed over the Chancellorship to the Social Democrat leader Ebert, who became President of the German Republic. Ebert, as his first action, had to hasten to Foch with Germany's acceptance of the Armistice terms. These, involving a retirement of German forces ten miles beyond the Rhine, the surrender of the fleet, and the practical disarmament of the Army and air force,[1] made it impossible for Germany to fight again in that war.

At 11 a.m. on 11th November 1918 all operations ceased on the Western Front. For the troops there the change went too deep for outward rejoicing; on the surface, life continued as usual except for the cessation of actual fighting. But in the back areas, as in London and Paris, the people and servicemen burst into demonstrations increasing in exuberance with the distance from the front. In Australia a false report from America set fire to public enthusiasm four days earlier, but that did not damp the genuine outburst of public relief when the true news arrived on November 12th; as in England, people flooded into the streets; flags broke out, bonfires blazed, bells rang, bands played, and for that day serious work was at an end.

The commanders of the A.I.F. were now suddenly faced by a problem in some ways opposite to that of the four previous years. It was certain that more than a year would pass before the last of the A.I.F. could be transported home. The Australian force had a reputation for admirable discipline in operations but for being less easy to handle when it had less to do. In place of the motive that had sustained it throughout the war—to make and keep itself fit to fight—there must be instilled a new motive to animate it during that trying year. The chief of its staff, Lieut.-General Brudenell White, had foreseen this; and besides initiating in 1917 the first investigations into demobilisation (with which the British War Office was

---

[1] The negotiations and terms are described in *Vol. VI, pp. 1045-7, 1049-52.* On November 10th the Kaiser, and on the 12th the Crown Prince, motored to Holland and were separately interned there.

then already concerning itself) he advised General Birdwood early in 1918 to authorise a scheme of army education. He was informed that the Canadians had already
established such a scheme and he foresaw that it would
expand into an activity of extreme benefit for the troops
after the Armistice.

The task of devising and organising this scheme was
given to an outstanding Australian, George Merrick
Long, Bishop of Bathurst, who happened to arrive in
France in May. As brigadier-general, with White's support and later Monash's, by Herculean labour, despite
the concentration of commanders and troops on winning
the war, Long succeeded in having a great part of his
staff ready and his scheme authorised by the time of the
Armistice. With the assistance of Mr Hughes and of
British and other authorities it was extended (in a scheme
of "Non-Military Employment"—more commonly known
among the troops as "Non-Military Enjoyment") to the
training of soldiers in industries, universities and technical colleges in Great Britain and even in America and
France. A representative committee from the Australian
universities under Professor E. R. Holme greatly helped.
In England 12,800 Australian soldiers and nurses went
through courses apart from lectures and classes at the
depots. In France some 47,000 enrolled, but probably
10,000 was the greatest number attending classes at any
one time. Though the education scheme, with both
classes and instructors constantly due for demobilisation,
achieved much less than had been hoped, it turned the
thoughts of the A.I.F. to reconstruction; gave—even to
those who did not take part—a sense of being cared for,
and enormously helped the A.I.F. in a most difficult
period.

The end of the war found Australian soldiers in
almost every theatre of operations; besides 92,000 in
France and 60,000 in England there were 17,000 in Egypt,
Palestine and Syria; in Mesopotamia, Persia and Kurdis-

tan were the wireless squadrons and the Australians in
the "Dunsterforce"; in Salonica Australian nurses staffed
four British hospitals, and in India, ten. The task of
repatriating the A.I.F. from Europe was entrusted by
Mr Hughes to General Monash, who worked with a
picked staff brought over from France. He at once
grasped that, whereas in the operations of an army at war
the immediate objective must be kept secret, in those of
an army at peace it was of the utmost importance to see
that each soldier, if possible, understood the plans and
realised the care that was being taken for his rehabilitation and for building the nation's future. Birdwood,
White and Long also had realised that the troops would
inevitably look to their education officers to explain the
government's plans for rehabilitation and to advise them
as to their training. This important part of the scheme,
however, was almost wrecked by the delay of the Australian government in sending particulars of its proposals.
Though Birdwood frequently asked for these from
November 1917 onwards, it was not until a year later—
on the day of the Armistice—that, after very strong cables
from Birdwood and the Official War Correspondent, the
information arrived.

The demobilisation scheme was similarly hampered
by the government's delay in deciding on the order of
priority; pride in the A.I.F. led the government to favour
the return of the men by regiments. Monash knew, however, that the troops, passionately longing for their
return, clung to the principle of "first come, first go".
The presence of Mr Hughes in London was of the utmost
value to Monash at this time; the Prime Minister finally
himself took the responsibility of provisionally agreeing
to this principle.

Upon it, therefore, the scheme was based, and it was
carried through without the disciplinary trouble that
occurred even in the British Army. The longest-enlisted
men had already just arrived in Australia on "Anzac

Leave", and the first step was to grant similar leave to the next batch. Monash next ordered each division to classify its men in order of their length of service, in "quotas" of 1000 each—that being a normal trainload, a normal shipload, and also a number readily organised as a battalion. Each "quota" was to have, if possible, its brass band, its education, staff, and organised provision for recreation. They were brought successively to the camps on Salisbury Plain. Through the energy of Mr Hughes and of the transport staff, ships were allotted by the British Shipping Control much more quickly than had been expected; and as each ship became available a quota was called on to fill it. The 40,000 convalescents went separately, under medical control and arrangements.

Partly because of the urgent desire of the Australian government and of the A.I.F. itself to get on with repatriation, partly, it has been said, because the British Command preferred to have more docile troops in the army of occupation,[2] the Australian divisions in France had not been sent to occupy the Rhineland—only an air squadron and a casualty clearing station represented the A.I.F. there. The divisions remained, under command of Lieut.-General Hobbs, mainly among the friendly Belgian towns between Dinant on the Meuse and Charleroi.

There the force spent six months, quickly shrinking. In March 1919 the 1st and 4th Divisions were combined, and the 2nd and 5th. In May the last 10,000 were brought from France to England, where 70,000 were now on Salisbury Plain. In the Middle East the Light Horse recovered in Tripoli and Philistia from the worst of their epidemics. The 7th Light Horse Regiment and Canterbury Mounted Rifles were for a short time sent with other troops to occupy Gallipoli Peninsula. Part of the Light Horse was delayed in Egypt during March and April to

---

[2] This may possibly be true, but the official historian could find no recorded evidence of it, and some to the contrary (see Vol. VI, p. 1072n).

protect life and property against a revolt by the natives.[3] Without a complaint the regiments abandoned their prospect of immediate home-coming and, after a few brushes, completely restored the country's quiet. In the summer they were embarked. Of the 155,000 Australian troops based on England, by the end of September only 10,000 were left. Over 15,000 soldiers' wives, fiancées and children were embarked without delay, mostly in "family ships" equipped with conveniences from playgrounds to baby powder.

The severest test to the discipline of the A.I.F. during demobilisation occurred when some of the troops on arriving transports found themselves quarantined almost within sight of their homes because of the discovery of, perhaps, one case of suspicious sickening for pneumonic influenza among 1000 men. But in only one such instance was there serious trouble—in most others the good sense of the men and the efforts of ships' captains and officers and quarantine authorities in organising recreation enabled this tedious delay to be borne with good humour; and as Australia was (to quote a report of the British Ministry of Health) "the only country which escaped, for at least some months, the terrifying type of influenza which, from October to November 1918, raged elsewhere", the soldiers' tolerance of this last trial was possibly of very great value to their nation.[4]

---

[3] For the affair at Surafend, where Anzacs and some British troops, incensed by murders by the Arabs, destroyed a village and killed many of its men, see *Vol. VII, p. 787-790.*

[4] See *Australian Official Medical History*, by Col. A. G. Butler, *Vol. III, pp. 782-5.*

CHAPTER XXX

THE PEACE TREATY

USEFUL though the presence of the Australian Prime Minister was at this juncture to the Australian military leaders in getting their troops quickly and smoothly home,[1] this had not been the main reason for Mr Hughes's prolonged stay in England. From long before the Armistice he had been determined to stay for the peace conference, and by a very stubborn fight he—and by separate initiative, the Canadian government—clinched the right, actually won for the Dominions by their troops, to be represented at the Peace Conference at Versailles. Early in 1915 the British government had pledged itself that Australia would be consulted "most fully" when the time came; and it was subsequently stated that this pledge would be observed in "the spirit as well as the letter" Actually, however, when the time came the British government, by concurring in President Wilson's reply to Germany agreeing to base the Peace Treaty upon his Fourteen Points, broke this pledge. The Australian government had not even been informed that the matter was under discussion.

Presumably this was due to the need for haste; but it so happened that the Australian government was highly critical of the Fourteen Points, being uncertain whether these might not imply a pledge of (1) free trade, (2) the giving up of the German colonies, and (3) the abandonment of the right to recover the cost of the war. In a speech in London of November 7th Hughes protested

---

1 Senator Pearce afterwards wisely came to London for the same purpose.

that Australia would not be bound by adverse interpretations on these points.

Strangely enough the Australian Cabinet, then headed by Mr W. A. Watt, did not think it reasonable for the Dominions to be represented as such at the Peace Conference, and had informed Mr Hughes that it would not support such a claim; and the proposal disturbed the British Foreign Office. But Mr Hughes had prepared his ground well. Himself immensely impressed by the part played by the Australian Corps in the final defeat of the German Army, he ensured that it should be made well known in Great Britain by inviting many parties of press leaders to visit the corps during its advance and even himself showing them over the ground recently won. He also, in October, rushed to Paris to support the French objection to any weakening of the future peace terms by reference to the Fourteen Points, an action which took him straight to the heart of Clemenceau and other French leaders. On December 2nd the Supreme War Council met in London to arrange the procedure at the Peace Conference. Next day, the Dominion representatives being present, the Conference agreed that, whereas the great powers would each have five representatives, British Dominions and India should, like the smaller powers, each have two, excepting New Zealand which would have one. These would, however, exercise no votes additional to those of the British delegation. Their inclusion was admitted to be the direct result of the general appreciation of their countries' war efforts.

At the conference, which met at Versailles on 12th January 1919, the control was in the hands of the great powers—indeed no other system would have permitted any headway in the immense task, or any hope of agreement. Sessions of the full conference were used only for formality—publicly to approve of decisions already made. From the first the Supreme War Council appointed itself as a Committee—the Council of Ten—to conduct business. Even this Committee, consisting of the leading representatives and foreign secretaries of the United States, Great Britain, France and Italy, with Japan now added, was soon found too large; secrets leaked in all directions, through staff or members. President Woodrow Wilson, and the Prime Ministers of Britain, France and Italy afterwards largely took control as a Council of Four (or, when Italy for a time withdrew dissatisfied) a Council of Three. The five foreign ministers formed a Council of Five to which some matters were delegated. The general body of delegates was employed on "Commissions" (or Committees) to which the Council distributed the detailed work of drawing the terms in various fields— War Offences, Reparations, League of Nations and so forth. In addition, each nation privately discussed every matter concerning itself at meetings of its own delegation.

Mr Hughes at once came into conflict with the Council of Five over its intention to hand over the occupied German colonies to various powers on trust to administer them in accordance with terms to be laid down in "mandates" to be issued by the projected League of Nations. The German colonies north of Australia were required by Australia for one reason and one only— protection from attack; German South-west Africa was needed for the same reason by the Union of South Africa. If the League of Nations laid down that immigration and trade to those territories were to be unrestricted, it might be impossible to prevent their falling into hands hostile to these Dominions. New Zealand stood with Australia in this contention, and Sir Robert Borden of Canada decided to support his Dominion colleagues. Accordingly, apparently by the good offices of Clemenceau and Lloyd George, the four Dominion Prime Ministers were suddenly admitted to a session of the Council of Five on January 24th, and strongly stated their case.

All the Continental powers—and the Japanese— desired to annex territory; and, though "in principle" the Council agreed to the mandate system, some of them were most willing to see if the British Dominions could break it down. President Wilson, however, saw the prospect of all his high aims being accepted "in principle" but completely abandoned in fact by reason of a swarm of exceptions. He held to the mandate system; and, when attacked in the press—not only in France and England but, by Mr Hughes's efforts, in the western states of America—he threatened to return to America and report this obstruction.

At this juncture, however, Lieut.-Commander John Latham, a Victorian lawyer on the staff of Sir Joseph Cook, suggested to Sir Maurice Hankey, secretary of the British Delegation and of the Council of Four, a form of mandate that should meet the views of both sides where the captured territory was remote from other powers but lay next to that of the nation to whom it was mandated: in these cases, Latham urged, the mandatory nation might be allowed to apply its own laws to the territory, subject to safeguards of native interests and to a prohibition against fortifying the territory or raising armed forces there except police. President Wilson accepted this, but Mr Hughes did not until after a heart to heart talk with Mr Lloyd George. "We gave up English and went into Welsh," said Mr Hughes afterwards; he was told that if the Dominions asked for more than this compromise they must go on without the help of the British government. That appears to have settled the matter.[2]

On this basis the League of Nations, when formed under the Peace Treaty, issued what were known as "C" class mandates over some of Germany's former possessions; south-west Africa was thus entrusted to the Union of South Africa; Samoa to New Zealand; New Guinea and the associated islands south of the equator to Australia; the former German islands north of the equator

---

[2] For the detailed story see *Vol. XI, pp. 771-787.*

to Japan; and the phosphate island of Nauru—in the fate of which, Mr Hughes complained, "big business" had an undue influence—to the British Empire, under which the responsibility and benefits were shared by Britain, Australia and New Zealand.

The German islands north of the equator, thus entrusted to Japan, had been among those which, at the beginning of the war, Australia was asked by the British government to occupy. When Japan came in, the Japanese Navy, also at the request of the British government, occupied Yap, but Japan informed Britain that the occupation was temporary and that she was ready to hand over to an Australian force. The British government passed this information to Australia on 13th October 1914, with the suggestion that Australian forces should relieve the Japanese as soon as possible. A special force was accordingly raised to take over this and other former German islands north of the equator. But in November 1914 the British government, on being informed that the expedition was about to sail, abruptly recommended that it should be stopped and that those islands—Pelews, Mariannes, Carolines and Marshalls—should for the present remain in Japanese hands, "leaving whole question of future to be settled at end of war".

There had evidently been some failure to inform the Australian government of a change in either Japan's or Britain's attitude[3] towards this problem; apparently the British government had found it necessary to ask the Japanese to undertake extensive tasks in those waters, and therefore could hardly request them to hand over the islands. Later, when Mr Hughes visited London in 1916, Sir Edward Grey asked him if he would object to the islands being handed to the Japanese. His reply was: "What is the use of my objecting. I am confronted with a *fait accompli*." In 1917 the Australian government, on

3 See Vol. IX, pp. 130-7; Vol. X, pp. 149-161; Vol. XI, pp. 763-4. For our government's astonishing carelessness in geography see Vol. XI, p. 766.

further inquiry from London, raised no objection to Britain's promising to support after the war Japan's claim to these islands. A week later this promise—together with a much less defensible one concerning German territory in China—was given to Japan by Lloyd George and the French government. Ultimately Japan received the islands under a "C" mandate, the terms of which her military leaders eventually broke.

The controversy over mandates was only the first of several in which Mr Hughes, whatever one may think of his manners, secured for Australia terms the vital importance of which for his nation has since been proved. The next arose upon a request from the Japanese delegates, headed by Baron Makino, for the inclusion, in the Covenant of the League of Nations, of a declaration that equal treatment must be given by all member states to the nationals of all other members, "making no distinction either in law or in fact on account of their nationality". Before bringing this forward the Japanese representatives had interviewed those of other nations. Mr Hughes told Baron Makino that Australia would have no objection to a declaration of national equality provided that it clearly stated that it did not confer any right to enter Australia—or any other country—except as the government of such country might determine. Makino replied that he sought only "a technical right of free entrance, and that there was no intention to act upon it".[4]

The proposal was temporarily dropped through a technicality, but was three times revived in slightly other forms. However, as Baron Makino refused to exclude by express words the interpretation that this gave the right to immigration, Mr Hughes still refused to agree, despite the assent not only of President Wilson but even of the Canadian and South African leaders. When the matter was brought to a vote in the Commission responsible for

---

[4] See W. M. Hughes, *The Splendid Adventure*, p. 359.

framing the basis of the League of Nations, the representatives of Italy, France, Greece, Czechoslovakia, Poland and China spoke in favour of the Japanese proposal. President Wilson, in the chair, was against a division, but the Japanese pressed for it, and the votes were 11 to 6 in its favour. But President Wilson knew that, if the declaration was made, Hughes would deliver "an inflammatory speech" at the solemn conference that was to ratify the Covenant, and would "raise a storm of protest not only in the Dominions but in the western part of the United States".[5] He therefore, to the amazement of the Committee, ruled that any amendment to the draft of the Covenant could be carried only by a unanimous vote. The Japanese, most astutely, made use of their reverse in order to obtain, as compensation, the former German rights in China. To this Wilson, being forced (like the Allies before him) into an act of opportunism, agreed. As a consequence the Japanese duly came into the League, contenting themselves with a protest at the full conference which, on April 28th, adopted the Covenant of the League of Nations.

In the Commission of the League that dealt with "Reparations" Mr Hughes was a vice-president and a leading spirit. He had been chairman of the British government's Committee appointed in 1918 to explore this problem; it had reported that the cost of the war to the Allies was £24,000 million (and that Germany should be able to pay one-twentieth of this annually as interest "when normal conditions are restored"). The British Treasury and Mr J. M. Keynes held on the other hand that one-twelfth of the former sum, that is, £2000 million, was the maximum safe figure of Germany's capacity to pay. Mr Hughes's attitude was probably not unconnected with his desire to return to Australia with the promise of a large war indemnity; Australia was estimated to

---

5 See *The Intimate Papers of Colonel House*, Vol. IV, p. 430 (quoted in Vol. XI, p. 794, footnote 70).

have spent £364 million on the war, and she had little return from war industry. But Wilson's Fourteen Points, as modified and accepted by the Allies, allowed only compensation for all damage to civilians and to their property.

On this point the Commission split. In the consequent dilemma the Council of Four seized on a suggestion by General Smuts that damage to civilian property included the capitalised amount of war pensions. This opened the door to vast demands, but no fixed sum was eventually set. Actually the leaders probably realised that the demand was impossibly large—the British delegation certainly did—but in view of the public expectation, for which some of them were partly responsible, they dared not ask for less. Australia's claim for £364 million—the actual war-time cost—was ruled out in one stroke, and her eventual share was based on her claim for £100 million for pensions, rehabilitation and loss to civilians and of civilian property.

Mr Hughes on his return home did not hide his disappointment. He informed his government that Australia's share would be "about a twenty-fifth of £2000 million spread over twenty, or fifty, or a million years more or less". Actually Australia received £5,571,720 before 1932 when the arrangement finally collapsed and payments ceased. A minor reparation was the eventual expropriation of German private property in New Guinea. Some compensation was also derived from the sale of German-owned goods, and from German ships that had been seized.

The Treaty of Versailles was signed by the German delegates in the famous Hall of Mirrors on 28th June 1919. Mr Hughes and Sir Joseph Cook signed for Australia, and—a condition of acceptance on which the Australian government, for one, insisted—the treaty was ratified by the Federal Parliament in September. Although it contained several provisions which—as its wisest builders

were aware—must some day be modified, and others that
held obvious seeds of future trouble, it was the result of
an earnest attempt to solve difficult problems, and its
arrangements were, on the whole, exceptionally fair—in-
comparably more so, if the Brest-Litovsk treaty is a guide,
than any treaty that would have been imposed by the
Germans. Wilson was satisfied because he felt that, if it
ultimately required modifications, there existed, in the
League of Nations, the machinery for making them.

CHAPTER XXXI

THE ANZAC LEGACY

ON 26th December 1919 General Monash, having almost completely repatriated the A.I.F., and so finished his last military task—in which the staff work was, he considered, "superior to anything with which we were connected during the war"—himself also returned home, and went quietly into civilian clothes to begin another outstanding service to his country as organiser of the great electricity undertaking of Victoria. Like him, the A.I.F. on its return merged quickly and quietly into the general population, an unworthy demonstration in Victoria by some of the inevitable riff-raff being quickly disclaimed by a huge meeting of ex-soldiers immediately called for that purpose and addressed by Elliott, Brand and other tried leaders on 23rd July 1919 in the Melbourne Domain.

The First A.I.F. officially ceased to exist on 1st April 1921. Its rehabilitation and pensioning—eventually administered mainly by the Department of "Repatriation"—were not finished when in 1939 the Second World War broke out. The number of pensions had reached its peak in 1931, when there were 283,322; but of these less than one-third were for servicemen and more than two-thirds for wives, widows or children of dead or (in some degree) disabled servicemen. The amount paid in that year was just under £8 million. The total number of pensions then began to fall until in 1942 it was 220,339,[1] when the amount paid was £7½ million. In rehabili-

---

[1] Pensions then, of course, began to increase owing to the Second World War. By 1945 there were again 283,000 pensioners to whom about £8 million was payable in respect of the First World War, and £3 million in respect of the Second.

tation, under the system established by Senator Millen and Sir Nicholas Lockyer, with Mr J. Nangle as Director for Vocational Training, over 74,343 soldiers applied for this training and 27,696 completed their courses in occupations varying from show-card writing to boat building, great assistance being given by both employers and employees.

The children of those soldiers who had lost their lives or been wholly incapacitated were educated at public expense. War gratuities (at 1s. 6d. a day from embarkation) were voted in 1919 to all ex-servicemen who had enlisted for service oversea, with a lower rate for those kept in Australia; the total being £27½ million. Under the War Service Homes Act over 37,000 soldiers (or their widows) were enabled to build or buy homes by assistance to the amount of £800 to £950; and after twenty-two years less than 2½ per cent of the payments for these homes were in arrear. The settling of soldiers on the land was much less successful, partly because the land allotted was in many cases unsuitable or too highly assessed, partly through failure to insist on the competence of the applicants. The system was managed by the State governments, the Federal government helping by an advance of £625 for each settler. Many of the properties were in the irrigation areas, some of which are still largely peopled by ex-soldiers. But nearly one-third of the settlers failed, and in 1929, after inquiry by an authority in land valuation, Mr Justice Pike, the Federal and State governments wrote off £23½ million over and above considerable losses of interest.

Twenty-one years after the war, when the Second World War broke out, there were still 2000 servicemen of the First World War under treatment in Australian hospitals, and nearly 50,000 attended at some time during the year as outpatients. For serious cases the "Repatriation" Department itself maintained one hospital in each State. Many severely disabled men, however, were carrying on their normal civilian occupations, overcoming their handicaps with extraordinary courage and ingenuity; the loss of one or even two limbs made astonishingly little difference in the civil life of some of these determined men.[2] It was constantly demonstrated that, in treating disablement, by far the happiest results were those in which the State was able to help men to help themselves.

In addition to all this effort at public expense, the returned servicemen or their families were greatly helped by voluntary effort, in particular through a great bequest for their benefit by the leading pastoralist in New South Wales, Sir Samuel McCaughey, who died in 1919. Combined with the profits of the soldiers' canteens, this formed a fund of over £1,300,000 which, carefully and sympathetically administered by the trustees, was mainly devoted to the education of the children of dead or disabled soldiers in certain ways complementary to the government scheme. Help of another kind was given by the ex-soldiers' organisations, much the strongest of these being the Returned Soldiers' and Sailors' Imperial League of Australia, which secured some measure of preference in employment for ex-servicemen throughout Australia—varying in the different States; and by perhaps the finest movement that emerged from the war—the Legacy Clubs, originated by General Gellibrand and some of those whom he formerly led—whose members now undertake, in place of their dead or disabled comrades, to guide and help those comrades' children.

The First World War cost Australia 215,000 battle casualties; the comparative figures[3] for the British Empire

---

[2] For typical cases see *Official Medical History*, Vol. III, pp. 840-3.

[3] The Australian military and medical statistics of the First World War may be found in the *Australian Official Medical History*, Vol. III, pp. 856-980, (see also *Vol. I* of that history); and in the *Australian Official History*, Vol. VI, pp. 1088-9 and Vol. XI, pp. 871-6, and 882-8.

	Population	Raised	Took the field	Killed and died of wounds	Wounded	Reported Prisoners	Total	Percentage	
								Troops in field to population	Battle casualties to troops in field
United Kingdom	48,089,249	5,704,416	5,399,563	702,410	1,662,625	170,389	2,535,424	11·2	47·1
Canada	8,361,000	624,964	422,405	56,625	149,732	3,729	210,086	5·0	49·7
Australia	4,875,325	416,809	331,781	59,342	152,171	4,084	215,045	6·8	64·8
New Zealand	1,099,449	128,525	98,950	16,654	41,317	530	58,501	8·9	58·6
South Africa	6,685,827	136,070	136,070	6,928	11,444	228	18,600	2·0	13·6
India	315,200,000	1,440,437	1,388,620	53,486	64,350	3,762	121,598	0·4	9·1

(mainly based on those of the British War Office, March 1922) are shown on the opposite page.

The military effort of the Dominions was not, as will be seen, proportionate to that of the Mother Country. In view of their distance from the main theatre, and their less advanced development, this was not expected of them. Nevertheless, if battle forces only are counted, Australians, with their five infantry divisions and the greater part of two cavalry ones, did not fall far short of the full proportionate contribution of their nation. Moreover, though Australia could not provide munitions, as did Canada, she was the only Dominion which furnished a considerable naval force. To the air force her contribution, like that of Canada and other British communities oversea, was outstanding, and she alone provided her own air force overseas as well as very many and notable entrants for the British one.[4] In money the cost of the war to Australia during 1914-19 was, as already stated, assessed at £364 million, and the post-war cost, up to the beginning of the Second World War, was about another £270 million.

. . .

If the cause that led Australians to enlist can be reduced to a single principle, it is the principle of protecting their homes and their freedom by sustaining a system of law

---

[4] For some of these, including Kingsford-Smith, Hinkler, Percival, Longmore, Taylor and Brearley, see *Vol. VIII, pp. xxv-xxviii.* Longmore and F. H. McNamara (who won the V.C. when flying in 1917 in Palestine) occupied high British commands in the Second World War.

Australians of both these forces competed for the prize offered in March 1919 by the Australian Government for their return home by air. The winners were Ross Smith with his brother Keith and Sergeants J. M. Bennett and W. H. Shiers, who in a Vickers-Vimy machine, reached Darwin on 10th December 1919 in just under twenty-eight days. Lieuts. R. J. P. Parer and J. C. McIntosh were forbidden to start, owing to the inadequacy of their D.H. 9, but disregarded this, and reached Darwin in seven months. Of other entrants, two were killed in England and two drowned near Corfu; others reached Crete and Java. For the full stories see *Vol. VIII, pp. 386-96.*

and order between nations. And as only twenty-one years passed before they had again to fight almost the same enemy in the same cause, some have questioned—as did the Mayor of San Francisco at the opening of the U.N.O. Conference on Anzac Day 1945—whether the Allies in the First World War achieved anything of value by their victory.

So far as Australia is concerned, there can be no such question. It is true that the Allies failed in their purpose, conceived during the struggle itself, to make this "a war to end war". Few, if any, even of their leaders had any conception that the maintenance of a free system in peace involves, on the part of those who believe in it, an effort almost as united—and at times, almost as vigorous—as that of war itself. The machinery set up in 1919 for peace— the League of Nations—failed perhaps partly because it did not offer the prospect of peaceful change when change by force had been ruled out; but mainly be- cause the powers, great and small, were unwilling to face the risk of using the machine they had erected. The Allies failed to achieve a "permanent" or even a lasting peace.

But at least they avoided a German victory. If in the struggle, which—according to Lichnowsky—Great Britain did her best to avoid, the might amassed by the Germans (when they forced the armament race of 1909-14) had resulted in German victory, the first term in the peace treaty would have been the abolition of the British Navy; and for the Australian nation this meant either sub- servience to Germany or extinction at the hands of the Japanese. But the Second World War found us still able and ready to fight for freedom; and that free men and women should have to risk everything in fighting for their freedom within twenty-one years of having saved it in an earlier struggle, is nothing new in history; rather it accords with the normal process by which freedom has been won and maintained.

What was abnormal was that British command of the sea had given us in Australia 126 years of freedom without fighting for it; and what was admirable in our conditions was the factor (or combination of factors) that during those peaceful years kept alive, and indeed apparently increased, the will and capacity of Australians to preserve that freedom. It may be conjectured that, as so often in history, the nation's virility was largely due to the comparative sanity and simplicity of the country life from which even the inhabitants of our great cities were not yet widely separated.

The main achievement of the Australian forces in 1914-18 was to help materially in winning a prolongation of the security of the Victorian era for at least part of the free world, including their own. But for Australia in particular they achieved something more. First, they won her a recognised place among the nations; her seat on the League was given in direct acknowledgment of the part played by her forces. Second, though less commonly realised, was the bringing of a new confidence into Australian national undertakings. Early in the war not a few Australians had watched with diffidence the departure of their force as an improvised contribution to the great armies of the Allies. That diffidence was a natural survival from the "colonial" days. The return of the A.I.F., its leaders covered with distinction, its ranks acclaimed overseas as one of the notable fighting forces of history, deeply, if insensibly, affected that outlook. The old phrase about the "tinpot navy" had died once and for all when the *Sydney* fought the *Emden*, if not before; and gradually even the most conservative Australians began to realise that the success of the A.I.F.—like that of other Dominion forces—while owing much to British tradition, owed much, also, to attributes of the new nation. It is true that the integrity of their leadership—the more vital of the two vital elements, character and brains, on which the great success of their higher command was firmly based—accorded with the best British tradition, as not only Birdwood but Bridges, White, Chauvel and Monash would have maintained; but the development of the extraordinarily capable regimental officers, whom British observers noted as an outstanding mark of the A.I.F. in 1918, was peculiarly Australian.

Admittedly the A.I.F.'s achievement was recognised by some of the people at home less quickly than by the British and French, and even the Germans, nearer to the scene of war. The opinion of the Australian Cabinet, that it would be unreasonable for their nation to have, or even ask for, a seat at the peace conference, was symptomatic of an attitude which the returning troops not uncommonly found in Australia, especially among people of education: they constantly met the belief that reports from overseas had naturally, or politely, exaggerated the A.I.F.'s contribution to the final campaign. It was not until the publication of Sir John Monash's book, *The Australian Victories in France in 1918*, that influential opinion in Australia recognised the performance of her troops for which leaders abroad, including Germans, were giving them credit.[5]

The crucial attribute of the A.I.F. was its discipline—or, perhaps, the compatibility of its discipline with the initiative and readiness to take risks that marked its men. As in every army, its discipline, to be effective, had to be based on the conditions and outlook of the nation. In their way, the critics from the colonial days were right: a people with Australian outlook and standards could not have produced an efficient army of the kind that those critics envisaged—that is, one imbued with the automatism of the old-time grenadier. But the Australian

---

[5] Though Monash's book contains exaggerations and inaccuracies, it does not overstate the fighting value of the A.I.F., nor does it really rate the force higher than did many leaders and writers, British, Allied and enemy, whose estimates can be found in the War Memorial records at Canberra.

commanders and the troops themselves, from highest to lowest, as a result of their outlook and of the natural relations between them, developed a system of discipline which, though outwardly that of the British Army, was in spirit more akin to that of the French. It aimed at the best and most reasonable use of the national material for the purpose in view. It succeeded because the troops wanted the object, and understood the methods, almost as thoroughly as their leaders.

The main condition for the success of this form of discipline was the careful selection of officers, on whose suitability even more depended than in the British Army, in which the prestige of social position or education automatically helped to give control. In the A.I.F., unit commanders used to pick from among their men those whom they themselves would most desire to have under them in action; and, contrary to the old British rule, the general practice was for these, when promoted, to serve in their old battalions, commanding comrades whom they knew, and commanded by the seniors who knew them and had selected them.

Anyone watching an Australian battalion on parade felt that in this year's corporals he saw next year's sergeants and the following year's subalterns. The influence of A.I.F. officers was strengthened by Birdwood's insistence that they must always see to the interests of their men before their own, and Monash's principle that "the staff was the servant of the troops". It was a point of honour that, at any rate when in the line, officers should receive the same food as the troops, and the platoon commander should take his meal in the trenches, among his men. The absence of social distinction encouraged the initiative which was the outstanding quality of Australian troops. Even in this abbreviated narrative the reader will have noted several instances in which a suggestion volunteered by some soldier to his officer at a critical moment resulted in an important achievement.

It is true that great damage was afterwards done to the Anzac tradition by caricatures, that became popular in Australia, of the indiscipline of her troops in the First World War, portraying the life of the "dinkum Aussie" as one of drunkenness, thieving and hooliganism—a caricature based on old soldiers' tales, which notoriously avoid the serious. Actually it was discipline—firmly based on the national habit of facing facts and going straight for the objective—that was responsible for the astonishing success which first gave to other nations confidence in Australia, and to the Australian nation confidence in itself.

Whether that confidence can be justified by achievement in peace as well as in war, only the future can show. The Second World War ended with the use by man of elemental forces of a kind that could dissolve him and, conceivably, all life on this planet, and even—as Shakespeare dreamed—"the great Globe itself". It may be hoped that human reason will bring these forces under unified control and overcome the monstrous danger of their use in war by surrendering those elements of national sovereignty ôn which war and its preparations are based. Such a consummation—which, in the not distant future, may be the only alternative to man's self-destruction—may be freely established by the nations; or it may be forced on the reluctant survivors by a victor after a third world war.

By what adjustments freedom, as known to the liberal world today, will be maintained under that new basis of human relationships, it is too early yet to foresee. But whatever the means still available to men for forcing their will upon others, these lessons of history will still be fundamental—that only in conditions ensuring freedom of thought and communication can mankind progress; and that such freedom can be maintained only by the qualities by which from Grecian times it has been won—by such qualities as our own people managed to preserve through the first 126 peaceful years of their existence—the readiness at any time to die for freedom, if necessary, and the virility to struggle for it.

In facing that necessity we now share with the New Zealanders one condition that was lacking to our young nations in 1915: we have passed through the test which until now, unfortunately, has necessarily been judged by mankind as the supreme one for men fit to be free; and we have emerged from that test with the Anzac tradition. In a Second World War that tradition has nobly served humanity.

May the day be near when it will be safely and gloriously fused in the tradition of a free mankind.

TERRITORIAL RECRUITMENT OF THE AUSTRALIAN IMPERIAL FORCE IN WORLD WAR I

		INFANTRY			LIGHT HORSE
1st Divn	1st Bde	(1st–4th Bns) N.S.W.	Divl and		part 4th Regt Vic.
	2nd Bde	(5th–8th Bns) Vic.	Corps		13th Regt Vic.
	3rd Bde	9th Bn Q'ld	Trps		
		10th Bn S. Aust.	1st Bde		1st Regt N.S.W.
		11th Bn S. Aust.			2nd Regt Q'ld
		12th Bn Tas. (also			3rd Regt S.A., Tas.
		W.A. and S.A.)			
4th Divn	4th Bde	13th Bn N.S.W.	2nd Bde		5th Regt Q'ld
		14th Bn Vic.			6th Regt N.S.W.
		15th Bn Q'ld, Tas.			7th Regt N.S.W.
		16th Bn W.A. and S.A.	3rd Bde		8th Regt Vic.
2nd Divn	5th Bde	(17th–20th Bns) N.S.W.			9th Regt S.A., Vic.
	6th Bde	(21st–24th Bns) Vic.			10th Regt W. Aust.
	7th Bde	25th Bn Q'ld	4th Bde		4th Regt Vic.
		26th Bn Q'ld			11th Regt Q'ld, S.A.
		27th Bn S. Aust.			12th Regt N.S.W.
		28th Bn W. Aust.	5th Bde		14th Regt ⎱ former
5th Divn	8th Bde	29th Bn Vic.			15th Regt ⎰ Camel Cps
		30th Bn N.S.W.			A French regiment of
		31st Bn Q'ld and Vic.			Spahis and Chas-
		32nd Bn S.A. and W.A.			seurs d'Afrique
3rd Divn	9th Bde	(33rd–36th Bns) N.S.W.			
	10th Bde	(37th–39th Bns) Vic.			
		40th Bn Tas.			
	11th Bde	41st Bn Q'ld			
		42nd Bn Q'ld			
		43rd Bn S. Aust.			
		44th Bn W. Aust.			
4th Divn	12th Bde	45th Bn N.S.W.			
		46th Bn Vic.			
		47th Bn Q'ld, Tas.			
		48th Bn S.A. and W.A.			
	13th Bde	49th Bn Q'ld			
		50th Bn S. Aust.			
		51st Bn W. Aust.			
		52nd Bn S.A., W.A.,			
		and Tas.			
5th Divn	14th Bde	(53rd–56th Bns) N.S.W.			
	15th Bde	(57th–60th Bns) Vic.			

INDEX

INDEX

Ranks shown after the surnames of officers and men are in general the highest held by them during events referred to in this volume.

Page numbers followed by n indicate that the reference is to a footnote on the page specified.

INDEX

37—os

INDEX

559

INDEX

INDEX